Cultivation of the ROSES

Cultivation of the ROSES

In the Open Ground and Under Glass; The Formation of the Rosarium; The Characters of Wild and Garden Roses; The Preparation of the Flowers for Exhibition; The Raising of New Varieties; and the Work of the Rose Garden in Every Season of the Year

by
SHIRLEY HIBBERD

2012
BIOTECH BOOKS
Delhi - 110 035

ISBN 81-7622-023-X

Original title: The Amateur's Rose Book, 1804

Published by : **BIOTECH BOOKS**
1123/74, Tri Nagar,
Delhi - 110 035
Phone : 27382765
e-mail: biotechbooks@yahoo.co.in

Showroom : 4762-63/23, Ansari Road, Darya Ganj,
New Delhi - 110 002
Phone: 23245578, 23244987

Laser Typesetting : **Classic Computer Services**
Delhi - 110 035

Printed at : **Chawla Offset Printers**
Delhi - 110 052

PRINTED IN INDIA

DEDICATION

to the

Right Rev. the Dean of Rochester

(REV. S. REYNOLDS HOLE)

Founder of the National Rose Show, and Author of "A Book About Roses"

Dear Friend,

The association of your name with my labours, which your acceptance of this Dedication ensures, enhances my enjoyment of Rose growing, and brings a welcome and pleasant presence to the very front of my book.

Accept herewith my hearty thanks and renewed assurances of esteem, and believe me.

Your fraternally

SHIRLEY HIBBERD

CONTENTS

INTRODUCTION

If on Creation's morn the King of Heaven
To shrubs and flowers a queen had given,
O, beauteous rose, he had anointed thee,
Of shrubs and flowers, the queen to be.
The spotless emblem of unnsullied truth;
The smile of beauty, and the glow of youth,
The garden's pride, the grace of vernal bowers,
The blush of meadows and the eye of flowers.
Thy beauties charm the gods above;
Thy fragrance is the breath of love.—SAPPHO.

Thirty years have elapsed since the first edition of the "Amateur's Rose Book" was published, and the high degree of popularity it has enjoyed throughout this long period is sufficient proof that it has amply fulfilled its promise, and been in every way adapted to the requirements of amateurs wanting a book on roses, at once brightly written and eminently practical. Its remarkable success has undoubtedly been in a large manner due to the fact that it has contained full information on many points of rose culture that, although of the utmost importance to the amateur, have been either wholly unnoticed in works on the same subject, or dealt with so briefly as to perplex rather than assist those who have had but little if any practical experience in the delightful art. More particularly has the subject of propagation been adequately dealt with, for it is believed to be of the highest importance to the amateur rosarian to have readily accessible the fullest possible information on the several methods of increase, that he may be in a position to adapt his course of procedure to the purpose for which the roses are required. A prominent position has also from the first been given to garden roses, which comprise some of the most beautiful varieties in cultivation, although their flowers are wanting in the size, fulness and form essential in blooms for exhibition in the ordinary classes. Whilst other books dealt almost exclusively with the production of exhibition blooms of the hybrid perpetuals and teas, the great value of all classes in the embellishment of the garden has been fully recognised, and properly so; for those who devote their attention to the production of show blooms form but a small proportion of the large body of amateurs who love and grow roses. The influence exercised by this work upon roses that belong exclusively to the garden has undoubtedly been great, and it is not too much to claim that it has been the means of preventing many of the most beautiful kinds from passing into oblivion. As one result of its teaching, there has been an enormous increase in the cultivation of roses, and it may be safely affirmed that during the past thirty years there has been more roses made and sold in this country, than in the preceding sixty-three years. It is equally certain that during the period in which the "Amateur's Rose Book" has been circulated and reprinted, with such revision as the additions to our knowledge have rendered necessary, the art of rose growing has made great advances, and the number of rosarians has increased to an enormous extent. It would be an act of disloyalty to the Queen of Flowers to attribute the ever-increasing enthusiasm of the amateurs of roses to any other cause than the inspiration of her beauty; but it will be readily acknowledged by all who render her homage, that by assisting to direct enthusiasm wisely, and present useful barriers against possible foibles and excesses, a well-written book must have afforded efficient help in popularising the flower, and thus extending the circle of its admirers and cultivators. After all, flowers full to contribute their full share to our enjoyment unless we talk about them, read about them, dream about them, and bring them at times into the midst of our intellectual being. It follows, that for the full enjoyment of roses, there must be books about them, and these, to be useful, must be written, not only by those who have a genuine love for them, but who have and sufficient experience to enable them to accurately describe the several details essential to success, and judiciously select from the large numbers of varieties in the several sections. Hence the importance of a work like the "Amateur's Rose Book," that records the observations and experiences of private or amateur cultivators, who are not only free from trade influences, but fully understand the wants of those in no way concerned with the commercial aspect of rose cultivation. It is of interest that the immensely increased and increasing trade in roses has been chiefly promoted by amateur writers, who, in giving publicity to the details of production as well as of cultivation, have actually improved the trade, and made the sale of roses far more profitable than it was before it will be seen that, as in previous editions, a considerable proportion of the book now in the reader's hands is occupied with directions and advices intended to facilitate the multiplication of stock and these directions and advices represent the latest conclusions on the subject. The seedling and cutting briers which are so largely employed as stocks by both private and trade growers receive for the first time the prominence that, by reason of their usefulness, they so well deserve. This is not the only feature to which attention may well be directed for the purpose of securing for the "Amateur's Rose Book," in its thoroughly revised form, a renewal and continuance and extension of the favour bestowed upon it during the many years it has been recognised as the standard work for amateur growers of the rose. It will be seen that the cultivation of roses in towns, the production and staging of exhibition blooms, the rules by which roses should be classified and judged, the vices of fashion in rose growing, the employment of roses for various decorative purposes, have specially received attention. To this edition has been added a synoptical catalogue, which is unquestionably the most complete that has yet been published, and will, it is hoped, be of much value in determining questions of classification and nomenclature, and also dates of introduction. In the chapters that follow, there is little to amuse the individual known as the "general reader"; but there is much, it is hoped, and indeed believed, to interest, to encourage, and to assist the amateur rosarian; and there may be something that will tend to improvement of a taste that is well founded, though by various accidents diverted from its proper course. This is essentially a "practical" book, and while it may not have many attractions for the idler in the rose garden, who probably thinks more of himself than his flowers, there can be no doubt that the ardent cultivator will derive much pleasure as well as instruction from its perusal among the roses.

Chapter 1

THE FAMILIES OF WILD ROSES

It is impossible to assign every garden rose its proper place in relation to the recognised species of wild roses. The origin of many garden roses is utterly unknown; a considerable proportion of the whole are the representatives of a succession of crosses between species and hybrids and varieties, and hence bear more or less resemblance to several of the more distinctive types. It is the tendency of floriculture to obliterate species, to the regret, and sometimes the chagrin, of the botanists; and the results of this tendency are markedly manifested in the various-named roses that obtain our attention on account of their beauty, without any regard whatever to their genealogy or blood relationships. The botanists have no good reason to complain. Our roses may baffle their endeavours to trace them to their several origins, but they do not supplant the species anywhere except in the garden: in the great world without the wild roses grow as freely and bloom as bravely as ever, and in every part of the northern hemisphere they who love the roses of the hedgerow, and the wood-side, and the breezy upland waste, have but to search for them in the season, and enjoy them to their hearts' content. When the botanists speak of the florists as destroyers of types, they talk sentimental nonsense, which is the more nonsensical because the complainants profess to be animated by lofty scientific motives, and to be strangers to sentiment altogether.

The order ROSACEAE is one of the most important sections of the vegetable kingdom, for it comprises not only the roses proper upon which we are about to discourse, but all our hardy fruits, such as the apple, pear, plum, peach, raspberry, and strawberry, besides a number of hardy ornamental trees and herbaceous plants, such as the thorn, the cotoneaster, the spiraea, and the potentilla. The best arrangement of the families of roses is that proposed by the late Dr. Lindley in his *Rosarum Monographia*, which will be followed here in all its essential features, for the very good reason that it affords the very best scientific basis available for a review of the affairs of the rose-garden, although fifty years have elapsed since it was compiled. There are about thirty species of roses known to botanists, and they are all natives of the northern hemisphere, and very nearly all are hardy in the milder climates of Britain, those that are not hardy needing only slight protection against the destructive weather of the late winter and early spring. The several species are, by the careful botanist whom we take for our guide, arranged in eleven families, as follows:

Feroces

This is a small group of roses bearing formidable armour, and hence their collective designation. They are bushes of from three to six feet high, deciduous, producing large and showy flowers of a deep red or purple colour. *Rosa ferox*, the "hedgehog rose," a native of the Caucasus, is a low shrub with thick, hoary branches, densely armed with permanent prickles; the flowers are handsome, but scentless, and there are no double varieties of it known. *R. kamtschatka* has deciduous spines and large deep red flowers. A very near ally of the last (and possibly identical with it), is *R. rugosa*, a Japanese rose, and described by Thunberg and Siebold. It is a half-rambling shrub, rising five feet high, producing numerous large deep-red or crimson flowers, in grand terminal corymbs, succeeded by brilliant scarlet hips of the size and shape of the pretty Siberian crab. Of this, a beautiful white variety has been introduced under the name of *R. rugosa alba*. The French raisers are endeavouring to obtain by the aid of the pollen of this splendid single rose, new characters to add to the attractions of the garden varieties. The Feroces, in their present rustic condition, are only adapted for hedges and for the rougher parts of shrubberies, but for such purposes are extremely showy, and as hardy as any roses known.

Bracteatae

Bracteatae is an interesting family, characterised by their floral leaves or bracts, downy stems and fruits, and bright green leaves, which last through the winter. The type is *R. bracteata*, obtained from China by Lord Macartney in 1795. It is a lovely, glossy-leaved bush, producing white flowers in great abundance late in the season, these being followed by large globose orange-red fruits. There are three good varieties in cultivation—*Macartney*, semi-double, pure white; *Alba odorata*, white, with yellow centre; and *Maria leoinda*, a pretty plant, of half-climbing habit, producing delicate bush flowers. This is well adapted for a rockery in a sheltered situation. *R. microphylla*, the small-leaved rose, introduced from China in 1823, is a compact bush, with beautiful small, finely-toothed leaflets, and solitary double, rosy-pink flowers. Of this species there is a series of varieties in cultivation, the principal of which are *Rubra-plena*, deep red; *Rugosa*, crimson; the *Old Purple*, deep carmine; and *Ma Surprise*, double white, with rose-coloured centre. *R. clinophylla* is a small shrub producing solitary white flowers and roundish fruit.

Cinnamomeae

The roses of this group mostly have long, narrow leaflets, flowers of medium size in clusters, and spherical fruits, that lose the calyx leaves ere arriving at maturity. *R. cinnamomea*, the Cinnamon Rose, is a native of Europe. It grows to a height of eight to ten feet, forming a stout stem, and has leaves composed of fine oblong leaflets, which are of a grey-green on the upper and glaucous green on the under surfaces. The flowers occur solitary or in clusters of two or three; they are of a pale carmine colour. *R. lucida* is distinguished by the brightness of its leaves; *R. laxa* is the loose or spreading rose; and *R. carolina*, the Carolina rose, inhabits marshy ground in North America. It has long stipules, the flowers are in clusters, of a rosy carmine colour, decidedly effective. *R. rapa*, the Turnip rose, another American species, is destitute of spines; the leaves acquire a reddish tinge in autumn; the flowers are in clusters, of a bright red, pink, or white, and often quite double. Its name refers to the spherical form of the fruit, which is crowned with calyx leaves in the manner of a turnip. It is a good garden rose for masses in the wilder parts of the garden. *R. maialis*, the May rose, a native of Europe, produces small flowers of a pale rose colour, which are followed by spherical orange-coloured fruits, which do not lose their calyx leaves. *Du Saint-*

Sacrament is an old and scarce variety of the cinnamon rose, with pleasing lilac-coloured flowers.

Pimpinellifoliae

The members of this family are called 'Burnet-leaved roses'. They are characterised by their numerous leaflets, which vary from seven to fifteen, some of them have and some have not spines, and they all retain calyx leaves until the fruit arrives at maturity. *R. spino issima* is the Scotch rose of gardens; the leaves of which resemble those of the pretty salad herb called Burnet. It is a small shrub, with small solitary flowers of a white colour, slightly stained with yellow in the centre. Of this species there are many varieties in cultivation, comprising the *Double white*, *Double yellow*, the colours of which correspond with their names; *Estelle*, and *Stanwell's*, rose-coloured. *R. sulphurea* is a bush, armed with spines and bristles; the flowers are large and double, and of a fine yellow colour. It appears to require an extremely moist soil. *R. alpina* is found growing wild in the higher regions of the south of Europe; it has a few purplish spines, the flowers are carmine-coloured, the fruits orange red. From this species, by crossing with the China roses, have been obtained the *Boursault* group, which are mostly smooth-stemmed, the habit climbing, and the flowers are large; double, and of various shades of crimson and purple.

Centifoliae

The hundred-leaved rose; represents an interesting and important group, from which many a gem "of purest ray serene" has been obtained to give light and lustre to our garden. The type of the group is *R. centifolia*, the Cabbage or Provence rose, which has large, unequal prickles, pendulous flowers, and oblong fruit. It is a native of Persia, and is probably the rose referred by Pliny in book XXI, of his *Natural History* (18, 25, 72, 73). Miller describes it as *R. provincialis* and pronounces it the most beautiful of all roses. A variety, said to have originated in Switzerland and named *R. centifolia muscosa*, is the "moss rose" of our gardens, the distinguishing character being the result of hypertrophy of the hairs and segments of the calyx. The most important allies of *R. centifolia* are *R. gallica*, the French rose, which has erect flowers and globose fruit; and *R. damascena*, the Damask or monthly rose, characterised by producing its flowers in corymbs, with reflexed sepals followed by elongated fruit. By the crossing and inter-crossing of these a large and valuable series of garden roses has been established the more important sections of which comprise the *Provence*, or *Cabbage*, the *Moss*, the *Hybrid Provence*, the *Damask*, the *Gallica*, the *Pompon*, and the *Portland* roses. The most distinct varieties in these sections are enumerated in the nursery catalogues, and are absolutely essential to the comprehensive rose-garden, although they all flower early and flower only once, and that most sweetly.

> "Would not this, sir, and a forest of feathers–if the rest of my fortunes turn Turk with me–with two Provincial roses on my razed shoes get me fellowship in a company of players, sir?"—*Hamlet*, III., 2.

Villosae

The Downy roses are characterised by straight prickles, persistent sepals, and a thickened disk. In a severe criticism of Lindley's arrangement this group would probably fall to pieces, and some of the fragments would coalesce with *R. canina*. The only important species in the family is *R. alba*, the white rose, which has rugose glaucous leaves, large and showy flowers, which vary in colour from white to rose, and oblong scarlet fruit. The named varieties constitute a beautiful group, and the best of them, as, for example, *Belle de Segur*, *Felicite* (Parmentier) and *Madame Legras*, are not surpassed by any roses of any class in cultivation.

Rubiginosae

This is a distinct family of sweet brier roses, characterised by the glandular under surface of the leaves, bristly prickles, and persistent sepals. *R. rubignosa* is the sweet brier, a native of Britain, usually met with on chalky soils in the south of England. This is a favourite everywhere for its pale carmine flowers and the sweet odour it emits when the leaves are slightly bruised, but too rugged a plant for a prominent position in the rose-garden. It is the "eglantere" of Chaucer-

> "That gave so passing a delicious smell,"

and the "eglantine" of the later poets—

> "The leaf of eglantine, whom not to slander,
> Out-sweetened not thy breath."
>
> —*Cymbeline*, IV., 2.

The eglantine of the French is *R. lutea*, a very pretty brier, with dark shilling leaves, and large, cup-shaped yellow flowers. From this have been obtained the *Capuchin brier*, which has flowers yellow outside and reddish brown within; the well-known *Harrisoni*, with double yellow flowers, once famous in English gardens; and *Persian yellow*, a fine double rose, still held in high esteem.

Caninae

The Dog roses are the most important of all the families recognised by botanists, for not only do the several species and varieties constitute the chief splendours of the rose-garden, but the formidable brier of the hedgerows supplies roots and stems for the sustenance and bold presentation of the choicest roses of the same family that have been obtained by long-continued and painstaking selections. It only needs a slight stretch of fancy to compel Shakespeare to witness that in his day the production of standard roses was understood, for he speaks of Pyramus as

"Of colour like the red rose on triumphant brier."

—*Midsummer Night's Dream*, II., 2.

The common Dog rose, *R. canina*, is the most common of all our native species, and, owing to its wide distribution, a very variable plant; for it is influenced by widely different conditions of soil and climate. Its most constant characteristics are hooked prickles, flowers pale rose or white, calyx segments pinnate, and not remaining attached to the fruit. The form of the fruit is ovoid-oblong, the colour bright scarlet. Amongst its many varieties, none have acquired renown as garden roses; but hitherto the rosarian has never bestowed a thought on the possible value of its pollen, though for ever absorbed in admiration of the actual value of its hungry roots and stalwart stem. *R. indica*, the common China rose, betrays its relation to the British brier in all its more prominent features, but is more refined throughout, and its varieties present peculiar attractions to the florist. *R. odorata*, the fragrant China rose, is (if, as a species, it exists at all) more brier-like in habit, forming long, stout rods, with hooked prickles, and showing on the sunny side of the stem those stains of purple which are always to be found on the young shoots of the dog rose. From the supposed *odorata*, crossed, perhaps, with *indica*, the Tea rose, *R. indica odorata*, has been derived; but whatever its origin, it takes the highest rank in the order of merit of all the roses in the garden, not excepting even the ever-useful and most popular of all roses, the so-called Hybrid Perpetual. The tea roses are for the most part tender in constitution; they have long shoots, with hooked spines, shining leaves, composed of few leaflets; large flowers, usually pale yellow or pale rose-coloured; and roundish fruit, of a reddish-scarlet colour. They are valued for their robust growth, rich glossy green foliage, and lengthened season of blooming, and for their lovely flowers. They bewilder the susceptible rosarian by their exquisite elegance of form, delicacy of colour and peculiarly refreshing fragrance, which though likened to that of a newly-opened sample of the choicest tea, is really distinct, and, we will venture to say, unlike all other odours, whether of flowers or leaves, and the most refined and blessed fragrance obtainable in the garden of the world. When from some other branch of the patrician family of roses a flower shall be obtained to surpass in all the proper qualities of a florist's flower that gem of gems, the *Souvenir d'un Ami,* we will revise the foregoing observations, and, in the interest of truth alone, modify the eulogy. The Tea rose was first seen in this country in 1793, since which date successive importations from China, and the persevering efforts of rosarians in raising seedlings, have resulted in securing for our enjoyment an immense number of named varieties, sufficiently distinct for horticultural purposes, and sufficiently alike to render them representatives of the highest qualities known amongst roses.

The Ever-flowering Rose, *R. semperflorens,* known also as the Bengal Rose, *R. bengalensis,* is in several respects distinct from the true China and Tea Roses. It is less robust in growth, it loses its stamens and petals at the same time, and the ovaries average fifteen in number; those of the Tea Rose averaging forty to fifty. Another and still smaller species of this group is *R. lawrenceana,* so named in honour of Miss Lawrence, who published a series of admirable drawings of roses. It is generally known as the Fairy Rose, and although grown in great quantities by florists who send plants to market, and more particularly by those who provide Covent Garden with perennial streams of floral wonders, it is rarely seen in private gardens, and still more rarely properly cultivated by amateurs. Its tender constitution renders it unfit for the open ground, and as a pot plant it requires more constant attention than amateurs or their gardeners can find time and mindfulness to bestow.

From the several reputed species thus briefly described have been obtained hybrids and crosses innumerable, and these are classified in accordance with their most obviously distinguishing features. The most important section, as already remarked, is that known as the *Tea Rose,* for which, in the, first instance, we are indebted to China, where, we may presume, it originated. The *Bourbon Rose* is occasionally classed as a species under the name *R. bourbonica,* but it is probably a hybrid from *R. indica* and the Red Four Seasons, a branch of the Damask race that was once famous in English gardens. The original plant was found growing in a hedge in the Isle of Bourbon; but of its origin nothing is known. By various crosses of the Bourbon, the ever-flowering and other members of the family Caninae, the *Hybrid Perpetuals,* have been obtained, and, as a rule, the best of these present the characteristics of the Bourbon type more strongly than any other, although in certain sections of the group, the Damask type is indicated as having taken part in the production of the perpetual race. Another distinct cross, or rather hybridization–for the parents were far separated in specific characters, has been accomplished between the Tea or Bengal and the Musk Rose, by *M. noisette,* a French gardener settled in America, the product being the *Noisette Rose,* noted for its free growth and abundant flowering, and especially for its late flowering; but is not held in high repute for either quality or fragrance. The first Noisette Rose was sent to France in 1814, since which time a distinct and large section of Noisettes has been established, many of which partake largely of the character of the Teas, while others lean towards the crimson China. *Marechal Niel,* a true Noisette, represents the highest quality of this race, and leans directly to the Teas. In addition to the foregoing there is a distinct group formed by the varieties known as *Hybrid Teas,* which have been obtained during the past twenty years by the inter-crossing of the Teas and Hybrid Perpetuals, and combine the characteristics of the two sections.

Systylae

The members of this family differ in but few and slight particulars from the last but one prominent characteristic is their confluent styles; whereas in Caninae the styles are free. *R. systyla* is one of our finest wild white roses; its shoots rising twelve feet high, and its flowers appearing in great plenty in June and July. *R. arvensis,* the Field Rose, produces slender trailing stems, armed with very few prickles, and pretty white flowers from June to August. It is probably one amongst many roses worn as badges during the wars of York and Lancaster. The *Ayrshire* Rose of gardens is an improved form of *R. arvensis.* The Evergreen Rose, *R. sempervirens,* is a native of the South of Europe. This is characterized by its persistent leaves and small round orange-coloured fruit. The Multiflora Rose, *R. multiflora,* is a native of China and Japan; the flowers are small and occur in dense clusters, the calyx leaves fall early, and the fruit is pear-shaped and of a bright red colour. The most important section in this family, however, is *R. moschata,* the Musk Rose, a native of the Northern parts of Africa, and now pretty plentifully distributed in the North of Europe. It is a robust habited shrub armed with hooked spines, producing white flowers in clusters; the calyx leaves fall early; the fruit is small, ovoid, and of a deep red colour. Its rich perfume constitutes an important article of commerce in the countries where it attains its highest perfection. It has been usefully employed by hybridizers in raising new varieties, and has no doubt contributed in a material degree to the formation of the important family of Noisettes. *R. setigera,* also known as *R. rubifolia,* is a native of North America, and the parent of the comparatively valueless *Prairie Roses,* which are characterized by semi-double pale rose or blush-coloured dowers, and smooth fruit about the size of a pea.

Banksianae

There are three species ranked under this head, and they are all of secondary importance. The true Banksian Rose, *R. banksice,* is a native of China, and decidedly tender in this country, a fact which in a peculiar manner militates against its popularity, for it is a charming rose, rising to a height of thirty feet in a warm situation, and producing showers, or rather sheets, of small elegant sweet-scented nodding flowers of a white, yellow, or salmon colour. *R. loevigata,* also known as *R. sinica,* the Georgian Rose, is a lovely climber with glossy leathery leaves, large solitary white flowers, and oblong spiny fruit, which carries its calyx leaves until full ripe. The Anemone-flowered Rose, *R. anemonoeflora,* produces small double flowers that bear a near resemblance to double anemones. It scarcely belongs to this family, but there appears to be no better place for it.

Berberidifolia

Berberidifolia, the Barberry-leaved Rose, is a pretty bush, producing yellow flowers. Its native country is the North of Persia, where it grows abundantly in salt marshes, and is used as fuel. It is scarcely known in gardens, but has nevertheless produced, by crossing with *R. clinophylla,* a pretty yellow hybrid named *Hardyi.*

Chapter 2

THE FAMILIES OF GARDEN ROSES

It will probably be convenient to many readers of this work if we here present a brief summary of the requirements of the rose as a garden flower, leaving for treatment in subsequent chapters those special points of rose culture which are calculated to interest the advanced amateur rather than the novice in rose-growing. The task before us is to present a practical treatise of so concise a nature as to be worthy to be designated "rose-growing in a nutshell," and which shall be so complete that those who desire simply a display of roses at the least possible cost of time and trouble shall find herein all the information needful to put them in the way of complete success.

Huc vina, et unguenta, et nimium brevis
Flores amoenos ferre jube rosae;
Dum res, et aetas, et sororum
Fila trium patiuntur atra.

The rose, in all its varieties and forms as a garden flower, requires a deep, rich, moist soil, a pure air, shelter from strong winds, and the most complete exposure to the sunshine. As a royal flower, it needs royal sustenance, and a starving system of treatment will never bring forth good roses, but will probably, instead, ensure for the practitioner disappointment, vexation, and loss. The mention of "varieties" and "forms" will perhaps perplex the beginner for a moment, and it is our duty, therefore, to explain at once the signification of these terms. There are many distinct families of roses, differing more or less in character and constitution, and these several families comprehend a number of varieties, which also differ more or less amongst themselves, though bearing, a general family likeness. Now, it will happen often that where certain classes of roses, or even certain varieties of one class, thrive exceedingly, others refuse to grow, or at the best grow weakly, and flower seldom. The beginner desires to be guarded against encountering a sudden disappointment through an injudicious selection of roses; for the first condition of success is to plant only such as are likely to prosper in the circumstances of soil and climate at command for rose-growing. We shall speak of the forms of roses before treating of the families and varieties. These may be roughly classed in two divisions: (1) Standard or Tree Roses; (2) Dwarf or Bush Roses. Each of these may be again divided into two sections: (1a) Standards budded or grafted on English briers; (1b) Standards on their own roots; (2a) Dwarfs budded or grafted on English and Italian briers or, (2b) Dwarfs on their own roots.

Standard Roses

Standard roses are noble objects when well made and judiciously managed, but ugly, unthrifty, and indeed disgraceful things when unsuitable sorts are selected for standards, or when they are subjected to a starving system of treatment. Nine-tenths of all the mistakes made by amateur gardeners are in connection with standard roses. They buy, and plant, and wait, and never see the beauty of the rose. They find their gardens filled with ugly sticks, which occasionally flaunt a ragged rose, that proves to be worse than no rose at all; and yet those same trees would have made handsome heads and myriads of noble flowers had they been properly treated in the first instance. Planting standard roses on grass, or in little beds on the margin of the grass, is usually the first step to failure in rose-growing; for the English brier is a hungry plant, and requires more food than it is possible for it to obtain when so situated. The standard rose requires a deep loam, well dug and plentifully manured, and will thrive on a well- cultivated clay, or on good peat. But it will scarcely live on chalk or sand; and, as a rule, whatever the soil may be, if the atmosphere of the spot is constantly loaded with coal smoke; it is not advisable to plant standard roses. As standard roses are in high favour with amateurs who do not make a study of rose-growing, it appears desirable to offer a few directions for the formation of a small rosarium, comprising standards chiefly, with dwarfs; for the front row. We will go as far away from the dwelling-house as possible, and mark out a piece of ground open to the sun, and sheltered by a belt of trees from the north. This shall be dug two spits deep, and plenty of good manure shall he incorporated with the soil as the work proceeds. As, whatever time of year the work commences, the ground must be ready for planting in October, it is a good plan to select and prepare the site as soon as the pressure of spring work is past, say in June, and immediately plant the ground with asters and balsams if flowers are appropriate, or with potatoes, if the appearance of the plot the first season is of no consequence. As we are now to deal with dwarfs as well as standards, it may be advisable to repeat that brier roses, whether dwarfs or standards, require a good deep moist loam, well manured and industriously broken up previous to planting. A good clay will suit them if there is no stint of labour in deep digging and breaking and manuring. Dwarfs, that are on own roots or Manettis, require a rather light rich loam, but are not particular, provided they can root deep, and are well fed. Nevertheless, the best way to prepare the ground, if it is a rather stiff loam, is to dress the front line where the dwarfs are to be planted with plenty of leaf-mould and rotten manure; and if rotted turf can be spared for it, the stuff will not be wasted. But let no one suppose that roses require elaborate preparations; any soil that will grow a good cabbage will grow a good rose, whether it is a cabbage rose or any other kind.

To obtain suitable trees is a matter involving no difficulty. A fastidious purchaser will manage to see and mark all the trees, and have the sorts according to a list made out before-hand. But there are very few people who have time to spare to buy roses in that way, and an order sent to any of the first- class trade growers, whose names are known well enough, specifying heights and numbers, and leaving the dealer to select the sorts, will be sure to result satisfactorily, and the cost of the whole will be about half what would be charged if the sorts and the trees were selected by the purchaser. We lately made a plantation of the kind under notice. We wrote to a well-known nursery for so many dozen standards, ranging from three to six feet, and said nothing about the numbers required of particular heights or sorts. When they came in, the men went to work in a systematic way. One pruned head and tail, and handed them over;

the next placed them in lots as to heights; the next carried them to their places, and laid them in bundles for planting. To have a plantation of roses as true to heights as an architect would require the columns of a portico, is out of the question–it simply cannot be done; but there is no difficulty in arranging them to form a very regular bank, if a fair proportion of each height is supplied in the first instance. As to arranging the colours, that is of no consequence; for any rose, whatever its style or colour will harmonise with any other rose.

The work of planting should be done with care. Fellows who blunder about, and hack and slash with spade and knife, ought not to be admitted amongst roses. They must be handled as old Izaak Walton advises the angler to handle frogs, that is, tenderly, as if you loved them. All the long roots must be cut back; all the wounded roots must be shortened so as to remove the injured parts; there must be no tugging and tearing, and care must be taken not to bruise the bark. In cutting back the heads, it must be remembered that the final pruning is to be done after they are planted; the cutting back before planting is to render them more convenient for handling, for the nurserymen send them in with all their huge whip-like shoots full length; it would not do for them to prune them. To say nothing of the time consumed, the process would prune the price out of them.

In planting, the ground should be measured off in lines, and it is best to begin with the tallest. If these average five feet high, they must be five feet apart in the row, or not more than five-and-twenty in a run of hundred feet. The next row should be five feet removed from the first, and the trees in it should average four feet high, and be put four feet asunder. The next row should be four feet from the second, and the trees in it should average three feet high, and be three feet apart in the row. If they are strong-growing sorts, and the soil is good, and the trees have already fine heads, give them a distance of four feet apart, and they will then touch each other, and make a solid line of leaf and bloom. The front row should be three feet from the last, and the bushes in it two feet apart, and set back two feet from the edge of the walk. The quickest way to plant is to lay down the line, place the trees, carefully laying out the roots near the surface, throw a little earth over, and tread very lightly, just enough to keep; them upright, and so on till the whole are in their places. Then go over them again, tread them firm, and stake them securely, and they may remain for months, if need be, without any further attention. The reason for planting loose in the first instance is this, that when the whole piece is planted you are sure to want to move a few, and make exchanges. It is therefore easy to take out any of them by a mere touch, and rearrange as needful, and there is no waste of labour. Besides, this sort of work should be done quickly, for we do not get much fine weather at the time for planting roses, and it does them much mischief to lay about: the sooner their roots are covered the better. By the system of merely placing them with a shovelful of stuff over the roots, the whole lot can be got into their places quickly; and come rain, frost, snow, or what else, they cannot suffer; they are safe, and if not finished for a week or two no harm can arise. The sooner the whole job is finished the better; but if every individual tree is finished right out at once, some may suffer through laying about with perhaps their roots not half covered; and at the best it is certain that a few will have to be lifted to get them all in such order as will satisfy an eye at all fastidious about arrangements.

Many years ago we advocated the use of iron stakes for rose-trees. Some growers contend that iron stakes do harm, and they go on using oak stakes instead. Now we are certain, from long observation and experience, that iron stakes do no harm, and that oak stakes, and, in fact, any kind of timber supports, are really injurious, and many a rose-tree is killed by the spread of fungus over its roots, through contact with decaying wood. Once in three years we boil up a cauldron of tar and pitch, thrust the ends of the iron stakes into the fire that boils the pot, and when the ends are rather hot dip them into the mixture. Two coats of paint on the length of the rod finishes them; they can be, placed close to the stems of the trees, care being taken in thrusting them down not to drive, them through the thick roots near the collar, and when the trees are tied up the stakes are almost invisible.

The pruning can be finished any time before the, 1st of March. It may be done as soon as the planting is finished, and before the trees are staked; for although winter pruning is not good for established roses, because it tends to make them grow too soon in spring, roses newly planted have enough check to prevent that, and autumn or winter pruning will not hurt them.

It is of the utmost importance for the full enjoyment of a plantation of roses to have them legibly and correctly labelled. If the calico labels the nurserymen put on are allowed to flutter in the wind all winter, the chances are that the writing will be washed out before spring. Therefore, to complete the labelling quickly is a matter of considerable importance. There are a thousand ways of forming and attaching labels to trees. Wooden labels smeared with white lead, and written on with a pencil while the paint is soft, answer admirably. Attach these with a copper wire, and take care not to cut the bark of the tree, and leave the, wire loose enough for the tree to swell. Once a year look at every label, and keep a list of all the sorts, in which you may make notes of their characters and behaviour.

Dwarf Roses

Dwarf roses are worthy of more attention than they obtain from amateurs; for, as a rule, they are considered very inferior things as compared with standards, even if the latter are of the consumptive, bogey, broomstick, worn-out bottle-brush kind frequently met with in the front gardens of suburban villas. Let us plant, say, a dozen of the more robust-habited perpetuals *on their own roots* in a border of deep rich loam, at about five feet apart in a straight line. For the sake of being concise, we will suppose them to consist of such sorts as La France, Jules Margottin, Baroness Rothschild, and Victor Verdier. These may be bought, perhaps in pots, and planted in April or May, and have regular supplies of water until July, to promote free growth from the first. Or they may be bought in the shape of strong bushes in October, and be then planted. In the following month of March they should be moderately pruned, but far less severely than it is the practice of gardeners to prune them. Say all the long rods are shortened to one-half their length, and the little twigs that bore flowers last year are removed altogether. By this course of treatment they will in time form large, compact, handsome bushes, producing roses of fine quality in great profusion, and in beauty of contour and richness of bloom probably surpassing by many degrees all the standard roses of the district.

Those mysterious words, "on their own roots", will perhaps perplex the novice, and, therefore, we return to the classification adopted above: (2a) Dwarfs on English and Italian briers; (2b) Dwarfs on their own roots. It was long the custom of the nurserymen to bud or graft the finer varieties almost exclusively on the Italian or Manetti brier, and so quickly may saleable roses be produced by this course of procedure, that it was rarely they adopted any other method for raising dwarf plants. But of recent years their practice has been modified, and cutting and seedling briers are largely used as stocks for dwarfs. The Manetti roses are comparatively cheap and answer well, because the Manetti stock imparts to the rose grafted on it a free-growing robust habit-in other words, the Manetti carries its roses well. The advantage of employing the Manetti may, for the present purpose, be regarded as consisting in rapidity; of growth, in consequence of which flowering bushes of a good size are obtained in less time than if the roses were on their own roots or the English brier, and the peculiar food-finding nature of the Manetti, which thrives on gravelly and other poor soils on which brier roses would pine or perish. For the amateur, the Manetti has one peculiar disadvantage. It is apt to throw up suckers, and if these are allowed to remain, they soon use up all the nourishment collected by the roots, and the consequence is that the rose perishes and the brier takes its place. A plantation of Manetti roses, in which suckers have been allowed to rise unchecked, may thus become absolutely worthless in the course of two seasons; but the mischief is easily prevented by watching for the peculiar blue-leaved growth of the Manetti stock, and cutting away the suckers to the point from which they spring. It is the rule with experienced rosarians to search Manetti roses well in the first instance, for the removal of any buds that appear below the graft, and they are usually planted so deep that the junction of stock and graft is covered with about two inches of soil. The results of such management usually are that there are no suckers from the root; but the rose forms roots of its own, while the deeply-buried roots of the Manetti perish, thus, at last, those which were planted as Manetti roses become Own-root roses.

The last-named are, without question, the best of all roses; but we cannot announce brier roses, however we may be enamoured of those on their own roots. Own-root roses are obtained by striking buds and cuttings, and by making layers or sowing seeds. When the branches consist of one plant and the roots of another, as must be the case with brier roses, there is more or less of conflict between them; but own-root roses are all of a piece, and roots and branches always agree in their times of growing, and their respective duties to each other. A singular advantage of own-root-roses is that if they throw up suckers these are so much gain to the garden, which is a very different case to that of suckers from briers, that are a nuisance any way, and may prove destructive in the end. Another singular advantage of own roots is, that in the event of a destructive frost, such as, for instance, occurred in the winter of 1860-61, they are likely to suffer only a little injury, whereas brier roses are likely to be killed outright, as actually occurred, and to a tremendous extent, in that disastrous winter. It is worthy of observation that if the frost kills a tree to the ground, the roots may be spared, and may in due time renew the plant. And here we see the difference in value of the two sorts of roses in the event of a destructive frost-those that were on brier stocks are gone entirely, because the suckers will be but worthless briers; but those on their own roots *will be renewed from the roots,* and thus for all practical purposes, they may be considered indestructible. It is an objection to own-root roses that in the first two seasons they grow slowly, and that is the only objection ever raised that is worth the consideration of a reasonable being: They are said to be difficult to produce, but that is untrue, and a trade grower should be the very last to give currency to the ridiculous doctrine that there is any difficulty in obtaining own-root roses from buds or cuttings.

As to the soil required for dwarf roses, those on Manetti stocks will, as above remarked, do pretty well on chalk or gravel, but on such unkind soils liberal preparation should be made for them. All kinds of own-root roses require a deep mellow, rich loam; some kinds, such as the Moss and Provence, will thrive in poor soils and in a smoky air; the Perpetuals and Bourbons need a thoroughly good soil of a substantial nature; the Chinas and Teas like a rather light soil, such as would be obtained by mixing plenty of old hot-bed manure, road sand, and rotted turf, with well-cultivated garden ground. But at this point generalities appear to be of less use, and it becomes desirable to particularize the treatment required by each of the several groups of roses, not only as to soil and climate, but also as to planting and pruning. For the convenience of the reader, we shall group the garden roses under two great divisions, in accordance with their seasons of flowering, those which flower once being designated Summer Roses, and those which flower more than once being designated Autumn Roses.

Summer Roses

Provence, Cabbage, and Moss Roses

These are all descended from *Rosa centifolia,* and have the same habit of growth, forming smallish bushes, with rather long whip-like shoots, which are armed with both spines and bristles. The commoner kinds are well adapted for town gardens, as they bear smoke well and make a good growth in poor soils, and their flowers are exquisitely beautiful. The better varieties of both Provence and Moss roses, however, require a good soil and a pure air, and should never be planted unless there is a probability of their receiving good attention. They are well adapted to form short standards on the brier, and they make neat bushes on their own roots. They require to be close pruned, every shoot to be cut back to within four or five buds of the base. The trade catalogues contain a section of "perpetual" flowering moss roses, which are thrown into a separate group, because they produce a second bloom. But they are perpetual only in the mind of an interested or very fanciful person, and should not be relied upon for any large supply of flowers in the autumn. These so-called perpetual Moss roses are, however, wondrous in beauty, and decidedly more delicate in constitution than the commoner sorts. It is well for a lover of Moss roses to obtain a few of the best on Manetti stocks, as they make better dwarfs than standards; but in a clay country brier stocks answer for them admirably.

Damask Roses

Damask roses are characterized by pale green pubescent leaves, which give them a distinctive appearance in the rosery. The common simple Damask or Monthly Rose is a capital town shrub, thriving in any kind of soil, and flowering most profusely. With us it is a glorious weed running wild in the shrubbery, and occasionally required to be forked out with as little ceremony as if it were but couch grass. There are some lovely named varieties of this group in cultivation, all of which make handsome standards for a strong soil, but are not less useful on the Manetti if the soil is poor. They require abundant manuring and rather close pruning. *Rosa alba* is a section of the Damask, and requires the same treatment.

The French Rose

The beautiful Gallica roses are invaluable for town gardens, and may be grown as either dwarfs or standards in any part of Britain where a rose of any kind could live at all, for they are very hardy. When grown for the supply of exhibition roses, the brier is the best stock for them; but as garden roses they are to be preferred as bushes, because of their upright growth, which renders them ungainly as standards. Though hardy and capable of bearing ill usage, they will abundantly repay for good culture. When grown for exhibition the trees should be severely disbudded early in June, and supplied with liquid manure until the bloom is over. They require rather close pruning, say to be cut back to within eight or nine buds of the base of the strongest shoots, and to within two buds of the base of the weakest. It is a peculiarly good quality of the French roses, that the cut flowers bear carriage well.

Hybrid China Roses

These are the produce of crosses with Chinas, Bourbons, and other kinds, the general likeness being Chinese. They have ample, luxurious, smooth, glossy foliage; the branches are generally long, the flowers of fine quality, and abundantly produced. The more robust and free-growing of the class make most elegant standards, and are equally adapted for poles and pillars. They do well on the brier for standards, but when grown for pillars, or to train on trellises, are to be preferred on the Manetti. They require a rich soil and abundance of water from April to the end of June, and to be liberally manured every autumn. In pruning, the sorts which make long rods must be very moderately cut back, and superfluous rods must be cut clean out to afford air and light for the rods left for flowering. Young plump rods that rise from the root should be encouraged, and old rods should be cut out to make room for them. The short, twiggy growers may be rather closely pruned.

Hybrid Bourbon Roses

These require the same treatment as the Hybrid China, and generally speaking, may be closely pruned with advantage, say, as a rule, to within five or six buds of the base of each shoot, and at the same time all the spurs that have produced bloom must be removed entirely. They may be pruned with other roses in the month of March; but, if in a sheltered situation, an earlier bloom may be obtained by pruning in November.

Austrian Brier

This little family comprises a few curiosities, and the two best hardy yellow roses known, namely, *Persian Yellow* and *Harrisoni.* They do well as standards on the English brier, and make good wall and pillar roses on their own roots, though rather too rustic in leafage for an elegant trellis. To ensure a plentiful bloom of the glorious Persian yellow, thin out the head carefully, but do not cut any of the shoots that are well placed for flowering. If every year a few shoots are cut out to the base, and the remainder left long, a plentiful supply of golden goblets will be the result. Harrisoni may be slightly pruned and carefully thinned, but close pruning is not to be thought of the common *Austrian briers,* with yellow and copper-coloured flowers, are useful for bouquets and decorative purposes, being small, neat, and very distinct.

Boursault Roses

Boursault roses are probably the produce of a, cross between the Alpine and the China roses. The varieties are well adapted for tall standards and for walls and pillars, as they grow freely, and present a gorgeous display of colour when in flower. They are mostly smooth-stemmed, the shoots long and pendulous, the foliage most luxuriant. They require a rich deep soil and to have no more pruning than suffices to keep them in order, and provide for the access of air and light to all the growth equally. If they are much shortened the bloom will be seriously diminished.

Ayrshire Roses

Ayrshire roses have no claims to attention as exhibition flowers, but they are remarkably hardy, thrive in any soil, and run mad with delight if allowed room to ramble. They are equally valuable to form large weeping standards, or to cover banks, rustic arbours, and to festoon dead trees and archways. When worked on tall English briers, a rich deep soil must be found for them; but when on their own roots any soil will do that is not waterlogged. They should be pruned only for the purpose of keeping them sufficiently thinned and orderly, for to be severely cut back is the worst thing that could happen to them short of being put upon the fire.

Scotch Roses

Scotch roses are neat-growing, but adapted for hedge-rows and shrubbery only, where they present their pretty wild flowers in plenty early in the spring. They do best on their own roots and require no pruning. Special mention may be made of *Stanwell's,* which has pink flowers, and *Sulphurea* the yellow Scotch rose.

Sempervirens or Evergreen Roses

Sempervirens or Evergreen roses are related to the Ayrshires, and have ample dark green leafage, which is retained the greater part of the winter, and large clusters of small but pretty flowers, which are mostly pale in colour.

Banksian Roses

The Banksian rose is of Chinese origin and is almost spineless, very smooth in leaf and stem, in growth a climber, blooming most profusely, the flowers occurring in large clusters. The double white form of *Rosa banksiae* was introduced into England from China in 1807, by William Kerr, and in due course dedicated to Lady Banks. Twenty years later, the double yellow-white variety was introduced, and in 1871 the single yellow form was sent to Kew by Mr. Hanbury. Banksian roses are tender, and require warm walls and a rich dry warm soil. The pruning should be done immediately the bloom is over, and be limited to cutting out the gross shoots.

ROSA BANKSIAE

Multiflora or Polyantha Roses

These roses are differ widely in character, and the several kinds now in cultivation form a group of much value in the garden. The type, *Rosa multiflora*, of Thunberg, and *R. polyantha*, of Siebold, is a native of Japan, and was introduced to European gardens in 1804, but it was not until some fifty years later that it became generally known in this country. It is extremely vigorous, has luxuriant foliage, and produces in great profusion its large clusters of pure white, deliciously fragrant, single flowers. It is invaluable for walls and arches, and, budded on a tall stem, makes a grand standard. From this species has been raised a race of dwarf perpetual flowering varieties.

ARCHES COVERED WITH *ROSA MULTIFLORA*

Autumnal Roses

Damask Perpetual

These roses, now but little grown, bloom superbly from July to October, are highly effective when planted in masses, by reason of their rich colours, and have a spicy and refreshing odour. All the varieties do well on the Italian brier, or on their own roots; and they make good standards on the English brier. They require a rich soil, and liberal watering during the summer, and to be rather closely pruned at the end of March or early part of April.

Hybrid Perpetual

This class is like Moses' serpent, it swallows up all the rest; or, rather, it would do so, were there not always a few resolute rosarian blessed with large and eclectic tastes to save the others from the total eclipse that constantly threatens them. Of their pedigrees, who shall tell? "Oh," says this amateur, who has reflected but little, "here you are—seedling from so and so". Yes, and so far good; but whence the origin of so and so? Let oblivion's curtain fall upon the origin of roses, and then we will confess that we cannot trace the perpetuals to their sources. And yet they are of quite modern origin, the first of the race (known to be such), *Princesse Helene,* dating back only to 1837. That China, Bourbon, and Damask, have mainly contributed to the formation of the race, may be clearly deduced from their more prominent characteristics; but we do find in them traces of Tea and Noisette, and in proportion as the blood of the last two tribes mingles with the stream, the roses manifesting it tend to detach themselves from the "perpetual" group, which has a certain unity and family likeness despite its mongrel character. They are for the most part vigorous growers, with purplish stems formidably armed, abundant darkish leaves, and very large double flowers, the colours of which range from flesh or bright rose to the deepest crimson, shaded with black or purple. It may be roughly said that the family cannot boast a single white or yellow rose; but, as a matter of fact, there are now in cultivation several good white varieties, and a yellow one is the perpetual and for ever-renewed promise of the French raisers. Being a very large family, derived from a variety of sources, it admits of being subdivided, according as certain varieties show more of the Damask or Bourbon or China strain. Thus our brave old friend *General Jacqueminot* has a decided Chinese complexion, and may be drafted to the China group some of these days. So, again, *Madame*

Louise Darzins may be relegated to the Noisettes; the almost forgotten *Duchess of Sutherland*, with its pale green leaves, will be consigned to the race of Damasks, and *Reine Victoria* will be pronounced Bourbon

As the hybrid perpetuals differ in origin and characters, so they differ also in constitution and floral merit. During the past ten years about five hundred new varieties have been put into commerce, and we may estimate that an average of fifty will be added to the lists every year for the rest of our days. Now, as no prudent amateur buys all the new roses, there is a broad margin for selection; and there need be no doubt of this, that a certain number in every batch of novelties may be rejected with the most perfect safety. In making selections our object will be to secure the best; and the question arises, what are the qualities most to be desired in a hybrid perpetual? In respect of the plant, there are two requirements—a good constitution, and a habit of blooming freely in the autumn. Very many so-called perpetuals bloom but sparely in the summer, and never show a flower in the autumn. Such are not worth growing unless they possess some very desirable qualities of flower; and above all things, the flowers should be very double and elegantly modelled, the globular forms being the best, as a rule. Many varieties that are quite second-rate in respect of habit are grown for the sake of some peculiar quality, and a good example of this is *Louis XIV*, which is so exquisitely beautiful", when you can catch it", that the amateur who loves high quality will be content and happy to have its half dozen flowers, while other varieties, not altogether wanting in quality, are producing their flowers by hundreds.

All the hybrid perpetuals require good culture, for their abundant and long-continued flowering exhausts the energies of the plants, and they must be sustained with a rich soil and periodical manuring, and, in the event of a dry season, abundant watering. To assist in the production of a plentiful autumn bloom, the trees should be slightly and carefully pruned as soon as the first bloom is past, and then the surface of the soil should be covered with a, thin coat of fat manure, or with a mixture of guano and wood ashes, and the whole lightly pricked over with a small fork. This treatment will promote vigorous root action, to the great advantage of the autumnal flowers. The finest flowers come at the tops of the strongest shoots; and if quality is more desired than quantity, all the buds except two or three so situated should be removed. They do not all make good standards, but they are, without exception, grown as standards in

H.P. SUZANNE MARIE RODOCANACHI

T. SOUVENIR D'ELISE VARDON

the nurseries, and immense numbers of these are planted in gardens every year, to serve, for all who can learn a lesson, as examples of "how not to do it". The most robust habited sorts are alone adapted for making old bones on the English brier; but they will all thrive on it for a few years, and give finer flowers than on any other stock, or than on their own roots. Amateurs who grow for exhibition bud their own briers, and, as a matter of fact, it is simply impossible to do justice to the rose in any garden, leaving the exhibition business out of the question, unless there is a plot of ground devoted to briers, and a certain, number of them are budded every summer. As for the pruning of hybrid perpetuals, it should be in great part regulated by the style of growth of the several varieties, those that grow most vigorously requiring to be less severely pruned than those that grow moderately. As a rule, however, they bear the knife well, and may be cut back rather close; but if too severely punished, the first bloom, which is always the best, will be lost. Every amateur who wishes to display a few roses to the utmost advantage, for the enjoyment of those of his friends who are not critical florists, should plant a lot of bushes—whether on own roots, cutting or seedling briers—of the most free-flowering sorts, and prune them very slightly. In a few years they will become remarkably handsome, and constitute noble adornments of the garden.

Bourbon Roses

These are invaluable for their fine autumnal flowers, and very often the weak-growing varieties produce flowers of higher quality than the more vigorous. These last, however, make fine pillar roses, and are to be preferred for standards. The remarks offered in the foregoing, paragraph on the hybrid perpetuals apply in every particular to the Bourbons, and therefore we may at once pass on to.

China or Bengal Roses

These are of comparatively small growth, forming neat dwarf bushes and compact headed standards when budded on short brier stocks. Amongst them are some splendid bedding roses, such as the *Common White China*, *Fabvier*, and *Mrs. Bosanquet*, and a few of them are sweet-scented. The *Common China*, with its profusion of pretty pink flowers, is invaluable for the margins of large beds and to form neat dividing screens or hedges. When a district once rural is swallowed up by the growth of a town, the common China is the very first amongst all the roses to show that the air has become too impure for many valued garden plants. It is, in respect of coal smoke a test plant, and we have for that reason called it the *Pilot Rose.* Where the common China thrives, the amateur of roses may take courage, and invest in a rosarium with some degree of confidence; but if it is found to be always in a poor state, rose-growing must be conducted with caution, for probably the atmosphere is loaded with smoke, and it will be hazardous to invest in roses. The China roses require a rather light soil, rich with leaf-mould and hot-bed manure. In pruning them, the longest shoots must be shortened back to keep the plants in order, but, generally speaking, the less pruning they have the better. The *Fairy or Lawrence* rose is too delicate for growing in the open ground, except in localities enjoying special advantages of climate; but as a greenhouse plant it is one of the most beautiful and interesting of all the roses known.

Tea-scented Roses

These are universally regarded as ranking higher than all other roses in the scale of floral excellencies. They are of less value, certainly, than the hybrid perpetuals, because less hardy, and less various in style and colouring; but their delicate fragrance, refined colours, and highly-finished outlines fill the true rosarian with the highest rapture, and engage him to bestow upon the tea roses the best of his attention, and the largest share of his love. To grow tea roses is indeed an object worthy the ambition of the most ardent horticulturist—the more to be esteemed, perhaps, because it is attended with difficulties. The shallow pretender who thinks to accomplish wonders without first preparing his mind and hands for the task, will surely be disappointed; for it is to skilful management alone that these coy and capricious flowers make the response that is desired. They appear to have been designed by nature to furnish the highest test of skill and patience in rose culture, and to afford constant evidence of the fact that the cultivation of roses does not consist in merely buying the plants and sticking them in the ground, and then pruning them with a knife and fork, according to the plan of the jobbing gardener, who thinks that trees of all kinds should be cut down and done away with.

The Tea roses have been known in this country since 1793, when an English amateur named Parsons could boast of possessing it. In 1803, Mr. Evans introduced two or three varieties; in 1809, Sir

A. Hume brought home the old blush-coloured variety; in 1824, Mr. Parkes introduced the yellow; and since then the number has increased considerably, both through successive importations from China and the raising of new varieties from seed in this country and in France. One, the most elegant and useful of the class, *Devoniensis*, was discovered growing in a garden in Devonshire by the late Mr. Pince, of the firm of Lucombe, Pince & Co., and was at once secured for the purposes of commerce.

In constitution the Tea roses vary considerably, the very famous *Gloire de Dijon* being as hardy as any rose in our gardens, wh le *La Boule d'or, Canary*, and others, are so tender that in the climate of London it is impossible to grow them well without the aid of glass, and even in the south of England they suffer in severe winters. The prevailing characteristics of the group are the production of long rods armed with hooked spines of a brownish or purplish colour; the leaves large, glossy, rather distant; the flowers large, semi-double, borne on long foot-stalks, and hence often presented drooping—an attitude favourable to their protection from wind and rain, though not desirable as regards their appearance–and roundish, reddish scarlet fruit. The colours vary from white to citron and rose pink, and the odour they emit may be likened to that of the finest sample of tea newly opened; say, for the sake of being precise, it is a sublime edition of the odour of first-rate orange-scented Pekoe.

To grow Tea roses well, a warm soil and a sheltered position are required; but all the robust varieties, the names of which are given in the lists at the end of this work, may be grown in the open ground in all parts of England south of the Trent, and beyond that line will require the protection of a wall. The weak-growing kinds, and especially those producing yellow flowers, require the protection of glass; and the truth must be told, that to grow a good collection of Teas there must be a spacious cool greenhouse, as well as an out-door rosery. A south wall may be richly adorned with the vigorous growing Teas, which answer better on the English brier than any other class, of roses, because, perhaps, of their near relation to it in vigour and constitution, for they belong to the same natural family of roses. The moderate growers make fine beds when grown on their own roots; and if a severe winter should kill them to the ground, they will be renewed from the roots if the beds are protected with moss or any other kind of dry litter, laid on quite loosely. They may all be grown as standards, but for this purpose the most vigorous growers are to be preferred; and if there is any fear of losing them in the winter, they may be lifted in November, and be planted in damp earth in a shed until the month of March, when they may be again planted. If it is not convenient to lift them, they may be protected with branches of brake or gorse, or even spruce, tied about their heads. It is not desirable to have Dwarf Tea roses on the Manetti, the best stock being the brier, raised from cuttings or seed. When dwarfs are grown for the production of exhibition blooms they should be planted in beds three feet wide and with three feet spaces between them, two rows to be put in each bed. In November, earth up with soil from the spaces, using sufficient to bury seven or eight inches of the lower part of the shoots. Dwarf Teas in beds on the lawn should be earthed up in a similar manner, as when this is done there is very little risk of losses even in severe winters. Should the shoots be killed to the surface of the soil they will be uninjured at the base and be in the best possible condition for making a vigorous growth. The soil should be removed in February.

When grown on English briers, the soil should be a deep, well-manured loam, or a well-worked clay; but when on their own roots they require a decidedly light, rich soil, such as may be secured by incorporating plenty of leaf-mould or rotted turf and old hotbed manure with a deep, well-cultivated loam. Copious supplies of water should be given in the growing season, and an established plantation may be greatly assisted by plentiful waterings with liquid manure, say the drainings from a dung-heap, diluted with soft water to the colour of the palest pale ale. To obtain large flowers, thin away all the buds except those at the tops of the strongest shoots.

To prune these roses requires a careful hand. The whole of the growth may be shortened back in the month of March, but the ripest and best-placed rods must be left a considerable length, and those that are not well placed should be cut out, or cut hard back to a bud so situated that a suitably-placed shoot may be expected of it. In the course of the summer a few very long rods will be produced, and a certain amount of twiggy growth. The latter may be left alone, but the long rods should have their points pinched out as soon as they begin to get firm; and this proceeding will promote the production of a plentiful crop of side shoots, bearing an immense number of the loveliest of flowers.

Noisette Roses

Noisette roses date from 1814, when Phillipe Noisette sent from America to his brother, Louis Noisette, a rose of his own raising from the Musk rose, crossed with the pollen of the Tea rose. The Noisette roses now constitute a small and somewhat distinct group, the proper characteristics of which are the production of long rods armed with hooked thorns, a plentiful and beautiful glossy leafage, and an immense profusion of flowers in large clusters. Those charming varieties, *Aimee Vibert*, *Ophirie*, and *Caroline Marniesse* may be regarded as typical Noisettes; but *Marechal Niel*, *Lamarque*, and *Triomphe des Rennes*, which we must class as Noisettes having much of the Tea character; and the pretty *Fellenberg*, with its brilliant crimson flowers, is very much of a China in constitution. They are all rather tender, but, generally speaking, the entire group may be grown as standards in the open ground, or with the aid of a wall, in any garden south of the Tweed; and a few of them, such as *Aimee Vibert*, *Jane Hardy*, *Reve d'Or*, *La Biche*, and *Celine Forestier* are as hardy as the hybrid perpetuals. The robust growers make fine standards on the brier, and superb pillar and wall roses on the Banksian, which is also a good stock for the more delicate habited of the Teas. When on their own roots they make nice beds, though rather straggling in growth. In pruning they should be well thinned out, as they always throw out more shoots than are wanted to make good heads, unless they are trained in to a wall full length, in which case it will be necessary occasionally to remove an old shoot and replace it with a young one. In respect of shortening the shoots left, it must be done with moderation, for severe pruning will never suit Noisette Roses.

Musk Roses

Whenever the literary history of the rose shall be written, the Musk rose, *Rosa moschata*, will furnish the subject for a chapter on Feasts of Roses, and perhaps another on the fables of the East, in which the rose holds a conspicuous place. The Musk rose is undoubtedly that which give its characteristics hues and odours to the celebrated "Gul Reazee," or "scattering," which forms the subject of many a Persian lay, and is introduced with the most refined taste in the last and lightest and fancifulest of the stories in Moore's great poem, "Lalla Rookh." It is impossible, indeed, to make even the slenderest acquaintance with oriental romance without observing that the Musk rose is a truly classical flower; less famous than the

Lotus, because less associated with superstitious rites and transcendental analogies; yet in another sense more famous, because more completely associated with the industry and pleasures of the people. It is probable the "Gul sad berk," or rose of a hundred leaves (*Rosa centifolia*), furnishes the principal part of the otto, or attar, whIch is so celebrated in Eastern commerce; but in many districts the Musk rose takes its place, and acquires an equal fame as a "source of wealth with that it otherwise enjoys as a source of imagery, allegory, and fanciful satire. According to Forster, the roses of Kashmire are the most celebrated in the East for brilliancy of colour and delicacy of odour, and thence we are wafted by the light-hearted poet to witness the festival of the scattering:

"Who has not heard of the Vale of Cashmere,
With its roses the brightest the world ever gave;
Its temples, and grottoes, and fountains as clear
As the love-lighted eyes that, hang over their wave?"

Moore's *Light of the Harem*

The supposed association of the rose and the bulbul, or nightingale, forms the subject of a thousand gay fancies and pictures and dreams. Jami says, "You may place a hundred handfuls of fragrant herbs and flowers before the nightingale, yet he wishes not in his constant heart for more than the sweet breath of his beloved rose". In the second part of the "Veiled Prophet" occurs that well-known and exquisitely musical and tender lyric—one of Moore's happiest efforts:

"There's a bower of roses by Bendemeer's stream,
And the nightingale sings round it all the day long;
In the time of my childhood 'twas like a sweet dream
To sit in the roses, and hear the bird's song.

That bower and its music I never forget,
But oft when alone, in the bloom of the year,
I think, Is the nightingale singing there yet?
Are the roses still bright by the calm Bendemeer?"

Having indulged a sprit of discursiveness so far, let us wind up this part of the subject with a genuine Persian fable, which may any day be used to illustrate the Scripture text, "A little leaven leaveneth the whole lump". A traveller, in passing through a country in Persia,

ROSA MICROPHYLLA

chanced to take into his hand a piece of clay which lay by the wayside, and to his surprise he found it to exhale the most delightful fragrance. "Thou art but a poor piece of clay," said he; "an unsightly, unattractive, poor piece of clay; yet how fragrant art thou! how refreshing! Whence hast thou this fragrance?" The clay replied, "I have been dwelling with the rose".

The White Musk is one of the famous old English roses, I quite uncared for by our amateurs, but much prized in many a cottage and farm-house garden. This is a free-growing rose, the flowers of which exhale a delicious fragrance in the cool of the evening, and thus very appropriately adapt themselves to the fancies of the poets, who picture it as the favourite flower of the nightingale. The treatment required by these roses is that recommended for Noisettes, which they closely resemble both in their habit of growth and style of blooming.

Macartney Roses

The true Macartney rose; *Rosa bracteata*, is a pretty single flower, with evergreen and glossy foliage. From this a few varieties have been raised, bearing the general designation of Macartney roses. Among the best of these is *Rosa Hardii*, a hybrid between a variety of bracteata and the single yellow Persian. This is a rather tender yellow rose, with evergreen foliage, worthy of culture in the greenhouse or orchard-house. *Maria Leonida*, with delicate blush flowers, is tolerably hardy, and is a pretty rose for a rockery or bank in a sheltered position.

Small-Leaved Roses

Rosa microphylla, the small-leaved rose, introduced from China in 1823, bears a close resemblance to the Macartney, and is believed to be one of its hybrids. Of the Microphyllas, *Rubra plena*, deep red, with prickly calyx, and *Rugosa*, with fine large crimson-purple flowers, are the only kinds that are worthy of attention. To do justice to these roses—which are in their way truly beautiful—they must, if grown out of doors, have a warm wall and a dry border. They require scarcely any pruning, and grow with vigour, though not to a large size. When grown under glass, their beautiful evergreen foliage is preserved in all its proper freshness, and adds very greatly to their value. To improve this race should be the object of every genuine lover of the rose.

Chapter 3

FORMING THE ROSARIUM

The formation of the Rosery, Rosarium, or Rose Garden, claims attention first amongst the many practical matters that are now before us. As the rosarium may be very humble or very grand, may suit the means of a bank clerk or gratify the ambition of a horticultural mogul, this chapter must be comprehensive, and deal with matters of taste and opinion, as well as matters of fact. It must be admitted, at the outset, that a rosarium worthy of the name is a good feature in a garden, and, as a rule, will prove to be the most popular of all distinct features, not excepting even the American garden, which should be indescribably gorgeous in June; or the Herbaceous border, which should be tasteful and brightly coloured during June, July, August, and September. But it must also be admitted, and in the interest of thousands of amateurs whose hearts are larger than their purses, the admission should be made here at the outset of our practical work, a rosarium worthy of the name is not absolutely necessary for the intellectual study and tasteful enjoyment of roses. We may cover walls, pillars, verandhs, arches, arbours, and fences with climbing roses; we may mix standard roses with the rhododendrons and deciduous shrubs in beds and borders; we may enliven the lawn with beds of dwarf roses, and appropriate a greenhouse to tea roses, and thus have a feast of roses comprising a number of distinct and delicate dishes, presented in convenient and agreeable succession, and yet lack, O genius of propriety! the pretentious thing properly and pleasingly designated a Rosarium! There must be a bit of ground, and some real sunshine, and a little leisure, to make, by the aid of roses, a rosarium; but the amateur who loves roses will derive entertainment from a small collection, even though the plants may be scattered. Whatever the extent of the rosarium, however, it must be founded on correct principles, and this will be the first subject of remark.

On the subject of soil we shall now say very little, as that has been considered in the last chapter, at some length. It is, however, proper here to remark that a rosarium of some sort may be made on almost any kind of soil, and in any case the selection of roses must be adapted to the soil, whether it be of the best or the worst possible nature. For example, if we wanted to form a rosarium on sand or chalk we should begin by excavating the soil so as to have it sunk below the general level, and we should carefully avoid brier roses as unsuitable, giving the preference to manetti or own root roses, as preferable for a hungry soil; and amongst the classes we should give preference to the moderate rather than the rampant growers, for the more robust the habit of the plant, the deeper and richer, as a rule, the soil should be.

As to the climate, the rose is somewhat fastidious, but the; worst of climates will produce roses of some sort; and the classes, and even the varieties, should be selected with a view to obtain from the climate, conditions of temperature, humidity, and exposure, the best possible results in the way of roses. All the high-class roses require full exposure to rain and sunshine, and, to some extent, to all the winds of heaven; but, as a rule, roses of good quality require shelter against the cruel east winds of March and April, and the destructive storms that occur at all seasons. Therefore, in selecting a site for a rose garden, or even a single small bed of roses, aspect and climate must be thought of as matters of primary importance, and the amateur must make the best of the conditions at his command. In districts well planted, there may be no necessity at all to provide shelter especially for roses, and it is well to keep always in mind, that if shaded by trees or walls, or exposed to a roasting heat, or subjected to the constant action of strong winds, roses will not thrive, and, therefore, if the conditions *ab initio* are against them, the conditions must be improved. The protection afforded by walls is better than none; but belts of shrubbery or hedges of beech, hornbeam, arbor vitae, privet, yew, or holly, are to be preferred both for the good of the roses, and the completeness of the picture they are to aid in producing. Hedges of roses are often recommended for the purpose of a boundary to the rosarium proper, but they are not sufficiently definite, and something else than roses is required to satisfy an exacting taste. In the scheme of a rosarium there may be provided suitable places for hedges of roses, and truly wonderful those hedges might be if judiciously managed; but the eye will range beyond them and look for a more distinctive boundary, such as a rich dark line of clipped yew or glistening holly would afford. In selecting a boundary fence we should object to quicks, because they are liable to the attacks of insect pests that also attack roses, and might serve as a nursery to breed destroyers of the rosarian's peace. If the rosarium is not within view from the house, beech or hornbeam may be employed with advantage; but on the other hand, if the rosarium constitutes a feature in the view from the windows, an evergreen hedge must be adopted, and the best is holly; but as it grows at the rate of only an inch in a century, yew is usually preferable; but arbor vitae is a capital plant for the purpose, as it may be clipped without injury. The cheapest and quickest evergreen fence may be made with privet, but it is not a choice material, and we do not recommend it.

In the disposition of the ground, it must be remembered that roses are thirsty, hungry things, and, therefore, it is not well to raise the site of any of the beds above the general level. As a matter of taste it will generally be found conducive to the enjoyment of roses to have the entire rosarium placed *below* the general level, and to provide a walk round it *on* the general level, to afford an advantageous view of the flowers, and at the same time ensure the concealment of the sticks. And this concession to taste will be good for the roses, unless the ground is actually swampy, for they love to be kept cool at the root in the heat of summer, and apart from matters of taste merely, a sunk rosery is more likely to be a success than one raised above the level. Another matter of importance, already slightly adverted to, is the placing of the rose garden, if possible, in a position where it will be seen only by those who seek for it; for it is not good for the roses or their owner that they should obtrude upon the scene commanded by the windows, for they are unattractive during, eight months out of twelve, and occasionally require attentions that cannot be comfortably afforded them when they are planted on the parade, under the constant eye of the general, whether he is in a mood for reviewing them or would fain forget them in the enjoyment of his matutinal rasher. In the suburbs of all our great towns we see what comes of the idea that roses should be planted near the house in conspicuous positions, for nine-tenths of all the entrance courts to snug villas are disgraced with things called standard roses, that rise out of the green turf like so many mops, or scare-crows, or machines for sweeping chimneys, and proclaim to, the passers by that "roses are *not* grown here, and it is to be feared, never will be!"

Yet one more condition of success in designing and arranging a, rosarium. It will be necessary occasionally to go amongst the trees to prune; label, and admire them. Hence the beds should be of convenient size, so that very much of the attentions to be paid the trees may proceed from the proper gravel walk or grass turf, and no temptation be offered to visitors to go into the midst of them to break their branches and tread the soil about their roots into a pavement. To make a rule prohibiting anyone from crossing the threshold to revel in the rosy thicket will be a folly, because the rule will be broken daily all the summer long; but it will be prudent so to dispose of the ground, and the trees, that visitors who love flowers in a general way, and are not severe critics of roses, may see the flowers advantageously and be satisfied. Moreover, it is a fine thing to protect our friends against temptation, especially if consenting to it should prove injurious to ourselves.

The reader who purposes to layout a grand rosarium will have no difficulty in finding examples that may be copied, or plans perfectly adapted to the ground intended for the scene of the enterprise. As a matter of general advice, it may be remarked that simplicity is much to be desired in the plan of a rosery, and that the production of a distinct and powerful display of colour will not be sought by a thorough amateur of roses. One of the most enjoyable displays of roses amongst many, large and small, that we are acquainted with, consists of a series of oblong beds, fifteen feet in length by five feet in width; arranged in regular order on the skirt of a wide lawn, and separated from the dressed grounds and the view from the windows by a belt of shrubbery, that also serves to shelter the roses from the north and west; to the east and south they are fully exposed. The beds are planted with showy standards in the centre, and bushes on the outside, and the shrubbery is lighted up with standards, which rise above the hollies, junipers, and berberries, and not only adorn, but visibly connect the shrubbery with the formal display of roses in the beds. A rose garden less happily

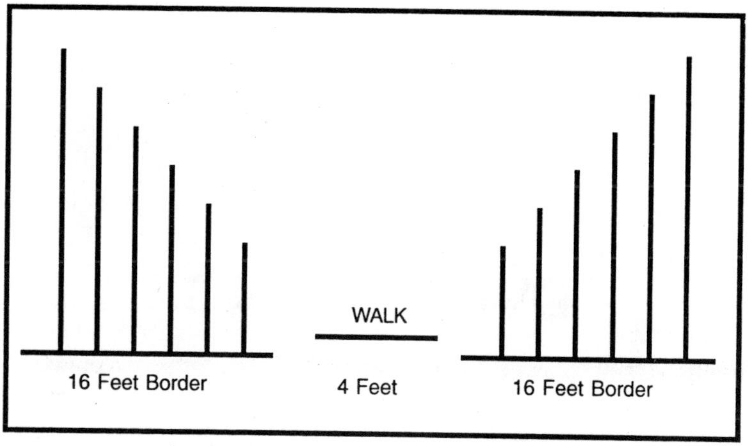

situated, and having no ample space of; grass turf to enhance the delicate beauty of the flowers, or encourage idle enjoyment of them, may be made very interesting and attractive. It may, indeed, be so arranged as to afford every facility for comparing and criticising varieties, and for making additions to the collections or alterations in the general scheme, as may be desired. Presuming we have a piece of ground 36 feet in width; it can be divided into two broad borders of equal width by the simple process of cutting a walk down the centre. If the walk is four feet wide and that width is the most suitable—we shall have on either side a sixteen feet border, which will afford sufficient, space for five rows of dwarfs, half standards, and standards, and one row of climbers trained to poles and chains. If a still greater space is available, there may be a narrow walk at the back, with a hedge of privet or some other close-growing shrub. The manner in which the trees should be arranged will be best explained by the diagram.

Simple as this arrangement unquestionably is, the effect produced when the roses are in bloom will be so extremely beautiful as to be a veritable surprise to those accustomed to roses grown in isolated beds, or scattered about the mixed borders. As a matter of course, the standards must be planted far enough apart to allow a careful amateur to pass readily amongst them without doing any damage.

Chapter 4

DWARF ROSES

Dwarf Roses are produced in a variety of ways, and with various kinds of materials. Some few of the methods are of the most simple nature, and demand the least imaginable amount of skill; others are complicated, and require the direction of trained hands and eyes, aided by considerable experience. We shall in this chapter describe as briefly as possible all the modes by which dwarf roses may be formed from plants already in the cultivator's possession, reserving the subject of raising roses from seed for separate treatment.

Suckers and Layers

The easiest of all methods of obtaining young plants suitable to form bush roses is to remove rooted suckers from thriving plants of sorts that are worth multiplying. Some kinds form suckers in plenty, others rarely produce them sufficiently far apart from the root stock to be suitable for separation. If a healthy sucker has grown freely all the summer, it may be taken off the ensuing autumn, and, if furnished with a few roots to begin with, will make a nice plant in the course of the next year, if carefully treated. To secure it, first remove the earth carefully from that part of the root stock whence the sucker proceeds; and, having traced it home, remove it by a clean cut with a sharp knife or fine saw. It will be prudent to, cut it down to one half, or even to one third its length before planting it. Select for it a sheltered nook, and plant in good mellow soil, and leave it to its fate. It would be better practice to plant it in a brick pit, with a view to afford it shelter during the first winter; but it will do nearly as well in the open

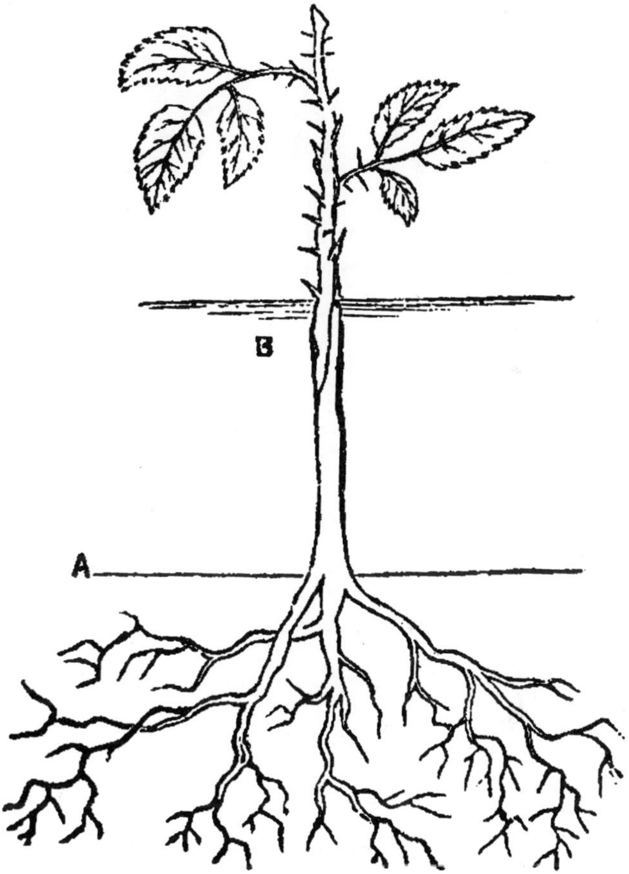

A: Original Ground Line
B: Present Ground Line

ground if planted rather deeply, and in a spot somewhat sheltered. If it be desired to raise a quantity of roses from rooted suckers, the parent plants may be induced to assist in the operation, even if they are not on their own roots. We will suppose that you are about to plant Manetti roses, and wish them to make roots of their own, with a view to increase of stock. You must first search for the

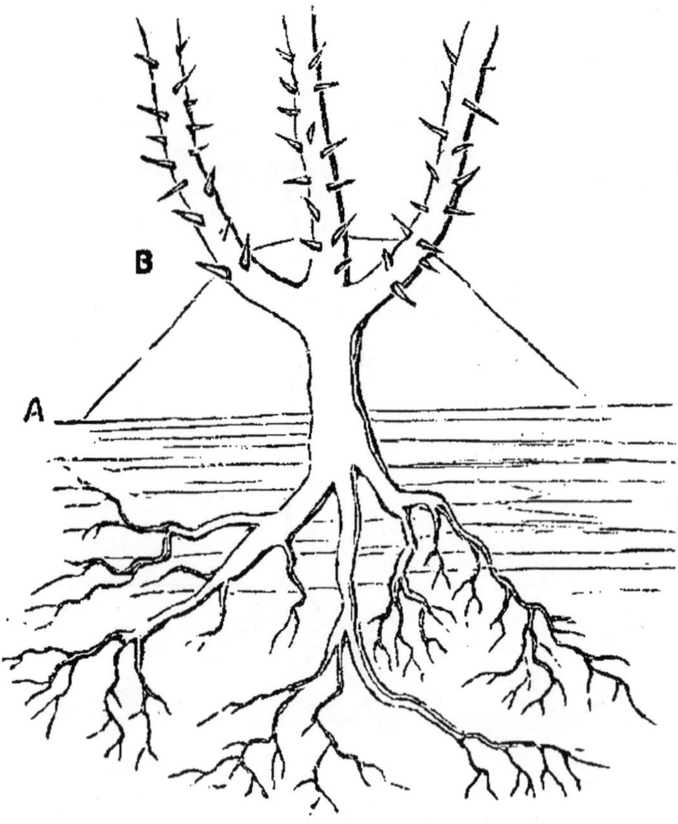

A: Original Ground Line
B: Present Ground Line

"work"—that is, the point where rose and stock are united by a kind of scar just above the roots. Just above or at the junction make a slight notch with a sharp knife by cutting out a little wedge-shaped piece (not of the stock, but) of the rose, as at B in the figure. Now plant it so that the notch is below the ground line, and wait for the result. It may be that the rose you desire to multiply is standing in the; ground, and has a number of shoots rising from a short stem close to the ground. This is often the state in which we find Manetti roses that were worked too high, or not planted deep enough, in the first instance. The treatment, however, is precisely the same. At the base of every shoot that is so situated as to be easily covered, a notch must be made, and then some fine earth or a mixture of leaf-mould and powdery manure must be heaped up from the original ground line A to cover the notches at figure. The size of the notch must be proportioned to the stoutness of the wood; it must always be deep enough to remove a portion of the true bark, but must never be so deep or so wide as to materially, weaken the stem, because, if it should snap in consequence, you will be the poorer instead of the richer for the proceeding. Unthrifty standards may be made to yield own-root roses by laying them down so that the base, of every good shoot may be covered with earth, as in the sub-joined rough figure.

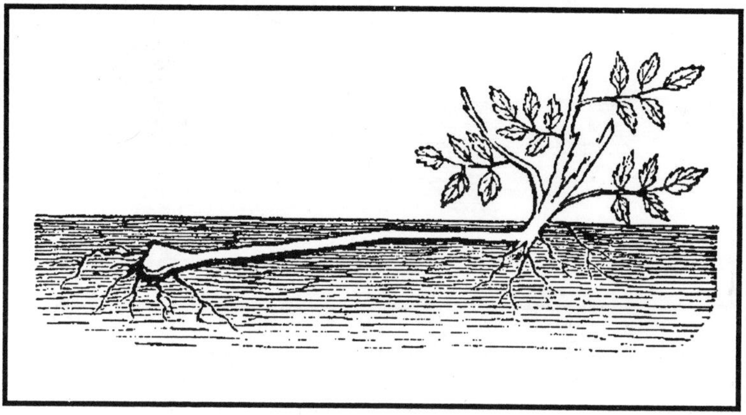

In resorting to this practice, it will be well for the amateur to bear; in mind that the brier will probably die, and therefore, if the shoots do not make roots of their own, they must die also. To make the more sure of success, it is advised to cut notches or tongues in the shoots, and cover with mellow sandy soil.

An enlargement of this simple plan consists in, "laying down" the rods in a way to induce them to form roots at any distance from the root stock or "collar." This is called "layering." It may be practised at any season, but the best time is in summer, when the shoots are about half ripe. If done too soon, the soft shoots die, through being placed in contact with the earth; if too late, the ripe shoots are liable to snap away at the base in bringing them down. First lay down a good rod, and fix it with a strong peg. Now release it, and cut a notch or a tongue on the under side, at any point where it admits of

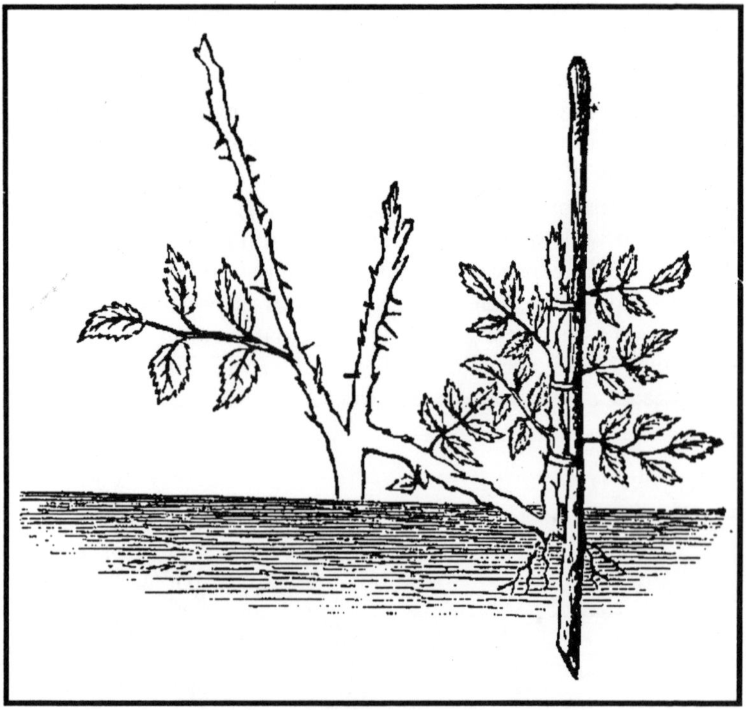

being covered most readily. Now fix it again as before, and heap a little mellow mixture, such as leaf-mould and pulverised manure, over the tongue, and the operation is completed. We have multiplied China roses in quantity by a variation of the usual mode of layering. We first cut a few inches of the softest growth from the point of a shoot, then strip off the leaves half its length, then bend it and thrust it down into a common pot, and fix it with a peg. The pot is soon full of roots; and, by severing the shoot, a detached and independent plant already potted is obtained, with the least imaginable trouble.

Circumposition

This is a modification of layering, but instead of bringing the branch to the earth we carry the earth to it. On several occasions we have resorted to this mode to ensure stock of a scarce variety, of which, perhaps, we had command of only one or two plants. We have planted them near a wire trellis, and instead of pruning the shoots have drawn each through a common flower-pot, which was

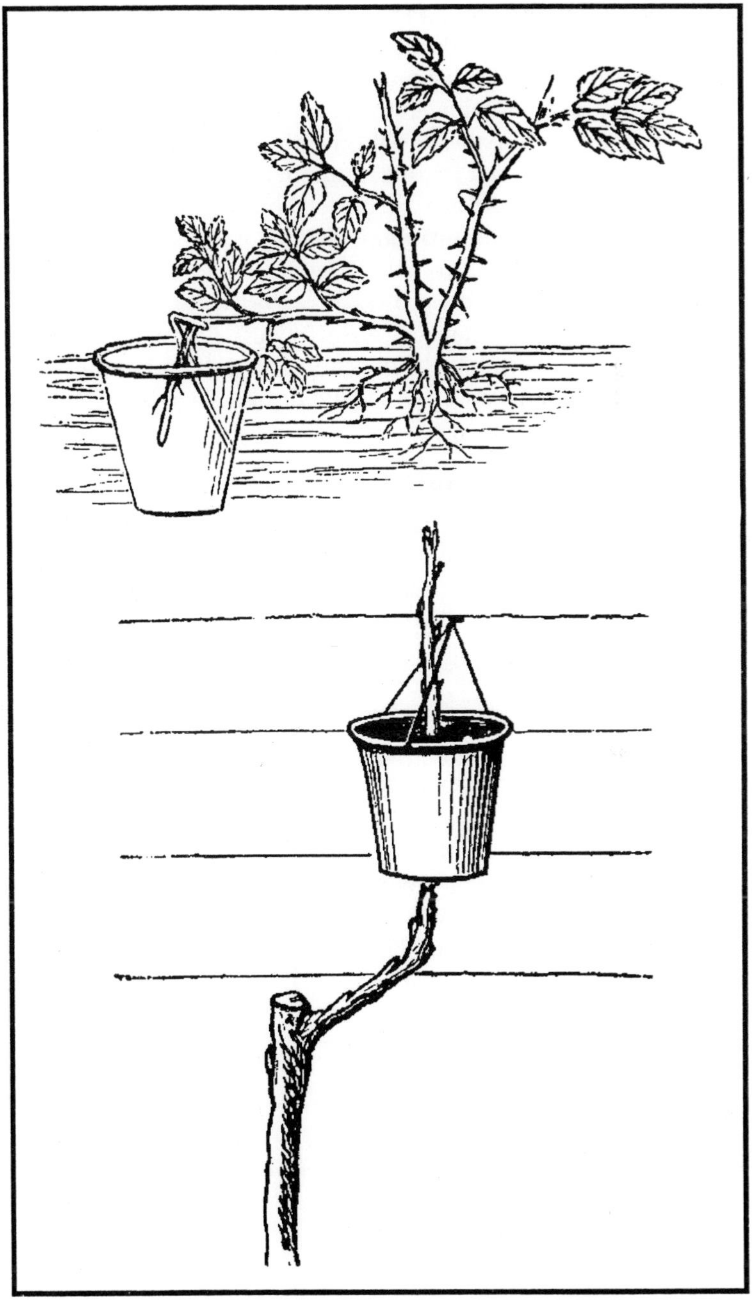

then fastened to the wire, and filled with fine soil. If kept always moist, the pot is filled with roots in the course of the season, and in the autumn the rooted shoot may be cut through close under the pot, and the pot then contains an independent plant. In this case the cutting of a notch expedites the rooting process, and it is all-important to give water regularly and in hot weather to clothe the pot with rough moss, which can be tied on with bast or string. If the shoot cannot be drawn through, break a pot into two equal parts, and bring them together to enclose the shoot, and tie them firmly. If there is no support for the pot already provided, it may be fixed to a stake, as in the figure annexed. A thrifty bush rose in a pot may be propagated by layering the shoots into pots plunged in the soil all around it. This plan answers well with flexible wiry-branched Teas and Noisettes.

Summer Cuttings

Summer cuttings afford an easy and cheap mode of producing dwarf roses on their own roots. There is no prettier practice in all the range of gardening operations than that which is to be described in this section, unless it be the one that follows–the propagation, not from, cuttings, but from eyes, or wood buds.

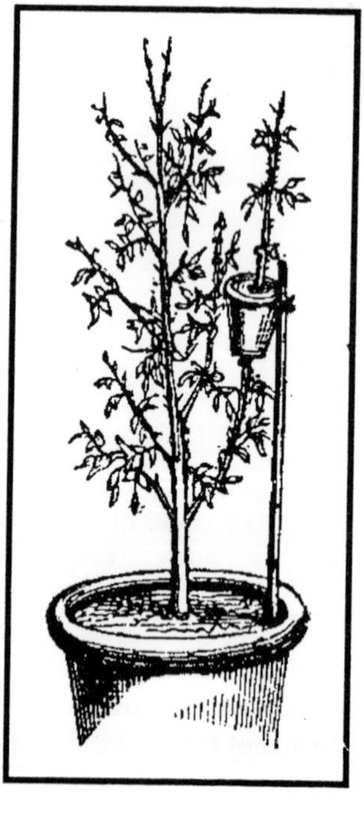

The primary requisites are roses to cut from, and a good frame or pit, and a few bell glasses or earthenware propagating boxes. The thoroughly skilful can do without even these simple appliances; but we advise the beginner to secure the aid of a frame on a half-spent hot-bed, or on a bed of common soil raised above the level, to catch as much as possible of the sun-heat. The cuttings must be kept rather dark, and constantly moist, and rather warm; but they must not be really wet, and they must have a little light, and a strong heat will kill instead of cure them.

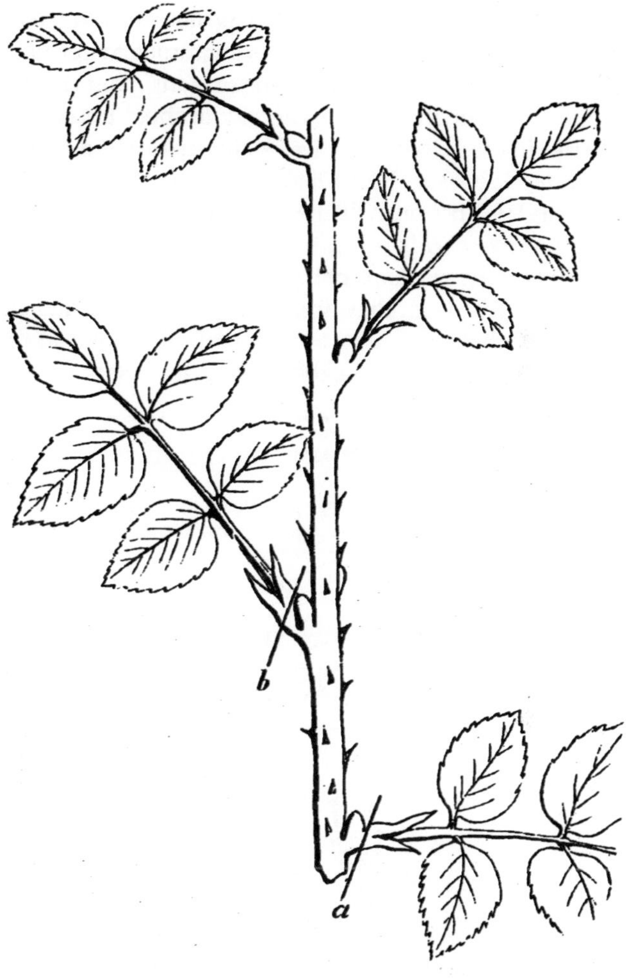

SUMMER CUTTING, WITH PUSHING BUDS.
Leaves to be Removed at *a* and *b*

It will be convenient to recognise the propagation from eyes, concurrently with the treatment of cuttings, because it is good practice to adopt both methods, for the more complete economy of all the wood that can be cut at the time the trees are full of nice half-grown shoots, which we may for general purposes consider to be the last week in June. The first step towards success is to cut judiciously, taking in every case firm shoots of the season, but avoiding always hard ripe wood as unsuitable. The model shoot for cutting is one that carries in the axil of every leaf-stalk a *visible* bud. This is called by cultivators a *pushing* bud. On old wood the buds are sometimes invisible, and will not push till the trees are pruned back next season. These are *dormant* buds. As autumn approaches, most of the buds on the upper parts of shoots of the season are invisible, and will not grow at all this season; they are, in fact, formed for next season's growth—and these also are dormant buds. But if we take a strong shoot which towers up above the flowers, and examine it, we shall

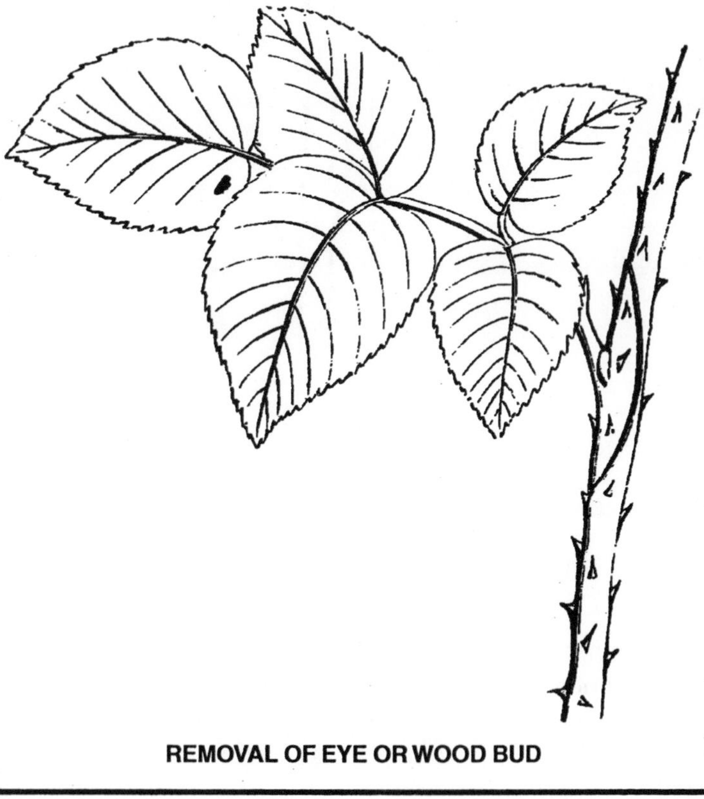

REMOVAL OF EYE OR WOOD BUD

see that the buds on the shoot are visible, nay plump; and we may guess, if fond of guessing, that when the July rains come many of those buds will push and form short side branches with flowers on them. These, then, are pushing buds, and such will best serve our purpose, though dormant buds may be used if none others are to be had, because the treatment will make them push when the proper time comes.

Take the knife and boldly cut away one of the strongest shoots of this year—not to the base, but within a fourth part of its length from the base. You may go quite to the base if you like, but we are thinking of providing you with cuttings without sacrificing the autumn bloom of the roses, and if you leave a fourth part of every shoot you cut, the buds on the part left will provide you with flowers shortly, and the process of obtaining the cuttings will be equivalent merely to a summer pruning. The very soft wood at the top of the shoot is not of much value to a beginner—cut it away, say three joints down. Now cut all the rest to lengths of, four joints each, as shown in the figure at page 51, with the knife remove the lowest pair of leaves by cutting them through as close to the stem as possible without hurting the bud at the base as shown at a and b. You have now the best-sized cutting for a beginner. Prepare as many as you like, plant them all in pans filled with sandy peat or leaf-mould, with an inch of sand on the top, and they will everyone root if you manage them properly. Proper management consists in planting them so deep that the second leaf from the top just escapes being covered with soil—in other words, plant them to the second joint, and no deeper. They must be kept shaded and moist—never wet, never dry; aired daily, but with caution—a mere peep at them daily for the first week will secure them air enough; after that time, the glasses may be taken off and wiped dry daily, and replaced after a few minutes.

When you have had a little practice in this way, you may make the cuttings with two joints only, and in this case you may do without a joint in the soil. Pass the knife clean through between the second and third joint, plant as before to the second joint, handle them carefully, and they will root from the "internodes"—that is, from the space between the joints to which they have been cut in preparing them.

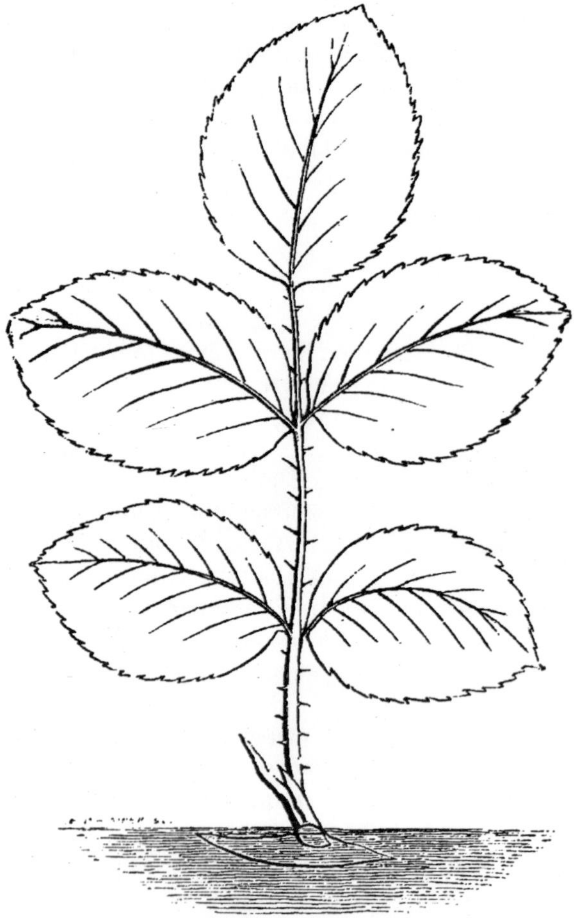

ROSE BUD INSERTED IN THE SOIL

Eyes or Wood Buds

The next practice will be to make one leaf and one joint suffice, with an inch of wood attached, and this is easily done, and ought to be done to prepare the practitioner for a skilful handling of eyes, which make better plants than cuttings, and, in fact, the best plants that can be had; they have the vigour of seedlings, with the advantage of being true to the several kinds from which the buds were taken.

Once more, cut from the tree a nice stout rod of this year. If the buds are pushing, good; but if pushed, they will not do. In other words, if you see the buds, and they look as if they meant to grow this season, you are safe; if they have already begun to grow, and have perhaps pushed to the extent of a sixteenth of an inch, reject them, for you will probably fail in all your efforts to persuade them to make roots. Having your nice, plump, green rod, half ripe, yet in a condition to peel easily—in fact, just such a rod as you would cut if you were intending to bud briers—you are in a fair way to proceed safely. Instead of preparing cuttings, take out each bud with its leaf by a crescent shaped cut as shown in the figure. This, in fact, is the same as if cut for budding, but the leaf is not to be removed, and the wood is not to be removed, so you escape all the "niggling" that is the stumbling-block of nine out of every ten amateur rosarians. Have your pans and glasses ready, the pans with a layer of peat or leaf-mould at the bottom, and at least an inch and a half of silver-sand at top. Plant the bud with the leaf upright, keep it moist and shaded, and in due time it will throw out roots from the edges of the bark all round, and then the leaf will fall, and the bud will start and grow.

Having succeeded in preparing the buds properly perhaps the principal difficulty will be to get them nicely dibbled in, so as to stand firm with all their leaves up above the soil. We always take the bud in the left hand, press a hole in the sand with a bit of stick held in the right hand, place the bud in the hole so deep as just to cover the point of the bud with the sand, and then press it firmly with the thumb placed on one side of it. They may be put very close together in the pans, and if the leaves are very large and when wetted fall over, clip off the top leaflet; the two leaflets then left will suffice to keep the bark healthy till it emits roots for its, own keeping. When planted the bud stands with its leaf erect as represented in the figure.

When a pan is filled, sprinkle the leaves; never mind wetting the sand—if that is just damp it is sufficient; put on the bell-glasses; put the pans into the frame; draw down the light, and take satisfaction to yourself that you have done something.

It is about 35 years since we were taught this plan of propagating roses, and remember as if but yesterday we were told, "All you've got to do, is to keep the leaves alive; if the buds are dry it don't matter". And so we always found it. There will be hundreds of persons at work on eyes this season through the appearance of these remarks, and there will be thousands of eyes lost through too much water. Remember then, not our lesson, but the lesson that was given to us, "Keep the leaves alive; if the buds are dry it don't matter". What is the use of water to a chip of wood that has no roots? Of no use at all; it must be kept plump, but a very little damp in the sand suffices for that. On the other hand, to keep the sap moving, and to preserve the vitality of what is now dependent on absorption only, the leaves must be always moist, and that is to be accomplished by frequent sprinkling, and by keeping them rather close shut up. But herein is another danger. If not daily aired—a few minutes will suffice for the first fortnight—the leaves will decay before the bark has thrown out roots. If this happens, the eyes are lost. But if kept always moist, always warm and close, and yet never saturated, the leaves will be green till roots begin to grow, and at the first start of the bud the leaf will turn yellow and fall, and up will rise the tender shoot to tell you that your work was ably done. Of course, the process of potting off must then commence and the little plants must have thereafter all the care needful to make big ones of them. They must be carefully potted in the smallest thumb pots, in light sandy soil, and be kept close and warm until they begin to grow more fully, and must then have more air and light by degrees.

But touching the making of eyes, we hope it will be understood that young wood and plump eyes are not imperatively needful. Old wood and dormant eyes will make plants, but the process is slower, and the proportion of losses is sure to be greater than with plump buds out from shoots of this season, on which at present none of the buds have begun to lengthen out in actual growth. Those who are used to budding only need select good budding wood—such shoots, in fact, as they would prefer to take buds from, for on these the leaves are fully matured, and capable of sustaining life in the bark and bud for a period of three or four weeks while the bark is forming a callus. Young immature leaves, and the buds at their base, are unfit for the purpose, and it will be a folly to use them, because they are sure to perish. If in the dibbling of the buds into the pans it is found difficult to make the leaves stand up as in the figure, take some fine twigs from an old birch-broom, and stick in to support the leaves, or put a few light stakes round the sides of the pans, and draw a few lengths of twine across, against which the leaves may rest. But all such small difficulties will soon vanish; the few manipulations needed are so simple, that any one with a will is sure soon to discover the way.

As to the subject of heat, a cold frame will answer perfectly in the height of summer in a good season if placed on an elevated bed in the full sun, and kept shaded from nine to six daily till the eyes are rooted. But a very gentle bottom-heat is preferable, and hence a nearly spent hotbed answers admirably. If a bed has to be made up for the purpose, let it be with rotten manure, and in fact the turning over and making up again of a bed which has been in use for early cucumbers will answer admirably, for when rotted manure is forked over and made up into a bed, there is always a gentle fermentation and a moderate heat which lasts a considerable time, and for this purpose will be sufficient. We can imagine an unpretending amateur planting separate eyes in thumb-pots and placing them under an ordinary hand-light, or one of the various plant covers manufactured on the common soil, in a rather shady place, and by covering the glass with canvas or mat all day, and taking it off at night, giving at the same time all needful attention to airing and sprinkling, getting his two or three dozen nice plants on their own roots, and being well repaid for his little trouble. We never did deal with eyes in such an offhand way, but we have rooted thousands of three-joint cuttings in separate thumb-pots under hand-lights on a border, and could get a comfortable living by that practice alone, if need be, for every rose is worth so much money.

In the production of stocks of roses from summer cuttings and eyes, it is essential to take great care of the young plants until, they are strong enough to bear, without injury, the adverse influences to which they are exposed when planted out. The best course will be to leave them undisturbed until the spring following, in the meantime protecting them from severe weather with the lights, supplemented, when necessary, by mats. In the spring, when the young shoots have attained a length of one or two inches, carefully remove them: from the soil and put them singly in small sixties. Handle them carefully, and proceed with the potting expeditiously, for both the roots and new growth are delicate and susceptible to injury. Use a light rich compost, press the soil firmly, and place them where they can be kept close and moist until they have recovered from the removal; then, harden off and, when well rooted, shift into five-inch pots.

Autumn Cuttings

In the latter part of September or first week of October, go over the rose beds and cut off all the straggling shoots, and as many as can be spared of strong ripe rods. Out them up into cuttings (excepting the soft points) about six to nine inches in length. Having previously dug and well broken a piece of ground, and then put upon the surface a good dressing of sand, which slightly stir in, tread the ground evenly all over, and smooth the surface; then take a spade, and begin at one end to open a slight trench; then place a row of the cuttings in about three inches apart, and three or four inches deep, after which close the soil upon them; then open the second row at about six-inches from the first, and proceed as before, and so on until all are planted. By autumn of the next year they will be nice plants, if occasionally stopped when freely growing during, the summer. It is the custom of many to put in winter prunings of roses in this way, and to be content if one in three or four make plants. The plan now recommended will ensure the rooting of nearly all. If the sap has gone down very few will root; but if the cuttings are made whilst the sap is still in motion, a callosity is formed before winter, and the cuttings are able in consequence to resist the inroad of excessive moisture during winter. It is better practice to plant them in old frames or pits, and give some kind of rough shelter during the worst of the winter weather. Many of them will flower the following season if allowed, but it is prudent to nip out the flower buds as soon as they appear. The mode of preparing and planting autumn cuttings is shown in the preceding page.

Spring Cuttings

Rose-growers are annually horrified at the idea of having to waste the spring prunings. The important principle of having the sap in full action before taking cuttings has a capital illustration in the propagation of the rose. Wait till May, and then take cuttings from roses in a house where they have been forced, and are going out of bloom, and you ought not to lose more than one in a thousand. But take prunings in a dormant state, put them over heat, and they are almost sure to perish. That peculiar process, the formation of a callus, which *must* take place before any cutting can throw out roots, requires the sap to be in very free flow, for the callus is formed of sap in the downward course. We do not say that it is impossible to strike

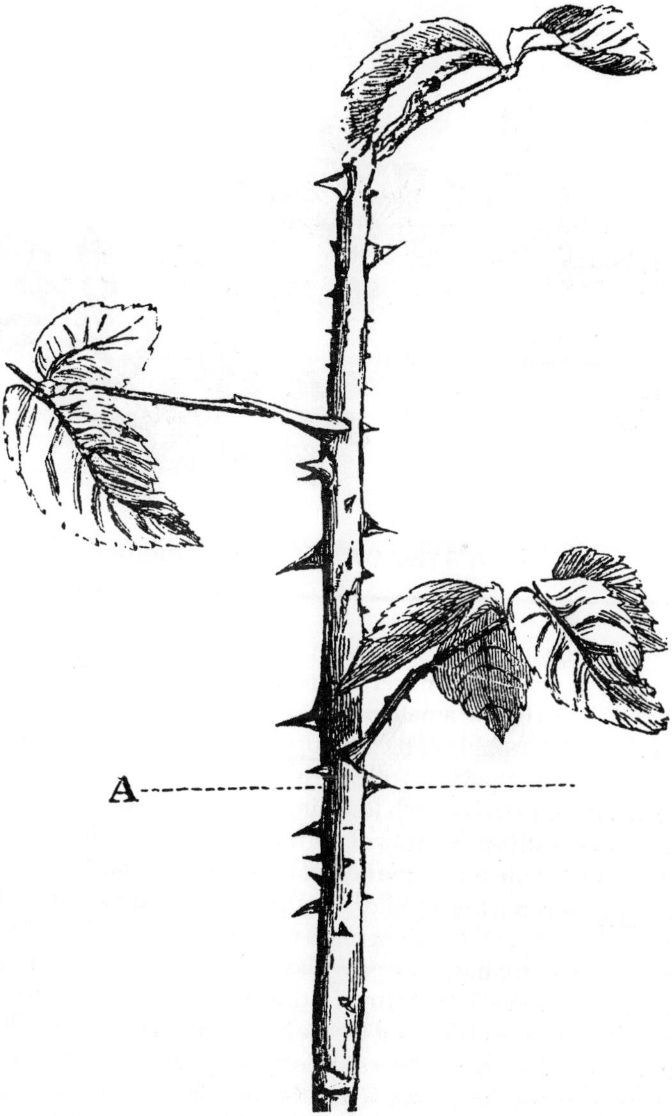

AUTUMN CUTTING PREPARED FOR PLANTING
To be planted as deep as the line *A*

HARDY'S YELLOW ROSE (ROSA HARDII)

the prunings of roses, because it is done every year at the rose nurseries, where they never waste one inch of anything that will make a plant; but no amateur would ever succeed in raising plants to pay for the trouble of picking up the prunings, and tallying the sorts. The only chance is with a brisk *dry* heat. The cuttings to be in sand, only the heel of each touching a hard tile, and the tops to be kept alive with an occasional sprinkle from the syringe. Lay the cuttings in a row across the bed of a propagating tank. Run under the upper ends a thick rod or a couple of laths to raise them to an angle, then cover the ends or heels with the sand, and keep the heat to 70° or 80°, till they root or wither. Of course, moisture must be supplied; let it be in the form of a daily sprinkling of the tops, with enough moisture in the sand for the heat to rise, and no more. If to be tried on a dung-bed, the heat should be fierce, and the cuttings might be thrust in bunches aslant. If in either case they callus properly, the tops will suddenly exhibit a healthy plump appearance, and the buds will begin to start; if they are failing, the leaves will begin to fall off, in which case it will be found, on uncovering them, that they are turning black and hastening to decay.

Chapter 5

THE PROPAGATION OF ROSES BY BUDS AND GRAFTS

Notwithstanding all we have said about the merits of own-root roses, those obtained by budding and grafting are valuable in their way, and as regards the supply of the exhibition table, there can be no question that the very finest flowers are to be looked for on young plants budded on healthy English briers. The Italian brier is of the greatest importance as a carrier of new roses into the market, and is, therefore, largely used by nurserymen, who would be compelled to charge a much higher price than at present rates for novelties, were they to put them on their own roots at once. For these, if for no other reasons, the amateur rosarian must learn the whole art and mystery of budding and grafting, and assuredly, as recreation, it will prove to those who love roses, one of the most agreeable in all the round of rural pursuits.

Standards on the English Brier

The Dog rose is chiefly used in this country in the production of standard roses. For this purpose it is admirably suited, being of vigorous constitution, and well adapted to nourish by far the larger proportion of all the roses known. These Dog roses, or, as they are usually termed, "briers" are managed so as to produce a few young stout shoots the first season after planting, and the buds of choice varieties of roses are inserted in these shoots. There they soon unite with the bark and wood of the brier, and in due time the shoots from these buds form the head of the tree, and all the shoots naturally belonging to the brier are removed. The brier is called the "stock", and the rose is usually spoken of as the "bud" or the "graft," and the place where the bud is inserted, close to the stem of the brier, is generally described as "the work".

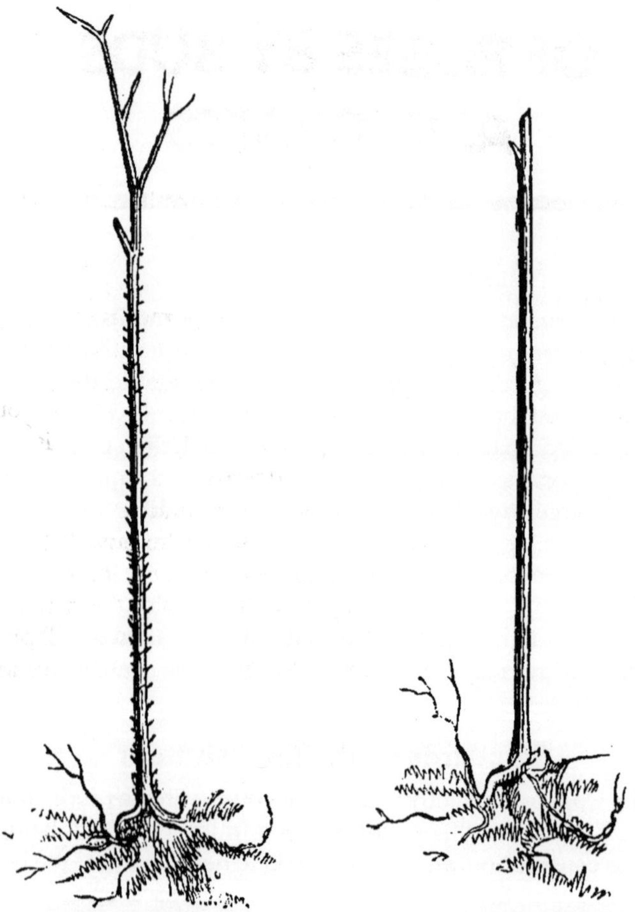

BRIER AS REMOVED FROM THE HEDGE

THE SAME PREPARED FOR PLANTING

November is the season to procure stocks, and they should be taken up carefully and planted with as little delay as possible. You must have them of different sizes and qualities, unless you pick from a large number just those that suit you, and pay a higher price. In sorting them over, give a preference to the straightest green and brown varieties. The lanky dry-looking dark grey sorts are not near so good as those that have a hearty-looking bark, with a stem clean and straight to the head, the colour being of less importance than the shape and size, and the more fibry roots they have the better. Briers are grubbed up so roughly, that you will probably get few with desirable roots; indeed, they cannot as a rule be had with such roots as gardeners delight in, but with huge woody underground stems, frequently of enormous size, and the older the stocks the larger the tap roots. They must first be sorted. Having laid them out in separate parcels, take a sharp saw and trim up the roots. In this operation a large portion of the tap root will have to be cut away, and in so doing cut so as to reduce it as much as possible without loss of fibres, for, though the absence of fibres is not a very serious objection, the more you have the better, because in the quick root action which most deciduous shrubs make after being moved in winter, the earliest and best roots will spring from those portions which are already furnished with fibres. Wherever a bud may be visible and like1y to produce a sucker in the following year, rub it off; and when the roots are brought to neat shape and compass, smooth over every portion that the saw has cut with a sharp knife. The heads will be trimmed off before you get them, but a little more trimming will be necessary. Remove all side shoots and reduce the stems to such a size as may be desirable, cutting each to a good bud or ring if the bud is plainly marked out close to it, that the bark may close over the cut part in the next summer's growth. But if you are in doubt, cut a few inches above where you expect the head to break, and the portion left will be useful to tie the tender shoots to, delaying the final removal of that portion till the graft has taken, and is able to heal the wound over.

Whatever wounds may occur, and every part fairly cut in the trimming up, should be *at once* smeared over with a preparation of half bees' wax and halt pitch, melted in a pipkin, and well mixed and melted together. The tops of the stocks may be dipped into the mixture while it is warm, and any wounds on the stem may be smeared over with a brush. This operation is useful as excluding the air from the injured portions, thereby aiding the formation of new bark to cover the abrasions. It is, however, very much neglected as troublesome; and in most cases the wounds heal over by the natural tendency of the plants to establish themselves in a healthy manner. The operation of removing the prickles is usually deferred till the season of budding; but it is better done at once, for at budding time the plants do not so well bear handling, and any wound causes an escape of sap, and the atmosphere is very destructive when acting on the exposed inner bark of the rose.

The removal of prickles is a matter of quite secondary importance. Those who are accustomed to handle roses suffer but little, however formidable the prickles may be, and where large numbers are grown, it consumes an, immense amount of time to detach them in detail.

In planting it is as well to economise space, for stocks need occupy but little room the first season. Take the sizes, and if possible make a row of each, or make two rows of each size, placing the rows in pairs, and leaving alleys between each pair only, so as to operate on each pair from the side next each alley. The best sizes for general stock are for the first row one foot, which make nice low border or pot plants; next eighteen inches, then two feet, two feet six inches, three feet, three feet six inches, and four feet for the last row. Any taller stocks planted for special purposes should be most carefully selected. Unless very strong and quite ripe they will not have sufficient vigour to take buds until perhaps the second season, or may in spite of you break half way down the stem, and compel you at last to cut them over equal with some of the dwarfest. When planted in rows, you need only leave space between for moderate freedom of action in superintending and managing; and in the rows they may be six or nine inches apart, the tallest not more than a foot at the most. Having planted them, drive a firm stake at the end of each row and run a lath or hazel rod along, and to the rod attach the head of each by a safe fastening. They will then be secure against wind, and kept neatly together for economy of space and facility of cultural operations.

Supposing adverse influences to work against you, stocks may be planted as late as February or March, or even to the middle of April; but every day's delay after the first week in November is a day lost, not in time merely, but in the strength and life of the plants, and in the chances of ultimate success. The later they are planted the later they break, and the more gaps occur from the presence of dead sticks in the rows.

Entering the Buds

As soon as the stocks begin to throw out shoots look over them occasionally, and rub off every bud that shows below the head, unless the top of the stock produces no shoots, in which case wait a little; and if the head is evidently weak, but a strong bud appears on the stem, cut the stock down to that bud, and let it push. One or two others will be pretty sure to appear in the vicinity, and you will probably get shoots for working, though at a lower height than the row to which the stock belongs. If a stock appears weakly and has been already shortened sufficiently, it is sometimes advisable to let a few superfluous shoots remain; for they help to increase the size and strength of the stock, for it is by the elaborating power of the foliage that wood is formed. At the same time, the best general rule is to allow only such shoots to remain as are really wanted. Two good shoots, well placed, are sufficient.

The best time to bud roses is from the middle of June to the end of August. The sooner it can be accomplished safely the better, but it is quite useless to attempt it unless the stocks are in a vigorous state and the sap rising freely, a condition indicated by the bark parting readily from the wood. After rain this happens with more certainty, and if the weather is cloudy there will be less evaporation, and hence fewer chances of failure. During hot weather it will be, desirable to cover every bud the instant it is entered with a cabbage or rhubarb leaf, which can be tied with a strip of bass, but as the buds do not take well in such weather defer the operation if you can until cloudy weather returns. The bark will never part so easily as after rain; and unless the bark of the bud and that of the stock be brought into conjunction quickly, and at a time when there is plenty of sap in the latter, and the atmospheric action somewhat reduced, there is the smallest possible chance of success. Choose cloudy weather, therefore; if immediately after a soaking rain all the better, and let the operation be performed either very early in the morning or in the evening. If all the circumstances are favourable, a well entered bud will begin to grow in a fortnight or three weeks after being entered; and will make a hard ripe shoot long before winter, from which of course the head is to be formed the following year.

Now a question of some importance arises. What is most likely to check the growth of a stock at budding time? Why, that common operation of pruning in the wild growth, which is generally practised by rose-growers under an impression that it throws the vigour of the shoots into the buds entered at their base. It is a great mistake to cut back the shoot to be worked, though in practice some shortening is generally necessary for convenience for it is impossible to enter the buds neatly and quickly with the head enveloped in a thicket of thorny sprays. In using the knife, therefore, for the mere purpose of getting in among the stocks conveniently, let it be borne in mind that the more the shoots are cut back the more is the flow of the sap checked, unless they remain for a time untouched, so as to throw out side shoots, by which time the sap will be in full flow again, and the buds will take as quickly as if they had been entered in the first instance without pruning back the shoots. Choose dull damp weather; if possible, cut only as many scions as can be made use of at once before the leaves flag; and take especial care to tally everyone correctly, so that the next season you may know exactly what your stock consists of.

Now, as to the particulars of the operation. The best heads are formed of one bud only, but to make more sure it is best to enter two or three, for if one fails the season is not thereby lost. It is best to limit the work of each brier to two shoots, and if both take, to remove the upper one by a clean slanting cut through the stock over the lower bud, as the head of the brier then heals over neatly, and the rose will last a lifetime. Many of the worked roses, through the want of attention to the healing of the head of the stock, soon get decayed half through just where rose and brier are united, and the consequence is a languid growth at top and a forest of suckers. The cut annexed represents a brier with two shoots fit for working–AA, the stem of the future standard rose; B, the top of the stock as pruned back last year, when planted in the nursery bed; C and D, the two shoots in which buds are to be inserted, D being the one we should prefer to form the head finally, because the stock can be cut through immediately over that shoot; whereas, if the head remains as now B will die back to C, and between C and D there will some day be a half thickness of dead wood, which is unfavourable to the forming of a head from C, but is entirely removed by a clean cut through the stock immediately over the base of D, which if performed in April, May, or June, will heal at once, and retain a flow of sap through the whole thickness of the

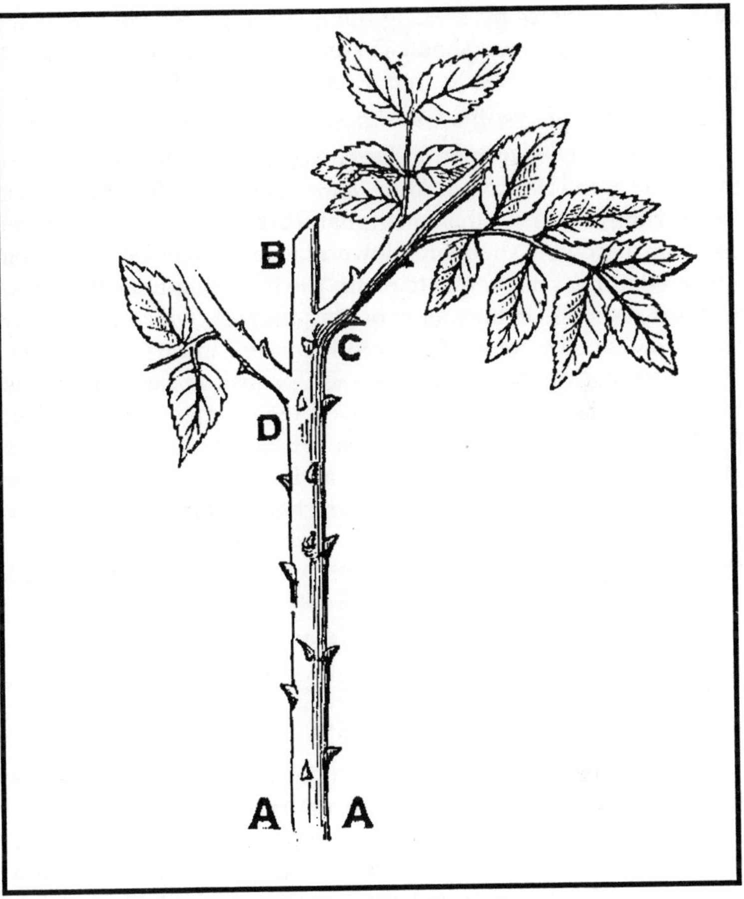

stock at its junction with the head. We need say no more about the stock except that the buds are to be entered on the upper sides of the two shoots, C and D, as close to the base of each shoot as possible; and if the cutting back of those shoots can be avoided till after the buds have taken, they will take more quickly and securely. Nevertheless, a moderate shortening is generally necessary for convenience.

A man who has both stocks and roses in the same garden, can choose his own time to obtain suitable buds. But the buds must be suitable, or the labour and the season will be lost; for if a bud fails it is hardly possible to enter another on the same shoot, though it may be done sometimes by making the incision on the side, or even underneath a vigorous shoot. These, however, are not such good positions as the upper side, from which the bud will start away and grow in a natural position from the first.

Much has been written on the choice of buds, but the truth is in this country the choice is limited, and much more depends on the free parting of the bark than on the nature of the bud, which may be cut from a growing shoot or a flowering shoot, or one that has just flowered but has not begun to push. The French use pushing buds with great success in the month of May, the sorts which succeed by that process being chiefly China and Noisette and Banksian roses. But briers in the open ground are not proper stocks for pushing buds, and they should never be used if the scale of the bud has opened so as to show the first incipient leaves. Choose a plump shoot, on which the leaves are large and perfect, and on which the side buds have not yet begun to grow. This will furnish about half a dozen buds, and the top of the shoot can be put in as a cutting; so that for every shoot cut, three or four briers or more may be worked, and one rose may be had on its own roots. The cut at page 52 shows how the bud should look, and how it should be cut. A portion of the stem with the accompanying leaf-stalk is to be cut in the form of a crescent; if the shoot is very stout, the segment may be a trifle longer than the engraver has represented it.

Take the shoot in the left hand, remove the leaf, but leave the base of the leaf-stalk untouched; enter the knife, which must have a keen smooth edge, above the bud; cut downwards and past the bud, and out again below it. Most amateurs use shields, of an inch or more in length. We prefer to have it not more than half an inch in length, but it requires some practice to insert them so small.

You have now removed a bud, and with it a segment of wood of this shape), and the cutting has the appearance of a in the next figure. You have now to remove the wood from the bud which is a nice operation, and not easily described. Sometimes a touch with the thumb-nail of the right hand, the bud being held in the left, will suffice to effect a separation between wood and bark, and then the removal is easily effected. Some people use a quill cut like a tooth-pick to act as a scoop to remove the wood, but no one will ever become a rose-grower by help of such contrivances. The back of the point of the budding knife may sometimes be required to loosen the bark, first at the upper end of the shield, and then the finger-nail will do the rest. The cut *b* shows the wood in process of separation from the bark; and *c* is the shield, that is, the bark with its bud and a fragment of the leaf-stalk, ready for insertion.

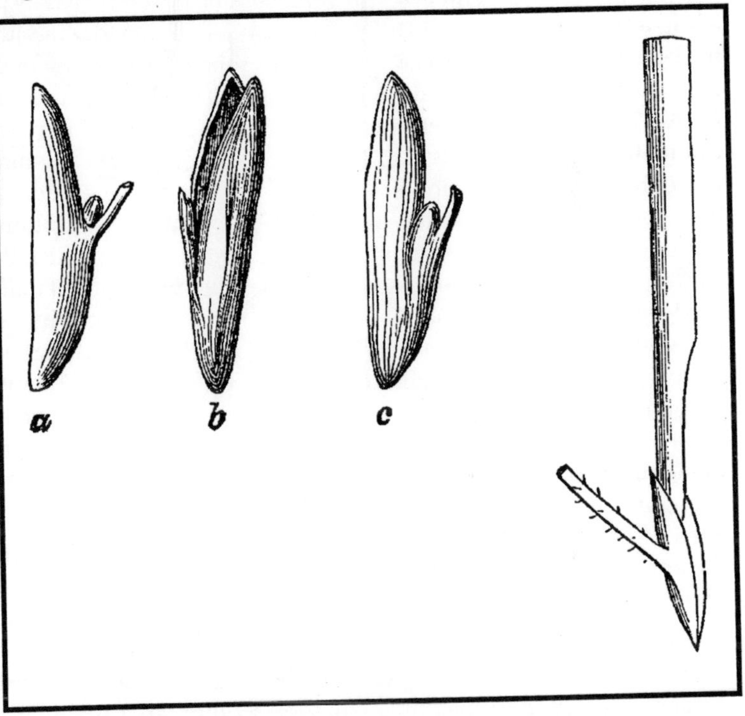

The shoot of the stock in which the bud is to be entered must have an incision made close to where it joins the stem, as at C and D in the cut at page 67, or as more distinctly shown here, where the shoot is shown with the **T** shaped incision slightly open, and ready to receive the bud. To make this incision, enter the point of the knife about an inch above the base of the shoot, press till you feel it go through the bark to the wood, *but do not cut the wood*: pass it downwards to the point where shoot and stem meet, and then make a similar cross cut to form the top of the **T**. Now take the ivory blade of the budding knife, and open this incision so as to lift up the bark slightly, and slide in the shield you have first prepared, and cut the top of the shield so that its edge exactly meets and fits the top of the **T** incision. It must fit there as neatly as if it belonged to the place

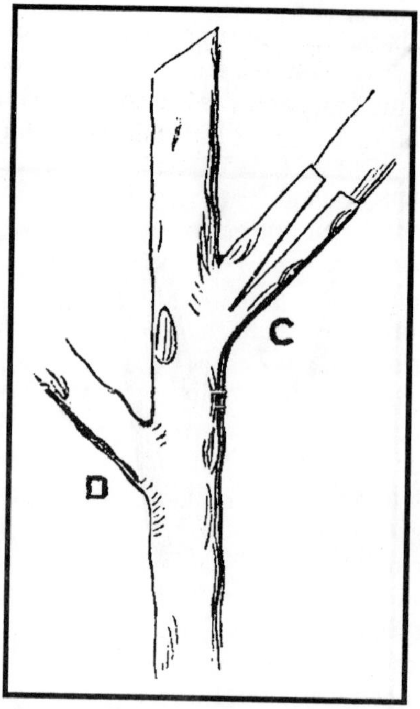

it occupies, and the lifted bark of the stem of the **T** must lap over it, so as to press the shield close to the wood of the shoot of the brier. The next and last job is to tie it up. Worsted is the best binding, but soft bast kept in a pot of water ready for use is nearly as good, and the material generally used. Place the middle of a strip of bast behind the shoot at the bottom of the incision, bring the ends across, and then proceed back and fore to bind it/ taking care to leave the bud peeping out, and finish off half an inch or so above the insertion, making it rather tighter there, but not to cut the stem, or squeeze the bud too hard. When tied it will have the appearance of the cut on the next page, and your work for the present is done.

All who have attempted to describe this operation have found it difficult. The fact is, the operation should *be seen* once at least. After once seeing it the beginner will soon acquire skill to overcome little difficulties, and at first a few failures are sure to happen.

Treatment after Budding

It must be obvious that an inserted bud is in a very artificial condition, at least for a considerable length of time. It is long before the yeoman stock can fairly agree with his delicate, courtly spouse, and, unless they both have a little coaxing, they may separate for ever, without the aid of a new divorce bill. The first step to prevent this is to make provision for supporting the shoot from the bud, the moment it is of sufficient length for a strip of bass to be passed round it. To the head of the stock tie a stiff short stick, of about the thickness of the finger or less. It must be stiff, so as not to budge a hair's breadth in the most threatening gale. To this stick tie the new shoot

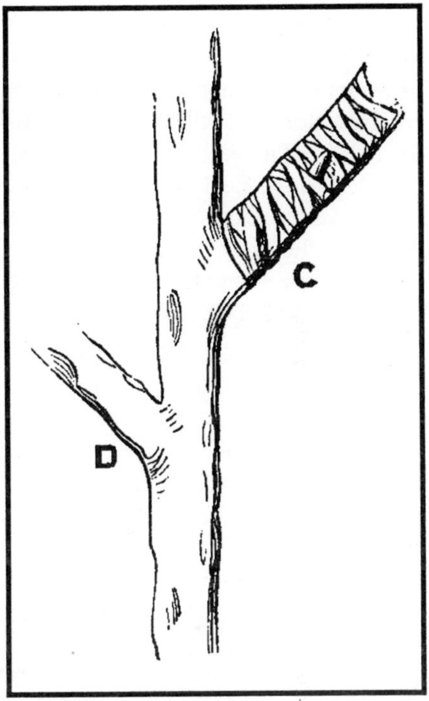

as it rises, and see at all times that your yet but partially united bud is safe against wind.

In very favourable circumstances the bud gets pretty well united in the course of about five weeks, sometimes eight, ten, or more weeks may elapse before the union may be considered good. At all events, six weeks after budding the heads should be looked over, and the ligatures loosened a little, or unbound and tied up again with broader strips of bast, and made a little, looser than before, but this must be very tenderly accomplished. The best way is to cut with the point of the knife that part of the binding which is just behind the bud, taking care, of course, not to go through the bark. If the bud is swelling, and the binding appears very tight, this loosening must be done. If the bud seems dormant, yet healthy, and the bast, only moderately tight, the binding may be left untouched till spring.

Supposing the bud to have taken, the character of the future head is to be determined by judicious pruning and stopping. There must be no undue haste to cut in the wild branches, because any sudden check to the flow of sap will disorganize the tree. But as soon as the sap is down, which happens at the end of October or the first week in November, slightly prune in the wild branches. Some growers cut them close down soon after budding, but beginners must leave them till autumn. Then trim up and shorten in the head, but use the knife moderately, and leave the tree neatly shaped, with a head somewhat proportioned to the root. The pruning must be tenderly accomplished, or the bud may be shaken to its injury.

If the bud pushes well in the autumn, it must be stopped by nipping off the top bud as soon as it is six inches long. This will cause its sap to concentrate about the rings of the bark, and in the ensuring spring it will be prepared to throw out side-shoots for the formation of a head. If, however, the head is small, or the position exposed to the north or east, it will be better to let the wild head remain untouched till March, or even so late as the first week in April; for the earlier you prune the earlier will new shoots push, and it is not desirable to force a tree into growth too early for it to make real and beneficial progress.

In March, the most important of all the pruning operations takes place. The wild branches are all cut away *except one bud above the inserted bud;* that is, one wild bud is left on the shoot which was worked, and this is called the *sap bud,* its office being to draw the sap upward, and help the pushing of the inserted bud. The sap flowing freely in that direction to the one wild bud hastens the completion of the union where the incision as made, and the entered bud is likely to make good progress. If no bud but that entered was left, the sap might not readily flow to it, and to get rid of its sap the plant would throw up side-shoots all the way up the stem, and perhaps suckers from the root; whereas the sap bud draws it upward, and encourages the kind of growth you want. If a knot forms below the inserted bud, and begins to push with it, it is well to allow it to remain for a time, for its presence will frequently assist the inserted bud by promoting a free flow of the abundant sap; but when the inserted bud seems strong enough to use the sap, the wild branch may be removed by a clean cut to its base.

When the March pruning takes place, the last job is to cut the top of the stock close over to the inserted bud, so that no more wild growth can take place above the bud to interfere with the formation of the head. It must be cut slightly aslant, and so close to the base of the shoot from the bud that there shall be scarcely the thickness of card-board above it; for the bud will have to help in barking it over; and if any length of wood is left above the bud it will either produce shoots of wild growth or die and eat into the stock, to the ruin of the tree. When cut over, the wound should be covered with clay paint or grafting wax.

The sap bud may now be expected to grow vigorously. It is better if it does so. When it has got two or three pairs of leaves, stop it by nipping off the top with the finger and thumb. Then, as the placed bud prepares to take the lead, cut ill the sap bud a little closer; but do not remove it utterly till about mid-summer, when it may be cut off close to the inserted bud, and that should be the end of all wild growth. Now you have made your roses, and may transplant them in the autumn to their blooming quarters in the garden or rosery.

It is necessary to suppose the reader to be familiar with the art of budding, in order to understand what remains to be said about it. From frequent observation, we are satisfied it matters not from what sort of wood we take the bud, whether from a flowering shoot or the growth of the season, provided the bud itself is of the right sort– plump enough to be visible, not plump enough to be on the point of opening into leaves, and the bark about it so full of sap as to separate easily from the wood of the shield. There is this advantage in working roses on strong stocks, that we get blooms the next season; and if the culture is thoroughly liberal and the buds are entered in June, the greater part of the wild wood cut away to force the bud, one season's growth from the bud is enough to make respectable heads. On their own roots they need another year to make a similar effect, and thus, by using foster roots, we steal a March on time.

Now, as to the process of budding. Roses differ among themselves as men do; some are tractable and some are stubborn. Jules Margottin will give good buds from the end of June to the middle of October, but Aimee Vibert will never give a bud such as a beginner can handle with safety. If you cannot remove the wood from the shield by a neat action of the thumb-nail, or the back of the point of the budding-knife, the nail being the best, let the wood remain, and make of it a summer graft in the same method as inserting a bud. Through not knowing this practice, or not thinking of it at the time of operating, many amateurs fail with roses that make thin wood and wiry buds; whereas by retaining the wood the difficulty is at an end, and you may work such a rose while the bud is invisible, especially after heavy rains, when the stocks are full of sap and ready to nourish them forthwith. Another point to be remembered in using plump buds from the shoots of the season, the shields of which perhaps are very soft, is this, that a little wood left in the eye of is no consequence at all. When you have peeled the bud there will be an obstinate bit of wood left, to get out which will probably destroy the eye altogether. You must throw that away and prepare another, which may share the same fate; and if you happen to have but one plant of the variety to be propagated the whole shoot may be cut up, and the chance of propagating lost for the season. Peel the shield as clean as you can without splitting it, and if a bit of wood remains in the eye, there leave it. The grand thing is to unite the edges of the two barks at the top cut, where the union will take place, and to have the shield pressed close to the wood in the incision on the stock, a result to be obtained only by binding it carefully. Another and still more important point is, not to mind the *apparent* loss of the eye when the shield has been dexterously separated. Immediately after flowering the bud is not always so prominent that you can be sure you have it safe after removing the wood; but be assured it is there. Insert the bud, tie such a bud not extra tight, but with an extra thickness of cotton wool to prevent exhaustion by evaporation, and it will come as certainly as the plumpest. Nevertheless, dismissing these exceptional cases, a visible bud from the growth of the season is to be preferred, and it is well if the removal of the wood is clean and complete.

Manetti Roses

The Manetti is the best stock for free-growing roses on soils unfavourable to the brier, and where roses on their own roots would starve. Nevertheless, the Manetti does well on stiff rich heavy soils, and is perhaps more adaptable in its nature than any variety of rose in cultivation. It takes its name from the raiser, Signor Manetti, of the Botanic Gardens at Monza. The best of this stock is that it may be worked later than any other stock, and if September pass by and you have lost the last chance of budding, then you can wait till March and graft your roses on its roots. Manettis, however, will not make standards. They must be worked as close to the ground as possible, and at the final planting the base of the shoot from the entered bud must be planted below the ground level to give the rose a chance of making roots for itself, which it will generally do, but *not always*. For chalky, gravelly, and sandy soils this is invaluable.

From the importance of this stock it would seem that there should follow a long chapter on the process of working it in the open ground during the summer. But in truth, there is no such necessity, for the process is precisely the same as we have already described in treating of the production of standard roses; but, as remarked above, the buds must be inserted close over the roots of the stock, for we need its roots only, and can make no use of the stem except for the production of the stock. However, it will be seen that in planting Manetti stocks sufficient space must be left in every alternate alley for the operator to work on his knees, for he will have to remove a little of the earth from the collar of the stock, in order to enter the buds as close to the roots as possible. When the buds begin to swell the shoots are to be cut close over and then the wild buds will start, and, generally speaking, they will not start until this be done. But there must be no haste about it. Some buds will swell up ready to start the same season, and others will continue quite dormant until the spring. Having thus hastily disposed of the summer budding of the Manetti, we must now treat more fully of another method by which it is utilized in the rose garden.

Spring Grafting

Spring Grafting of the Manetti is rather more difficult than budding briers in summer, but when the details are thoroughly mastered, and proper care bestowed, upon the stocks and scions until they are united, there will be but very few failures. It is not difficult to understand why so few private cultivators have hitherto taken advantage of this mode of propagation, for the simple reason that, unless they are for some time in the propagating department of a good nursery, in which roses are regarded as one of the chief specialities, they have no means of acquiring a proper knowledge of it.

To be able to take advantage of this method of producing a stock of dwarf roses for bedding or pot culture, it will first of all be necessary to provide a sufficient number of Manetti stocks. They require to be lifted carefully with a spade or fork, to prevent injury to the roots. The proper time for this operation is from the latter part of September to the middle of November. Have a supply of small sixty-sized pots in readiness, and a mixture of turfy loam and manure, and pot them separately first removing all the roots produced up the stem, and trim those produced at the bottom sufficiently to allow of the stocks being potted without difficulty. After they are potted, place them close together in a sheltered corner, and throw over them sufficient decayed tan or cocoanut fibre refuse to preserve the roots from frost. They will then be ready for working as soon as the scions are sufficiently advanced.

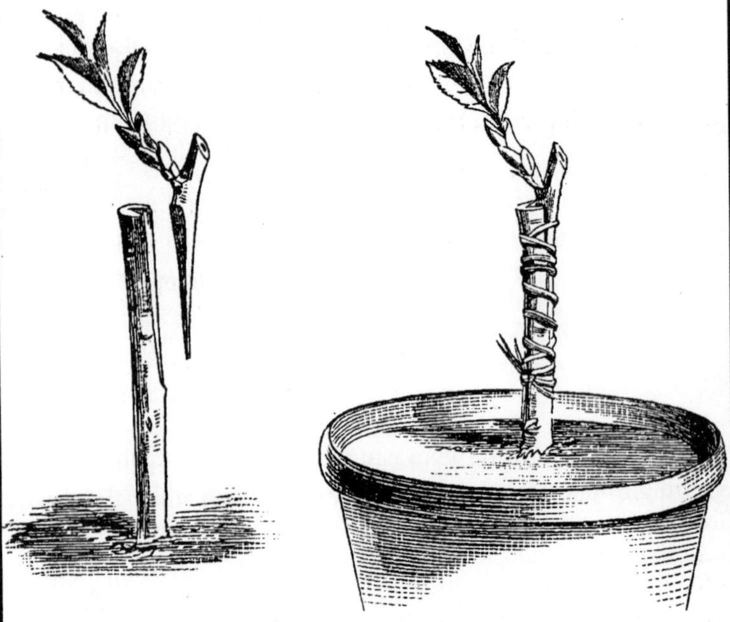

PREPARED STOCK AND SCION

THE PROPER WAY TO JOIN THE STOCK AND SCION

The scions are of course obtained from plants that have been forced. To prepare them for the forcing house they are take up in October or November, and potted (unless they are already in pots), and placed in a cold house for a month. By that time they will have made a few new roots, and may then be pruned and started. It is desirable to commence with a moderate heat, increasing it as the growth progresses, but at no time is a very high temperature requisite. Syringe them twice a day, and admit a little air on favourable occasions.

The scions should be formed of half-ripened wood, and, generally speaking they will be ready for taking off about the first or second week in March. One eye or bud to each scion will be sufficient, and they should be prepared exactly as shown in the annexed sketch. The stock is cut down to within an inch or so of the surface of the soil, leaving just room enough to put the scion on. The manner of preparing the stock is also clearly shown, so that no further description is necessary; but it is proper to remark that both the scion and stock must be cut so as to ensure an exact fit. It will be seen that a triangular piece is taken out of one side of the stock sloping off to the lower end of the cut, and also that the scion is cut so as to exactly fit upon both sides. When fitted together as shown in the second figure, bind them firmly with a piece of bast and cover the wound with a little properly-prepared grafting clay, or any of the mastics, which may be purchased of the principal nurserymen. Place the pots on a mild bottom-heat and keep the house close, and maintain a moderate degree of atmospheric humidity.

When a junction is effected shift them into five-inch pots; and sink them low enough to quite cover the stock. In a few days they will be nicely established, and may be gradually hardened off and placed in a cold frame or otherwise disposed of. They must not be placed in the cold frame too early in the season, for it is important to guard against their receiving a check of any kind at this stage. After they are removed to the frame they will require the same management as the ordinary stock of roses in pots.

Grafting Brier Standards

This plan may be adopted where buds of the preceding autumn have failed. To succeed, the sap must be rising freely in the stocks, as indicated by the swelling of the wood and buds, and the stock must be in advance of the scion, that is, in a condition of greater vigour; and to insure this condition the scions are cut some time before they are to be used, so as to reduce their strength, and fit them to take up sap from the stock.

The stocks should be in good condition, well rooted, and *about* to grow vigorously. In February, procure the scions. If you have some good roses from which you can take scions, cut off with a sharp knife some strong shoots that have not begun their spring growth, cutting them their full length; tally each lot of shoots as soon as taken, and tie in separate bundles those of different kinds. These must be kept alive for some weeks with great care, and the best way is first to cut off any of the top buds that are open, and then to stick the thickest ends of the shoots into moist clay, pressed tightly to them, and place the whole in pots of moist mould, and stow them away in some dry shed or cool green house, where they will not be subject to the action of sun, rain, or wind; they may be kept just moist for three weeks, and if they are in a very dry place it will be as well to strew a little damp moss amongst them.

At the expiration of three weeks, those least fit for grafting will be shrunk, and must be picked out and thrown away; but the best will be still plump, and in a desirable condition for use. The first week in March is the best time in most seasons for grafting briers. The made of operation is nearly the same as described for the Manetti; but it will be prudent perhaps to describe it. The stock is cut over horizontally, and a slit or wedge made in it vertically, one and a half or two inches long, a strong sharp knife being better than a chisel for the purpose. It must be a clean cut down the centre of the wood, without any jagging or tearing of the bark. As soon as the slit is made, take the scion in the left hand, cut away the portion that was buried in the clay, and cut away from the head of the scion as much as may be necessary to reduce it to two or three good buds in the

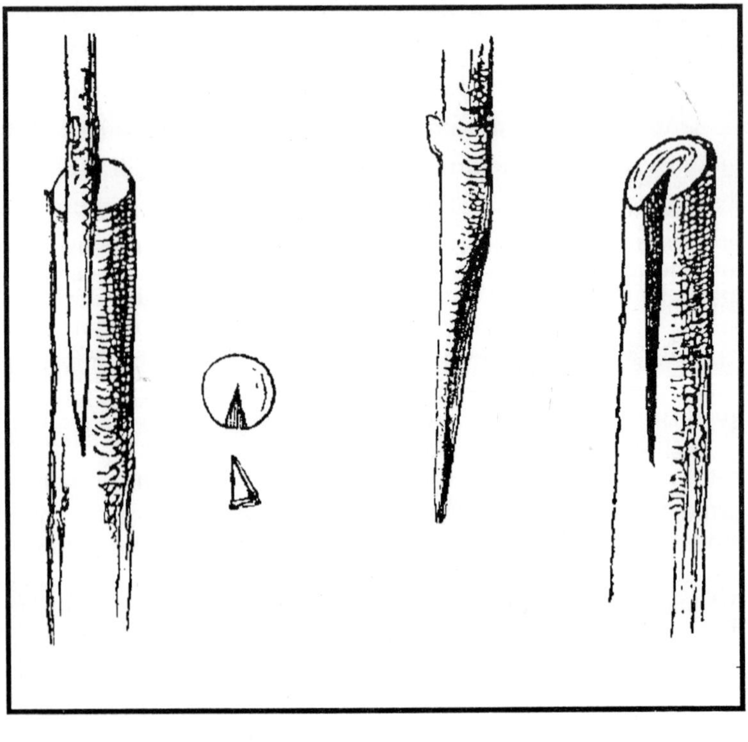

middle of the shoot; then cut the lower end to a long wedge, proportionate to the length of the slit in the stock, and with the lowest bud only just above the top or thickest part of the wedge. No dirt or chips must be about either of the cut parts, and the bark must be as whole and untorn as possible, not a scrap removed beyond what comes away in cutting a clean wedge. Now open a slit in the stock by means of a hard wooden tally or ivory wedge, and holding the thickest part or front of the scion outwards, insert it in the slit, and allow the stock to close and pinch it; they ought to fit very neatly, and the inner bark of the scion ought to touch the inner bark of the stock all the way down, and the outer bark of each should meet neatly down the outside of the cleft. Now prepare another scion in the same way, withdraw the ivory wedge, and insert that on the opposite side of the stock, and in the same way proceed till you have three or four scions inserted, though a couple will be enough for middling-sized stocks, and in the first attempts no more should be tried.

In binding up, it will be best to use broad strips of good bast, and to pass it round so that it shall be impossible for the scions to shift, either owing to the weather, or the swelling of the stock, or the accession of a flow of sap. When neatly, but not too tightly, bound up, cover the whole over with grafting clay, to exclude the atmosphere entirely from every portion that has been cut. Of course the cleft in the centre of the stock between the scions must be bound over with bast to prevent the clay from touching the split wood, which will unite in time by the flow of the sap. A bundle of soft moss should then be tied round the head of the stock and the scion, still further to defend both from the atmosphere, and preserve moisture to the bark. In dry weather the moss must be occasionally wetted; but if the water trickles through any crevice in the clay or bandages, and gains access to the head of the stock, it will do much mischief, and may cause the loss of the scions. Grafts inserted near the ground may be covered with mould after the clay is put on.

Grafting completed, you have now to hope for a speedy union and the perfect healing of the wounds that have been made. About mid-summer, remove the clay and loosen the ligature, and apply a coat of mixture, leaving the point of the pushing bud free. This must be done just after rain, when the clay will be soft and easily removed,

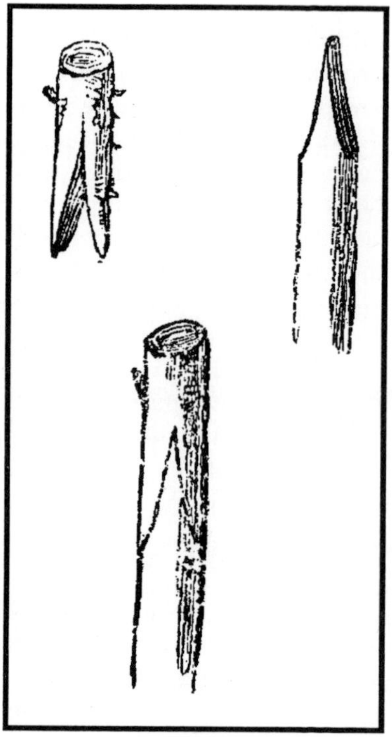

and the scion in a condition not to feel a shock from exposure to the air. Any grafts that have not taken should then be cut away, and every portion of dead wood on the stock where it has been worked cut clean away to the scions that have taken, and the wounds covered with mixture; but if all fall, knock off the clay and cut the stock down to the first wild branch that has broken out below the graft, and thus get a new head to bud upon in the autumn. But there must be no haste in inferring that the grafts have failed; they sometimes lie dormant a long while, and then push vigorously. At all events, as long as the bark and buds of the scion remain plump there is nothing to fear, and when once a good leaf opens on the scion the union hastens, and ultimate success is certain.

Those who are practised in grafting usually have their favourite methods for various subjects, and it really does not matter by what particular method roses are grafted provided the work is properly done. It has been our custom to pot in autumn, a lot of the small suckers that sometimes rise at the bast of a brier. These potted suckers make nice stocks to graft in spring with shoots of roses selected of exactly their own thickness. The saddle graft is the best for these small stocks. They are cut close over near the rim of the pot; the head is then cut to the shape of a wedge, by taking a slice off each side, the graft is cut to fit it, and after being tied with bast and painted with grafting wax, they are placed in a warm damp part of the greenhouse or stove and they unite directly. The grafts ought to have only one or two buds each.

Chapter 6

STOCKS FOR ROSES

Thus far as regards the making of roses on foster roots, we have put the cart before the horse. But advisedly so, for it is not to be expected of any amateur to enter seriously into the business of producing stocks until expertness has been acquired in budding and grafting them. The beginner will buy stocks, the adept will raise them. It is proper, therefore, at this stage to say something on the subject.

The English Brier

The English brier is the only stock employed to produce standards or tree roses, and usually they arc obtained ready made from wood sides and hedgerows. It is prudent, to plant and bud a fresh lot of briers every year, so as to keep the rosarium supplied with thrifty young plants, as accidents; may cause blanks in the rank and file, and it is also well to allow a certain number of recently budded briers to flower in the nursery piece without transplanting, as it often happens that these young trees in their first season produce the finest exhibition flowers, and may be trusted to cut from. Usually the briers are grubbed up in a rough, and more or less destructive manner, and in consequence many of them never thrive in the garden, and a certain number of deaths may be expected in every new plantation. The amateur who can superintend the lifting and planting will do well, for many a fine straight stem will be saved from rough usage, and will be secured with a reasonable proportion of roots wherewith to begin life again in the garden. The month of

November is the proper time for the operation, and it should be carried on with spirit, the ground being first deeply dug and liberally manured to receive the briers, and these being planted as soon as possible after they are taken up, for exposure to the atmosphere is extremely injurious to their roots.

Seedling Briers

Seedling Briers are largely employed by trade growers for dwarf roses more particularly the teas. It is an extremely easy matter to raise them, but the amateur is advised to be content with raising a few at first and carefully determining their relative value before proceeding far in the business. As we have several kinds of wild roses, it may be proper to remark that the fruits or "heps" of *Rosa canina*, the Dog Rose, are of an oblong form and a shining scarlet colour. They should be gathered in October or November, and be laid up of layers with said—first a layer of sand, then a layer of heps, and so on until all are buried. A damp place should be selected, as the object of "stratifying" is to promote the decay of the skin and pulp and thus separate the seeds for sowing in the spring. A small quantity may be stratified in a wooden box or a large flower pot, and a very good place to keep them all the winter is under the stage of the greenhouse, as they will be often seen and hence not forgotten. In February or March pick out the seeds and sow them while they are still damp. Any good ground in an open situation will serve as a seed bed, but if the quantity is small, it will be best to sow in pans and boxes and keep them in cold frames until the plants appear. In any case they must be transplanted as soon as large enough, and as vigorous stocks are required, the best plan is to plant them in showery weather, on ground prepared for the purpose by deep digging and liberal manuring.

Hitherto seedling briers have been employed for the production of dwarf roses only by spring grafting. But they may also be budded. The practice followed is to insert the bud or graft low down close over the roots, the result being, if the work is well done, thrifty, free-growing bushes. But there is no reason why the amateur should not raise stocks for standards from seed if he wishes it, and we are bound to say that we have obtained from seedlings, the straightest and finest stocks ever seen, and had the advantage of control over their roots from the very first. But carefully lifted hedgerow briers answer so well and are so easily obtained, that no one should enter upon the raising of seedlings either in great haste or in a wholesale manner unless fortified with a good reason and some amount of experience. There is, moreover, an objection to the use of seedling briers in their pertinaceous production of suckers. This is in some part the consequence of checking their natural tendency to run up into strong, straight rods, but if they are grafted close over the roots the heading down of the stock is inevitable. All that can be done is to cut out the suckers to give the grafts a chance of taking and keeping the whole of the supply of sap from the roots.

The Natural Suckers

The Natural Suckers that rise from briers at some distance from the stock may be turned to account to make pretty little standard pot roses. To promote their rooting, uncover them early in the season and carefully cut a small notch on the under side near the base or point of the stock from which they spring, and cover them with rich light soil. By November they will probably have a good wig of roots of their own and may then be removed and potted, and the next season budded. Or they may be budded as they stand before they are lifted, but it must be on the stem or *gun barrel budding*, and of course, this will be done at the same time as the head of the stock proper is budded. As this system should be clearly understood, we return to the subject of budding in order to describe it.

Run your eye along them from head to foot. Say the sucker is three feet high, at two feet from the ground, the young wood is in just the same state of greenness and ripeness as the base of the summer shoot, which you have just budded, on the top of the stock. Instead of waiting till next season, bud it there at once just under one of the leaf-rings, "gun-barrel" fashion; and six inches higher up on the opposite side, also under a leaf-ring, and with the top of the shield on the line of the leaf-ring, enter another bud, and you will have a fine plant next season. The operation is easier than the usual method of working. Make an incision like the letter I on the stem, then a cross-cut on top to make the usual **T**, but let the incision and the shield be a little longer then usual with top-shoots. In fact, use the largest shields you can get from very plump rods, to suit the robust nature of the wood you work on. Tie up and tally; in 14 days loosen; in a month from entering remove the binding, and you will be surprised at the growth of the new shoots. They will soon distance those entered in the usual way on side-shoots of hard briers. Thus

brier and rose begin the world together. There is no conflict between youth and age, and roots and shoots are of equal vigour. In November lift and pot them, and put the pots in a plunge bed with a few wires or rails to tie the heads to, and they can be protected in severe weather, as in the sub-joined figure.

Briers From Cuttings

Briers from cuttings enjoy a well-deserved popularity as stocks for dwarf roses, and are extensively employed in the nurseries, especially where tea-scented varieties are largely grown. Medium-sized shoots should be selected for propagating purposes, and the cuttings should be prepared as advised for autumn cuttings of roses, with the exception that two buds only should be allowed above the surface, and the buds be carefully removed from the portion underground. The cuttings should be inserted in the beds during October, and be allowed one year's growth in the cutting bed. In the autumn of the year following they should be transplanted, and if this operation is carefully performed, they Will be in capital condition for budding in the next summer.

Manetti Stocks

Manetti stocks may be propagated by layers and cuttings. As to the first, make them as already advised for named roses. As to the second, put in cuttings in the months of October as advised for autumn cuttings in the chapter on own root roses. This is really all that need be said on this important subject; but on the supposition that a beginner may turn to this part of the book first, we will provide a short code for the culture of this stock. The first step will be to procure in the autumn one or two dozen well established plants, according to the number of stocks likely to be required. Plant them in an out-of-the-way corner of the garden, at a distance of two feet apart each way, and prune them to within four or six inches of the ground-level. In the course of the season each plant will produce number of shoots, nearly all of which may be made available for propagating purposes in the autumn. All the shoots which are as thick as an ordinary lead-pencil will he quite large enough, for cuttings. In selecting the cutting in October, take them off just above the first or second joint from the base, and then cut them up into lengths of six or seven inches according to the distance the joints are a part. As a rule, each shoot will make two good cuttings. The soft part of the shoot towards the end is not suitable for making cuttings and should be rejected. In preparing them, cut them just under the lower joint and an inch or so above the one nearest the top. To check as far as possible the natural tendency of the Manetti to produce suckers, remove the eyes from all the joints excepting the one at the top. When prepared, make a trench just deep enough to bury the cuttings so that the top bud will be an inch or so above the level where the trench is filled in. They should be laid in regularly at a distance of about three inches apart in the rows, and the latter must be far enough apart to allow for cutting down the weeds during the summer without difficulty. They will require no further attention during the summer season, and by the autumn they will be nicely rooted, and may be taken up and potted for grafting in the spring following, or planted out in nursery beds for budding in the summer. When they are taken from the cutting bed trim the shoots. slightly, and, if necessary, the roots may also be pruned; but root-pruning, is not necessary excepting when there is a difficulty in putting them into small pots. The shoots should be pruned back to, within a few joints of the ground-level annually, even if they are not required for propagating purposes, otherwise there will be a difficulty in procuring a sufficient supply of good stocks the following season. Every rosarian should plant out, two or three Manettis in an out-of-the-way part of the garden and leave them to grow in their own way without pruning. They will after a few years produce a nice crop of pretty pink flowers annually, and at any time will supply an abundance of cuttings if required.

Various Other Stocks

Various other stocks may be employed for dwarf roses. The old *Maiden's Blush*, the *Comnon Boursault*, the Hybrid China rose *Descartes*, and the Hybrid Perpetual *Napoleon*, are useful stocks, as they root freely from cuttings, and are somewhat hardier than others in their several classes. Finally, the rosarian who raises seedling roses from heps of named sorts may turn to account all the rejected ones as stocks, and as a rule they will answer admirably.

Chapter 7
GARDEN ROSES

As all roses are garden roses, and the wildest of wild briers is not to be despised when adorning a rough rockery, we must explain the purport of this chapter. A proper distinction may be made between roses that are intended to enrich a garden scene and afford entertainment to those who are not amateurs of roses, and those others that are grown chiefly to delight the critical eye, and perhaps to represent their owner in a glorious contest under canvas on the occasion of the district Rose Show. The exhibitor may care nothing about beds of roses, or arches of roses, or handsome weeping roses, but rejoice in straight lines of hard mop-headed standards from which he is accustomed to cull flowers of wonderful size and symmetry. But we must think of those who care little for exhibitions, but much for garden roses, and a few observations may be proper to the book and this particular part of it.

Standard Roses

Standard roses may be employed to produce an interesting and beautiful feature of a garden, as suggested in the description of our own arrangement of them at page 43. But generally speaking they seem best adapted to make the garden hideous, for everywhere we see poor mop-headed things dotting lawns and borders like so many criminals consigned to a lingering death. The custom of planting standards in "pincushion" beds is not to be commended, for they are ugly during at least eight months in the year, and when at their

STANDARD ROSE

best the few flowers produced do not pay for their keeping. The necessary digging and scratching of the beds to adorn them with bedding plants injures the roots of the trees, and that by lowering their vigour increases their ugliness. Still worse is the selection for such purposes of the stiff-habited kinds that throw their branches up in the fashion of a birch broom and persistently refuse to show a single line of grace or beauty. When planted in files five or six deep, and extending a considerable length, the stiff-habited kinds cease to obtrude their harsh outlines and pleasingly harmonize with the rest. But standards may be planted on the lawn with the best effect, and we present a sketch of one which we selected in the garden as a model for the purpose. We require a graceful growth and a habit of flowering freely, and we find several of the hardier Teas, Noisettes, Bourbons, and Perpetuals admirably adapted to the purpose. For a peculiar position a strong stock worked with Common Ayrshire would produce a tree that an artist would delight to sketch, but the quality of the flowers would not delight a florist. What a charming standard does *Aimee Vibert* make, especially if in the pruning it is carefully thinned out and never shortened. It is a perfect garden rose. For a blaze of colour take *Thomas Mills*, or *Victor Verdier*, or *Jules Margottin*. For delicacy take *Bourbon Queen*. For a great head on a tall brier to help to enrich a rural nook take *Blairi No.2*. For a sheltered corner take *Gloire de Dijon, Grace Darling, Souvenir de la Malmaison*, and you will have glorious garden roses. If standards are planted with a view to close them in with turf, provide a fair-sized bed in the first instance, and fill it with a mixture of loam from rotted turf, and a fourth part of decidedly fat manure, taking away the hard old soil from the spot to a depth of two feet. Plant early, plant firm, stake with care, and keep the bed open for one whole season and then close it in with turf. By this mode of procedure you may expect a fine tree instead of a starveling, and you will do still better if you never turf to the stem at all, but keep the bed open and fill it with such a pretty bedding rose as *Mignonette*, taking care to lay on the surface a good coat of manure every winter.

Dwarf Roses

Dwarf roses are not sufficiently esteemed as garden ornaments. They make fine beds if wisely selected and properly managed, and many of the stiff-habited kinds that we should reject for standards will be found serviceable to make thrifty bushes and huge pyramids of flower. Many folks who love their gardens would be shocked if we implored them for their own sakes to root out the starving standards that line the walks and form ghastly centres to pincushion beds. But they would be not less overjoyed than convinced if we were to replace the standards with great bushes of *Alba* roses unpruned, or with strong plants on their own roots of *Ulrich Brunner, fils, General Jacqueminot, Baronne Prevost, Madame Domage,* and *Glory of Waltham*. But we should want beds to plant them in; it would be no use to paste them into holes, or merely chop over the old stuff and think the roses would never find out the quality of it.

There are various modes of pruning and training roses to render them useful as garden ornaments. One very good way is to slightly shorten the strongest shoots in the month of March, and otherwise leave them to grow as they please. We have some gigantic bushes that have never been touched with the knife for at least twenty years, and they are wonderful for health and splendour, but of course they do not produce roses fit for exhibition. A capital mode of pruning to form handsome bushes is suggested by the sub-joined figure at page 91.

When the plant is pruned the best shoot near the centre is left unpruned, and the rest of the shoots are cut back to two or three eyes. The effect is surprising, for on such sorts as *General Jacqueminot* or *Madame de Cambaceres* there will be found in the season from one to two hundred flowers expanded at one time. For this mode we are indebted to M. Van Hulle, of the Botanical Gardens, Ghent.

Another effective mode of training dwarf roses is to *peg them down* full length, so as to carpet the ground with their leaves and flowers. A serious objection to this procedure is to be found in the fact that when the pegged-down rods are in flower new rods will be rising and must be allowed to rise. The mode of procedure is very simple. The rods are allowed to remain their full length until the wood is about half ripe, and then they are slightly shortened to get rid of the soft tops, and being carefully bent down are fixed to the ground with strong pegs as shown in the figure at page 92.

The beginner will experience at least one difficulty in accomplishing the pegging, for the hardest rods will snap near the ground. Nine times in ten the snapping of the shoots is of no consequence, for if the bark continues whole on the underside it will maintain itself and flower as well as if it had remained unhurt.

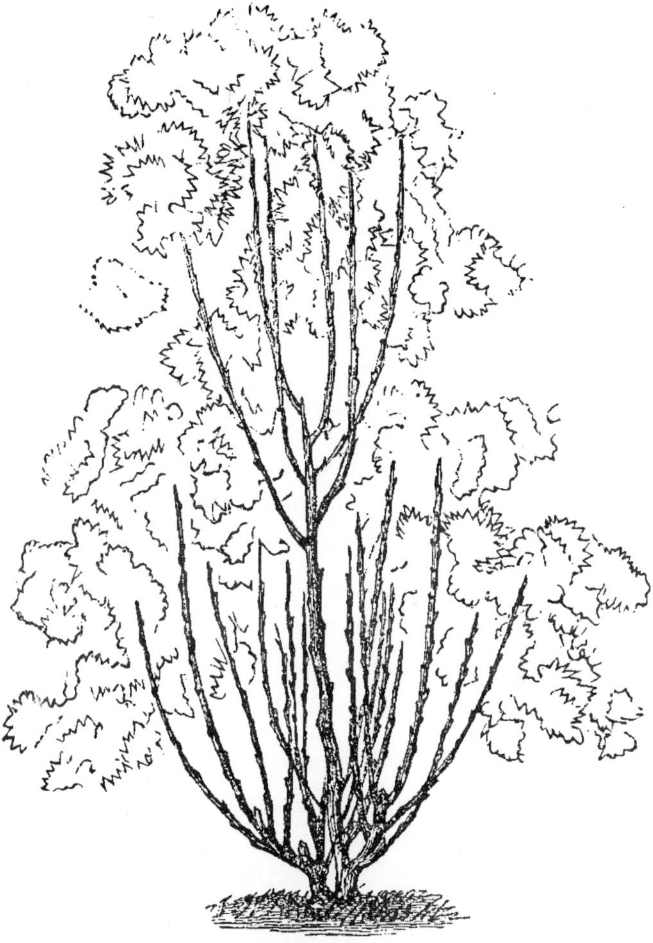

CAPITAL MODE OF PRUNING FOR HANDSOME BUSHES

When we have had some unusually hard rods to deal with, we have cut a tongue by an upward cut about an inch long at some point near the base of the shoot where the bending would be most convenient. But if they are laid in summer while still soft, but fully grown, there will be less danger of a snap and the beds will be tidy all the autumn and winter. We have found them flower better, however, when laid down in spring, and for that reason have

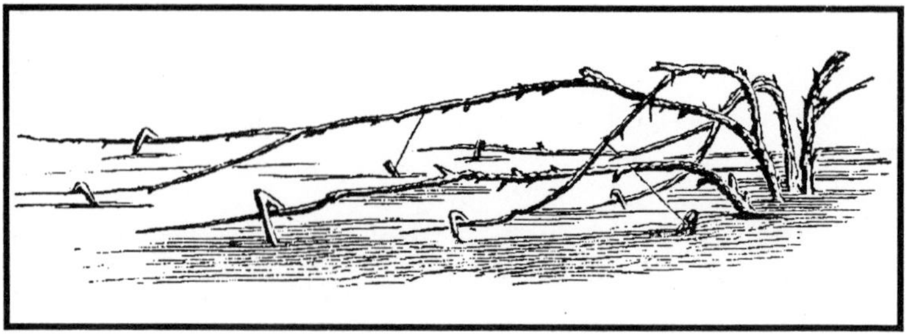

adopted the practice of cutting a tongue. Every year the pegging must be repeated, the old rods being cut away to the ground line, and a fresh lot being laid down in their place.

A variation of the method may be resorted to for the production of another kind of effect. We will suppose we have a fair lot of own root roses before us in the early days of March, and we must decide about the pruning and training. The first step to success will be to

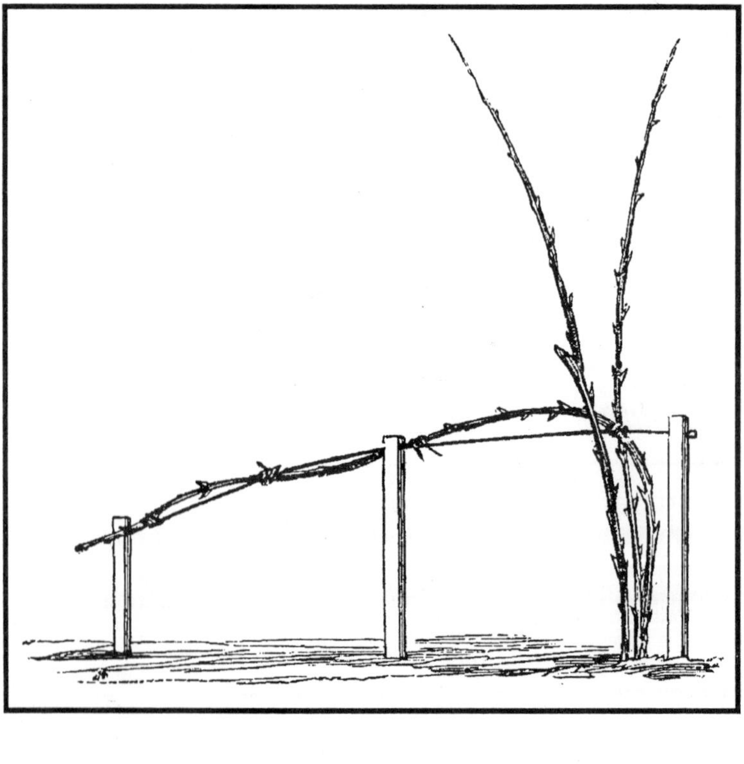

find our way amongst them without doing mischief, or having one's face torn with their hooked thorns. Hence, if we plant on purpose for this effect, we shall provide by the original arrangements for convenient access to the centre of the bed. The next thing will be to drive in some stout stakes, say ranging from four feet in the centre to two feet at the outside and to run stout galvanized wires from the centre to the circumference in the way that the wires of an umbrella are arranged. Now we tie the rods to the wires and produce a regular convex surface of wood bristling with plump buds, which in due time will clothe with leaves and flowers the whole of the dome of umbrella, whereof the suggestive skeleton is in part before you.

It is proper to advise the amateur not to resort to this plan without taking thought of all the details. What shall the centre consist of? A grand standard of a somewhat drooping habit, rising above the highest part of the trained rods, would make a nice finish to the scheme; and so would a gigantic bush rose or a small wire pavilion clothed with clematis, or climbing roses. The finish on the outside will be an easy matter, for we may select at will amongst the dwarfest of the roses, and the pompone cabbage rose would do nicely but best of all, perhaps, the common China.

In the elementary scheme of this bed you have a proposal for an elaborate and extensive display of roses. Let us therefore layout a compartment as a quatrefoil or cinquefoil, and the chord of every

semicircle should measure fifteen to twenty feet at least, and there should be openings at their intersections, for convenience-sake, to the centre. Here we may have standard roses, or we may have a pavilion covered with climbing roses; and then we might call the whole affair a rosarium. There is no end to the modifications of the idea, but in every case provision must be made for access to the machinery, for there will be need for occasional visitation and tidivating all the spring and summer, and even, perhaps, far into the autumn.

Bedding Roses

Bedding roses may be obtained by the more simple plan of selecting sorts of dwarf habit and planting them in groups and masses, and keeping them in strict order by very close pruning. The *Common China* is one of the best bedding roses known, but the dwarf growing *Chinas, Noisettes,* and *Bourbons* afford a number of varieties admirably adapted for beds. Thus amongst the China or Bengal roses we meet with *Archduke Charles, Fabvier, Ducher,* and *Little Pet,* all good bedders. The Noisettes offer *Fellenberg, Ophirie,* and *Amiee Vibert;* and from the Bourbons we may select *Armosa, Baronne de Maynard, Madame Baron Veillard,* and *Queen of Bedders.*

The dwarf *Polyantha* roses are in every way suitable, as they bloom freely throughout the summer. We may select with advantage *Blanche Rehatel, Gloire de Polyantha, Mignonette, Paquerette* and *Perle d' Or.*

In planting masses of such roses, a sunny situation should be chosen, and the beds should consist of good loam, deeply dug, and enriched with plenty of rotten manure and leaf mould. Substantial beds they must be, but rather light than heavy, and well drained, but not raised above the level. If pot roses on their own roots can be obtained, they are to be preferred; but Manettis will serve the purpose. The planting should be done in the latter days of May, say as soon after the 20th as possible, for that is about the date at which the last sharp frost occurs, and pot roses that have been ill frames all the winter might be seriously injured if caught by a frost immediately after they were planted in the open ground. The distances must be regulated by the sorts, but as a rule they may average two feet apart; and if the beds are rather thin the first season, it will be well to plant geraniums or other showy bedders to fill up. A broad border of roses, consisting wholly of dwarfs, arranged in the order of their relative vigour, the back rows consisting of perpetuals, would constitute a noble garden feature; and as own root roses in great part take care of themselves, fetch their own water, renew themselves from the root if cut down by frost, and last, with proper care, beyond any ordinary human lifetime, such a border may be pronounced one of the cheapest elegancies within the range of the amateur gardener's operations. To give it a finish, a boundary fence of roses would be appropriate, and for this we should prefer the most showy and vigorous of the pillar roses, such as *Red Rover, Climbing Victor Verdier, Glory of Waltham,* and *Princess Louise.*

Chapter 8

EXHIBITION ROSES

When the judges retire from within the ropes, and the eager crowd rushes past the wavering policemen, and the tables are stormed, and the ladies win all the front places, and those who have not lost their hands are busy with notebooks, and from every wave of the great crowd arise splashes of sound resembling such words as "Wonderful !" "Surprising !" "Delightful !" and "Are they real?" "Yes, they are indeed roses !"–when these things occur you may conclude you are at a rose show, and perhaps the first question you will ask yourself or somebody else is, "By what magical means are such glorious flowers produced ?"

The magical means comprise careful selection, honest cultivation, and tasteful disposal of the flowers. To succeed as an exhibitor the amateur must put his heart into the work, must master all the details of planting, pruning, and budding, and train his eye by constant observation and comparison to the appreciation of the distinctive qualities of the flowers, as well as the modes of procedure followed by different cultivators. How far a good soil aids the exhibitor may be estimated by the relative success of a certain few of the most eminent trade growers. It should not be prudent to mention names, but we may properly suggest that those who most frequently and continuously take the highest awards—the challenge trophies and silver cups for seventy-two varieties and forty eight trebles at the principal exhibitions-the folks who have longest and loudest held a lead in this way, al ways hail from a strong soil, and are generally found to be great in growing roses on the English brier.

Others who follow them closely, or, while showing well in certain extra classes, carefully abstain from competing in the sections where both quantity and quality are required, will be found to be located on gravelly or sandy soil, and to be assiduous cultivators of the Italian brier. The amateur must always bear in mind that a genial climate, a rich mellow soil, and a considerable amount of moisture both in the earth and the air, are the needful aids to skilful manipulation; and although he may not be able to command any of them as the accidents of locality, he must do all that art suggests as possible to remedy the defects of nature–that is, if he hopes to succeed with roses.

In presenting the queen of flowers in a competitive exhibition, considerable *finesse* is required. You may have superb roses, but unless you show them properly they will be lost, and flowers of inferior shape and substance may win the prize over the head of yours. If exhibiting is in your mind, you must occasionally visit rose shows, and make note of the manner in which the flowers are arranged, and especially of the differences in appearance between those that win and those that lose. You will very soon learn that skilful handling of the flower has nearly as much to do with success under canvas as skilful cultivation has in the open air. Now, whatever your ideas as to how roses *should be* shown, be you content in the first instance to walk the way of the world, and conform to all established rules, taking comfort by this, consideration, that there have been original thinkers in the field–aye, and men of rare sound taste, too, and yet after all they have attained to nothing better than wooden boxes covered with moss in which to stage their competitive flowers.

The regulation boxes are made of inch deal, all of the same. breadth, namely, eighteen inches; all of the same height, namely, six inches at back and four in front, and of various lengths, according to the number of roses. For twenty-four roses the length is four feet; for eighteen roses, three feet; for twelve roses, two feet two inches. The twenty-four box is the largest, and for convenience of carriage is rather too large; and hence many exhibitors have a number of boxes made to hold eighteen each, and if they want to show seventy-two varieties, they put four boxes in a row, and cover the whole with moss, and so make one continuous bed of the whole. The boxes should have covers one inch larger every way, and inside, all round, should have a narrow beading half an inch from the bottom of the lid; this will rest on the edge of the boxes, and leave space between for the roses, which cannot be too closely confined, provided solely that nothing touches them. It is necessary to have holes pierced at equal distances for the roses, and to provide zinc tubes,

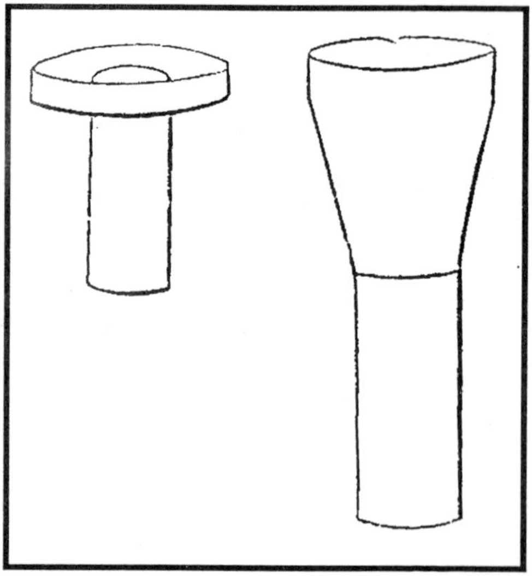

with moveable tops, to hold the flowers. These should be of the regulation pattern, and the best way to secure a supply is first to beg one of an exhibitor—and any exhibitor will say "Yes" on the instant—and go to a tinman for a supply, giving him the one you have begged for a model.

Before cutting the flowers, it is desirable to have printed or carefully written a number of neat cards bearing the names of varieties to be shown. At the last moment you will of course modify your plan more or less and therefore you must have spare flowers and spare cards to meet all probable emergencies. The cards are usually three inches long and one inch wide, but you may have them smaller, provided always that the names are legible. Some exhibitors place the labels on edge in front of the roses; others insert them in neat cleft sticks which stand up slightly above the flowers. To keep the labels in lots, alphabetically arranged, is easy enough; and it is a particularly convenient way for one whose hands are likely to tremble in finally touching up the flowers preparatory to quitting the tent at one end as the judges come in at the other.

To select good flowers is of course one step towards success. For days in advance of the show you will have your eye on certain: thumping buds that sit amidst buxom bright green leaves, and promise each to count one–or more than one–in the judging. Now

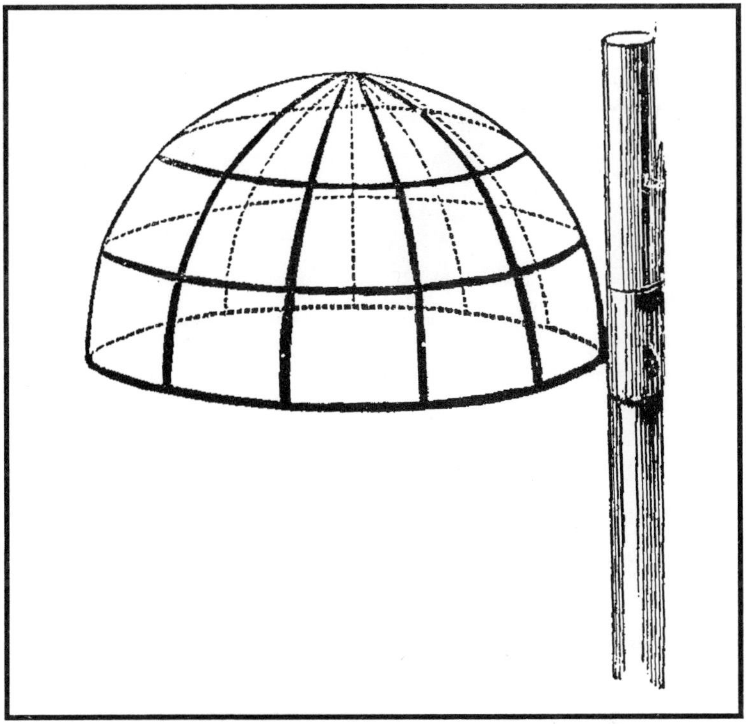

you must be prepared with a number of wire shades eight to ten inches in diameter, and five to six inches, deep, made to slide up and down a stake, and to be fixed where required by inserting a wedge in the sliding socket. Never use the shade unless you feel that it is really required; for in dull weather delicate flowers will attain perfection without it; but if an east wind and a scorching sun, or a sou'-wester with heavy rain, prevail, the shades must be used to protect the more highly-finished flowers, and especially such as are of thin texture and light colour. The caps must be covered with fresh cabbage or rhubarb leaves, or paper. A shade may be improvised by means of a board and a flower pot, as in the sub-joined figure. The board must have a hole in the centre and a slit cut from it to the edge to pass the stalk of the flower through. The boards will of course be firmly fixed to stakes, and the flower pots will have their bottoms knocked out and covered with wire gauze or glass. In place of a flower pot a bell glass may be used.

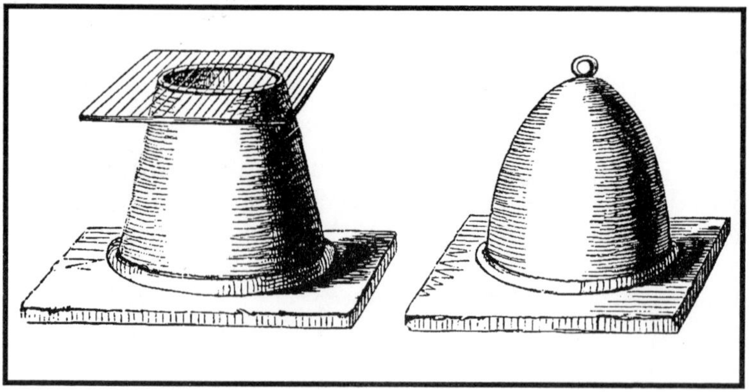

To have cards and moss and boxes in readiness will be one good step towards achieving conquest in the strife. You will, of course, have severely thinned the buds on your best trees, especially if they stand remote from the garden in a nursery quarter, and you will have supplied with regular doses of liquid manure such of them as may have appeared to need it, taking care also not to overfeed any, lest, instead of huge *perfect* roses, they should present ugly green centres. Very well. You have next to cut the flowers. Now, the best time for this business is the morning of the show, and you cannot be too early, for the flowers will hold their own longer if you can cut them before the sun has shed one rayon their perishable petals. It is good practice to cut and stage them at once; therefore your boxes and tubes should be taken to the garden shed the night before, and your man should be encouraged to meet you on the ground at daybreak by any kind of encouragement you consider best adapted to his constitution. If he is one of the right sort, it; will be enough to say, "Call me at three, Sanders, and don't cut a flower until I come".

Always cut your finest flowers first, and arrange them as you proceed, to ensure a telling effect, placing the largest at the back, and putting the yellows as far apart as possible, and taking care to have light flowers at each end of the lot, and here and there in the back row to draw out the eyes of the judges, but in such a way as not to betray any strict formality. If you have but a few light flowers, and put them close together near the centre, you will spoil the very best of the dark flowers that happen to be on the outsides. Spread the light as equally as possible, but take care to have enough about the boundary line. Always work up to your best flowers; do not use them to bring others out, but, while staging nothing but what is good, lead up by judicious arrangement of colours to your thumpers, to ensure their counting their full value in the judging. A little dressing will be required as you proceed, and you will have to learn the art by practice, although in essence it is most simple, and essentially honest. You are not to stick petals into flowers that show goggle eyes, but you may cleverly clip off the decayed edge of a petal, or twitch a petal out if necessary. A very large Mamiaison, not quite out, may perhaps be improved by giving it a gentle squeeze between the finger and thumb, and then the removal of the stained outside petal may make a fine flower of it. An ivory dressing-stick will be found useful. It should be the size of your middle finger, flat, and rounded at one end. If in any difficulty about obtaining it, ask a lady friend to show you the ivories employed in netting, and borrow one for practice. By deftly handling this, holding the rose at the base between the thumb and two fingers of the left hand, you may regulate the petals if they are a little disorderly, gently curling them in towards the centre.

To provide moss may prove a more difficult task than providing roses. If it is not green and bright, you will be better off without it; but as there is nothing so good as moss, you must be at some trouble to secure it if you can. The Dean of Rochester recommended a lining of zinc for the boxes, and in this growing the dwarf Lycopodium, *Selaginella apoda,* to form a rich green bed for the roses. But this adds so enormously to the weight of the boxes, that it should not be used. The late C.J. Perry, of Castle Bromwich—one of truest florists and heartiest of men who has helped a show in modern times—once spoilt the look of a magnificent box of twenty-four at; the Crystal Palace by bedding them on cut sprays of the common lycopodium, *Selaginella denticulata,* which had a most tweedy appearance. What, then, you will ask, is a rosarian to do if he cannot obtain real moss of the proper fairy-like texture and colour? The answer is easy. Let the boxes be nicely painted and varnished a full dark-green colour, or covered with dark-green velvet–the velvet covering being preferable; and set up the flowers without moss, and every rose will appear to the judicial, as well as to the public eye, in its proper beauty.

When you have done all, be patient and hopeful. If you win, be not vain; if you lose, be not downhearted; and, above all things, do not openly or inwardly abuse the judges, for remember that they perhaps know more about roses than you do, and after all they are but fallible men, and must have a margin for error in common with other people.

"Thus fears the man whom virtue, beacon-like,
Hath fix'd upon the hills of eminence;
At him the tempests of mad envy strike,
And rage against his piles of innocence:
But still the more they wrong him, and the more
They seek to keep his worth from being known,
They daily make it greater than before,
And cause his fame the further to be blown.
When, therefore, no self-doting arrogance,
But virtues covered, with a modest veil,
Break through obscurity, and thee advance
To place where envy shall thy worth assail,
Discourage not thyself, but stand the shocks
Of wrath and fury. Let them snarl and bite,
Pursue thee with detraction, slander, mocks,
And all the venomed engines of despight,
Thou art above the malice, and the blaze
Of thy celestial fire shall shine so clear,
That their besotted souls thou shalt amaze,
And make thy splendours to their shame appear."

—George Wither

Chapter 9
THE CHARACTERS OF ROSES

Roses are variously described as "cupped," "globular," "imbricated," and as otherwise distinguished by some peculiarity of form. It is a matter of considerable importance to the rose amateur to be able to picture in the "mind's eye" any given rose from a printed description; but to this end the terms employed must have a definite signification, and the descriptions must be precise and true. It is not desirable–and, happily, it is not possible, to have all roses cast, in the same mould. The exquisite form and delicate colouring of the common cabbage rose do not in the least detract from our enjoyment of the dense globular or semi-conical form of a fine tea-rose, such as *Souvenir d'un Ami*, or the tazza-shape of a glowing perpetual like *John Hopper*. As, however, all merit is comparative, so the relative merits of roses depend much on their forms, and in any practical scale of the order of properties form should certainly hold the first place. We may sometimes accept with gladness some particular variety for the sake of its colour and perfume; but, if we have any range of choice, those of best forms will be selected first, and amongst the several forms that are recognized some will certainly rank higher than others. It is with a view to assist the critical amateur to a right appreciation of the more distinctive forms of roses, and to promote uniformity of practice in the employment of descriptive terms, that we submit the accompanying sketches of six distinct types, which we propose shall be recognized as admissible to the great class of "show roses", and shall henceforth be known by the designations we have adopted for them.

The Globular Rose

The Globular rose is certainly the finest of all known forms; but, as "variety is charming," we do not wish to see the stands at a rose show occupied with roses of this type only. Its near approxi-mation to a spherical outline satisfies the eye, and that same outline favours depth of petal, uniformity of contour, and concealment of the centre. A very considerable number of the finest show roses are of this form, the centres being full of small petals, and the exterior petals broad, stout, and richly folded, each sweetly embracing the portion of the periphery which its outline covers. When we view the rose from above, the petals are seen to graduate regularly in size from the centre to the circumference, and their regular convexity produces a most delicate series of shadings of the prevailing colour, whatever

GLOBULAR ROSE

that may happen to be. It is a good point if the colour deepens towards the centre of the flower, and the centre of every petal; and this will be the case if the petals are "shell-shaped", because every part of the surface will receive the light at a different angle to every other part, and the colour will be intensified towards the hollow of the shell.

The Cup-shaped Rose

The cup-shaped rose is an elegant modification of the globular, the result of a greater depth–and, usually, less breadth–of petal. This form is well adapted to display any peculiar colour, and it is generally elegant in the bud. But it is not always satisfactory when viewed from above, for the centre is rarely well concealed, and many of the smaller petals are lost to view, because hidden by those that rise above them. Nevertheless, we have some lovely roses of this type, and it may be said of it that the more it tends towards the

CUP-SHAPED ROSE

globular the better. It is a good point in a cup-shaped rose to be well rounded at the base; if it narrows down sharply to the calyx, it is in that respect faulty.

The Tazza-shaped Rose

The Tazza-shaped rose is a modification of the globular, resulting from a shortening of the petals, which are often wider than their depth. Roses described as "compact" are usually tazza-shaped. It is a most desirable form if the centre is good, but the interior of the flower is so fully revealed that it must be thoroughly well filled to bear severe criticism. The petals should be shell-shaped, their edges slightly clasping, and they should be stout in substance, to sustain the fine formal outline of the flower.

TAZZA-SHAPED ROSE

The Imbricated or Expanded Rose

The imbricated or expanded rose affords a very agreeable change from the three foregoings. In this the petals are numerous and comparatively small, rising tier above tier to the centre, which

IMBRICATED/EXPANDED ROSE

should consist of small petals without a, trace of an eye, for that indeed is more bearable in a cup-shaped flower. The general contour of the flower is flat land broad, and, therefore, extreme regularity, good colour, and a camellia-like substance, are required to compensate for obvious defects. We have some very pretty roses of this type, but it is not well to take seed from them, although if they are good in colour and substance, they may be turned to account to supply pollen to the globular and cup-shaped. Too often roses of this class are wanting in substance, and tend to most objectionable features.

The Reflexed

The reflexed is a good form of the imbricated, as the petals curl outward, and present the shade of the inner surfaces in alternate lines or waves to the shade of their outer surfaces. If nicely filled up, in the style of a high-centred dahlia, this is a fine form of rose, but as every petal is revealed, the utmost regularity is required, and the flower should be "full of stuff", that is, it should consist of an

REFLEXED ROSE

immense number of petals, and display no trace of an eye, the stamens being all converted into petals. We have not many good examples of this type, and the best of them tend to roughness in the centre, and a general confusion throughout. When, however, there are two or three delicate shades of colour, the flower is admitted by all true rosarians; to be beautiful, even if, according to the "properties", its faults are obvious, and we have to regret that Nature is wilful and eccentric.

The Quartered Rose

The quartered rose is generally objectionable, and can only be recognised as admissible in a show class because, in spite of our rules and harsh empiricism, very many quartered roses are so lovely that we would sooner burn and forget our rules than lose these roses. It is not well to cite examples in setting forth a system for technical guidance, but in illustration of this type of rose we must mention *La Ville de Bruxelles* and *Souvenir de la Malmaison* as lovely roses that please us even by their defects. In this form flatness is a striking characteristic, but the chief peculiarity is that the petals are

QUARTERED ROSE

arranged in groups in such a manner that there are usually four or five distinct whorls of them in a concentrical arrangement, the principal shadows of which suggest to the eye the possibility, and even the probability, that the flower may divide from the axis into a series of radial divisions. A rose of this type must have some very pleasing characteristics of colour, size, or fragrance, or all these qualities combined, to compensate for its defects of form, for a quartered rose is objectionable from first to last, for the simple reason that it is quartered.

> "From fairest creatures we desire increase,
> That thereby Beauty's Rose might never die."

In judging roses, form, size, and freshness are the three grand qualifications. In comparison with these, colour is quite of secondary importance, and as to novelty it is on its own account of no account at all. When a new variety presents a new and desirable quality, then novelty shall count for something; but in the garden, on the dinner table, in the button-hole, and under exhibition canvas, one good old rose is always to be preferred to fifty new and bad ones. At every show where proper encouragement is afforded to roses, there should be a separate class for the new ones, because the amateur who boldly speculates in novelties cannot always wait until his latest purchases are thoroughly established, and the trade are naturally anxious to present examples of the newest of the new, and it is impossible to obtain from recently-introduced varieties such flowers as they would produce after being in the country a few years. Hence, to put the newest in the same stand with the oldest is unfair as a rule, for the tremendous vigour of an established favourite may result in the eclipse of a novelty presenting some very desirable qualities as yet only partially developed. But nothing will and

STRIPED ROSE, MADAME DESIREE GIRAUD

nothing need prevent the insertion of examples of the newest in the same stands with the oldest, if the first happen to be equal in size and substance to their veteran competitors. We must judge roses as we see them with the bodily eye, and not by the prophetic vision; and it is a matter of no small importance that no rose, however good, can be shown so well in the first season of its occupation of the English garden. The hard forcing it is subjected to for the purpose of making stock will suffice to take the substance out of its flowers and deceive us as to its capabilities. *Form* is the most important, certainly, of all properties; next in rank we place size; but if size is accompanied with any degree of coarseness, such as rough petals or any trace of an eye, it is a fault rather than a merit of the flower. Nor is *freshness* or *condition* of small account, for a rose that has become papery or cambricy, or stained or shrivelled, is as nothing or worse than nothing. We are not to consider what it has been any more than in respect of a green rose-bud of the size of a hazle-nut we are to consider what it will be. A stand of small flowers nicely formed and fresh and clean should carry off the palm from a stand of the largest that have lost form and character by reason of staleness. As to *colour*, "variety is charming", and the brighter and purer and more various, the colours the better. The exhibitor who has "half an eye" will take care to arrange his colours so that all will tell, and will even make a little sacrifice of form and size to ensure a certain brightness of colour requisite in the arrangement of a pleasing group.

Chapter 10

CLIMBING ROSES

The rose grower must never confound together the idea of a climbing with that of a pillar rose, for the simple reason that they are very distinct in their characters, and to a great extent require different treatment. Climbing roses may be grown on pillars, and *vice versa*; but a genuine climber is not best adapted for a pillar, nor is a genuine pillar rose best adapted for a trellis or wall. But as the leading principles of their respective cultivation agree in some points, and as for decorative purposes they very closely assimilate, there would be a strict propriety in considering them together, if we could afford room to do so, especially as the treatment needed by one would serve to illustrate and explain that necessary for the other. As a rule, fast-growing roses, of pendulous and rambling habit, such as *Boursault* or *Rampante* for instance, make the best climbers; but these generally produce inferior flowers, though when seen *en masse* their appearance when in full bloom is delightful. But for pillars, varieties of the highest floral excellence may be chosen, such for instance as *Charles Margottin, Red Rover, Glory of Waltham, Madame Fillion,* and others that hear inspection individually, and exhibit characters consistent with the important and conspicuous places assigned them. Bearing these differences in mind, let us consider now the uses and abuses of climbing roses.

The object first sought is to cover the wall, trellis, or arch quickly, but not with such haste as to prejudice the future well-doing of the trees. For all the better class of climbers the first thing requisite is to prepare the soil, so that when planted they will have every help to free growth. No matter what the position or the circumstances in which the roses are to be planted, the soil should be deeply stirred and liberally manured some time before planting takes place. For these roses are hungry, and if starved the leaders become hard in the bark, and are reluctant to make side-shoots; and instead of making a vigorous growth at one effort there is a succession of spasmodic efforts at growth all through the season, especially after rain, that prevents the formation of flower-buds. But for Ayrshire roses no great preparation is necessary, unless the soil happens to be poor peat, sand, or chalk, in which case some good loam must be introduced at the stations where they are to be planted. In nearly every case of planting climbing roses, plants on their own roots are to be preferred. If not on their own roots, they should be on short brier stocks. Some kinds seem to do well budded as on their own roots, and for the first year or two grow quicker. We remember once covering a great breadth of wall with one plant of Grevillea in three years, the plant being worked on a brier about six inches from the ground; and another plant on its own roots, in a similar position close by, had not made more than half that growth in the same period; but after the third year, there was no great difference between them.

In common with other roses, the climbers may be planted at any time between November and March if they have been previously growing out of doors, and as many of them are precocious in their movements in spring, autumn planting is to be preferred. But in any case of planting out of pots, if the plants have been sheltered or grown for some time under glass, it will be best to wait till April or even May, and then turn them out carefully, loosening the ball of earth, but not stripping their roots entirely.

It will depend on the varieties planted, how they are to be dealt with from the day of planting. Ayrshire and Sempervirens roses require very little pruning at any time, whether in youth or age; but Boursaults, Rosomenes, Teas, and Noisettes require careful pruning to insure a regular distribution of the flowering wood, and prevent increase of altitude at the expense of growth at the base. Any of these roses left to grow as they please will soon become mere bunches of leaves at the ends of long naked shoots. It is the business of the cultivator to prevent this. If the plants are strong when planted in autumn, tie them in sufficiently to keep them safe against wind, and so leave them till spring. At the end of February cut them down to within two eyes of the base of each shoot and on no account begin with more than three shoots to each tree. The object of deferring cutting down till spring is to prevent the premature starting of the buds at the base, for should there come a sharp frost after mild weather those buds may be killed back after having grown a few inches. From the three shoots supposed to be cut down there will probably start eight or nine shoots. Retain five of these, and cut or nip out the remainder as soon as you can determine which push the strongest; the weakest are to be removed. Supposing you have but one main shoot to begin with, cut it down to three, four, or five eyes, and from these form the plant. Train in all shoots regularly, never let them hang about, or the growth will be checked and they will flower prematurely. (When they are established they may be allowed to fall over if the position allows of negligent growth, and they will bloom the more freely for it). At the next season's pruning, cut back all the shoots at least half their length, no matter what the length may be, and at the same time remove any weak, or ill-placed, or imperfectly ripened shoots, leaving a bud at the base if another shoot is wanted in the place from which a poor shoot was removed. The next season cut back to a uniform length, but not severely, all the leading shoots, and shorten in very moderately all the laterals, and thenceforward prune very little, no more in fact than is sufficient to prevent crowding at anyone place or the usurpation of the principal vigour of the tree by anyone leading shoot. To keep a wall or trellis well clothed, it is needful to have an eye to the strong shoots that occasionally rise from the base. It will be well to allow one of these to rise every year, train it over the shoots that are already nailed in, and at the next pruning remove one of the old main shoots by a clean cut at the base, and let the young shoot replace it.

Arches and Trellises

If the summits and connecting chains and rods only require to be covered, plant climbing roses worked on tall stems and train their heads over, and only prune sufficiently to regulate the growth. For this purpose those of the Sempervirens section are invaluable; and as they retain their leaves till spring, you have the advantage of verdure in winter with roses in summer. When in bloom they are magnificent, the clusters showing from a dozen to forty or fifty roses each. The deepest coloured rose of this section is *Princess Marie*, reddish pink, the flowers nicely cupped, and produced in large clusters. The next brightest coloured is *Flora,* flowers of a pleasing rose, a brilliant object when full out, the plant less decidedly evergreen than the rest of the family. The purest white of the race is *Donna Maria,* which has rich deep green, glossy foliage. Another good white is *Rampante,* a tremendous bloomer. The most fragrant is *Banksiaeflora,* with straw centre, very double. But the favourite of the race is *Felicite Perpetue,* a remarkably rapid grower, with lovely foliage, and myriads of little globular creamy blossoms. There are many others, the best of which are *Leopoldine d'Orleans,* white, tipped red, and *Myrianthes,* with beautifully formed rosy-blush flowers most delicate and graceful in all its aspects.

Trellises and Dividing Screens

When worked roses are planted to run over the summits of arches and temples, the low trellises and chains connecting the principal supports of the arches may be covered with Hybrid Perpetual and Bourbon varieties, or with *Rose de Rosomene,* which is very vividly coloured, and most profuse in flowering, though a poor rose when compared with any of the florists' varieties. Among the H. P. and B. sections, any of the vigorous growing kinds may be selected, and of Teas, Hybrid Teas and Noisettes there are many suitable.

Banks, Trees, and Wildernesses

In wild scenes, and where truly rustic roses are required, the Ayrshires answer admirably, being of rapid wiry growth, and requiring only to be trained–if trained–the first season, after which they will take care of themselves, and festoon dead or living trees, ruins, gateways, and other rough elevations most gracefully and profusely. To start them well give every plant a square yard of prepared soil, consisting of good loam and one-third manure, or if the staple is clay, break it up and manure it without introducing loam, and if they have but a moderate share of daylight they will grow in the confusion of a glorious wilderness, and make good hold for themselves wherever they go. Ayrshire and Sempervirens roses furnish precisely the kind of materials needed for the banks of wilderness walks and for open spots in woodlands, and to clothe mounds and knolls where mere weeds wo1ud be obnoxious, and choicer plants out of place. Let the ground be well dug over and manured, and then plant the varieties in masses of a dozen of one kind together, the plants five feet apart every way, and after that an occasional dressing of manure on the surface is all they require. Even that is unnecessary on good clay or loamy soils.

Wall Roses

All the foregoing may be turned to good account on walls, but as walls are good positions, they should be appropriated to the best roses that can be obtained for them. We shall not soon forget a *bijou* rose garden in which was a great breadth of wall on one side of the dwelling house, fitted from the eaves to the ground. line with a wooden trellis, completely covered with *Jaundtre* and *Wistaria sinensis* freely intermixed, and one mass of bloom throughout; such a curious blending of fawn colour and bluish purple as it would be equally impossible to describe or imagine. It is prudent to have a wall intended for roses fitted with a trellis to which the gardener will *tie* the roses instead of having to *nail* them; but instead of wood, let it be stout galvanized wire run through eyelet-hole nails. This plan preserves the wall, and is better for the roses than the nails and shreds.

The most splendid and certain of all wall roses are the *Boursaults*. They grow fast, are thoroughly hardy, bloom in immense clusters, and are truly gorgeous in the display they make, but they do not last long. To grow *Boursaults* well cut them down close at the first start, and after that merely shorten the seasonal growth, and thin out the weak spray and any soft or misplaced shoots, and they will never fail to be beautiful in their season. They require a good soil, but the aspect is comparatively of little consequence. The best is *Gracilis*, which is a rapid grower and of pendulous habit, with handsome foliage. The flowers are of all intensely brilliant rose colour. *Inermis*, bright red, is a lively rose, and of most luxuriant habit. *Amadis*, with purplish crimson flowers, is a favourite about London. At some places it appears to come spontaneously, like an efflorescence of the brick walls. It is a truly deserving rose, and superb on a pillar.

In the Multiflora section we have the finest wall rose known, but which happens to be only fit for a south wall in the south of England, being unfortunately very tender. This is *Laure Davoust*, arose which claims admiration for its lovely foliage, and large flowers, produced in immense clusters, the colour a curious mixture of lilac and blush. *Russelliana*, rosy lilac, is a trifle more hardy, but needs a

FELICITE PERPETUE ON CHURCH PORCH

south or west wall. *Grevillea*, or the *Seven Sisters* rose, is the best known of this, class; and a superb rose it is, growing with marvellous rapidity, and if capable of ensuring the climate, presenting a magnificent spectacle when in bloom, the flowers being in great clusters, and exhibiting various shades, of rose, and purple and deep crimson. It is a troublesome rose to grow, owing chiefly to its habit of beginning to push early in the season, and its unfitness to endure the sharp frosts which usually occur in this country in the month of May. The specific form *Rosa multiflora*, more generally known as *R. polyantha*, is the most useful rose for covering large wall spaces in the section, as it is vigorous in growth, and its small white flowers are produced in enormous profusion.

Banksian roses are of the same delicate constitution as the Multifloras, but where they can be grown, they are exquisitely beautiful. Travellers by the South-Eastern Rail way may in the season have a feast of these lovely roses by keeping a look out after passing Croydon, as at several of the stations south of that town the walls are covered with them, and they grow most luxuriantly, and flower in dense sheets of white and yellow uniformly from head to foot. Banksian roses require a rich, dry soil, a warm exposure, safe shelter from east winds, as they bloom in May, when the weather is frequently as cold as in January; and in pruning, any long rods may be cut away, but the small side shoots must be left their full length or there will be no bloom. If they produce gross shoots late in the season cut them clean away in September, unless they are wanted to fill up gaps, in which case tie the shoot down to as nearly a horizontal line as possible. This will check the growth, and tend to its more perfect ripening. The next spring, it can be trained into the place where required. The best of this series is undoubtedly *Jaune Perin*, with yellow flowers of good size, that is for a Banksian; and *Fortuniana*, with double snow white flowers, also larger than the ordinary type of a Banksian. But the old White and less old Yellow Banksian are beautiful in their way; and where Banksian roses can be grown without risk, they should certainly have a place.

Lastly, there are some useful hybrid climbing roses, partaking more or less of the characters of the preceding sections, which merit the attention of those who have occasion to use climbers in plenty. *Laurae Davoust*, classed above as a Multiflora, is in reality a hybrid, though showing a predominance, of the Multiflora character. *Cheshunt Hybrid* is a showy purple crimson rose, and well adapted

WILLIAM ALLEN RICHARDSON ON WALL

for an arch or portico. *Madame d' Arblay*, pure white, flowering in immense clusters, is invaluable for its beauty and rapid growth. It is almost a Sempervirens. *The Garland*, lilac and blush, sometimes opening white and changing to pink, is a free growing climber, producing fragrant flowers in large clusters, and in habit closely related to the Sempervirens. Especially valuable for walls is *William Allen Richardson*, a vigorous growing Noisette bearing rich fawn-coloured flowers in great profusion. When planted in a moderately rich border and trained to a sunny wall, it will present an effective appearance, and afford liberal supplies of flowers for vases and bouquets.

It frequently happens that after some years of good service roses on walls become poor and flowerless, and thus ceasing to be subjects of admiration, the few attentions formerly bestowed upon them are discontinued, so that when they most need help they obtain the least, as is often the case with those of our own kith and kin who have bestowed their strength in the service of mankind. The question will often arise how are aged wall roses to be rejuvenated, how shall we restore to them their wonted vigour, that they in return may present us with their wonted bloom? Usually the cause of decline in these roses is that their rapacious roots have exhausted the soil all around them of its nourishment; and they have become decrepit; not by age but by starvation. The process of rejuvenating comprises two operations–a dressing of the soil, and a severe pruning. In the month of September open a trench in a semicircle, two feet distant from the stem of the tree, and remove from this the soil to the depth of eighteen inches, and to a breadth of two feet. At the same time remove some of the surface soil for the space of two feet round the stem where the soil has not been dug. Fill up the trench with a mixture of a turfy loam two parts, and rotten dung one part, and lay

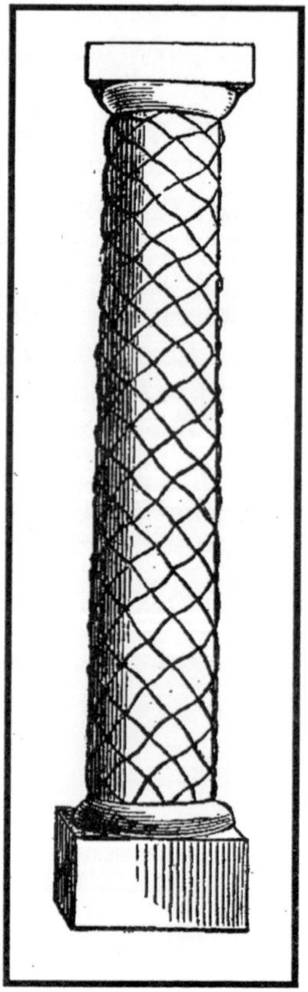

The roses clustering o'er my portal
Breathe welcome to you, fellow mortal

over the roots which have not been disturbed, six inches of half-rotten manure. In the month of March following cut the rose to within six inches of the ground, and that same summer it will throw up a new set of stems, and flower plentifully the succeeding spring.

The sub-joined illustration represents the mode adopted by an amateur for giving his friends a welcome by adorning his doorway with garlands of roses. The pillars are clothed with wire net of large mesh, and to this the sprays are tied and kept in perfect order without using nails, or the least appearance of untidiness.

The less robust of the climbing roses are well adapted to form picturesque weeping standards for the lawn, in which case it is advisable to plant in the first place young thrifty briers in well-made beds, and afterwards bud and train *in situ*. It must never be forgotten that an *established* brier is always to, be preferred to one recently transplanted, if vigorous growing roses are to be grafted or budded upon it. We occasionally meet with standards ten, twelve, or even fifteen feet high, and, as a matter of fact, there are some such now in the various nurseries. These gigantic standards are ungainly enough, but they suggest what might be done by a cultivator who could command extraordinary briers. Let us suppose one of these briers planted and left alone for one season, and then budded with a first-class climbing rose. We might, next season, make it the centre of a pavilion, for by simply training the growth over a suitable frame-work, It would form a tent of its own branches, and make a far more magnificent, though not less substantial, specimen than a weeping ash.

Chapter 11

PILLAR ROSES

The best pillar roses are those that grow from six to twelve feet high, and produce flowers of a quality good enough for exhibition. If climbing roses are used, the flowers will be of poor quality, though there may perchance be plenty of them; and in the majority of cases the pillars will be less uniformly clothed, though they may have a certain picturesqueness, which only true climbing roses can impart to them. Climbing roses are unsuitable, because usually they grow too fast and free. A moderate growth with a superior style of flowers are qualities to be preferred in forming objects that are likely to be closely and frequently inspected, and that under ally circumstances are subjected to closer and more critical scrutiny than roses trained over arches, banks, and the roofs of temples and arbours. The more vigorous growing varieties of Hybrid Perpetuals, Bourbons, Hybrid Bourbons, Moss, Damask, Hybrid China, and a few of the hardiest of the Teas and Noisettes, are those usually selected to form pillar roses. No rule can be laid down as to the class of roots to be preferred, for that depends so much on the character of the rose to be planted, and the soil in which it must be grown; and in the general remarks on the families of roses, numerous advices are offered as to the treatment of individual varieties so as to insure the most vigorous growth.

The culture of pillar roses certainly demands some skill; but it is a skill easily acquired by the observant and inquiring cultivator. Let us consider the several points in regular order, so as to dismiss all simple matters with a word, and deal with difficulties as they come before us at such length as their relative importance may demand.

Planting Pillar Roses

In any case the soil must be well drained, liberally manured, deeply stirred, and in a sound condition. It should be of such quality as to produce good wheat or cauliflowers or it will never produce pillar roses. A pillar rose will require at least one square yard of soil which must not be occupied with shrubs, or grass, or in fact anything but annuals and other flowering plants of humble growth, all the summer; and every autumn this soil must be enriched with dressings of half rotten stable manure. As the pillars need not, and had better not, be fixed till the roses are in their third year, it only remains, after having prepared the soil, to plant firm, and insert one or two ordinary four-feet stakes. If Manetti roses are planted, be sure to place them sufficiently deep to have the point where graft and stock meet two inches below the ground line. Whatever tends to increase the vigour of a rose–such as top-dressings in summer, abundant supplies of water, etc.-must be given to pillar roses; for it is not only desirable to clothe the pillars, but to do so with *stout wood*, which can only be accomplished by feeding liberally. Let us suppose the roses planted, they are then to be cut down to within one or two buds of the base, and allowed to grow the first season as they please, and the more vigorously the better.

Pruning Pillar Roses

The second season they will require pruning. Now, to prune them properly, the rosarian must bear in mind that it is much easier to induce a tree to grow to its full height than to induce it to form regular tiers of flowering wood all the way from its roots to its summit. This is true of apples, pears, plums, vines, and hundreds of other trees. Keep the leading shoots upright, and do not prune it at all, and it will grow with great vigour, so as continually to increase its length till it attains its maximum height; but in the meantime, the leading bud having monopolized the sap, there will be but few side-branches formed, and consequently there will be little or no flowering wood produced. The sap of a tree always rushes upwards; hence, if the leading shoots be trained out of the perpendicular, the side buds are developed, and these assume a vertical form in the majority of cases. It is true that trees, *do* produce side-branches without the aid

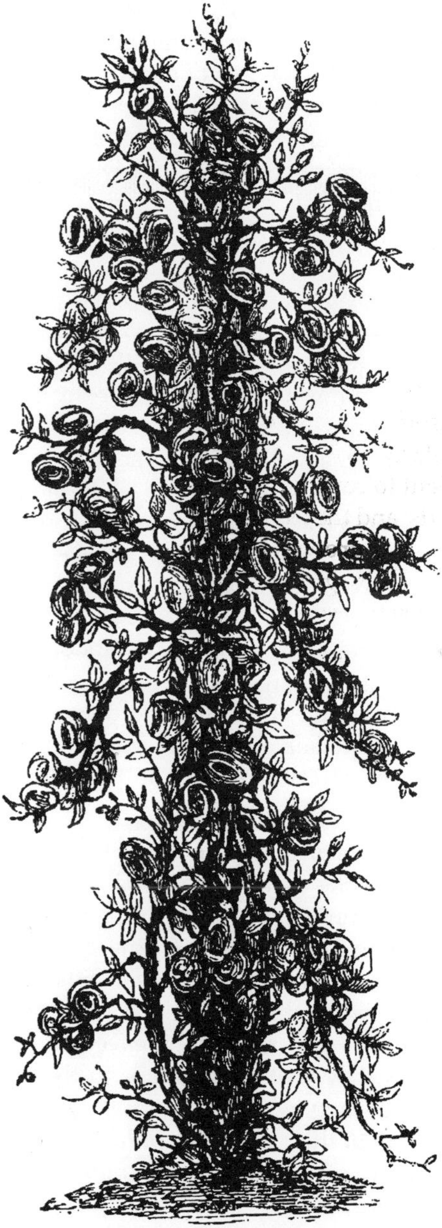

ROSE PILLAR, FURNISHED

of the pruner, and that these often take a horizontal or oblique direction; nevertheless, the general tendency of the sap is upwards, and one of the first consequences of allowing a tree to grow in its own way is to cause the formation of a bare stem for some distance from the ground line; and that tendency is of itself a sufficient argument for pruning pillar roses. In a word, if the pruning is neglected, they soon acquire their full height, but have naked stems; whereas, if properly pruned, these stems will be clothed from head to foot with flowering branches. The pruning in the second year will consist in removing by a clean cut, to within one or two buds of their base, all long, weak shoots, reserving two or three of the strongest shoots, and shortening these about one-third or one-half of their whole length. If any doubt as to the application of these instructions, let the rose itself furnish a hint. If it has attained to a great height, and is so regularly furnished with side-shoots as to be already very nearly sufficient to cover a pillar, prune all the side-shoots back to about four buds, and the leaders only a fourth or fifth of their whole length. If it has not grown much, cut it back very hard, removing quite half of the entire growth, so as to conform pretty nearly to this rule–*the more growth, the less pruning, the less growth, the more pruning*. Having accomplished the pruning, lay the shoots down full length on the ground, and fix them with a few strong pegs, so that the wind may not blow them about. This will cause, the buds to break–that is to say, will cause the formation of side-shoots the whole length of the rods; and by the end of April, or the 1st of May at latest, they must be tied up to their poles or pillars.

The third season's pruning must be on the same principle as in the preceding year; the cultivator must be more anxious about obtaining plenty of furniture–that is, of hiding the pillar with a plentiful side-growth from the ground upwards. He need not think much about getting the rose to the top of the pillar; it will go there in time, and perhaps sooner than will be good for its ultimate beauty; and if it does not, it is only needful to leave one or two long rods unshortened, and they will soon mount to the summit of their ambition. To begin, then, with the pruning, let us first determine about the furniture of the base of the pillar. Here we find already plenty of weak spray, some well-placed strong shoots, and perhaps a certain proportion of wiry twigs that produced flowers the previous season. All the weak spray should be cut clean out, leaving only the buds at the base to break again; the same with the wood

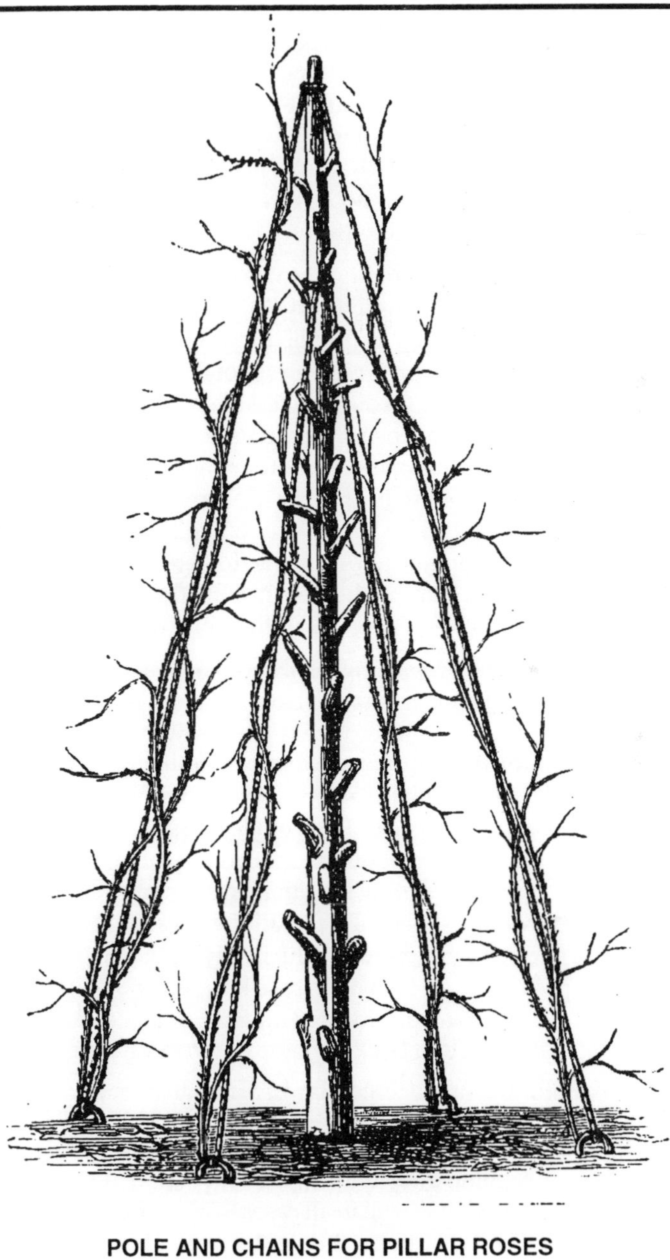

POLE AND CHAINS FOR PILLAR ROSES

that flowered the previous year. But the strong side-shoots may be cut to six or eight buds from the base. Where the pillar is bare, cut a few shoots very close, so as to get some vigorous growth to fill up the gaps; where crowded, thin away the weakest of the shoots, and leave those that are best placed for flowering. Proceed thus till you arrive at the top, then shorten back the leading shoots according to their length and strength, but not severely, to a plump bud, to carry the growth upward the next season.

After this pruning there ought to be an abundant bloom; and from this time forth there must be very little pruning; the cultivator's principal care will be to keep the tree liberally nourished, and provide for the occasional *renewal of the main shoots*, for those originally formed will in time be debilitated through excessive production of flowers. It is a good rule with Provence, Perpetuals, and Bourbons to prune in the short ripe side-shoots to from four to six eyes throughout. These shortened shoots will produce flowers plentifully; and as effect is more desirable than the quality of individual flowers, it is best, after fairly pruning, to allow all the flowers that are produced to come to perfection, helping the tree through the flowering season with copious supplies of water and with strong top-dressings..

The renewing or repairing of the pillar is accomplished by means of the strong shoots that rise from the base. As these appear, tie them in loosely, so as to induce a free growth; prune them as recommended for the first formation of the pillar, and as soon as they reach half way up the pillar, and, are tolerably well furnished with side-shoots, remove one of the old leaders, and let the young one take its place. When an abundance of young shoots is produced, some must be cut away entirely to within one bud of their base; from the bud left a flowering shoot will generally be developed next season, or it may be another strong shoot, which may be useful, though not wanted the previous year; in which case keep it; if not, either pinch it back, and cause it to form a mass of laterals, or leave it to grow its full length, and then cut it back as before. Two more remarks seem needful to complete these directions. By training the leading shoots straight up the pillars they will grow with more vigour; by training them regularly round and round the pole, the growth will be more moderate and regular, and there will be an earlier disposition to form flowering wood. It is well in all cases to allow new shoots to go straight up, and to twist them the next season after the pruning.

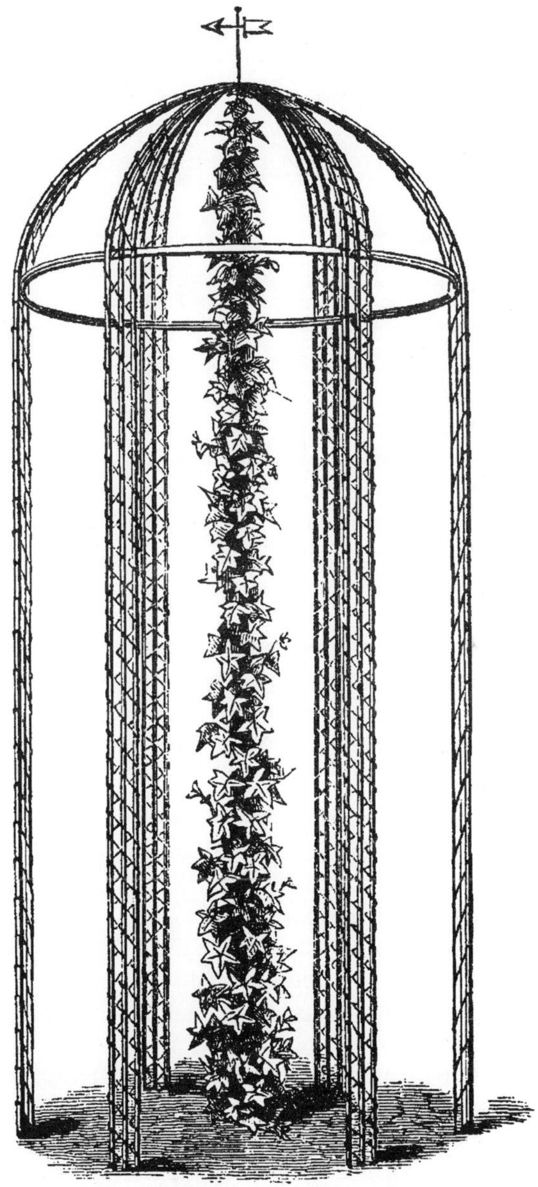

TRELLIS PAVILION FOR PILLAR ROSES

This secures strong wood in the first year, and plenty of laterals in the second. The last remark is, that poles and pillars should not exceed twelve feet; and when it is determined to have them of that height, the most robust-growing pillar roses should be selected. The better kinas of Hybrid Perpetuals and Bourbons do best on pillars of six to eight feet; if taken higher, it is difficult to keep them furnished at bottom.

We may now offer a few remarks as to the poles and pillars themselves. It is best not to insert these till the roses have grown two years, and when inserted, it must be in a way to stand firm during a gale. Larch poles, with short snags, and the bulky portion of the roots attached, make the best of pillars, for when planted they have a firm hold of the soil, and are not easily blown out of the perpendicular. Old stems of yew are very durable; ash poles require frequent renewal, and being slight it is best to put two or three close together, and brace them securely with copper or galvanized wire, so as to form one stout pillar. In all cases, it is best if the lower parts of the posts can be charred, as this prevents the growth of mycelium, by which so many roses are destroyed, owing to the proximity of decaying wood to their roots. The superiority of iron must not be overlooked, for not only is wood perishable, but the soundest wooden pole may be snapped short off by a gale. If iron poles are adopted, they should be one inch in diameter, with triple prongs proportionately stout, and the prongs should be from one to two feet in length, proportionate to the height of the pole above ground.

When climbing roses are used conjointly with genuine pillar roses, very beautiful effects may be produced. The climbers may be trained as fast as they will grow, without any pruning, to cover the roof of a temple, and the pillar roses trained to the trellis supports, which by a regular course of pruning they may be made to cover completely. To form a simple rose temple is a matter of no great difficulty, as suitable breadths of stout galvanized wire trellis can be obtained at a cheap rate, and the roof might be either of zinc or copper, or left open by continuing the breadth of trellis in a graceful curve to the apex. There can be nothing more suitable for the centre of a rosarium; and, besides its elegance as all architectural object, it serves the useful purpose of displaying varieties that are only seen to advantage when allowed to grow to vast dimensions. Other and more simple methods of training will occur to the ingenious rosarian,

ROSES ON PILLARS AND CHAINS

THE DOG ROSE

as, for instance, the *designs annexed*, which will explain themselves to consist of tall poles sustained by trellises, chains, or wire ropes. In the case of poles and chains, the poles may be covered with a climbing rose, or with ivy, the dark green of which will show up the roses trained to the chains very effectually.

Ah ! see, whose fayre thing doest faille to see,
In springing floure the image of thy day !
Ah ! see the Virgin Rose, how sweetly shee
Doth first press foorth with bashful modestee,
That fairer seems the lesse ye see her may.
Lo ! see soone after how more bold and free
Her bared bosome she doth broad displaye.
Lo ! see soone after, how she fades and falls away.

—*Spenser*

Chapter 12

ROSES UNDER GLASS

The cultivation of roses in the greenhouse and conservatory is attended with some amount of difficulty, and should never be attempted until experience has been obtained in the management of roses in the open ground. The best proof of the difficulty of growing roses under glass is afforded by the periodical exhibitions of pot roses, both at special and general horticultural exhibitions. The reader will ask, with surprise, perhaps, if it is not usual to see at the great London flower shows in the months of April and May, displays of pot roses that are equally remarkable for perfection of training and growth as for the profusion and splendour of their flowers? The reply must be that these magnificent roses illustrate the whole of the case we have to consider, for they are invariably presented by experienced trading firms that devote a large share of their energies to rose growing. Probably there are not so many as half a dozen trading firms in the whole range of the British islands capable of finishing pot roses as they are finished by the competitors whose productions have for many years past constituted leading attractions at the Crystal Palace and Regent's Park. There are thousands of trade and amateur cultivators who can grow roses superbly both for the decoration of the garden and to cut for exhibition, but the number of those who can manage pot roses in the very highest style, may be counted on the fingers, and leave fingers to spare. From time to time spirited amateur cultivators of the highest talent, men who have attained numerous honours in pelargoniums, cinerarias, heaths, and other exhibition plants of widely different character, resolve on entering the lists with the leading growers of pot roses, and they invariably fail. The explanation is not hard to find. To do perfect justice to pot roses, the cultivator should have nothing else on his mind. They are the most exacting of all known plants; they surpass ericas and orchids in the amount and minuteness of the attention they require; and when first-rate cultivators fail in their management, it is usually because they have many other things to think of, and the roses are the most emphatic to resent even the semblance of neglect. Any lover of roses who has acquired experience in handling them, and is really skilful in the art, may attain to proficiency in the production of pot specimens, if he will devote himself to the work rather as a duty than a pastime, and allow nothing to divert his attention from it. There is no mystery to be unfolded, no secret to be taught, no peculiar difficulty to be explained. The rose is not well adapted for pot culture, and being liable at all times to suffer from heat, cold, drought, damp, mildew, vermin, and mismanagement, these several enemies become additionally dangerous the more the plant is subjected to artificial conditions of existence. A rose in the open ground can fetch its own water if there is any moisture in the soil within two or three feet of the surface, and it can drink as much as it likes of the dew of heaven all night long; but a rose in a pot is entirely dependent on the discretion of the cultivator for food, water, air, light, and other necessaries of life, lacking any of which, or having excess of any, it is in danger, and if it does not die, must part with its health and beauty. The amateur who has but little time for gardening, had best not attempt to grow specimen pot roses, but he may find recreation in growing pot roses that will be useful, and a credit to his skill, without entering on the higher walks of the art, if he will be content with such small triumphs as come within the range of his opportunities and appliances.

The simplest, and in many respects the most enjoyable way of growing roses under glass, is by planting them out on well made borders. The sub-joined figure represents a rough span-roofed house of low pitch, in which a friend who grows roses for Covent Garden Market, produces the principal part of his supply. The house is ventilated at the sides and along the ridge, and being a very light and inexpensive structure, it is necessary to support the ridge line with two rows of iron gag pipes, or as they are termed in the trade, "gas tubing". The beds in which the roses are planted are raised

ROSE-HOUSE WITH ROSES PEGGED DOWN

above the level and supported by rough boarding, but as a matter of course a brick wall would be preferable. These beds consist of two feet depth of a first-rate mixture, resting on two feet depth of large brick rubble. The mixture may be said to consist of three parts loam from rotted turf of one spit only, one part, fat manure, and one part rough gritty stuff consisting of broken brick, sharp sand, and the coarser part of charrings from a garden smother. The greater-portion of the roses are pegged down on the bed; others are trained up the rafters and the gas tubes, which we must now call pillars, and the result is a delightful garden of roses, wherein during the sometimes bleak weather of March and April, a lover of them would be delighted with the fresh and ample green leafage and the swelling buds, with here and there a precious flower full out, to afford a foretaste of the "feast of roses" that is nearly ready. As this house is not heated, the difficulties of management are few. The crop is all cut and sold before the end of May, and then the lights are taken off that the roses may enjoy sunshine, and rain, and dew, to perfect their growth for the following season. With the assistance of a little artificial heat, such as would be afforded by a single four-inch hot-water pipe fixed round the bed, the roses may be had in bloom a month or so earlier, but fire heat has its disadvantages, for when the plants are started into growth early in the year they require constant attention and more care throughout the whole period of growth in keeping insect pests under. Roses are especially susceptible to the attacks of green fly when grown under glass, and when fire heat is employed great care is necessary in regulating the temperature, ventilation and atmospheric moisture, or the aphides will multiply at a rapid rate and do irreparable mischief. Therefore it will in all cases be preferable to dispense with fire heat in the amateurs' rose house, and depend wholly upon solar warmth for the acceleration of the blooming period. A movable roof, as in this case, is a great advantage, for when the roses are fully exposed they require but little attention as compared with those grown in structures from which the lights cannot be removed.

The rose house described above is not, however, exactly the kind of structure most suitable for the majority of a nateur rosarians, the rough-and-ready method of the trade grower being accompanied with too many rough-and-ready appearances to be at all consistent with the neatness that should characterise a private garden. A span-roof structure of plain yet elegant design would be far more preferable.

It would be much more pleasing in appearance, and the interior could be so arranged as to admit of the plants being readily attended to and their flowers fully enjoyed.

The structure should be fixed somewhat below the general level, the roof have a sharp pitch, and the glass be continued to the ground line. The proper position for such a house is one running north and south, as it then benefits by sunshine the whole time the sun is above the horizon. The steep pitch favours the gathering of sun heat in the spring, for the merest gleam of the early sun that touches the roof exercises a beneficial influence, light and heat being quickly dispersed from above, while at the same time the air is put in motion. In a district where cats abound a steep roof is a protection against them, for they will hold wittenagemotes and courts of love on glass roofs of easy slope, and should the heaviest delegates or the entire court fall through, a little mischief will follow inside. The sinking of the basement below the general level answers two important purposes. In winter frost does little harm, and it must be very severe to be felt at all; in summer the roots of the roses are kept cool, and consequently they hold their leaves longer, make stouter wood, and ripen their wood more completely. It is particularly important to secure, in connection with the low basement and steep roof, the most perfect drainage and ventilation. In the example before us, the drainage consists of common tunnel and sole drains under the centre line of each border, and these drains terminate in a drain of large bore outside. The walk may be concreted, and be, therefore, as dry in winter as in summer, and yet every drop of surplus water in the borders be quickly drawn away. As for the ventilation, that may be amply provided for by movable lights on either side, near the apex of the roof, and openings in the side walls. A house of this make may, of course, be of any length, but it should not be less than ten feet in width, to allow for a three feet walk and borders three-and-a-half feet each. A better, and, we may as well say, a proper minimum width is 16 feet, to allow for walk four feet and borders six feet each. It is not necessary for ensuring a good and early bloom to provide for such a house any heating apparatus, but if forcing is intended, there must be a good service of hot-water pipes, for a flue is not to be thought of, and fermenting materials would make a barbarous mess. However, as a matter of fact (tell it not in Gath), a great body of tan or stable manure, in a right state of age and moisture, might be laid up along the central walk–using the walk as a trench made for the purpose–with wonderful effect, to promote a strong and early bloom with a delightfully bright green leafage. If any wavering amateur wants a word of advice to "turn the scale," our advice is have no artificial heat at all, but be content with the lovely roses that will begin to open in April, and rise to a fulgid flush in May, for these may be enjoyed without expense or trouble, or fear of disaster; but the instant you take Promethean fire among roses you become a candidate for Promethean pains and penalties. In a kindly season the roses will begin to flower in the first week of April, and if they are cut freely, and not one is allowed to run to seed, and the management otherwise is what it should be, there will be plenty of flowers up to the end of June, when all unexpanded buds should be nipped out, to prevent further exhaustion, and give the plants a chance of recruiting for their next display.

In planting a house of this description the roses must be arranged in the two side borders, and the way we planted our house may be worth telling to those who are fond of Tea Roses and have no prospect of growing them successfully in the open ground. It was originally 35 feet long, but as the roses wanted more room, the length was increased and the roses were lifted, the border renovated, and the trees were planted at a greater distance apart than was allowed them in the first instance. As enlarged, the house measures 50 feet long, 16 feet wide, and is 12 feet high from the path to the ridge. It is, therefore, strictly a miniature rose-house. The borders are 80 inches wide, and are kept up by means of stout planks, neatly planned, and painted stone colour. The walk is sunk 15 inches below the top edges of the boards, and it consists of a mixture of fine gravel mixed with Portland cement, laid down on a bottom of hard stuff, and then watered and rolled while wet with a garden roller. It has the fresh colour of good gravel, and is as hard as a pavement. The borders were prepared with great care; for Tea roses will not endure damp at the roots in winter, and they require a light, rich soil. First, then, along the centre of each border is laid a drain to carry superfluous water quite away. These drains communicate with the main drain which passes the house, and thus all stagnation of water in the soil is prevented. Over these drains is laid about six inches of broken brick and tile, and then twenty-four inches of soil, consisting of thin slicings of, turf from a loamy pasture previously laid up and the grass quite rotted, hot-bed manure, leaf mould, the top pulverised crumbs from a bank of clay, and old plaster broken fine, equal parts all through. It is full of nourishment, firm and yet light, and the roses root into it as they do in forest loam in pots; that is, they make masses of fibre, and no rambling fleshy roots. The roses were in each of the borders planted in three lines, the weak growers in the front, and the more robust kind in the centre and back of the border. They *are all on their own roots*, which is the best way for free growth, good flowers, and never to be plagued with suckers. They were all planted in August, and were all small plants in 60 and 54-sized pots, and most of them bloomed well the first, autumn, immediately after being planted out.

There are ninety Tea roses planted out in the borders, namely, forty-five on each side, in three rows of fifteen each. In the front line, being moderate growers, are *Amazone, Andre Schwariz, Cleopatra, Comtesse de Nodaillac, Devoniensis, Elise Fugier, Ernest Metz, Etoile de Lyon, Francisca Kruger, Hon. Edith Gifford, Homere, Innocente Pirola, Isabella Sprunt, J. B. Varonne, Jean Pernet, Joseph Metral, Jules Finger, La Boule d'Or, Madame Chedane Guinnoiseau, Madame de St. Joseph, Madame Honore Defresne, Marie Guillot, Marie van Houtte, Medea, Mons. Furtado, Narcisse, Papa Gontier, President, Princess Beatrice, Princess de Sagar, Rubens, Sappho, Souvenir de Madame Levet, Triomphe de Pernet pere, Viviand Morel.* In the centre and back rows are *Albert de Blotais, Anna Olivier, Belle Lyonnaise, Bouquet d'Or, Caroline de Kuster, Catherine Mermet, Christine de Noue, Comtesse de Nodaillac, Comtesse Riza du Parc, Duchesse d' Auestadt, Ethel Brownlow, Henriette de Beauvan, Jean Dacher, La Soleil, Madame Berard, Madame Angele Jacquier, Madame Cusin, Madame Hippolyte Jamain, Madame Hoste, Madame Lambard, Madame Margttin, Madame Moreau, Madame Eugene Verdier, Madame Willermos, Mons. Furtado, Mons. Desir, Mrs. James Wilson, Niphetos, Perle des Jardins, Princesse Vera, Safrano, Souvenir De Gabrielle Drevet, Souvenir de Paul Neyron, Souvenir de S.A. Prince, Souvenir d'Elise, Vardon, Souvenir de Madame Metral, Souvenir d'un Ami, Souvenir de Therese, Levet, Sunset, The Bride.* Some of the varieties are repeated, but those enumerated comprise the finest in the several lines of colour and include several that are of special value in bouquets and button holes in the bud state.

In a larger house the vigorous growers might be taken up the rafters, and allowed there to form festoons. Several of the Noisettes would serve for the same purpose. *Marechal Niel, Ophirie* and *Lamarque,* would make magnificent climbers under glass. In the case of a lean-to, Noisettes and Banksians might be planted against the back wall. It should be a fixed rule to grow roses and roses only in a house ostensibly devoted to roses, for nothing else will properly mix with them when planted out; and the reader need not be told that planted-out roses are much less trouble to manage than in pots, and they grow and bloom with considerably more vigor when the roots have the run of a border.

The conditions essential to success in the cultivation of roses planted out under glass, in the manner here described, are free ventilation, an abundance of moisture and a rich soil. The ventilation requires careful regulation early in the season, when the new growth is being made, for if subjected to sharp currents of air during easterly winds the foliage will become a prey to mildew; on the other hand the plants will, during periods of cold and damp, be attacked by mildew, and in bright sunny weather be infested with green-fly unless air is admitted freely and sharp droughts may be avoided by opening the ventilators on one side only. Liberal supplies of water are required from the time the new growth commences until the bloom begins to expand, but the watering must not be over-done, and the border be kept in a constantly saturated state. Roses that have occupied the border for a considerable period will derive material assistance from occasional supplies of liquid manure, and if there is any difficulty in supplying them with it, apply a top dressing about once a month of some good artificial fertiliser. In using artificial fertilisers during the season of growth, apply them when the soil is moist. The borders may be further enriched by an autumn or winter dressing of half-rotted manure from the farm or stable yard.

Forced Roses

Pot roses for the conservatory and for plunging in the flower garden may be obtained in fine condition with very little trouble. In the development of our "plunging system", many years since, pot roses were largely employed and with unvarying success, the system securing a bright growth and early bloom with but little trouble. The earliest in flower answer admirably for conservatory decoration, and the latest with the earliest, after they have stood some time in the conservatory, are valuable to fill plunge beds out of doors after the potted tulips, hyacinths, and alyssums have had their day. For a little bijou plunge ground in a sheltered nook near a window, this system of dressing is the most complete of any; but the scheme of operations must comprise a display of roses in the month of May. But it does not require a plunge ground to turn to account a lot of pot roses that have been skilfully forced, for no matter how many you may have you will probably wish you had more, and as there is some risk in putting them out of doors even in the month of May, it will be safer practice to employ them all in the conservatory and the corridors and the entrance hall until they lose their freshness, and then promptly remove them and provide other seasonable furniture to succeed.

With a view to render this chapter minutely practical, we kept an account of a lot of pot roses from the first stage of production to the last, and when they were in their prime we had Portraints of two of them painted, copies of which we now present in illustration of this record of operations. We began by budding a lot of short young briers in a nursery piece. These, as they grew, were several times pinched back, and being at the same time well fed, made a free-spreading growth, the result being round compact heads without any, long rods or crossing branches. They were allowed two seasons' growth, and were then considered ripe for potting. When taken up they were slightly pruned back, and every incipient sucker carefully cut away from the roots. This took place in the autumn of the second year after budding; and that there may be no confusion in the reader's mind as to the time allowed, we set forth the order of procedure chronologically, supposing operations to commence in 1894:

In the summer of 1894 insert buds.
In the summer of 1895 pinch and regulate.
In the summer of 1896 pinch and regulate.
In the autumn of 1896 pot for forcing.

If the cultivator cannot devote so much time to production, he must go to a nursery and buy, and he will have no difficulty in obtaining plants properly prepared to reward him for his trouble.

But to return to the record. These little trees were potted in 8, 9, and 10-inch pots, in every case the smallest pot being selected, to allow reasonable room for the roots, for the sooner the new roots touch the sides of the pot the better. The compost consisted of the top crumbs of a heap of clay that had long been laid up, frozen in winter and baked in summer, with mellow turfy loam, rather fat old hot-bed manure, and gritty leaf mould (consisting for the most part of grass mowing and sweepings of gravel walks), equal parts all

POT ROSE COUPE D'HEBE

POT ROSE COUPE D'HEBE

through. In some cases they were potted with the stem close to the pot, but whenever the roots would allow they were placed neatly in the centre "ship-shape," and in every case the shortened roots were carefully spread out, and the compost was rammed in with a wooden rammer until it was as hard as a brick-bat. They were then all plunged to the rim in a bed of leaves in the open air, and taken very little notice of till the middle of April the next year. Then a great bed of long dung was made up *in the open air;* the bed two feet deep in a sheltered spot, in fact on the south side of an old hedge. When the bed was nicely warm (about 60°), the pots were plunged in it nearly to their rims, and every night a few cans of water were plunged as well, and out of these cans those that wanted water were supplied next morning. They were never searched for maggot, they were never washed or dusted for fly, they were bright as new waxwork from the first leaves they pushed, and the young wood came thick as lead-pencils, with thumping flower buds in plenty. As soon as the buds were showing fairly we began to help them with guano, but in a very rough way. About a tablespoonful was put into a two-gallon can every night when the cans were filled and placed on the plunge-bed. As soon as a few flowers were open the guano was discontinued, but plenty of water was given, and a few of the rather wiry-growing kinds were assisted by means of twigs and ties to carry their blooms nicely, but as a rule they held their flowers nobly, and took care of themselves. A few frosts occurred late in the season, but they were untouched, the hedge sheltered them, and the constantly-escaping warmth of the bed preserved about them a genial atmosphere. At the end of May there was a good show of flowers, and the bed was cold. They were then transferred to a sheltered forecourt, where a display of some sort is always required, and were there plunged to the rim; and they flowered freely till the end of June, and were then beginning to lose their looks. through being under the shade of trees.

The next process consisted in removing them back to the plunge-bed, but before they were placed upon it they were slightly pruned and pinched, then plunged as before, without the aid of artificial heat, but with all the assistance of a cool and constantly-moist condition of their roots. Now guano was used again, and as fast as flower-buds appeared they were nipped out. By the end of September they were quite at rest, and were lifted out, and only just in time to prevent a second growth, for the roots were pushing into the plunge material, and a warm autumn would have renewed their activities. They were now carefully pruned with a view to the formation of handsome round heads. They were next shaken out, the roots moderate]y shortened in and repotted–some in the same pots they came out of, some in pots a size larger, and in every case an endeavour was made to get the stems in the centre, as they were now to be considered pot roses in the properest sense of the word. They were housed in a cool, clean, light pit, were fully exposed to the weather till Christmas, and were then placed in a large light pit on a bed of warm leaves, and they, began to push nicely. About the middle of February they were placed in a house with a low-span roof, the pots standing on a wooden floor over which was strewed a couple of inches of rotten hops. A service of 4-inch pipes kept this house at an average of 45° by night and 50° to 60° by day, according to weather. Very little air was given for some time, but as the season advanced air was admitted freely on fine days. A temperature of 70° was allowed sometimes, when the wind was in the east and the sun shone brightly, and syringing was practised daily. Once more, as soon as the flower-buds appeared, a pinch of guano was put in the water-can as before. In the month of April the house was as rich in leaves and flowers as any rose garden in July–richer, in fact, for roses properly forced are ten times more lovely in both leaf and bloom than the best that can be grown in the open air. The sorts included Teas, Perpetuals, and Bourbons.

The novice will be prepared to protest that his idea of forcing roses is to have them in flower at Christmas, and to save contention, we agree with him that the idea is sound and proper, and must be encouraged in such a book as this. Very well, good friend, you shall have a nice bloom at Christmas if you will follow our instructions, and it is proper to inform you at once that, *to do the thing well*, you should go through the practice thus far prescribed, and the result will be that you will have a grand lot of pot roses of your own making to begin with, and from these you will make your selection of such as are to be forced according to our now expanded idea.

As it is rather sharp practice to secure a good bloom of roses on Christmas Day, it must now be remarked that healthy thrifty plants that were slightly forced the previous season will answer better than plants taken up from the open ground. And as many as possible should be set aside for forcing without disturbing their roots, but those that are not repotted must be assisted by a careful removal of the top crust of soil, in place of which a mixture of fat manure and sweet gritty leaf mould should be laid on and pressed with some force into all the hollows and crevices. Life is short and Art is long, so the poet tells us. If this tedious system of producing roses for forcing does not suit your notion of enjoying life, you must go to a nursery and buy the plants ready made, and it will be well to remember that if the nurseryman charges a high price for them, he has to be paid, for the years of attention the plants have had, and it may be—we shall not insist lawyer fashion on this point—he has to be paid also for the number of years he has devoted to his business to become master of it.

But to return to the pot roses. The business now before us begins on 1st of August. If you begin later and fail, please not to blame the Rose Book. In selecting the plants, give the preference to such as have made a good plump growth, and are beginning to become brownish or purplish, indicating a desirable ripening of the wood. If they must be repotted, they must, and there is an end of that matter; but a certain number, say one half, must really be refreshed at top without disturbing the roots at all, or you cannot make sure of flowers at Christmas. Those that were potted may perhaps be put into the same pots again, after having been carefully picked over, but in any case pots only one size larger must be used, they must be finished with a good ramming, and the operator must endeavour to disturb the roots that are close home as little as possible.

Having settled the potting, put the plants on a sunny south border, every pot standing on a tile or slate. Mind, there must be no plunging, for the sun must shine on the pots as well as the branches, and regular supplies of water must be given, for although we want no new growth above, we do want the roots to work quietly into the new stuff, and we must have the wood and the dormant buds kept in health and condition. It will be well to surround each pot with a lot of short stakes, to which the head of the plant may be tied out, both to improve its shape and promote the perfect ripening of the wood. Tie them out as hard as you can without snapping or straining, and the result will be a thrifty swelling of the buds at the base of the shoots, and a consequent equalization of the growth and bloom.

We will suppose the 1st of September has arrived. Now the trees must be put under cover and kept cool and dry. Perhaps the best place for them is an orchard-house, the ventilators and doors being left open night and day. A structure may be extemporized by taking a large cucumber frame, and placing it on four large flower pots or any other suitable supports at the corners. It will be well to make it *slope to the north*, for the cooler the trees are kept the better. Put the plants in the frame, each on a brick or tile, and put on the lights, and give them no water. The breeze blowing through will constitute an *artificial winter*, and the trees will be deluded thereby into a state of rest.

We will suppose the 1st of October has arrived, and now the business of the cultivator will be to take off the lights and let the rain beat on the trees if it chooses to do so, and in the meantime, he must prune them and prepare them for forcing, taking care to have them all housed before the month is out. After pruning, paint them all over, using a *soft* brush, with a mixture consisting of soft soap and

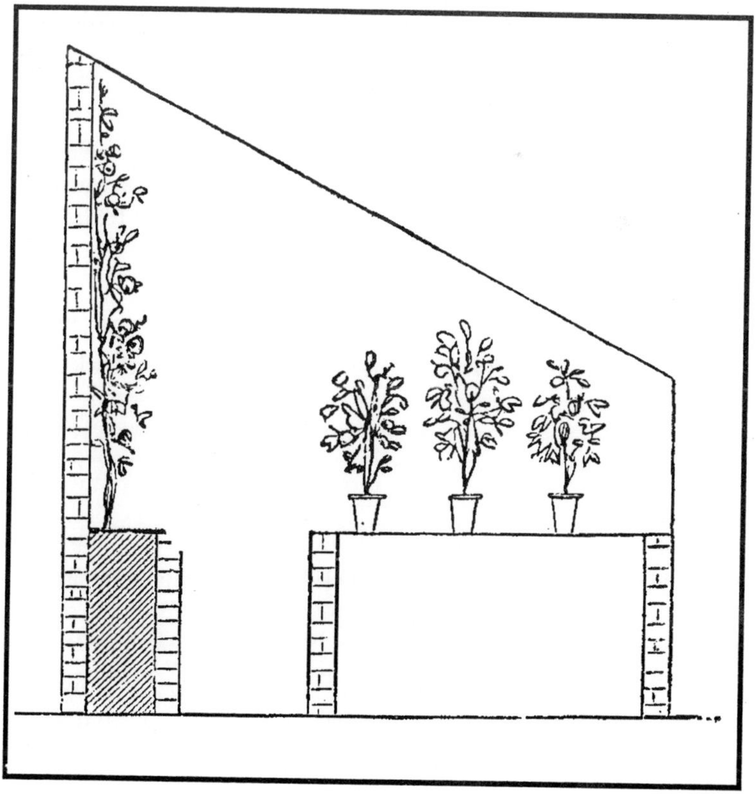

clay made into a thin paste with tobacco liquor. The way in which they are pruned is of some consequence, for if pruned "too hard", that is, if the shoots are cut too close back to the old wood, the flowers will be pruned out of them. Be careful, therefore, and prune tenderly, remembering that for early forcing the buds at the ends of the shoots are the most likely to open well, and a plentiful bloom is of more consequence than a perfectly-balanced plant. Keep the roots moderately moist, and the heads of the trees as cool as possible, continuing by this treatment their artificial winter.

We will now suppose the 1st of November has arrived, and the routine of forcing must commence. The best structure for the purpose is a lean-to with a good stage in front, and it will economize the back wall to plant it with *Devoniensis*, *Marechal Niel*, and such, as shown in the sub-joined figure. But any sort of house or pit will do, provided it is light, and can be kept at a moderately warm temperature–say 60° to 65° by day, and 50° to 55° by night, in dull sunless weather such as we usually experience in November and December, with a rise of 5 to 10 degrees when the sun shines. This rise of the temperature during sunshine must be accompanied with extra air, but very much depends upon whether the plants are placed close to the glass, in a very light structure, as well as upon the condition of the plants as to ripeness and plumpness of wood. If the plants are in fine condition, with hard wood and promising well, they may enjoy a rise of 5° or even 10° with sunshine, without harm; but the safest plan is to adopt the minimum temperatures given above, and if the plants break strongly, and put on a dark green and vigorous foliage, it will be a sign that a cautious increase of temperature may be indulged in; but if, on the contrary, the foliage is thin and pale, and the shoots weak, the contrary course must be pursued, and more air admitted. It may be no harm indeed to observe here that *slow* forcing is safer and easier for beginners than *fast* forcing; the practitioner must therefore make his own choice.

It is somewhat difficult to calculate the precise time it will take to bring the plants into flower, so much depending upon the amount of sunlight we may or may not get, and the condition the plants are in when taken in to force. It will be better, therefore, to introduce a few plants at intervals of a fortnight, beginning early in November. If a moderate degree of bottom-heat can be secured to the roots, it will be well; this may be accomplished in various ways, such as plunging in tan, leaves, or other fermenting material, or over a tank, or even upon a rack placed above the pipes or flue by which the house is heated; if by the latter mode, especial care must be taken to preserve a moist atmosphere about them by frequent syringings of the heated surface, and by painting some part of the same with sulphur, to keep off red spider. Watering must also be looked to, to see that when given it is in sufficient quantity to pass out at the bottom of the pot; and the water should be in a tepid state, and slight]y coloured with some liquid manure, such as the drainage from a farmyard or cowhouse; but if it has to be made for the purpose, steep deer, sheep, or horse droppings with a little soot (tied up in a bag) in water, in preference to stirring guano or other artificial manure in the watering can, as in early forcing any sudden or severe stimulation of the roots may cause the flower-buds to fall unopened.

Green-fly must be looked for, and the usual remedy, tobacco smoke, applied without loss of time. Frequent syringing overhead with tepid water will do wonders to keep down green-fly and red spider.

After the plants have flowered, they must have protection in some structure where they can finish their growth, and be protected from injury until the season is sufficiently advanced to allow of their being placed out of doors. If you follow these instructions faithful]y, you will, in the depth of winter, enjoy:

A bower of Arcadian sweets,
With Flora still in her prime,
A fortress to which she retreats
From the cruel assaults of the clime.
And when earth wears a mantle of snow,
Have her *roses* as fresh and as gay
As the fairest and sweetest that blow
On the beautiful bosom of May.

Pot Roses for Exhibition

We may now, having acquired experience, take a bolder flight, and grow pot roses for exhibition. The sizes of the pots in which roses are grown for exhibition must be determined by the schedules of the shows whereat they are to be exhibited. But it is impossible to grow roses fit for show in less sized pots than nine inches diameter;

SPECIMEN POT ROSE, EDWARD MORREN

and for grand specimens the pots must be fifteen inches in diameter. Between these two extremes the cultivator must take his choice, according to the requirements of the schedule and his own means and taste. As a rule, the best plants to show are bushes from eighteen to thirty-six inches high, worked on the cutting or seedling brier. Large pyramids like the one figured are the most effective, but they are only suitable for the great trade growers. From the first it must be borne in mind that to exhibit twelve the cultivator should have in hand at least 36, and so on for every distinct effort at exhibiting; for it is impossible to rely upon having so many in bloom and in exhibition condition for such and such a day. If a hundred were grown, it might be difficult to find a dozen fit for show on a day perhaps well adapted to roses generally. But as the dates of shows are fixed before anyone knows what sort of season it will be, the exhibitor must have two strings to his bow, first plenty of plants, and secondly skilful management. Supposing stems to be preferred, the selection must be made in October or November, from a batch of

budded plants that have been grown with a view to be flowered as specimens. Choose from these such as have a regular disposition of stout hard wood; if the shoots are as regular as the ribs of an umbrella, the better for the shape of the trees hereafter. But it is equally important to see that the roots are good, and of such a kind that the plants can be potted in the centres of the pots; for if there are huge knobs of underground timber, such as often occurs on old briers, they cannot be potted properly, and must be rejected. Having selected the plants, proceed to shorten the longer shoots about a third of their length, and then pot them, using two parts sound turfy loam and one part rotten stable dung, and ramming the soil into the pots quite hard. Place the pots on a hard pavement of stone or slate out of doors, and fill in between the pots with sawdust or old tan. To protect them against injury by frost, a few uprights and rails may be arranged on which to throw mats or nets, as in the cut.

In case of very severe frost throw a little loose dry straw or hay amongst them, and they will escape unhurt. At the latter part of February, take them out and prune them. This must be done with care, and according to the rules laid down for pruning the particular groups and varieties. The operator must have in view the formation of a close and symmetrical head, and symmetry must be thought of more than size, because the size can be enlarged from year to year; but it is very difficult, if the head is badly shaped in the first instance, to improve it afterwards. Where two branches cross each other close to the work remove one of them, and that the weakest or the one most twisted out of a natural position. Shorten all the strong shoots to within an average of six buds of their base, and the weak shoots to an average of two buds of their base. They must have liberal culture all the summer, abundance of water till the middle of July, after that but little. They ought to be in an airy position and enjoy full sunshine, and it is very important to arrange them after pruning so as to allow plenty of room for a circulation of air amongst them, and so that any plant can be got at readily without having to reach across another, and perhaps break a valuable bud or shoot in the operation. Take notice how they grow. Those that throw out their branches horizontally, and obliquely, and with tolerable regularity, may be left to grow in their own way. Others will grow too upright and rigid ever to make nice heads without help. Carefully draw down the outside shoots of these with strands of twisted bast, and tie them down either to their own stems or to a piece of bast, passed below the rim of the pot. If drawn down while young and soft, they will harden into the required position. It does not seem needful to enlarge upon the necessity of keeping the plants free of fly and mildew. If these get the upper hand, your chances of a prize next season are lessened.

Having grown, them well throughout the summer, it is important to have the wood well ripened. This will perhaps require no special care. If the autumn is warm and sunny, there will be no fear of the wood ripening; but if it is a wet and cold autumn some precautions must be taken, such as placing all those that look greenest and growing under glass, and supplying them with abundant ventilation and very little water. Or if there is no room for them under glass range them under a wall or fence facing south, and let the pots be exposed to all weathers till there is danger of frost, and then return them to the bed for the winter.

All further operations are to be conducted with a view to prepare the plants for exhibition the next season. In October or early in November, shift those with the finest heads and most robust growth into larger pots, removing at the same time some of the soil from their roots and using to fill in half turfy loam and half rotten dung. Those that do not require larger pots should be turned out, and have some of the soil removed, and be repotted into the same pots. Every pot rose should be repotted or top-dressed once a year, whether grown for exhibition or any other purpose. At every potting, let the soil be fully two inches below the level of the rim of the pot—in the case of large pots, three inches. This will allow of an inch or more of fresh sheep or deer's dung to be spread as a top dressing as soon as the plants begin to grow in spring, which will materially assist in producing a fine bloom. It is best to make quite a separate affair of the pruning, so as to secure the repotting of the whole stock early, as the formation of fresh roots cannot take place too soon after the season's growth is completed. As for the pruning, that must take place according to the dates at which the plants are required to be in bloom; and here it is proper to inform the amateur, that with all his care he must not depend on having anyone batch or any one plant in perfection by a given date, and that is one reason why he should grow a considerably greater number of plants than he would ever purpose to exhibit at one time. But we lessen this difficulty: first, by having plenty of plants; next, by pruning them in batches at different times; and lastly, by forcing some, allowing others to bloom at their natural season, and retarding others. If the collection is large, pruning should be performed once a month, from November to the end of April. Warm greenhouse treatment from Christmas will bring the first pruned batch into bloom early, and thence the supply may be kept up till it is seen whether the season will be an early or late one. If there appears to be a little difficulty to the extent of a week or so in securing a certain number of plants in perfection for a given date, the use of a gentle hot-bed out of doors will hasten, and placing the plants in a cool north aspect shaded at mid-day by trees, will retard them a week. All these measures of hastening and retarding should be determined on at least six weeks before the date of the show.

The management of roses on their own roots will not greatly differ from that of plants worked on stems. It is desirable in the first instance to remove the three or four lowest buds from the young plants so as to form clean stout stems. To have these stems strong they should grow the first season of potting to their full height, which, if they are well fed, may vary from two to six feet. The next season they are to be cut down to three buds, and from those three the cultivator proceeds to form a close bush, the base of which is within an inch or two of the rim of the pot. These bushes on their own roots are really better adapted for pot culture than the plants worked on briers; but it is impossible to get them to exhibition size in the same time. The pruning and training out of these bushes will require but a slight variation of the directions given above, the niceties of the culture are to be acquired only by practice; and it is better at this point to leave the rosarian to his own resources than attempt to explain every possible detail. But it may be well to say that there can be little progress made in the pot culture of roses, whether for exhibition or home use, without the aid of glass. Teas and Noisettes, which make the most beautiful of pot roses, require protection in winter and spring; and there are times when even Perpetual and Provence roses in pots must be housed to screen them from the inclemency of the blast. Potted plants occasion more trouble than those in the open ground; but that trouble we suppose furnishes the rosarian with just the kind of recreation he needs, and he will not be slow to discover that success depends much more on constant attention than on extraordinary skill. Let it be the rule to deal with every difficulty promptly, then neither fly, nor mildew, nor drought, nor frost will he able to do much harm—sheer industry will prove a talisman, and the constant worker will win the day.

The Dew-Drop and the Rose

A rose in the moonshine lay quietly sleeping,
Where zephyrs were timidly creeping, creeping;
A dew-drop crept silently into its breast,
Without waking the rose from its moonlight rest.

When morning dawned, the rose was waking,
While glimmering leaves were shaking, shaking,
And finding a dew-drop so near to her heart,
She prayed he would ne'er from her bosom depart.
She folded him close in the warmth of her love,
As the wings of the mother fold round a young dove.

The morning was dawning, the rose was waking,
And rustling leaves were shaking, shaking.

The gleams of the sun came slily glancing
Where leaves on the branches were dancing, dancing;
And on the green moss where the rose had been sleeping,

The golden glances came peeping, peeping.
The rose felt a joy in her fragrant breast,
When she saw her loved dew-drop still lying at rest;
But while she was watching her loved one's eye,
He dissolved as a dream and soared up to the sky.
The sorrowful rose hung her head in weeping,
While the dew-drop went upward creeping, creeping.

So the morning of life may have blessings to cheer it,
And love, like the dew, gem the blossoming heart;
Though the joy of a life may be gathering near it,
That joy, like the dew-drop, soon, soon, must depart.
But still 'tis for ever a sweet consolation,
If that which we cherish pertains to the sky.
For the fond hope is left in our gloomy probation,
That the dew-drop *we* cherished still sparkles on high.

There are gardens above where the spirits we love
Will be taken like dews from the roses of this;
Where nought can destroy, they awake in their joy,
To dwell peacefully ever in regions of bliss.

So to heavenly hopes we may gladly be waking,
Though the heart in its sorrow is breaking, breaking.

—*s.n.*

Chapter 13

SEEDLING ROSES

In previous pages a few remarks are made on the raising of seedling briers. An amateur intending to raise roses of high quality might follow the short code there provided in some twenty lines, and in due time become eminently successful. It is proper, however, to the plan of this book, that the subject should be treated at greater length, and with some circumstantiality.

It is generally believed by amateurs that to raise seedling roses is a most difficult and tedious business; but that is a mistake. There can be nothing easier. To obtain thereby varieties worth naming is another matter, but it would be a serious mistake to suppose that elaborate manipulations in hybridizing, or as we should more properly say, crossing, are necessary. Very few of all the roses that are in the catalogues have been obtained by systematic crossing; they have for the most part been obtained in the same way as good geraniums, good carnations, good *dahlias*, and good chrysanthemums are obtained; by simply saving seed from the best varieties, and carefully raising plants therefrom. It is nevertheless a fact, that, as a rule, systematic crossing gives the best results, and the rosarian may, therefore, be properly advised to operate on selected flowers with a view to obtain seed of a character predetermined by the operator. If he is not disposed to make so refined a pastime of raising seedlings, he may be content to save seed as he can get it, and take his chance of what it may produce.

Our climate is not quite favourable to the raising of new roses, and that is the principal reason why we have so greatly depended upon the French raisers for novelties. Nevertheless, the many splendid varieties that have been raised in this country not only prove the possibility, but afford encouragement to the English amateur, who, in a fine autumn, may ensure abundance of seed, and in a wet and cold autumn must rest from his labours, or gather, perhaps, a score of ripe heps instead of hundreds or thousands. How then is the seed to be obtained? The simplest mode of procedure will be to plant out in a sunny position, on rather poor soil, a selection of the very finest roses known. The site should be dry and breezy; if shut in by trees, or in any degree swampy, it will not produce good seed. A luxuriant growth is not to be desired; in fact, a somewhat starving and roasting condition favour seed production, but the seed-producing plants should not be starved to the extent of impairing their health, for, above all things, we want vigour in roses, and debilitated parents are not likely to produce robust progeny. Every inferior rose that can be got at within a mile of the seed ground should be grubbed up and burnt, and consequently the seed grower must purify his own garden of such, and that will be no hardship, for the best roses anywhere and anyhow must be better than the worst. In the first place the selection should comprise all the first-class typical roses; next, all the most distinct and beautiful of the several classes. The collection should be comprehensive, save and except in this respect, that every variety known to have a weakly constitution, however highly esteemed for its flowers, should be carefully excluded. We have too many weak habited varieties already, and the English raiser should as carefully as possible guard against adding to their number. In selecting for the plantation, any kind of roots will do, and it might be a saving of expense to take from a nursery all the ugly plants of the best kinds, because the shape and attitude are matters of no consequence at all if the object is seed saving merely.

It is an important matter to ensure that the seed is ripe before it is gathered, and on this point mistakes may easily be made. It happens with heps as with grapes, that they often acquire a fine colour in advance of perfect ripening, and as a rule, a hep is not ripe when it is of a brilliant red colour, and if the harvesting of good seed is our object we must wait until the heps are black or nearly so. It may be proper to remark here, that the seed-producing trees should have a little, but not much, care. Above all things they must be kept in good health, and any that show a persistent tendency to mildew should be rooted out and burnt. They will require no more pruning than suffices to keep them in order, for the more flowers they produce the better. The novice may reasonably suppose that better seed could be obtained from a few first-class flowers than from allowing the flowers to come freely and to lose somewhat of their substance and doubleness. But the fact is just otherwise. By a somewhat starving system of cultivation, which results in rendering many first-class varieties "goggle-eyed", through deficiency of petals, we secure a fine sample of seed, from which, in all probability, there will result a fair proportion of seedlings characterized by a excessive fulness, for the *doubling tendency is in the strain* and will come out at last if encouraged by good cultivation.

The heps having been gathered may be treated in several different ways. The most simple is to stratify them in layers with sand in a damp place, and leave them until March, and then to rub out the seeds and sow in the ground in rows two feet apart, the seeds being six inches apart in the row. Another simple mode of dealing with them is to sow the complete heps in rows as soon as gathered without any attempt to separate the seeds from the pulp. This is Nature's way of raising seedling roses, and although it is a rough way, it has this advantage, that the seedling plants have their proper vigour, for the seed is buried as soon as it is ripe. The result of this method is that the seedlings rise in clusters, and therefore, the heps should be put at least a foot apart in rows two feet apart.

Another method of procedure is to break open the heps and separate the seeds, and sow in pans and boxes, and keep them in frames or pits, or under the stage of a greenhouse all the winter. This is the best method, for it ensures early germination without drying of the seed, and gives the cultivator command of the seedling plants from the first. In such a case we should prefer to pot all the earliest plants and flower them in a cool airy greenhouse, and plant out all the late ones and wait a little longer for their flowers. Now the inexperienced amateur will want to know how long he must wait to see the flower of the seedlings? Well, comparatively speaking, no time at all. If seedling roses start early, most of them will flower the first season and the remainder will flower the second. We have flowered seedlings in pots in 45 days from the date of sowing the seed; but, as a rule, they need five or six months' growing before they flower, and those that flower latest are generally the best. Probably some of those that flower first deserve to be saved, for they present lovely little flowers, sometimes quite novel in colour, and as round as cherries and not much larger. Some day a prophetic amateur will be wise enough to keep some of the best of the most precocious seedling roses, and by this conservative procedure provide. us with a companion race to the Lawrence or Fairy roses, which have been too much over-shadowed by the thumpers and thunderers of the exhibitions.

The raiser of seedlings must make much of promises. Whatever promises well must be kept and propagated. A seedling rose never declares itself as "first in the throng" by its first flower, or even by its first half-dozen. Remember that, all you aspirants for floral fame. You must have prophetic insight or you will be continually consigning to the rubbish heap possible competitors with Marechal Niel, or Gloire de Dijon, or Alfred K. Williams, or Mrs. Paul, or some other variety. Let us suppose now that you have a flower of promise. In the first place bring pencil and note-book, give the plant a provisional name or number, and make an entry descriptive of both leafage and flowers; and a very rough and hasty description will suffice. Next adopt whatever measures are most convenient for its multiplication. You may enter a few buds in brier or Manetti stocks, and you may also put a few cuttings or eyes in pans of sandy soil over a gentle hot-bed, so as to ensure a few plants on their own roots. When the cool autumn days return you must separate the plant from the crowd and give it a separate place on rich soil in an open situation, and it must be moderately pruned back to ensure bloom the next season from the ripest wood, and thus, giving it a good chance, you may hope for a reward of your labours. The second bloom will surpass the first, and not unseldom the third bloom will surpass the second; but in the third year your seedling will probably be at the best, and you may make up your mind whether it is best to keep it, sell it, or burn it. Be not troubled if after the careful trial of three years you have to burn many, but not withstanding such a painful expectation, do the thing well or do not dabble in seedlings at all. You must make stock of every promising plant, and you must courageously destroy all the evidently inferior ones, and of these you will have plenty. In the event of a seedling turning up a trump–and I hope the dear reader who purchased and not borrowed this book will have many such–what an advantage it will be to have ready-made stock of it; and, on the other hand, what a disadvantage will you be at if a seedling comes out grandly in the second or third year and you find you have but one plant?–the propagation on promise having had no attention.

It may be well to offer a few advices to amateurs who propose to "make assurance double sure" by careful manipulations of selected flowers. If you have the patience to examine the pedigrees of roses–of which we have comparatively few that are authentic–you will find that the pollen parent is the most important of the two. The old rule of going to a flower of high colour for pollen and to one of good form for seed has been considerably modified by recent experiments and observations. Look to your pollen parent first of all, and, generally speaking, think of *form, substance,* and *colour*, without reference to doubleness, because amongst the seedlings from varieties that are strong in form, and substance, and colour, a goodly proportion of thoroughly double flowers will come, for as a matter of fact, doubleness is more easily obtained than any other quality. This is not orthodox teaching, but it is true. Hitherto writers have made it a point that seeds should be obtained as much as possible from double flowers. Our advice is that you starve the doubles into singles, looking for form, substance, and colour, without reference to doubleness, and trusting to your own power to *make petals* when you want them, provided you secure seedlings remarkable for perfection of form, distinctness, delicacy or richness of colour, the substance of a calf skin or piece of pile velvet, or the parchment of a big drum of the very best maker. Pray don't be in a worry about doubleness, so long as you take seed from first-rate varieties, for the doubleness is in the blood, and will come out as time and blood and sunshine contribute to the stamina of the plant.

Chapter 14

ROSES IN TOWN GARDENS

It might be prudent sometimes to advise the owner of a town garden to give up all idea of growing roses, but prudence is of no avail when we have to deal with those whose mainspring of action is sentiment. Roses are required in every garden, no matter what may be its size, soil, situation, or surroundings, and a book about roses must provide for all possible circumstances, and in some way or other accommodate every taste. As we are bound to keep facts in view at every step, we may as well at once face the fact of first importance at starting. The closer the proximity of a garden to a large smoky town, the greater is the probability that it will not nicely accommodate roses. Many of our large old English towns that are innocent of factories, and but rarely disturbed with the dust of roadway traffic, have good gardens and grand roses in their very midst; but wherever there is a large consumption of coal, the atmosphere is rendered unfavourable to roses, and those who desire to grow roses must encounter a few difficulties, and after all be content with flowers some degrees inferior to such as, with similar means at command, might be produced in a purer air. But the town amateur may take courage if he will at the same time take care. The writer of this cultivated roses for fifteen years in a garden three-and-a-half miles distant as the crow flies, northward, from St. Paul's Cathedral, and with such success that he frequently presented them at public exhibitions and obtained the approbation of experienced judges, and not un-seldom carried off the highest honours of the show. It was in order to impress upon amateurs the possibilities of rose growing in the suburbs of London that we put upon the table at the first great rose show held in the Crystal Palace, the collection of Moss, Perpetual, and China roses which attracted the attention, and secured the admiration, of the visitors, among them being Dean Hole, a, most discriminating critic of the qualities of roses. Thirteen years after the event we met Dean Hole (not for the first time, happily), and his first remark was in reference to those "London roses," and his agreeable recollections of them as bright examples of town gardening. Let the town amateur take courage then, but let him also take care, for to buy roses haphazard and plant them anyhow will not answer in the furnishing of a town garden.

The Form

The reader who doats on standards will perhaps think enough has been said in their dispraise in these pages, but it remains yet to warn the townsman that they are the very worst of roses for his purpose. In the suburbs of all our great towns we see a certain number of entrance courts made hideous with starving standard roses that have neither shape nor make at any time, that are leafless and scraggy half the year, and during the other half show a few unhealthy leaves, amid which, for a very brief period, a few flowers appear that are scarcely equal in form, substance, and colour, to those imitation roses that are sculptured out of beet roots and sold in the streets of London city in the depth of winter at one penny each. We have made a study of a fine entrance court that lies in the way of our daily rambles. It should constitute a beautiful approach to a respectable mansion, but the owner has evidently made up his mind to make it characteristic by a display of rose trees, and it must be confessed he has succeeded, though it may be doubted if his success is of the kind he intended, or, as we should say, to his heart's content. The beds were in the first instance raised above the level, and then were thickly planted with nice young trees that were at once severally pruned and presented thenceforward a most wobegone appearance. At the end of three years we made a sketch of the principal bed, and here it is, faithful to the fact, and we should hope it will serve as a warning to every townsman who comes to this book for help in the enjoyment of the sweetest of flowers. Now if those beds had not been raised above the level, had they been deeply dug and well manured, and planted with a well-considered selection of Perpetuals, Bourbons, and Noisettes on their own roots, they would in all probability have

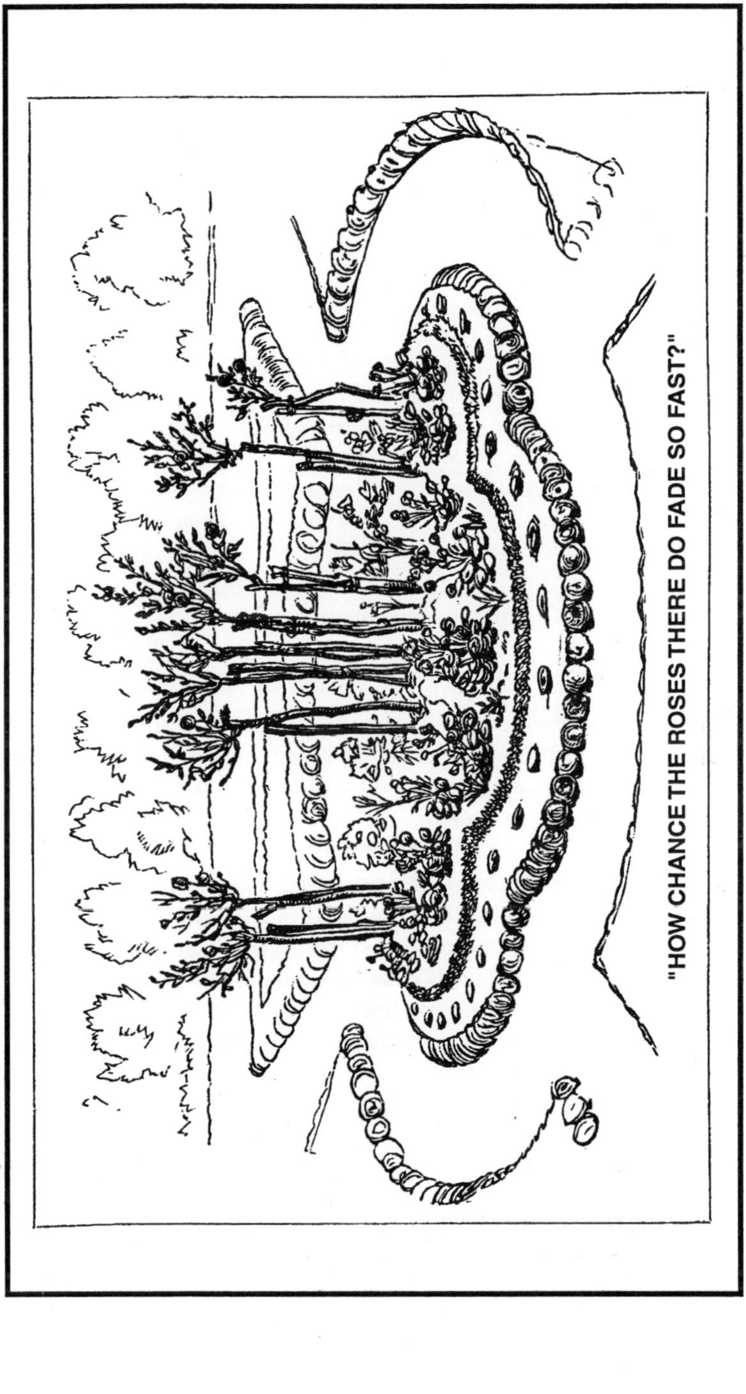

"HOW CHANCE THE ROSES THERE DO FADE SO FAST?"

quickly acquired a free and healthy growth, covering the ground with buxom leafage, and during a considerable portion of the summer and autumn presented a glorious glow of welcome flowers, and not one rigid stick visible to mar the contour of the mass. As a matter of taste, roses are not appropriate to entrance courts, for they are leafless at a time when the place should have a rich and bright appearance with thriving evergreens that look a welcome to the invited guest. But we will not discuss the question of taste; our business is to advise on the growing of roses, leaving the amateur to gratify every whim, provided only he will do justice to the Queen of Flowers.

It should be understood then at starting, that the brier needs a good soil and a somewhat pure air, and the town amateur should not begin with brier roses, but obtain experience first with bushes, and then extend his operations and adopt standards cautiously. It is an interesting fact that the taller the standard the more favourable should be the conditions for its sustenance. Hence the nearer the town we pitch our tent, the shorter must be the standards if we will have them, and only in the open country and in a good garden should the tallest standards be planted.

If we observe how the dog-rose grows wild, we shall find the stoutest and most lusty growths along the hedgerows of a clay country, where their roots get plenty of moisture, and very often some stronger stuff from the byre and the manure heap, but where there is never any stagnant wet. A bit of real clay, that has been laid up all the winter to pulverize, is, when enriched with manure, the best possible soil in which to plant briers for budding, and also all flowering standard roses, which are the same briers in another stage of cultivation. If the smoke of towns does harm to the rose, a bad state of the soil does much more harm to the root, and the more attention is paid to this basis of operations, the more will the field widen for the growth of roses in towns. But the closer we come to the centre of a town, the more must we incline to short roses, and at last give up standards altogether.

The state of the case may be represented by a diagram, and suburban gardeners are recommended to adapt the diagram to their own geographical position in regard to the towns to which they are attached. Suppose we begin in the centre of the city of London, there we should use none but roses on their own roots; travelling outwards, in anyone direction, we may at last use short briers, and further on, taller briers, and so on as the distance increases. The taller they are in towns, the greater is the difficulty of keeping them alive. In the suburbs of London we should consider it safe to plant half standards at four miles from the Post Office; and at one mile more, full standards; and at six miles they might be of any height desired, to form weeping roses on lawns and back rows of broad banks. Here then is the diagram, which may be considered as representing the gradation of heights, on a radius of six miles from St. Paul's Cathedral.

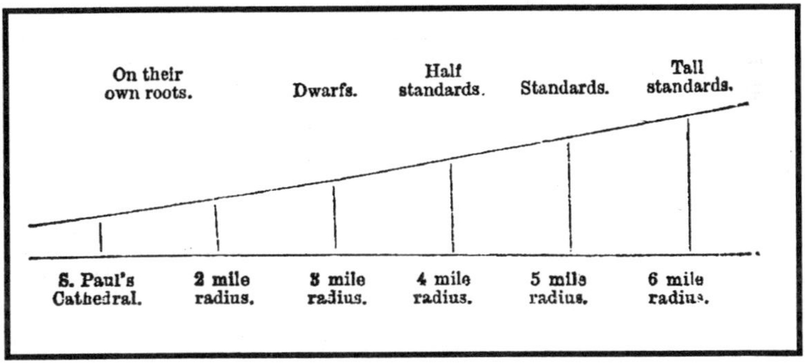

Whatever exceptions may be made to such a rule must still be in accordance with the principle it involves. It may happen that in the four-mile radius the air and soil offer the best conditions for roses of every size, shape, and variety; and such was almost the case at Stoke Newington; and it may be that even at the five-mile radius, the proximity of a floorcloth factory or a hungry soil compel the amateur to consider himself on equal terms with those who live two or three miles nearer to the great town.

The Situation

The first step towards securing a nice rose garden in the vicinity of a town is to select the most sunny and breezy spot the garden affords. To plant on borders near walls or live fences is about as unwise as to plant on grass. If the garden opens at the rear on meadow land, or is otherwise countryfied and breezy, there is the spot for roses. But, generally speaking, the very centre of the garden is the most favoured site, and there it may be convenient to layout a compartment for roses, and so screen it from the windows, that its poverty of appearance in winter shall not obtrude on the daily vision, while in the summer, when all is bright and fair, a walk to the rose garden will afford a delicious preparation for breakfast-more delicious, perhaps, than the breakfast itself !

The Soil

It must be borne in mind that the soil of a town garden is not usually the best that can be found for roses. The soil, indeed, is not impoverished by the smoke that pollutes the air, or by the houses that interrupt the free play of the sunshine. But just you watch the series of transformations which have for their object to change the country into the town, and you will perceive that every separate stage of the process is like a veto against roses. In the first change the farmers and gardeners, knowing the land will soon be let or sold, do their utmost to take the heart out of it. The fences are patched anyhow, the land is hard cropped without manure, and whatever is likely to exhaust it, is sure to be adopted in the routine of operations. Then the builders come, and their first business is to strip off the top crust and sell it as turf or garden mould, and at one fell swoop the very best of the soil is carted away. Next, the houses are run up, and the townsman florist locates himself on a soil that has lost its heart; and if he fails in rose growing he is apt to blame the smoke alone, when perhaps it is but a small offender. In any case, the intending planter must consider if the soil is good enough for his purpose, and in spite of all that has happened, it may be. If it will grow a first-rate cauliflower, if trees and shrubs generally make a lusty growth upon it, he is pretty safe, and fair digging and manuring will suffice to prepare a foundation for rosarian successes. But if the soil is not good it must be improved by carting in the top turfy spit from a fat meadow, and incorporating with it a fourth or fifth part of good stable manure, and with this mixture the rose bed should be made; the bad stuff being taken out to make room for it. To raise the rose bed above the level, is, as a rule, bad practice, for towns are so effectually drained that raised beds are too dry for roses, rhododendrons, lilies, and other plants that thrive best when their roots are cool and moist, and it will be found that where elm trees continue healthy and vigorous, roses generally do well, because the moisture that suits the big trees is congenial to the little ones.

Planting

The next business will be to plant the roses, and the best general advice that can be given in regard to selecting them will comprise two major points. In the first place select in the several classes that are available for the purpose those varieties that are described as vigorous growers. As to these classes we shall have something to say presently. If you cannot discover whether any particular variety is of vigorous habit, see if it is entered in the list of "garden roses", for that list comprises none but vigorous kinds that are noted for abundant flowering. The next point of importance is, that the plants should consist for the most part of own-root or Manetti roses a few standards may be planted with them, and they should be such good growing and free-flowering sorts as *Brightness of Cheshunt*, *Eugene Appert*, *Jules Margottin*, *Anna Alexieff*, and *General Jacqueminot*. If the plants are to be taken from the open ground, have them home and plant them during fine weather in October. Plant the Manettis six inches deep, to encourage roots from the scar where the graft was inserted, plant the briers no deeper than suffices to fairly cover the roots, and when the planting is finished tread the ground over, to make it thoroughly firm, unless rain comes on before the work is finished, in which case finish the planting if you can and defer the treading until the ground is pretty dry and does not become a mere paste under your feet. It is well to advise, moreover, that you plant rather thickly, for a thin rose bed has a poor appearance; and finally, that you prune all of them rather close back as soon as the planting is finished. If the plants ate purchased in pots in spring you must not be in haste to plant, because having in all probability been kept in pits all the winter, they will be rather tender, and should a sharp frost occur soon after they are planted they may suffer considerably. Wait for dull mild weather; then plant them carefully and quickly; tread the ground firm, and if rain does not quickly come give them plentiful supplies of water.

As this chapter may be read by some who are in haste to begin rose growing, and have had but little experience in gardening, a word of caution as to the meaning of the direction "plant firm" may be useful. It is only by seeing how things are done in various places that it is possible to know how to advise amateurs for their advantage. We call to mind a notable case of failure which will illustrate the importance of the remark just made on treading of the roots of newly-planted roses. A gentleman fond of roses sent for us to have a look at a plantation which had cost him a large sum of money only to give him vexation, and make the best piece of ground in his garden a specimen of utter failure. He had purchased yellow loam of admirable quality at about a guinea a load, in order to give the roses such a soil as is recommended in the books; he had purchased manure in quantity at six shillings a load; and lastly, paid seven pounds per hundred for a fine lot of dwarf Hybrid Perpetuals. When we saw them in the month of June they looked so miserable we could scarcely avoid laughing; but preserving a suitable gravity we looked about for leaves and flowers. A few of both were to be seen, but the leaves were more black than green; the few flowers were small, ragged, thin, and ridiculous. The plants had a starved look, and the general tone of the whole piece was that of a mass of blackish-green, scrubby, sticks, much like the vegetation one sees on the banks of the Tyne where coal-smoke influences the shrubs in a way which makes one regret it does not quite kill them. The owner had planted them with his own hands; he had pruned them admirably, taking his method from the books; and he had prepared for them a soil in which roses might have been grown to take first prizes at any flower show. But, alas! he had planted them so loose, that by taking a stem in the hand and pulling gently the entire bush came out as easily as would happen in drawing a radish immediately after rain. What was to be done? The remedy was simple enough. We began with one bed, trod it all over backwards and forwards, made the soil as firm as a pavement, and recommended that all the rest be served in the same way, and then the beds to have about two inches of half-rotten dung spread all over them. We saw no more of them that season, but in the June following called in to have a look at the roses, and they were one mass of healthy green foliage and thumping flowers. Thus, you see, we may do right in all things but one, and the omission of that one, or the doing of that one wrong, may make a wreck of our enterprise.

Management

To keep the roses going, it will be well to supply them with water, root and branch, during dry weather in the summer months. But this must be done properly. Many town gardeners waste their energies in dribbling water about where it is not wanted, and in such small quantities that it does more harm than good. The way to water roses is to soak the ground well morning and night for two or three days in succession, and then give no more for about ten days, when the heavy watering should be repeated. If fresh house sewage can be obtained, they may have almost any quantity from the end of

April to the end of July, after which they should, have no more for the season. If it is strong it must be diluted, and independent altogether of possible poisoning of the plants by strong sewage, it will be found that very weak sewage is the most beneficial–in fact, strong liquid manure of any kind is not good for any kind of plant, however gross a feeder it may naturally be. The overhead watering should be accomplished by means of a good barrel engine. The water should be soft and clean; therefore, although ditch and pond will be the best for the roots, it will not do for washing the foliage, for it injures the trees by leaving on the leaves a muddy deposit. The engine should be filled in the morning and left standing in the sun all day. In the evening it should be taken to the roses and made to deliver upon them a fine shower. If there is any green-fly upon them, the water must be directed with force to the under sides of the leaves, with a view to drift the fly away into the indefinable limbo. For other matters of management, other chapters must be consulted.

The Selection of Sorts

The Selection of Sorts is a matter of the utmost importance. The rosarian who is determined to go forward, and has no fear of difficulties, will patiently test many kinds of roses, and make his garden, so far, a trial ground. He will be surprised as he goes on (provided only that he goes on prudently and does everything well), at the vast range of selection that is open to the townsman, for in truth, we may grow in a satisfactory manner an immense number of good roses, in the near neighbourhood of the permanent smoke cloud, if the spot is somewhat open so as to enjoy the best air and sunshine possible in the district, and the soil is prepared in a sensible manner. But our business is to provide the safest possible, path for the beginner, and we advise him in the first place to secure some of the more vigorous of the Summer Roses, and pay less attention than is usually given to the Autumnal Roses.

Amongst the summer roses, the Provence, Damask, and Gallica classes will supply several splendid varieties that endure smoke patiently, and thrive under the partial deprivation of sunshine, which must be their lot in a town garden. Such varieties as *Common Cabbage,* which, in beauty, is not surpassed by any rose in the world; *Maiden's Blush, Common Damask, Luxembourg, La Ville de Bruxelles, Ohl,* and *Transon Goubault,* will be sure to present a fair crop of their handsome flowers, and although they only flower once, it is better to ensure that one display than trust over much to the sorts that should flower twice or thrice, but, when put to the town test, refuse perhaps to flower at all. Among the Hybrid China and Bourbon are many good summer roses that may be recommended, such as *Blairii* (Nos. 1 and 2), *Brennus, Charles Lawson, Madame Isaac Pereire, Paul Ricaut, Vivid, Chenedole,* and *Fulqens.*

The best of the Autumnal roses are the Perpetuals, Bourbons, and Noisettes. From these select the sorts that are described as *growing vigorously and flowering freely* in preference to those that are in high repute as show flowers. Happily there are several first-rate show varieties available, such as *Princess Mary of Cambridge, Dr. Andry, Duke of Edinburgh, Victor Verdier, Florence Paul, General Jacqueminot, Paul Neyron, Senateur Vaisse, Thomas Mills, Ulrich Brunner.* But beware of that distinct, snowy dark-leaved race represented by Geant des Batailles, Lord Raglan, and Lord Clyde, for they will become unsightly with mildew before the summer is half gone, and create vexation instead of pleasure. A few of the Noisettes, such as *Aimée Vibert, Ophirie,* and *Fellenberg* will succeed; but the shy-flowering varieties are useless. From the Teas you may select with safety the grand old *Gloire de Dijon,* for it is one of the best of town roses, and *Devoniensis* may succeed; but for any other Teas you must wait, and when you plant them take all the responsibility on yourself. Not many Chinas will be available, but you may expect to do well with *Fabvier* and *Cramoisie,* which are gorgeously coloured and as nearly alike as two peas. Finally, plant in far-separated parts of the garden a few of the *Common China,* and be guided by it in your future movements. Let it have good soil and a sunny situation, and so long as it thrives, you may speculate rather freely in all kinds of roses. If common China does not thrive you may be sure that your range of selection is restricted. It is the first of all roses to give warning of danger, and for that reason we have designated it the Pilot Rose.

The townsman who loves roses must not depend solely on the open ground for supplies of flowers. He must take advantage of the better climate that may be secured by the employment of glass, and by good greenhouse culture secure a plentiful bloom of the lovely Teas that the cruel conditions outside forbid him to grow in the open ground. With wool netting, to exclude the blacks, a good border on a bed of large rubble, and syringe and engine frequently at work, a rose garden of the most delightful kind may be enjoyed in the very heart of a great city. All that is wanted from the actual locality is sunshine; everything else may be brought to the spot, and even the common air may be in some degree filtered and purified. But the house must be built in a full flood of light, and if that cannot be obtained in the back garden, we may ensure it by going on the roof. The work needs only to be done well, and then, within hearing of Bow bells, there may be enjoyed a genuine rose garden, over the entrance of which might be appropriately inscribed the lines of Mrs Hemans:

"How much of memory dwells amidst thy bloom,
Rose! ever wearing beauty for thy dower;
The bridal day, the festival, the tomb,
Thou hast thy part in each thou stateliest flower.
Therefore with thy sweet breath come floating by
A thousand images of love and grief;
Dreams filled with tokens of mortality,
Deep thoughts of all things beautiful and brief.
Not such thy spells o'er those that hail'd thee first,
In the clear light of Eden's golden day,
There, thy rich leaves to crimson glory burst,
Linked with no dim remembrance of decay."

Chapter 15

THE FAIRY ROSE

The "Fairy" or "Lawrence" roses are so highly esteemed as pot plants, that they are grown for the flower markets in thousands, and always meet with a ready sale, even at times when the general trade in flowers is otherwise at a standstill. As thousands are sold, there must be thousands of purchasers, and we may reasonably guess that nine-tenths of the whole number try to keep their roses, and hope to see them flower again. To how many of them all is it vouchsafed to have a full gratification of the honourable desire? We can only answer the question vaguely, as another guess, that not more than one per cent of the whole number sees the flowers of the fairy roses a second time, that is to say, in another and distinct season of bloom. These roses are easy enough to grow, if you go the right way about it, and in that respect, they agree with all other known plants. But they differ from many other subjects of our care in this respect, that if we make a mistake at any point, or give way to any degree of carelessness, the fairy roses vanish, or if they deign live, it is for the entertainment of aphis, acarus, or mildew; perhaps, for all three; and while entertaining these new and disreputable acquaintances, they ignore the feelings of their vexed possessor. In any and every case, the management of pot roses by amateurs is a troublesome business; but there are no pot roses so in haste to cause disappointment as these, and when the disappointment comes, it is bitter, because between the fairy rose, as we see it in perfection in the flower market, and the fairy rose, as we may m see it two months afterwards, the difference is as great as any one could desire, who would treat dramatically the aspirations and experiences of the amateur rosarian. The writer has tasted the sorrows and joys that accompany the management of these fickle fames, having had to learn through failure the secrets of success, and having at last succeeded so far as to beat the market growers in all save time. For whereas, they could carry nice plants into market in the very early days of spring, the writer could carry far nicer plants into the dwelling house to adorn the window or the dinner table, about a fortnight later than the time at which the first batch were sent to Covent Garden. And as to the date of flowering, the market grower always has the advantage, for he can devote a house, or many houses to the stock of one plant, while the amateur, who does not want hundreds or thousands of the same thing, must fill a house with mixtures, and take his chance, and then; as a matter of course, however complete his practice and routine may be, the market grower is bound to beat him in something or other. Beware then, ye amateurs of roses, and be content to have your Lawrencianas in flower a fortnight later than those that are first sent to market; and if you are a month later you need not fret, because the later the better for you, for the more you force fairy roses, the more surely do you open the door wide for all the plagues of Egypt, and some other plagues that Egypt never heard of, to walk in and sprinkle the ashes of death on your garland of flowers.

It may be said with the most perfect truth, that the man who can grow a fuchsia well, can do perfect justice to the fairy rose. If fuchsias and Lawrence roses were grown in the same house, they would agree perfectly, and would either prosper or perish together, according as the treatment might be right or wrong. Let it be borne in mind, therefore, that the Lawrence roses are of that tender hardy class of plants, that require the aid of glass, except in the extreme southern and western counties, and when under glass, require the coolest possible treatment–that is to say, coolest in the thermometric, and not the moral sense of the word.

All experienced cultivators are well aware that whenever a plant is grown in a temperature higher than that of its native country, or whenever its season of development is artificially hastened (as when a plant that should flower in summer, is forced to flower in winter or spring), it becomes the ready prey of numerous animal and vegetable parasites. Now it is particularly worthy of remark that the fairy roses are quite healthy and hearty–in their own peculiar way, indeed, robust–so long as we grow them in the cool house, and make no attempt to force them whatever. They may be wintered nicely with geraniums, just as fuchsias are; they may be allowed to shake off their leaves, and be kept for awhile under the stage, just as fuchsias are treated in some gardens. But they like warmth, moisture, light, and are in haste to grow in the early spring if a little encouraged, precisely as fuchsias are. In this point they differ, that whereas some amount of shade does not hurt fuchsias; but the fairy roses must have the fullest amount of light possible, or their delicate wiry shoots become drawn and weak, and the flowers fall over, instead of holding their heads up jauntily on foot- stalks of sufficient toughness and substance.

To propagate these roses, is so easy a matter, that an experienced hand will make a plant of every inch of wood that can be cut, and as a good plant consists of a dense mass of shoots, ten good plants should soon, if required, give birth to a thousand. There are two seasons in the year for taking cuttings. The best cuttings are those obtained from plants that have been forced, and have made a free and kindly growth afterwards. The plants that have flowered under cool treatment will supply an abundance of cuttings in the early days of September. In any case, young, half-ripe wood must be selected, and the cuttings must be put into a mixture of equal parts of powdery peat and silver sand, and be kept on a gentle bottom heat with plenty of atmospheric moisture until rooted, and then should be potted off singly, in thumb pots, in any good sandy compost, and should be kept warm and moist, until the pots are full of roots, and should then be shifted into sixties, and allowed to cool down gently, and take a good rest preparatory to being shifted into forty-eights for flowering.

The soil for these plants should in any case be light, and the pots carefully drained; but as to the quality of the soil otherwise they are not at all particular. They will grow superbly in good fibry peat with plenty of sand, and they will do quite as well in mellow turfy loam with sufficient sharp grit; but the strong soil that more vigorous habited roses require is really not suited for them, for if the soil be too heavy, or the pots not well drained, they soon become covered with mildew, and to restore them to health will be a difficult task. A light fuchsia compost will suit them admirably, and they should be shaken out every year when the new growth is completed, and be wholly or partly repotted, when a goodly proportion of thoroughly rotten

A FAIRY ROSE

hot-bed manure may be added to promote a vigorous bloom. As a definite prescription is always valued (by such as have confidence in the prescriber), we propose, as a compost for fairy roses, two parts loam from top spit of pasture, the fibre quite broken down; and one part each of siliceous grit, rotten hot-bed manure, and clean leaf mould. This will be light and rich, and they will grow like radishes in it if they have fair play as respects air, light, and moisture.

To force fairy roses is easy enough for those who have had some experience in forcing in a general way. They do well with *Deutzia gracilis*, *Astible japonica*, and of course with Tea and China roses in the forcing-house, the principal point being to force *gently*, for if you drive them, off go the buds; and as the buds fall, mildew or fly, or red spider will appear, and then, where are you? Let echo answer, "Where are you?" Extreme of heat, extreme of cold, extreme of moisture, extreme of dryness–any extreme, even of wind and sunshine, is ruin to fairy roses. They must be treated like healthy people who are slightly "hipped". They must not have over-much food or drink, or air or sunshine, and yet if they are kept unduly close, Death will soon mark them for his own. Nevertheless, though so fastidious, I would sooner trust a ploughman with a lot of fairy roses than the starving, prohibiting Dr. Sangrado, whose ambition it was to say "No", and who gratified his ambition with a vengeance. These coy plants may be better coaxed with a "Yes" than a "No", for if they ask for water and you say "No", they will instantly shake off all their leaves and refuse to be comforted.

Now the reader will begin to ask what is to be done with the plagues these plants are subject to. The proper answer is, that if the case is a bad one, nothing should be done to cure, and that killing is the procedure for the prudent. We must confess we have seen several sudden outbreaks of aphis in our stock of fairy roses, but rarely saw red spider or mildew. We disposed of the aphis in all off-hand way, by simply providing a pail full of pure water from the kitchen boiler, and cooling it down to 150° F, and then we turned the plants head downwards into it and gave them a brisk rinsing. The spider and the mildew we have completely cured by the aid of a solution of Gishurst Compound, which we found peculiarly efficacious when used of a moderate degree of strength and quite hot. But when used on tender foliage, as in the case of that of the fairy roses produced in the forcing pit, it should be carefully syringed off with pure water. The best course is to use the insecticide late in the afternoon and syringe the plants with water early in the following morning. The plants may be either syringed with the solution or be dipped in it; but dipping is preferable, as every leaf is then saturated with it; and if they are laid on their side for a short time over the vessel in which they have been dipped, a great economy in material will be effected.

The books say that these roses may be planted out, but those who obtain them honestly are advised to be a little cautious as to planting out. Several times we have planted out surplus stock of well-hardened thrifty plants in May, but the next winter killed them so completely that there were no marks of their whereabouts left. In the Scilly Islands, and in some sheltered nooks on the coasts of Devon and Somerset,

> "Where spices breathe and fragrant roses smile",

they may do very well, if planted out on a dry, light, nourishing soil; but even in such favoured spots we should prefer to grow them as pot plants, for their exquisite beauty can only be fully appreciated when they are seen close under the eye, and pot culture ensures the early bloom that is so great a charm with such delicately-habited plants as these.

Chapter 16

YELLOW ROSES

The "Golden Rose" of history is the most renowned of emblematic flowers, and yet by not a few amongst many who are at once ambitious, and simple minded, would be less valued than the golden rose of the garden. The rosarian cherishes an ideal estimate of the golden rose that he has grown or will grow, for to him it is a sort of fiction founded on fact; he has never seen, and mayhap never will see the perfect flower that constantly delights his inward eye, and is the most welcome fantasy of his dreaming.

There are more yellow flowers than of any other colour, and yet we prize yellow roses above all other roses, and take considerable care to insure their plentiful production and perfect development. The *blue* rose is at present a "fancy flower", a thing of the imagination, hoped for, and indeed expected by rosarians who take superficial views of the workings of nature, but by such as have observed with intelligent eyes, it is generally agreed that there is no reasonable prospect of the production of a *blue* rose at any time or anywhere except in the dream of an enthusiast. But the yellow rose is one of the most agreeable of the many realities of the rose garden. It is not the Noisette or the Tea-scented groups only that furnish us with yellow flowers, but several other families dispute with these regal roses for favour with those who love "cups of gold", and hence a chapter on yellow roses must range rather wide in the selection of examples. Nor is the subject insusceptible of illustration from dreams and fancies, for there are those who hope for yellow moss roses and yellow perpetuals, and not a few who believe that such things really exist. As a matter of fact, our lively friends of the flowery persuasion on the other side of the channel, have actually announced yellow moss and perpetual roses as ready for confiding purchasers, but it has not been our good fortune to see any of them in flower, and for the present we do not believe in their existence. That, hypothetically, they are to be desired, there can be no question. A yellow moss rose of good quality would startle civilized society out of its accustomed propriety, and a yellow perpetual to flower all the summer long in the open ground, and make sheets of golden bloom in the proper rose season in the early days of July, would be the greatest possible "acquisition" to the rose garden that has ever been accomplished, not excluding the introduction of the honourable, puissant, redoubtable, heroic, and all-conquering Maréchal Niel. Now, to speak for ourselves, we do not expect ever to see a *blue* rose, and we have not yet seen a yellow moss or a yellow perpetual. But in the possibility of the last two we fully believe, and therefore feel bound to urge on all those choice spirits whose delight it is to raise floral novelties, the propriety of labouring with a view to secure such desirable additions to the rose catalogue. It may contribute towards this happy end, and at the same time promote the enjoyment of yellow roses everywhere, if we now offer a few observations on the several classes of yellow roses, and the cultivation they severally require.

Macartney

In the Macartney section there are several varieties that show more or less of the coveted colour. *Alba odorata* has white flowers, which are yellowish in the centre. *Hardy's Rose*, the result of a cross between *R. involucrata* and *R. berberidifolia*, has flowers of a pale yellow, spotted with purple at the base. *Rosa hardii* was raised by M. Hardy, of the Jardin de Luxembourg, in the year 1836. In all its characteristics it is very distinct, but alas! it has no constitution, and, in consequence, on cold clay soils all it usually does, after being carefully planted, is to dwindle away. But we have done well with it planted in a peat border, in a sunny lean-to house in a very damp position, and attribute our success to the free ventilation afforded during summer, and the very small amount of artificial heat employed in winter to keep frost out. The amateur intending to breed from this plant would do well to plant it in peat in a brick pit, as it would then be completely under command, and as nearly as possible in the condition of a rose in the open ground, but enjoying perfect shelter. As a matter of policy, however, we should advise the amateur to go anywhere for pollen rather than to Hardy's Rose.

Scotch

In this section occur several yellow roses, and they all produce seed abundantly. The growth is dwarf, excessively spiny, and they multiply rapidly by suckers, which rise up some distance from the parent plant. The flowers are always more or less double, very small, globular like little balls, and agreeably fragrant. The varieties are only to be met with in old gardens, as they are all quite out of fashion. We should select, with a view to possible uses in hybridizing, the following: *Josephus*, a good plant, with light yellow flowers; *Mary Stewart*, lemon yellow; *Mrs. Hay*, tawny straw colour; *True Yellow*, pale yellow in bud, creamy white when expended. They should all be grown as bushes, for they make miserable standards. Any soil will suit them, but they require pure air. A hedge of True Yellow would make a pretty feature in some out-of-the-way spot, but would not be good enough for the rosarium proper. They are strictly summer roses.

Sulphurea

Sulphurea is a relation of the Scotch rose. It has pale green glaucous leaves, erect shoots, which are covered with long prickles. The *Double Yellow* has flowers of large size, very double, and a lovely yellow colour. It is, unfortunately, without odour. It is an old, very old rose, with an incorrigible habit of bursting just when it should open beautifully. Patkinson, writing in 1629, says: it is "so thicke and double, that very often it breaketh out on one side or another, and but few of them abiding whole and faire in our country, and the time of flowering being subject to much raine and showers; many, therefore, doe either plant it against a wall, or other ways defend it by covering". Occasionally, when warm rains have been followed by bright sun, this rose will open properly, and is then extremely beautiful, but to "catch it" thus happily is a rare event. Every observant cultivator who knows the variety has "made an effort" to overcome its eccentricities, but with small success. A rather light but rich soil and exposure to the north, appear to be favourable conditions, and without a question it thrives better on its own roots than on any kind of stock on which it has ever been tried. An important element, in the production of perfect flowers is *age*, for the older the tree the better; therefore the Double Yellow may teach the rosarian patience. The tree should be pruned immediately after flowering; not indeed to shorten, but to thin out the shoots so as to secure the most perfect ripening of those that are left. The *Yellow Pompon* is a small variety of Sulphurea, the flowers are globular, quite double, and of a bright yellow colour. All the roses of this section flower in the early summer.

Alba

In this group occur a few which may be regarded as having a yellow tendency. They are *Belle aurora*, white, tinged with yellow; *Blanche Belgique*, white, tinted sulphur; *Buff*, pale buff, small; *Madame legras*, creamy white. They are hardy, good growers, require no particular treatment, and thrive well on any kind of free stock as well as on their own roots. They flower in summer only.

Austrian Brier

This is a section consisting almost wholly of yellow roses. They are all closely related to our old friend of the cottage-garden, the sweet brier, or Eglantine of English writers, and the one called *Globe Yellow* is the Eglantine of the French. The following are beautiful and useful yellow roses: *Bicolor*, single, copper and yellow; *Copper*, single, reddish copper; *Double Yellow*, or *Williams*, raised by Mr. Williams, of Pitmaston, double bright yellow; *Globe Yellow*, a very thrifty variety, producing globular flowers of a bright lemon colour; *Harrisoni*, double, cupped, golden yellow, habit of the tree pendulous, flowering early and soon over; *Italian Yellow*, pale straw colour; *Persian Yellow*, large double, globular, rich deep yellow, a grand rose of its class; *Single Yellow*, or *Capuchin Brier*, large and single, cupped, bright, primrose yellow. Harrisoni and Persian Yellow make fine standards, and flower freely, but their beauty is soon past. They should be pruned close every alternate year, and as the process prunes the flowers out, they will of course, under such treatment, flower only once in two years. It is possible, by cutting out a certain quantity of wood every year, to insure an annual bloom, but it is better practice to flower them every other year, for then a rich display is secured instead of a poor display annually. They are summer-flowering roses, and produce an abundance of seed.

Tea-Scented

These might be described as a group of golden roses, save that amongst them are several veritable Teas that have rosy, creamy, and blush-tinted flowers. If we stop to praise them, we shall be led away and possibly lost; therefore, we will ask Horatius to dedicate the golden rose with the lily and the ivy to festivity and love, and then give attention to practical matters:

"Neu desint epulis rosae,
Neu vivax apium, neu breve lilium.
Omnes in Damalin putres
Deponent oculos; nec Damalis novo
Divelletur adultero,
Lascivis hederis ambitiosior."

Carm. i. 36, 15.

The yellow Teas differ in habit and merit considerably, but all except one are somewhat tender, and to enjoy them thoroughly, it is necessary to plant them out in a span-roofed house, or to grow them in pots with the aid of a good brick pit. The free-growing sorts make fine standards, and are unequalled as wall-roses, for they run to a great height quickly, and flower abundantly if the points of the shoots are pinched out as soon as the rods have attained their full length. The weak growers make neat bushes if regularly pruned back to promote a sufficient growth of side-shoots, and they are most prodigal of their flowers in autumn if out of doors, but when grown under glass they flower delightfully in the month of May, and again in August. The English brier is the best stock for all the strong-growing sorts, and of all roses in the world that thrive on the brier, no matter what the height of the stem or the aspect, or even the relative purity of the air, *Gloire de Dijon* surpasses them in hardiness and general usefulness. Indeed, we place Maréchal Niel, which we class as a Noisette, second in rank of relative merit to this most thrifty of the Teas, and although for the present no one will agree with us, the time will come when all experienced rosarians will declare the judgment to be correct. The weak growers do well on the seedling brier, and all do well on their own roots, and their own are the best roots they can have when they are planted in open borders; because as they are likely to be killed to the ground-line in a severe winter, they will renew themselves from the roots, and recover in one season, but if on foster roots they never recover—it is the stock alone that survives. As the weak growers make good pot plants, and the strong growers run fast and soon cover a wall, a profitable way of appropriating a house to yellow roses is to have a border for the runners, and train them up the wall, while the pot plants are placed on a stage in the usual way. In a house with a broad roof, a succession of festoons may be obtained by planting strong growing yellow Teas to clothe the rafters. This would be a good way of insuring a free bloom on some of the shy Noisettes, the display in a good season fitting to Hamlet's expression, a "majestical roof fretted with golden fire".

It will be of some service to the amateur, perhaps, if we run through the list of yellow Teas in alphabetical order, and make such remarks on the more important of them as appear necessary. *Adrienne Christophle*, a strong grower, confusedly coloured yellow, copper, and peach, but sometimes comes pure yellow, first rate. *Beaute de l'Europe*, deep yellow, suffused copper, large, full, and of superb form. *Belle Lyonnaise*, rich canary-yellow, passing to white, tinted salmon, large and of good form. *Chateau de Bergeries*, pale canary-yellow, deep yellow in the centre, large, firm in bud. *Comtesse de Frigneuse*, an effective shade of canary-yellow, large and full; vigorous. *Devoniensis*, creamy white, with tinge of buff or yellow. *Duchesse de Auerstaldt*, bright yellow, large; vigorous and free. *Duchesse de Braganza*, bright canary-yellow, large and full; vigorous and free. *Edouard Gautier*, buff yellow, shaded rose, large and globular; free. *Etoile de Lyon*, saffron-yellow, bright yellow in the centre, large, superb form; fine habit. *Francisca Kruger*, rich yellow, shaded copper and peach, large, full, and highly finished. *Fiirst Bismarck*, yellow, tinted rose, large and full; *Gloire de Dijon*, too well known to need a character but it is proper to observe that it has a fine constitution and seeds freely, it is well adapted to breed from, and probably the pollen of Maréchal Niel is the best that can be found to fertilize it. *Isabella, Sprunt*, a strong grower, a fine habit, a most valuable pot-rose, forces well, flowers well formed, colour sulphur-yellow. *Jean Pernet*, a vigorous grower, clear yellow, good. *La Boule d'Or*, a strong grower, well adapted for a rafter or pillar in the rose-house, as it flowers freely; in colour it is not as its name implies, a ball or bowl of gold, for it is neither compact in make nor of a good yellow colour; but it flowers most profusely, and we must pronounce it a good variety to grow but not good enough to breed from. *Louise de Savoie*, a strong grower, fine in form and substance, clear, pale yellow, and deliciously scented; makes a fine pot-plant. *Mdlle. Cecile Berthod*, a strong grower, the flowers large and full, colour sulphur-yellow, a superb pot-rose, and one of the best of its class for forcing. *Madame Charles*, rich apricot; a moderate grower, and the flowers of medium size. *Madame Eugène Verdier*, rich chamois yellow, the flowers large, finely formed and sweet, and the growth vigorous. *Madame Falcot* is a famous rose, and highly appreciated for its beautiful buds. *Madame Levet* has finely-formed flowers of a bright yellow hue, suffused with rose, and a vigorous habit. *Madame Honorée Defresne*, deep yellow, the reverse of petals tinged with copper. *Madame Hoste*, a superb flower of a clear yellow colour; free and good. *Madame Margottin*, deep lemon-yellow, centre rich yellow; flowers large and full. *Madame Pierre Guillot*, rich orange-yellow, shaded copper and suffused rose. *Madame Scipion Cochet*, bright canary-yellow, shading to white and suffused rose. *Medea*, a beautiful rose of a pleasing canary-yellow colour. *Narcisse* is hardy in the neighbourhood of London, and makes a good standard, the flowers large, rather thin, delicate pale yellow; good. *Niphetos* is a strong grower and a capital type for a seeding rose; the flowers are large, full, and vary from pure white to pale yellow. *Perle de Lyon* is a strong grower with handsome dark foliage, hardier than most, the flowers are large, full, and stout, varying in colour from apricot to deep yellow; a glorious golden rose. *Reine des Pays Bas* is a pillar or wall rose, as it makes long rods that flower profusely, and it may be grown as a standard or bush; the flowers are moderately full, the colour pale sulphur. *Perfection de Montplaisir* is a weak grower; forces well; the flowers come in plenty, they are smallish, the form good, colour canary-yellow. *Sunset* is a sport from Perle des Jardins; the flowers are of a deep apricot-yellow; one of the best for forcing. *Vicomtesse de Cazes* is another of the famous Teas, a moderate grower, but strong enough to make a good standard, somewhat hardy, and one of the freest to flower in all this family; the flowers are large, full of stout petals, the colour coppery-yellow shading to gold-yellow at the edges.

Noisette

This section is rich in yellow roses, and the best of them are hardier than the Teas. Among the yellow Noisettes there are a few which will thrive anywhere, and require very little care to insure an abundant bloom; but these are not the kinds that the rosarian becomes excited about.

We come near to true yellow in *Solfaterre,* which has always been a favourite. The colour is pale sulphur, the flowers are large and very double, and the tree grows with great vigour. Very like it is *Lamarque,* a most beautiful sulphur-yellow rose, and one of the finest wall-roses known. *Triomphe de Rennes,* a true Noisette, with large canary-coloured flowers, is hardier than the two foregoing, and bears the smoke of towns tolerably well. At Stoke Newington it grows and blooms superbly as a standard, exposed to all the winds of heaven. *Celine forestier* is another true Noisette, of vigorous habit, as hardy as the last, and very adaptable to any situation where a rose of any kind will grow. The flowers are pale yellow, pure and bright, large and full, and are freely produced if the tree is scarcely at all pruned. The best way to manage it is to cut back a few of the longest rods every spring, leaving always about half the shoots to flower, and the other half to grow. In a good season, the shoots that were pruned will flower in the autumn as well as those left unpruned. It bears smoke well, and grows freely on any free stock. The best place for it is on a west wall, where the strong shoots can be trained in their full length, or as a standard on a brier; for when grown as a bush it is too straggling unless much pinched in, and that is apt to endanger the flowering, though the stubby side-shoots which follow are sure to flower the next season if left alone. *Madame C. Kuster* is another vigorous grower, with a decided trace of the Tea rose in its constitution. This requires a warm wall, and grows best when worked on the seedling brier, but it will do on the Manetti. The flowers are pale yellow, with deeper centre, and if the tree is well fed, the flowers are large and full.

Among the strong growers we have now six left; of these we shall dispose of five, and reserve the sixth for a separate paragraph. *Cloth of Gold* is truly magnificent when brought to perfection; the colour pure gold, the form globular, very large and double. *Isabella Gray* differs from it in being a shade deeper in colour towards the centre. When well grown, the flowers open freely, but are rather deficient in form. Very often, however, this rose does not open well, and it is shy in blooming under all ordinary circumstances. *Jane Hardy* flowers deep golden yellow, small but pretty; the habit that of a climber, and too tender to be used as a standard. *L'Ideale,* a fine wall-rose, and invaluable for the supply of cut flowers; the blooms of medium size, and attractively coloured yellow, chamois, and red. *William Allen Richardson*, vigorous in growth and profuse in blooming; the flowers of medium size, deep yellow, shaded fawn.

Of the yellow roses enumerated above, there are four that call for special consideration as to the best means of securing a plentiful and an *annual* crop of flowers. These are Cloth of Gold, Solfaterre, Isabella Gray, and Jane Hardy. We omit from this consideration Maréchal Niel, because it never fails to flower freely when planted in a suitable position. It is a fortunate thing that if we hit upon the right method of managing anyone of these, that same method will apply to all the rest.

These delicately-constituted roses require a deep, rich, dry, warm soil. If wall and border could both be moderately heated, without covering with glass, there is no doubt these varieties would surpass everything, in the way of roses, ever seen. To do so would be quite possible, but the majority of cultivators, and, for our own part, we cast our lot with the majority as having common sense on its side prefer to attempt their culture with the heat of the sun alone. It will be understood from these remarks, that to plant any of these roses in a bleak position on undrained soil, or in poor, sour, pasty stuff, would be the height of folly. They might live, but they would neither grow nor bloom. A south wall has been pronounced by more than one authority as unfit for them; but this is a mistake. The fact is, the place cannot be too hot; but as tender plants on south walls are in more danger in winter than plants of the some kind on north walls, the cultivator must make amends by protecting, and there is nothing better for the purpose than a stout canvas fixed to a lath above the top line of the trees, and drawn down at night. The use of protection is perhaps of more importance in spring than winter; for, having secured a hot position and a thorough good border, the next step towards success is to promote *an early and vigorous growth.* Early formation of strong wood allows of its more perfect ripening by summer-heat; and if the wood be well ripened, there will be plenty of bloom to a certainty. There are two more points for the cultivator to fix in his memory—namely, to use the knife as little as possible, and to exercise patience, for these roses must be well established, and have had some years of growth, before they acquire a blooming condition. We must now speak of them separately, as to their individual needs and peculiarities.

Cloth of Gold will do as well on a brier as any rose known. It will also do well on the Banksian. It will also do for a time on Celine and Manetti stocks, but unless its makes roots of its own, and so becomes independent of the stock, it may perish just as it acquires the proper age to be in perfection. It is important to bud on *established stocks*, because, when the junction has been effected, the rose makes that quick and early growth which is so essential to success; whereas, if the stock be only half rooted, the first shoots of the rose rise weak, and never afterwards acquire their proper vigour. As the shoots rise, train them their full length upright till June, then unnail them, and nail in again in the, form of half circles, or as near that figure as possible, as in the sub-joined diagram. This bending of the shoots will promote the ripening of the wood; and if the season is hot and dry there will be an abundant production the next year of golden trusses *on the upper parts of the shoots*. As soon as the bloom is over, cut half the shoots back to plump buds at the base, train the shoots from these buds upright, and bend as before. By this treatment the trees will bloom again in autumn.

It really does not matter what stock *Isabella Gray* is worked on; but it must have a warm and dry position. To promote the tormation of spurs it is necessary to hasten the growth by giving abundance of water, alternating with liquid manure, early in the spring, and to train in all the wood its full length and cease watering about the middle of July. As soon as these shoots begin to ripen, there will

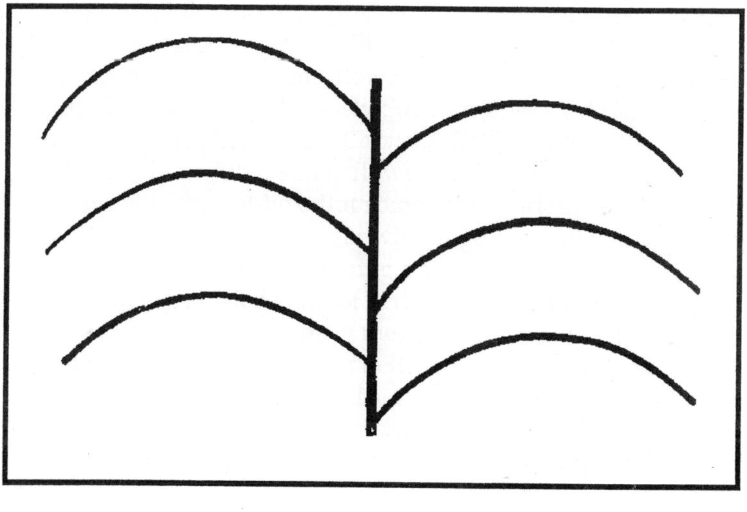

probably appear a second growth of shoots from the base, and these shoots must be suppressed, otherwise the formation of spurs will be prevented. If the season is tolerably dry, and the tree has plenty of sun, it will at once throw out spurs and bloom freely. As soon as the side spurs begin to push, the critical moment is past, the tree will low devote its energies to the production of flowers instead of new wood, and it may be assisted again with liquid manure. The next spring cut back a portion of these shoots, to induce a strong growth of new wood to go through the same process as the year before, and perchance on the shoots not pruned a few (or many) blooms will appear in May or June.

The first year that *Isabella Gray* was sent out, and when rose growers had no other subject to talk about, so thoroughly did it engross their attention, we purchased some plants in five-inch pots, worked on Boursault stocks, which consisted entirely of bloom spurs, the buds having been taken from ripe wood. There were some eight or ten wiry branches upon each, forming very compact little bushes. These little plants bloomed in the greenhouse in May, most beautifully, being completely covered with small but very perfect blossoms, of a rather pale gold colour, two or three shades paler indeed than the flowers usually come out of doors. When the bloom was over, they were cut back very close, and the pots were dropped into larger ones and rich soil rammed in between. They soon produced shoots which naturally broke into spurs, and bloomed tolerably well in the autumn. After blooming they were shaken out, repotted into seven-inch pots, and slightly shortened. In February they were put in a, warm house and again bloomed as before; but the flowers were always pale, though they were always kept near the glass. In the winter of 1860 these plants were in an unheated structure, the pots were frozen through, and they perished in company with a good collection of camellias that shared the same fate. They had, however, taught us a very useful lesson, and that we hand over to all whom it may concern.

It is quite certain that any rose grower, who has a warm wall and a dry border, may secure two crops of bloom every season from any of the yellow Noisette and Tea roses. Start them early, protect the young growth while spring frosts prevail; let the unpruned wood produce its flowers, then cut it back and get an autumn bloom from the shoots of the season; or treat the spurs as apple and pear spurs which continue fruitful, and instead of cutting out the wood which produced them, shorten in the spurs to one or two buds as soon as the first bloom is over, and so cause them to renew themselves and flower again the same season.

The yellow Noisettes of less vigorous habit, should except in the most favoured localities, be grown under glass. *Le Pactole*, a fine yellow, requires a warm wall, but does better under glass, and makes a good pot-plant. *Cornelia Koch*, delicate straw colour, and *Smith's Yellow*, lemon-colour or yellowish straw, are good forcing roses, but of little use out of doors. The best way to manage them as pot-plants is to train them spirally. They should be on their own roots to make nice plants. *Clara Wendel*, fawn, with yellow centre must be grown under glass. *Vitellina*, colours mixed as in Jaune Desprez, but occasionally the yellow predominates; a vigorous grower, and flowers well after a hot season.

Maréchal Niel

Maréchal Niel, the most popular of the yellow roses, is occasionally classed in the trade catalogues with the Teas, but it is unquestionably a Noisette, and remarkably hardy. Throughout the southern and midland counties it can be grown out-of-doors in the greatest perfection, and with but small risk of its being cut off by the winter's frost. In the north it can also be grown moderately well in a warm position against a wall, but the chances are that about every third or fourth winter it will be cut down to the ground even with considerable protection. It is on record that in the neighbourhood of Derby it withstood the effects of the severe winter of 1866-67 without injury, but it is very certain that in Yorkshire it is killed with the thermometer considerably above zero. In sheltered nooks of such favoured spots as Worthing and Bonchurch, Isle of Wight, it will be found quite at home, and in the neighbourhood of London the shelter of a good wall is sufficient for it, provided the station is well drained.

Whether grown under glass or against a wall out-of-doors, the details of management will not be found to differ materially. At the commencement, strong plants on their own roots should be selected, as preferable to those on the brier or Manetti stock; but if there is any difficulty in securing them on their own roots, those worked on the brier should have the preference. We have budded it on Gloire de Dijon, the latter being a stout plant on the English brier, and it grew vigorously and flowered freely; the position being sheltered and suitable. Some rosarians act upon the belief that it is not well able to support itself on its own roots, whereas there is not another rose in cultivation that will do better on its own roots. As a proof of this, it is only necessary to refer to a gigantic specimen in the nurseries of Messrs Kelway and Son, at Langport, Somerset. This specimen covered the back wall and roof of a large orchard-house to a length of forty feet, and would in one season have covered the whole of the roof, and run another forty feet if the space could have been spared for it. In its third season, it produced upwards of one thousand flowers, besides furnishing sufficient cuttings for the propagation of five hundred plants. The large specimen in the nurseries of the late Mr. Harrison, at Darlington, Which produced 3000 blooms in the year 1872, when it covered an area of nearly 650 sugerficial feet of the roof of the house in which it is planted, was worked upon the Manetti; but immediately it was turned out of the pot it pushed out roots of its own accord, and may be virtually considered on its "own roots". The vigorous constitution of the Maréchal is as much a matter for wonder as the fine form and rich colour of the flowers. We have measured a shoot made in one season, on a plant in Messrs. Veitch's nursery at Coombe Wood, and found it a trifle over 20 feet. This plant is on a short English brier stock, and is planted in a border next the wall of a lean-to rose-house.

The best way of cultivating Maréchal Niel under glass is to plant it in a border or large pot or box, and train it just under the rafters. The rose-house will be the most appropriate place for it, although it is entitled to rank high as a conservatory climber. Sound turfy loam and partly-decayed manure chopped up roughly, and incorporated together at the rate of three parts of the first to one of the second, forms as perfect a compost as can be prepared for it. A few bones broken up moderately will be of considerable service in maintaining the fertility and porosity of the soil. When it is necessary to use pots or boxes, let them be of a large size, for it will be difficult to repot the plants when trained to the roof; but when growing in large pots they may, with the assistance of annual top-dressings, be kept in a healthy condition for several years, more especially if encouraged to root through.

Rosarians differ somewhat in their opinions as to the manner in which the Maréchal should be pruned, and some go so far as to assert that it should be pruned in the most moderate manner only, whilst others contend that it may be pruned severely. It is an easy matter for anyone practically acquainted with the matter to effect a reconciliation between the two extremes, for in the one case allusion is made to the long rods which healthy plants will produce, whilst in the other the lateral growth is referred to. In reality, this rose requires pruning in much the same manner as other vigorous-growing varieties, for the strong rods require to be simply shortened back to a moderate extent, whilst the lateral shoots must be cut back to the first or second bud; and, in addition, all weak shoots must be entirely removed to prevent overcrowding. It must be understood that, if the long, vigorous shoots are pruned severely, other strong shoots will be produced; whilst, on the other hand, if the tops are simply taken off, and the rods placed, as far as practicable, in a horizontal position, laterals bearing flowers will push from nearly every bud, and a grand display of colour be the result.

Yes, every flower that blows
I passed unheeded by,
Till this enchanting Rose
Had fixed my wand'ring eye.
It scented every breeze
That wanton'd o'er the stream,
Or trembled through the trees
To meet the morning beam.

—*Cunningham*

Chapter 17

HEDGEROW AND WILDERNESS ROSES

Who can view the ripened rose, nor seek
To wear it? Who can curiously behold
The smoothness and the sheen of beauty's cheek,
Nor feel the heart can never all grow old?

Thus far we have considered the management and uses of the rose as a garden flower; but it must be allowed to stray beyond the garden and take part in beautifying the wilder scenes that lie around, as on the boundaries of the play ground; amongst the rough sunny rockeries; on the mount where the rustic arbour commands a view of the country; and in all the more open and dressy parts of the wilderness and orchard. But our way to the wilderness lies through the garden, and as we proceed we may be asked about certain hedges and partitions and bowers for which roses are required, and that may be better furnished with roses than with aught else. It will occur to the practical mind that the climbing roses afford the best of material for the kind of work we have in mind now; but we must begin by saying that there are many varieties not classed as climbers that have higher claims than climbers proper for good positions in the garden. Of pillars and trellises and chains we have spoken already; but of bowers and hedges we have as yet said nothing. In the case of a bower of the rustic sort, formed, perhaps, of larch poles and stout wire-work, we would not trust to roses alone, but have a mixture, to ensure a rich dense covering and a variety of effects, Suppose we plant our bower with *Gloire de Dijon* rose, *Jackmani* clematis, and *Pyrus japonica.* This combination comprises plants about equal in vigour and growth, very different in colour and character, yet of a nature to associate well in clothing a place intended for shade and shelter, and to render a bower beautiful from early spring until the actual commencement of winter. In all garden scenes, garden roses should be planted and hence for the hedges that enclose the rosery, and ally dividing screens and partitions that are to consist of roses, the strong-growing Hybrid Perpetuals, Noisettes, and hardy Teas are to be preferred to the more rampant Multifloras and Sempervirens. A most effective hedge may be made by means of arched wires fixed to split larch poles, forming a continuous trellis three feet wide and four feet high, planted throughout with *Gloire de Rosomene*, with *Aimée Vibert* at intervals of ten or twelve feet throughout. It is customary to plant standards in a garden hedge to break the line, and when all goes well, the arrangement is most effective. The standards should be tall enough to stand clear above the top line of the hedge, and should have large round heads, and produce an abundance of the most showy flowers. Such varieties as *Madame Domage* or *Jules Margottin* we should consider suitable, and in one length of hedge, or one set of hedges, all within view at once, we should allow only one variety for standards, or at the very utmost, three varieties, and these should be planted so as to alternate regularly, and it would be better if they did not all flower at the, same time. A capital hedge may be made without the standards, and in the case of enclosing a rosery, we should, as a matter of taste, certainly prefer the unbroken line of neatly-trained and nicely-rounded growth of dwarf roses of vigorous habit, of one sort only, or at the utmost, of three, without any standards.

One of the best of the roses for hedges is *Rosa rugosa*, as so well shown in the accompanying illustration of the hedge in the beautiful gardens of G.F. Wilson, Esq., at Wisley, Surrey, where its suitability for hedgerows was first demonstrated in the United Kingdom. Planted twelve inches apart in soil that has been well prepared by liberal manuring and deep digging, and supported by a rough trellis, it will in a few years form dense hedges impregnable to cattle, and of an exceedingly ornamental character. The hedges are, indeed, highly attractive from the end of the spring until late in the autumn, for the beautiful flowers are succeeded by a heavy crop of the handsome fruits which retain their rich colours until late in the year.

HEDGE OF ROSA RUGOSA AT WISLEY

Beautiful garden hedges may be made, without the aid of poles or wires, by selecting varieties of a somewhat stiff habit of growth, and perhaps, the *Common China* should have first consideration, for the soft quiet colour of its flowers would not interfere with the enjoyment of the choicer and richer qualities of the roses encompassed and sheltered by it, for the frame should, at least, not be grander than the picture.

In the case of a hedge apart from the rosery, however, greater variety may be desirable, and a great feast may be derived from a mixture of many kinds of roses, provided they nearly agree in growth, for we must have a vigorous and leafy growth, and abundance of bloom. The groups to select from for such a purpose are the Perpetuals, the Noisettes, and the Teas. The best possible plants are those on their own roots, for that disposes of the difficulty of suckers; but Manettis, planted fully six inches deep, will answer admirably if a sharp look out be kept for any growth that may arise from the stock. The ground should be deeply trenched and heavily manured, and the planting should be completed early in the autumn, unless the plants are to be turned out of pots, and then the best time to plant is April. If just a yard apart in a straight line they will have space enough to develop their characters fully; but a quicker effect may be insured by allowing only two feet space between them. They should be allowed to grow without a check; and have the help of abundance of water the first season. In the month of March following they should be cut down to within four inches of the ground, and again left to grow in their own way. It will be well now to provide stakes and wires of a rough, cheap kind, to give regularity to the front line of the hedge, and there can be nothing more effectual than such a fence as

is here represented. If manure can be spared, let the roots have a top dressing every autumn, and if it be possible to give water in abundance, let them have liberal supplies during the months of May and June. The pruning, after the wires are furnished, will consist in moderately shortening the best rods, cutting out the weak ones, and cutting down to four inches from the ground all the plants that have failed to grow with a proper degree of vigour.

When we enter upon wilder scenes we shall require wilder roses, and must plant them in the *négligé* style. The casual pile of stones in the paddock, or the pseudo rockery that has been made up to screen the rubbish yard, may be vastly improved by a screen of such dense-growing Noisettes as *Ophirie* and *Miss Glegg*; and the ever-desirable Sempervirens *Félicité Perpétue* with its gracious corymbs of flesh white flowers. Another good use of such roses is to clothe the stems of decrepit trees and associate with ivy on ruins, and the more sunny parts of rockeries and sloping banks. The open glades in the pleasure ground and park may be agreeably enriched by clumps of *Scotch* roses, and for the same purpose, *Common Damask*, *Common Provence*, and the *Common Sweet Brier*, are eminently suitable. There is ample room for selection; but it would be bad taste to plant the finest exhibition varieties in the wilderness, and, generally speaking, a vigorous rustic growth is required to harmonize with the surroundings.

The snowy lily pressed with heavy rain,
Which fills her cup with showers up to the brink,
The weary stalk no longer can sustain
The head, but low beneath the burden sink.
Or should the virgin rose her leaves display,
And ope her bosom to the blaze of day,
Down drops her double ruff, and all her charms decay.
Languid and dying. seems the purple flower,
Fainting through heat, low hangs her drooping head;
But if revived by a soft falling shower,
Again her lively beauties she doth spread,
And with new pride her silken leaves display;
And while the sun doth now more gently play,
Lays out her swelling bosom to the smiling day.

—*Giles Fletcher*

Chapter 18

ROSES FOR DECORATIONS

To make the best use of roses in decorative works requires more than an ordinary degree of skill. If they are grouped with such garish flowers as scarlet geraniums, they are eclipsed completely, and the combination is a muddle of colouring, better calculated to give pain than pleasure to a cultivated eye. It is always necessary, before cutting roses for bouquets or epergnes, to consider what kind of materials they are to be associated with, for if not nicely matched in style and colour, they are either lost or become prominently objectionable. With orchids, eucharis, and stephanotis, they group well; but with asters and pelargoniums they are less happy. However, it must be admitted, as a matter of fact, that roses may be tastefully combined with any class of flowers, and it will depend on the skill of the artist to establish harmonies where none were apparent in the first instance. With ferns and grasses in sufficient plenty and variety at command, many combinations, otherwise incongruous, may be rendered acceptable, for these elegant neutral agents harmonize discordant elements, and bridge over a difficulty, if wisely employed to tone down and soften the more distinctive of the showy flowers. One great persuasion to the employment of roses in decorations is to be found in the fact that the sight of roses always affords delight. If they were heaped up with cabbages on the dinner table, the guests would say, "We do not care about the cabbages (in that way you know), but, oh! the roses". If you were to send a very bad set of decorations to the flower show, taking care, however, to put some good roses in with other flowers, your friends would be sure to say, "Those roses ought

H.P. AMERICAN BELLE, IN VASE

to have won the prize for you–they were, indeed, lovely roses". The sentiment in favour of the flowers is a great point gained, but we must not be led astray by it.

In any and every case it must be borne in mind that roses soon drop and fall to pieces if exposed to a hot dry air for any length of time, and whatever the state of the air, they must have their stems in water, or their freshness will soon be gone for ever. Hence it is not desirable to employ them in suspended wreaths, or in any way which renders it impossible to keep them in contact with moisture. Hence, for one who is unprovided with the little button-hole phial, a rose is the worst of all flowers for a button-hole decoration. When roses are to be employed in epergnes and vases, they must be cut with a sufficient length of stem to reach the water, and care must be taken in fitting up, that all the roses are safely fixed in this respect, or they will probably not last out the occasion for their use. Very many of the most valuable decoration flowers, such as lapageria, stephanotis, and orchids, and even eucharis, will retain their freshness not only for several hours, but for several days, without any aid whatever; and pelargoniums, which are sadly given to fall to pieces, will hold together nearly as well without water as with it, at least for twenty-four hours, in an atmosphere more than ordinarily hot and dry. But the roses must be sustained, or they will be worse than useless.

In dressing a dinner table with roses, it is important to suit the colouring to the kind of light under which the flowers are to be seen. If the table is dressed for a day-light meal, the utmost latitude of colouring is allowable, provided, of course, that a tasteful picture is the result. We may have in juxta-position the exquisite flowers of Maréchal Niel and Louis XIV.; the first, a great tassel of gold; the second, a purple plum, ready to burst with vinous juices, and such decisive colouring may be as tasteful as it is dashing. But, under gas light, such colouring would be altogether wrong, and, in fact, all roses of decidedly purple tint appear dirty by gas light, and the best yellow roses do not come to much under similar circumstances. All the shades of pure rose, carmine and crimson, come out grandly by gas light, and the brightest of the latter acquire a tone of rich scarlet. All the white and blush roses are exquisitely delicate, and show themselves admirably amongst light sprays of ferns and grasses. But the buff and yellow flowers are less desirable, and the more decidedly blue the flower is, the more certainly is it unfit for use in a gas-light decoration. Some of the unimportant roses, that our heroes

HYBRID TEA, Mrs. W.C. WHITNEY, IN VASE

of the exhibition look down upon, such as Aimée Vibert, Common Provence, Fellenberg, Model of Perfection, and Cramoisie, are invaluable for decorative purposes, for, indeed, show roses, however perfect, are not always the most suitable.

When these needful precautions are fully observed, roses may be adapted to every style of floral decoration, from the exquisite method of some artists in this department to the more dashing and precise and hard style of others. For the wedding breakfast, a simple basket or vase containing a few white tea-scented or other roses, tastefully arranged with white bouvardias, carmine gloxinias, creamy gardenias, and elegant fern fronds, may be more acceptable than the best epergnes and vases.

If it is intended to make a feature of roses on the dinner-table, a rich, bold, daring style is to be preferred, as in the decorated table of which an illustration is given. This precise mode of dressing, in which a formal arrangement predominates, quickly degenerates into vulgarism if the requisite talent be lacking; but it is wondrously effective when well done, and suits roses perfectly. In this group the centre piece had a base of silvered glass, with a margin of small flowers. The lowest tazza had circles of scarlet geranium, white eucharis, and crimson roses relieved with sprays of astilbe, stipa, milium, and maiden-hair. The middle tazza was dressed with pink heaths and white and crimson roses, with grasses and ferns to soften the outlines. The trumpet top was filled with astilbe and scarlet geraniums, with grasses, to give a feathery finish. The side vases were modified repetitions of the centre, the roses constituting characteristic furniture of the tazzas.

A simple, but most effective, mode of displaying roses on the dinner table may be accomplished by bedding them in living lycopodiums. The only way to do it well is to prepare for the purpose a set of zinc pans, in which the lycopodium is to be grown, so as to be ready on the instant of being required. In the centre of each pan an empty flower-pot is placed, and around it is a sufficient mass of sandy peat. The lycopodium is then planted, and the pans are taken care of in the fern-house, where they soon become richly clothed with the most elegant vegetation. The best plant for the purpose is the close-growing *Selaginella apus*, better known by its nursery name of *Lycopodium apoda*. The more common and rampant growing, *S. denticulata*, answers well, and there are several others available.

When these receptacles are brought into requisition, the empty flower-pots are lifted out, and other pots, containing suitable plants, are inserted in the cavities; and the roses, being placed in small tin tubes filled with water, are thrust into the soil, and the flowers are thus embedded in the most sumptuous cushions of green moss it is possible to obtain.

In preparing for an elaborate gas-light display, the safest course is to arrange all the important colouring by gas light, even if it has to be done twenty-four hours in advance. It is a question, of course, if at the end of the period the flowers will look as well as at the beginning. We can answer that if the work is well done, and the place in which the vases and other dressed receptacles are put until wanted, is somewhat dark, and damp, and still, they will keep perfectly, and even if a few flowers should look the worse for the keeping, it will be an easy matter at the last moment to remove them and insert fresh-cut flowers of the same colours in their places. The great advantage is that complete success may be ensured; whereas there is great risk of a mistake, in fact, of an entensive muddle, when decorations are prepared by day light for the purpose of being displayed by artificial light. And here it will be well to recommend a mode of procedure we have adopted with complete success. In dressing vases and baskets some hours in advance of the time for the display, we have taken care to dip every flower and leaf and fern frond into clear tepid water, and then to gently beat the water out of it, so as to render every leaf and flower quite dry to all appearance. They are then grouped with the usual care to place the stems in contact with water, and put away in a cool store-room, and when brought out for use look as fresh and bright as when first fitted. The advantage of dipping them in tepid water is that a certain amount of moisture is retained by them even when it appears to have been beaten out. Even the dry-looking fronds of adiantums hold a little, and, generally speaking, flowers of all kinds hold a considerable quantity, lodged at the base of the petals, where, for a time at least, it tends more directly to keep them together, and with their proper, freshness unimpaired, than the water they have access to by means of their stems.

Roses may be employed to great advantage in the decoration of the drawing-room and boudoir, as they present an exceedingly beautiful appearance in fancy baskets, china-glass, and other bowls, vases, or specimen glasses, and placed on tables and wall-brackets. Elaborate grouping, that is so highly effective on the dinner-table, is

DINNER-TABLE, DECORATED WITH ROSES AND MIXED FLOWERS

quite unsuitable for these apartments, and, as a rule, the arrangements should be of the simplest description. Whether the blooms are placed singly in specimen glasses or from twelve to fifteen in a bowl, they should have a sufficient length of stem for them to stand well above the top of the receptacle, and show a portion of their foliage. In no way, when used for indoor decorations, do roses produce such a delightful effect as when cut with long stems and arranged in vases, as in the case of *American Belle* and *Mrs. W.C. Whitney*, of which illustrations are given. For this style of arrangement, well-developed blooms are essential, and its general adoption may be recommended, if only for the purpose of excluding from the house the miserable flowers that are so frequently met with in reception-rooms.

It will happen sometimes that you wish to use roses that do not open kindly, or that you wish to revive quickly roses that have become somewhat faded. In this case, plunge the stems into water as hot as the hand can bear, and the wished-for result will soon follow. The magician who makes a flower expand before an audience cannot, with all his machinery and skill, surpass the trick of compelling a sullen rose to expand by this simple process. A little manipulating with finger and thumb will be another help in the case of hard half-opened rose buds in cold weather. We may find in the garden, in the dark dull days or November, large promising buds on Souvenir de la Malmaison, Maréchal Niel, Gloire de Dijon, and other late-flowering roses, If we leave them, they will slowly decay and fall without expanding; but we may save them by such gentle means as are here indicated, and make thereby a garland of roses for fire-side enjoyment in the deadest days of the year. Thus the last rose of summer may live in substance for our bodily eyes as truly as it lives in the poet's verses for the delight of our inward vision:

'Tis the last rose of summer
Left blooming alone;
All her lovely companions
Are faded and gone;
No flower of her kindred,
No rose bud is nigh,
To reflect back her blushes,
Or give sigh for sigh.

Button-hole roses should not occupy much of our space, for there is really not much to be said about them. A half-blown moss rose is as perfect a button-hole flower as the world affords, and a bit of grass or fern can always be found to go with it if desired. Two or three flowers of the Austrian brier may be turned to account for the purpose, with a sprig of maiden-hair fern or a leaf of coleus or begonia—*chacun à son gout*. When a button-hole rose is presented, the case is, perhaps, different to the selection for one's own wearing. It may be proper then to consider delightful floral philosophy of Perdita, or take advice of Alphonse Karr or Thomas Moore, or, better than all, to interpret the language of flowers by the language of the heart.

"________Not words, for they
But half can tell love's feeling;
Sweet flowers alone can say
What passion fears revealing.
A once bright rose's withered leaf,
A towering lily broken,—
Oh! these may paint a grief
No words could e'er have spoken."

Chapter 19

THE ENEMIES OF THE ROSE

The "consuming canker" that secretly hollows out the plump red buds, and leaves it as a shell to wither on the tree, may be regarded as the leader of a host of harpies that wage warfare against the welfare of the rose. The amateur will soon become familiar with them all and happy will he be if they disturb not his rest, nor press upon him the cruel suggestion that rose-growing is accompanied with more plague than profit. The "grub," the "fly", are the captains of the army of enemies, and, they lead a formidable host that have for allies the east wind, the summer drought, the winter frost, and the blundering human hand that will do wrong, and generally errs most gravely by attempting too much. In respect of the principal insect enemies of the rose, a golden rule may be offered for the comfort of the anxious amateur, and that is—*Good Cultivation*. Do full justice to the trees in respect of soil, planting, watering, mulching, pruning, and manuring, and they will be but rarely seriously injured by these plagues; for they seek out first the starving roses. They attack the trees that have been badly used; they swarm to the garden of the sluggard, where the "thorn and the thistle grow broader and higher", and, generally speaking, are to be regarded as proofs that the trees are not thriving, and need some improvement at the root. Of course, good cultivation is not all-sufficient for the prevention of injury from insect pests, and it is therefore necessary that the rosarian should be well acquainted with the habits of the kinds that prey upon his favourites, and the best means of compassing their destruction when they attack the trees. With a view to assisting him in this important matter, a short description of the most destructive and the most effectual means of exterminating them are given. With regard to the remedial measures, it is important to constantly bear in mind that they should be adopted immediately the pests make their appearance, and not deferred, as is so often the case, until they have become well established, and the trees have been seriously injured.

Rose Aphis (*Aphis rosa*)

Rose Aphis (*Aphis rosa*) is usually very troublesome, more particularly when the growth has been checked by cold or otherwise unfavourable weather, or is very slowly developed in consequence of an impoverished condition of the soil. In the case of this pest, it is especially necessary to resort to repressive measures immediately it makes its appearance, for it multiplies at an extremely rapid rate when unchecked, and quickly does an immense amount of damage. It cannot be doubted, that many of the destructive visitations of "fly" on roses are prepared for by the frosts that usually come in the middle of May, when the sap is flowing freely, and development of leaf and wood is in full activity. The sudden check occasioned by unseasonable cold corrupts the juices, and renders them more palatable to the insects than the juices of an unchecked healthy tree would be; while, concurrently with the destruction that rapidly ensues on the settlement and multiplication of the insects, the growth of the tree is arrested, and it cannot quickly outgrow the destruction as a healthy tree would do, if we remove some portion of its leaves, or even cut off a considerable number of its branches; therefore, we may properly begin to advise that to prevent the spread of aphis, the trees should by every possible means, be encouraged to grow vigorously. Late pruning and shelter afford protection from the May frosts, that are the precursors of "blight" in the rose garden and orchard, and liberal manuring and watering will carry the trees through many a trial with little harm, when, by the proper advance of the season, they are capable of appropriating considerable supplies of sustenance. But the green fly will sometimes come when the trees are placed under the best possible conditions for making a healthy and vigorous growth, and the rosarian must therefore be ever on the alert, and be prepared to wage warfare against the invaders.

The immense value of pure water as an insecticide must be insisted upon. At present, very few cultivators believe in it; but the day will come when reason will prevail, and the syringe and water engine be appreciated at their true value. The regular and vigorous use of the water engine amongst roses, will render the lodgment of fly upon healthy trees next to impossible. If the plague is confined to a few shoots, the hand syringe may be sufficient to discharge a killing shower, and scatter the enemy to the devouring elements. Washing the trees in a thorough and systematic manner involves a considerable amount of labour; but it will be justified by the results, for the water will, by moistening the soil, be of service in promoting a vigorous growth as well as being useful in keeping the shoots free from the aphis. There are a considerable number of preparations that may be used with good effect, and it is with pleasure we confess that we have tried all the insecticides that have been advertised during the past forty years, and found them equal to the professions of the introducers, therefore the novice who buys a preparation described as an infallible destroyer of green fly on roses may at least give it a fair trial without trembling for the result; it is therefore unnecessary to recommend the preparation of any particular maker, and we will at once proceed to show the earnest rosarian how he may prepare at home washes that are efficient and inexpensive. There are several good washes that anyone can prepare with but little trouble, but the best are those containing tobacco juice, paraffin, or quaesia, and one of these should be used. In preparing the wash containing tobacco well mix in two gallons of hot water one and a half pounds of soft soap, and then add the juice obtained from steeping four ounces of tobacco in a quart of water, which should be poured over the tobacco when boiling. Well mix, and when required for use add the solution to twenty-five gallons of water. A decoction of quassia is prepared by well-boiling quassia chips in water, the proportions to be ten ounces to each gallon, and while quite hot stirring in about an ounce of soft soap. When used, dilute by adding nine gallons of water to each gallon of the extract. One precaution is necessary, and that is, to put the chips in cold water, and bring it slowly to the boiling point. This quassia wash is somewhat uncertain in its action, unless soft soap is added, for should there be a smart shower soon after its application, much of it will be washed off before it has had the desired effect. Moreover, the skin of the aphis is covered with a mealy secretion, which repels insecticides that do not contain anything of an adhesive nature. An effectual paraffin wash is made by adding one pound of soft soap to a gallon of water, and boiling for a few minutes; then add a pint of paraffin and agitate vigorously until well mixed with the soapy water. Bottle whilst warm, and in using add one reputed quart bottle of the preparation to fifteen gallons of water. It is important not to exceed the strength stated or to repeat at frequent intervals, as a paraffin wash that is perfectly harmless when applied once may be injurious if repeated at an interval of a week or ten days. After the expansion of blooms has commenced, the wash of soft soap and tobacco should alone be used, because of the objectionable odour left by the paraffin. The soft soap and tobacco wash is unquestionably the best for general use, for it is very effective and perfectly safe, provided, of course, the strength recommended is not exceeded. These washes may be applied by the hand syringe or garden engine, but a knapsack pump or other spraying machine is preferable because of the more thorough application of the insecticide and the greater economy of material. With a sprayer the whole of the foliage and wood call; be saturated without any appreciable quantity falling on the surface of the border. Tobacco powder may also be used with good effect in waging warfare against aphides, provided care is taken to apply it when the foliage is moist, to ensure its adhering. Under glass the plants may be kept perfectly free from aphides by fumigating with tobacco or tobacco paper. In fumigating roses it is important to have the foliage quite dry and to avoid very strong doses. The house should be just filled with the smoke, and if necessary, the fumigation be repeated after an interval of about three days. It is essential that the material be damp, not wet, when used, and that it be not allowed to burst into a flame, or indeed for the fire to burn through to the top.

Rose Caddice Sawfly (*Lyda inanita*)

Although less common than some other pests that prey upon the rose, damage is frequently done by the larvae or grubs. The fly makes its appearance at the end of May and is readily recognised by the golden hue of its wings. The female soon commences to deposit its eggs upon the leaves, and the grubs when hatched roll themselves up in cases formed with strips of the leaves, of the shape shown in the accompanying illustration. The strip, about an eighth of an inch in width, is attached to the body of the caterpillar, and as it is lengthened it is wound round it until completely covered.

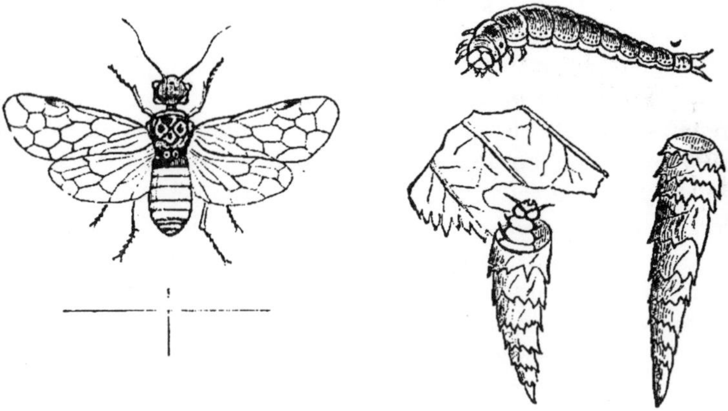

ROSE CADDICE SAWFLY, WITH LARVAE

The caterpillar then detaches the case from the leaf and falls to the ground, where it remains until the following May. Hand picking is the best way of dealing with these grubs.

Antler Rose Sawfly (*Cladius difformis*)

Several of the sawflies are injurious to the rose in a larval state, and this is one of the most destructive, the grubs eating both the foliage and the succulent shoots. The attack of this pest is indicated by the small perforations in the leaf and the jagged appearance of the margins. If the under side of a riddled leaf is examined, the bright green caterpillars will be found curled up as in the figure given herewith, or stretched out and holding on by their feet to the leaves they are busily engaged in devouring. The male fly is black and engage shining, and the female, of which a characteristic illustration is given, has iridescent wings suffused with brown. Much may be done in keeping the pest in subjection by handpicking, or by spraying the trees with a wash of tobacco and quassia or Paris green. The latter should be used in the paste form, and in the proportion of a quarter of an ounce to six gallons of water, but as it is a deadly poison, the greatest possible care must be taken in preparing and applying it. The preparation of quassia and tobacco is harmless, and therefore the best for general use. The caterpillars may be

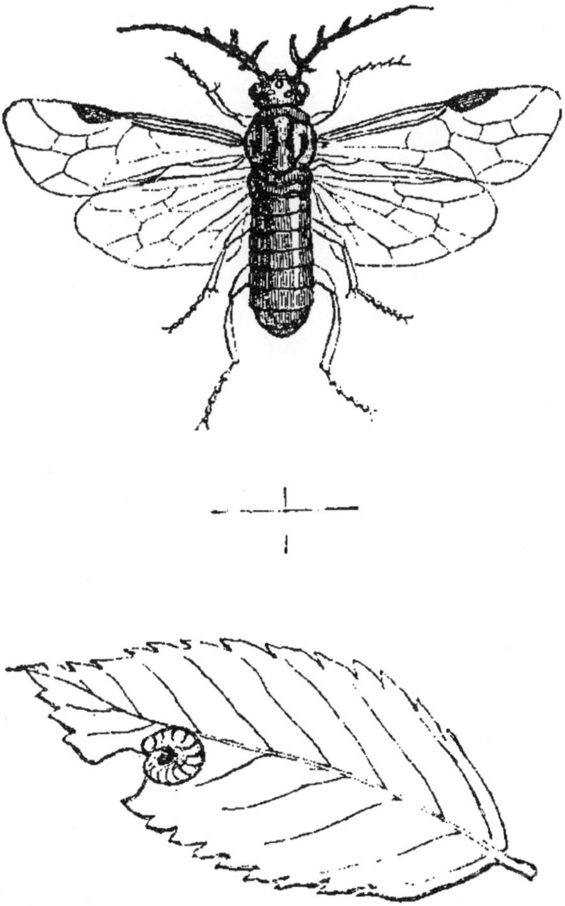

ANTLER ROSE SAWFLY, WITH GRUB

dislodged by a sharp shake of the tree, and if a piece of canvas is previously laid down, they can be readily gathered up and destroyed.

Rose Grub Moth (*Tortrix bergmanniana*)

It is a common pest in the rose garden, and where no steps are taken to keep it under considerable damage is frequently done. The

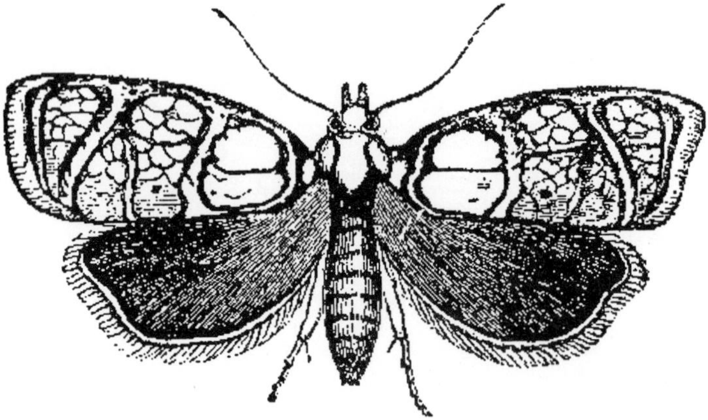

ROSE GRUB MOTH

moth is of a bright yellow colour, with brown markings, and deposits its eggs on the young growth. The caterpillars are hatched out in about three weeks, and they make their way to the upper leaflets, which they proceed to glue together, as a protection to themselves. When ensconced in these they can be readily crushed between the finger and thumb, and this summary course of procedure is undoubtedly the best method of dealing with them.

Rose Moth (*Tinea rhodophagella*)

It is very plentiful in some districts, and the larvae frequently do considerable damage. It is therefore essential that in all cases an effort should be made to keep the pest in subjection. The moths are small, and silvery grey marked with black on the wings; they make their appearance in May and soon begin to deposit their eggs on the buds and new growth. The caterpillars are produced in June, and make for themselves cases of portions of the leaves, and when full grown they descend to the ground and bury themselves an inch or so below the surface, where they remain throughout the winter. The most simple and efficient method of preventing the increase of the moth is to remove the surface soil during the winter, and either burn it or bury it to the depth of several feet in another part of the garden.

Common Vapourer, or Tussock Moth [*Bombyx (Orgyia) antiqua*]

It does not confine itself wholly to the roses, but its caterpillars are sufficiently partial to the foliage to justify its being included among the enemies of the flower. The females are small, wingless, and of a dull brown colour; and the males comparatively large, bright brown, the upper wings marked with dark lines and a white spot, as shown in the accompanying figures. The eggs are deposited in clusters upon the branches, to which they are firmly attached. The majority of the eggs are hatched in the autumn, but those of the late moths remain unhatched until the spring. The caterpillars are slate colour, furnished with tufts of hair, and marked with black spots and red tubercles. They feed upon the leaves, usually doing much damage, and when full grown they take refuge among the partly-devoured leaves on the stems, or on a fence or wall. Here they spin cocoons and change into pupae or chrysalids, from which the moths emerge in a few weeks. Where the caterpillars are troublesome, a careful search should be made for the eggs, which are invariably deposited near the webs. Spraying with a wash of soft soap and quassia is the best method of destroying the caterpillars.

Lackey Moth (*Bombyx neusteria*)

The caterpillars of this moth, so destructive in orchards and fruit gardens, occasionally attack roses and do considerable damage. The moths make their appearance towards the end of the summer, and are brownish with darker markings. The eggs are deposited before the autumn is far advanced, in bands on shoots of the current year, and remain until early in the following May, when they hatch. The black hairy caterpillars form web nests, in which they live at night and also in wet weather. When they have attained their full size they separate and locate themselves in sheltered positions against walls or fences, and change into the pupa state, in which they remain until the perfect insect emerges towards the end of the summer. Where the moth is known to abound, the clusters of eggs should be searched for, and the shoots bearing them be cut away and burnt. The web nests should be cut off and destroyed where the caterpillars are within them.

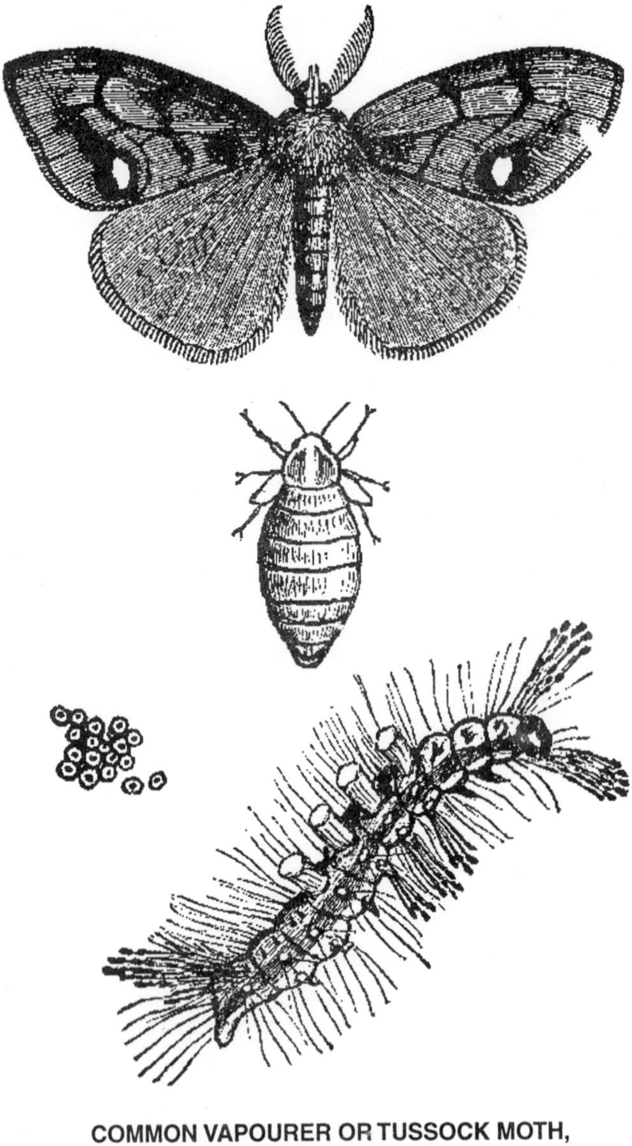

COMMON VAPOURER OR TUSSOCK MOTH,
MALE AND FEMALE MOTHS, EGGS,
AND CATERPILLAR

Golden Rose Beetle (*Cetonia aurata*)

It is sufficiently formidable to merit attention. The beetle is bright green, shaded with a rich golden hue, and is of large size and very handsome. Its depredations consist in eating the petals of the flowers when expanding, and rendering them worthless either for exhibition or house decoration, the blooms of light varieties being the most susceptible to attack. Handpicking is the most effectual remedy, and not difficult, because of the showy appearance of the beetles; the grubs should be destroyed when turned up in digging over the soil.

Mildew is without question an evidence of debility, but it may be the accident of the season and not the fault of the cultivator. The plague usually follows close upon a time of drought or of excessively hot days followed by excessively cold nights with a keen east wind and a sky wonderfully blue. The plant is checked by sudden and extreme and oft-repeated changes of temperature, and debilitation is the result. Here, again, whatever restores the vigour of the plant makes an end of the mildew; but as a matter of fact, when mildew has really obtained what gardeners call a "firm holt," it continues to the end of the season. The best of all preparations are those which, as in the case of Gishurst compound, contain sulphur. Dry flowers of sulphur dusted over the foliage is at once the simplest, and as a

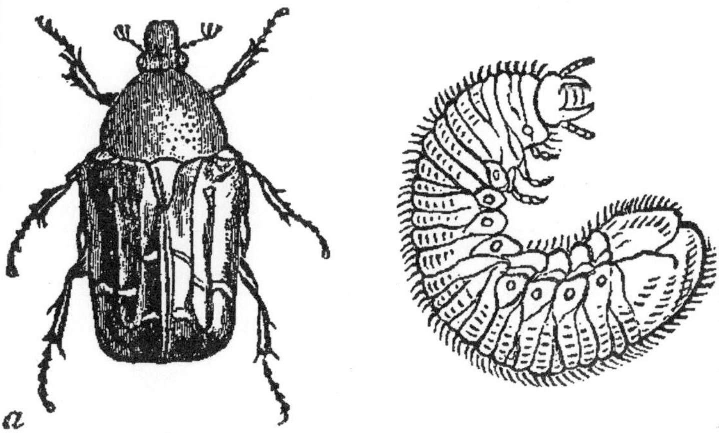

GOLDEN ROSE BEETLE, WITH GRUB

rule the surest remedy, provided it is applied with care, to cover all the affected parts of leaves and bark while they are moist and will hold the powder. Under glass, mildew is caused by a damp, close atmosphere, and the best means of eradicating it is to dust the foliage with sulphur and carefully increase the ventilation.

Winter Moth (*Cheimatihia brumata*)

The caterpillars of this moth are so cosmopolitan in their tastes that they will feed almost as readily upon the foliage of the rose tree as upon that of the apple, pear, and plum. The moths emerge from

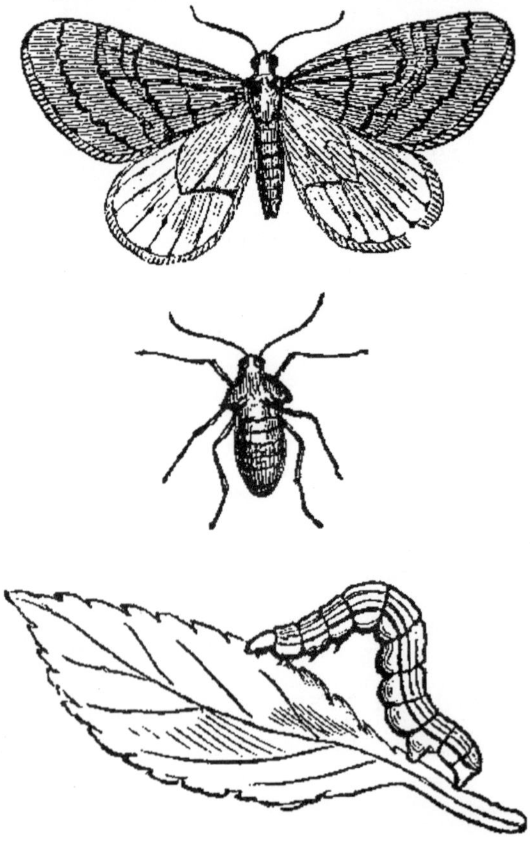

WINTER MOTH, CATERPILLAR, WINGED MALE, AND WINGLESS FEMALE

the chrysalids in October and November, and, as shown in the illustration, the female is small and practically wingless; she ascends the tree by means of the stem, and deposits the eggs on buds or twigs, or in crevices of the bark. They remain upon the wood until March, when hatching commences. The caterpillars are variable in colour and range from green to brown, and immediately they are hatched commence to attack the tender shoots and leaves. They attain their full development by the end of May or the beginning of June, when they leave the trees, bury themselves immediately below the surface, and change to chrysalids, in which state they remain until the autumn. In the case of standards, the female moths can be prevented from ascending the trees by putting a band of grease-proof paper round the stem, ten or twelve inches from the ground, and then smearing good cart grease upon it. Spraying the trees early in the spring with a wash of paraffin and soft soap, prepared as advised in speaking of the Rose Aphis, is a good remedy, as also is a mixture of Paris green, but the use of arsenical preparations is not advisable in the rose garden.

The Little Friends of the Rose

The Little friends of the rose are by no means few in number, and should have brief mention here. The common sparrow is one of the most active and assiduous, for if left alone sparrows will banquet on green fly, and pick, pick, pick for leaf rollers, and nibblers, and excavators of all sorts. If you find your roses are becoming dreadfully clothed with aphis, and you really have no time to pult or poison them, you may adopt an efficacious method of enlisting the sparrows in your service. Two or three times a day, sprinkle a handful of grain or bread crumbs amongst the roses. The sparrows will soon appreciate your bounty, and having cleared the ground, will next proceed to clear the trees, taking the best care possible to repay your kindness. To render this plan a perfect success, you should keep the sparrows always on the look out, and never supplied very bountifully: so as far as possible, institute frequent sprinklings of infinitesimal bounties.

Make yourself acquainted with the larvae of the ladybird, or *coccinella*, for these are greedy devourers of aphis, and touch no vegetable food whatever. The larvae of the *syrphidae*, again, are indefatigable destroyers of the same pest. Still more destructive to aphis, than either of the foregoing, are the larvae of the lace-winged fly (*Chrysopa perla*), a sort of ephemera, with golden eyes and green wings. This fly lays its eggs in a manner which causes them to appear like minute fungi, for every egg is on a transparent stalk, the latter being a kind of gluten deposited with the egg, and drawn out by the parent to elevate the egg out of the reach of danger. These stalked eggs may often be seen like microscopic fans fixed on the edges of rose leaves, and on the youngest shoots of the lilac, The ichneumon fly (*Ophion luteum*), is another friend of the rosarian, for its larvae feed on caterpillars, and the more of them we can find amongst the roses the better.

Chapter 20

SENDING ROSES BY RAIL AND POST

Go, lovely rose !
Tell her that wastes her time on me,
That now she knows,
When I resemble her to thee
How sweet and fair she seems to be.

Every lover of flowers knows the importance of being enabled to send them safely on long journeys as messengers of love, or as replies to the possible question, "Does my old friend remember me?" It is our fortune or misfortune to receive parcels of plants and flowers daily, nine-tenths of which are so badly packed that we can make nothing of them, whether they are sent to be admired, named, judged, or to illustrate botanical problems. The remaining tenth or thereabouts are so wonderfully well packed that although days may have elapsed in the course of their transit, and the weather may have been suitable for hay-making, they come out of the package to all appearance as fresh as they went into it, and we marvel that while it is easy work to pack and post flowers for a long journey, very few amongst the many who make the endeavour succeed in the accomplishment of their heart's desire.

Flowers vary in their capabilities for travel. A spray of lapageria, bearing many of its noble thick-textured flowers, might travel in a chip box without any harm five hundred miles in the hottest weather

But a bunch of roses in the same kind of box would not hold together in a journey of fifty miles; indeed, they would shrivel and separate into their component parts before they reached the post office, if put into a chip or card-board box without moisture-holding packing on a hot summer day. The usual failing in the sending of flowers by post is packing them in dry cotton wool, which robs them of their moisture, and appears to be peculiarly adapted to rob them also of all proper form and colour, for the very worst examples that come to our hands are those packed in this absorbent material in boxes that offer no resistance to the action of heat and dry air. A rose or a truss of scarlet geranium may be regarded as affording the best possible test of skill in packing and posting flowers, for from the instant of their being cut, they are in haste to fall to pieces, unless sustained by suitable surroundings.

In order to furnish the reader with some useful information, we will suppose we are called upon to send roses of all kinds and sizes, in all sorts of ways, by post or rail, or messenger, on long and short journeys, in all sorts of weather. We shall cut a few half-expanded flowers of Austrian briers, and having placed them between three or four freshly cut leaves of Irish ivy, shall put them in a common paper envelope, and seal them up and trust them to the post without fear. A certain amount of crushing they must be subjected to, but a twelve hour's journey will not destroy their character, for the ivy leaves will hold them firmly but softly, and impart to them moisture sufficient to sustain them for many hours. Large flowers, and especially such as are of succulent texture, cannot be transmitted in this way; it is indeed adapted only to such as are scarcely more substantial than a primrose or a buttercup.

We will now gather a pretty little bunch of roses of fine quality, and adopt measures to despatch them safely a considerable distance. We shall bribe the doorkeeper of the household storeroom to find us an empty barrel of the kind that mustard, arrowroot, and other farinaceous comforts are usually packed in, both for sale and keeping. Having obtained the barrel, we shall bore a small hole in it with a bradawl at each end, and provide a length of string of a size that will pass the holes easily. The next business will be to tie the roses to the string as close together as possible, then pass one end of the string with the roses heads downwards, through the hole in the bottom of the barrel, and fill in carefully between the roses with damp moss, or fresh grass mowings, or fresh leaves of any kind, those of the privet being perhaps the most suitable. Finally draw the other end of the string through the lid, shut up the roses and tie the two ends of the string over the outside, and your flowers are prepared for a long journey. You might throw the box from hand to hand, as the Duke of Queensbury's twenty-four cricketers contrived to send a cricket ball fifty miles within the space of an hour.

Larger undertakings must be conducted on the same principle; the flowers must be fixed in the first instance, and then carefully bedded in moss, grass mowings or green leaves; the grand thing is to *prevent evaporation*. If the flowers are actually wet, they will decay at a most rapid rate; if actually dry, they will surely all to pieces. Having secured a wooden box of suitable size, it will be advisable to cut a few narrow laths to fit inside, and then proceed to pack the roses. You are not tied down to one particular mode of procedure, but will do well to take your first lesson in this wise. On the bottom of the box put a layer of fresh ivy or privet leaves, and then a layer of roses, which are to be covered with leaves very lightly. Now put one or two of the laths across to fix them firmly without pressure, and fix the laths in their places by means of brads driven from the outside. Proceed in this way until the box is filled, taking care of course to finish up with a layer of leaves in the top. When this package is nailed down, it may be tossed and kicked about in any way for days together, and the roses will come out almost as fresh as they went in. If a tin box is selected, a slight wooden cage should be made to fit it; and the flowers should be tied to the cage and be lightly bedded with leaves. If the weather be hot and the journey long, tie the flowers in bunches with fresh moss round the stems, and dip the cage and the flowers into water, and then pack with moss or leaves and despatch as soon as possible. It is better however to be content with the natural moisture of moss or leaves, than to resort to the use of water, for wet flowers long confined are almost sure to be more or less injured by decay or the outer petals. Tin foil, and oiled paper, and gutta percha paper, may be employed to advantage in packing flowers with a view to arrest evaporation, but fresh moss or privet leaves will generally suffice as preservatives, and will be rendered the more effectual, if large cabbage leaves were laid above and below the packing, so that they will not come into contact with the flowers.

From such rough and ready means of packing roses, we may turn to the properly constructed bouquet carrier, which will require more careful description, and the help of figures. We begin then with a tin box, round or square, ten inches high, and eight inches wide, in the sub-joined figures. That the lid should fit closely and lock safely are matters of evident necessity; the lid is to be perforated

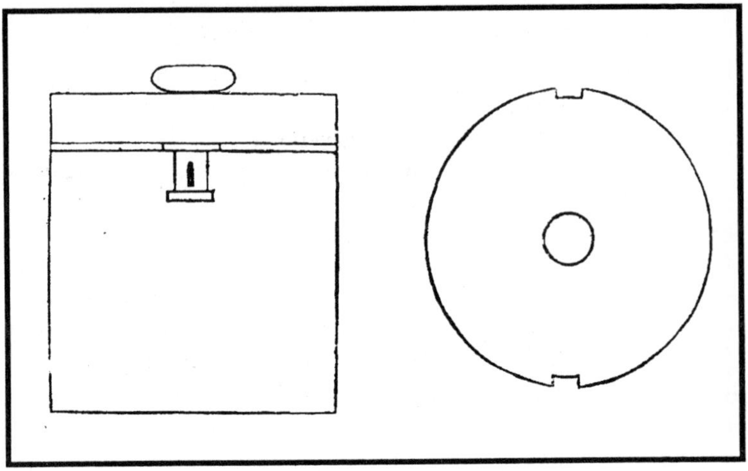

with six small holes close to the handle. There must be prepared a till tray to fit the inside, as in the second figure, which of course is adapted for a circular, box. In the centre of this tray is an aperture through which the stem of the bouquet is passed; the purpose of the tray is to keep the bouquet steady. The tray is fitted with two upright pieces of tin one inch wide soldered on the rim, and long enough to press against the lid when the tray is in its place, as at A in the next figure, two brackets are soldered to the sides of the box, as at B (see figure at next page). The bouquet is then fixed to the tray by means of two pins underneath. The tray is then lowered to rest on the brackets, and the result is such an arrangement as the sectional sketch indicates. The figure shows the bouquet standing in water, but few handfuls of fresh damp moss will suffice if the weather is cool, and the box is likely to arrive at its destination in the course of a few hours. A very slight alteration of the arrangements will make a first-rate fruit or sandwich box of this, and by taking out the tray it might be made to carry a small outfit of apparel for a pleasure tour.

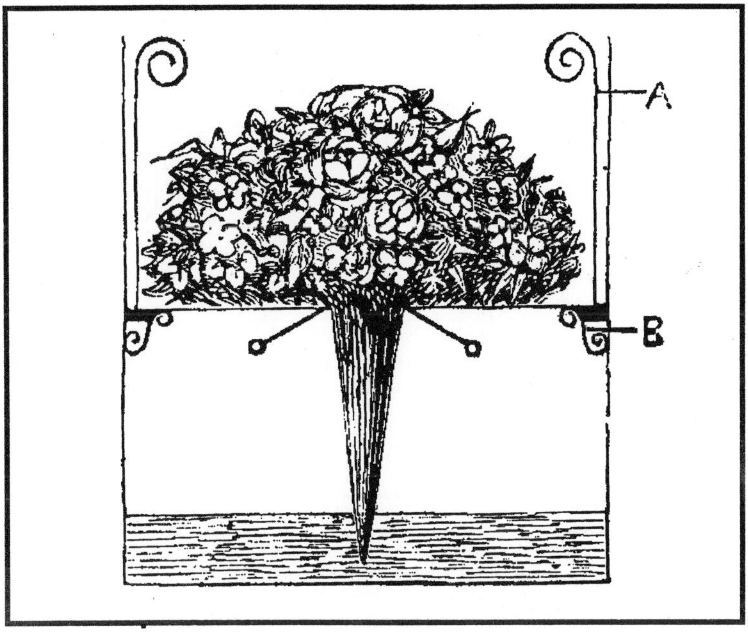

The next practice will be to provide a box to carry a number of separate cut flowers. The depth should be four inches, with handle and padlock; the tray should be made on precisely the same plan as in the former case as regards the handles (A A) that press against

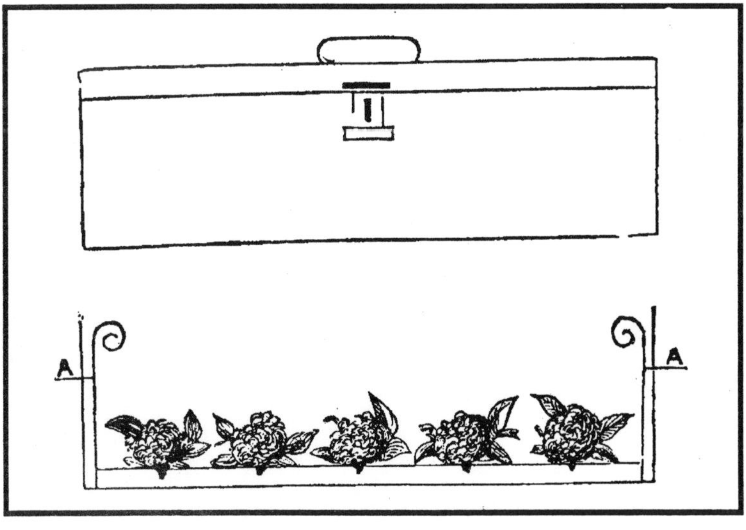

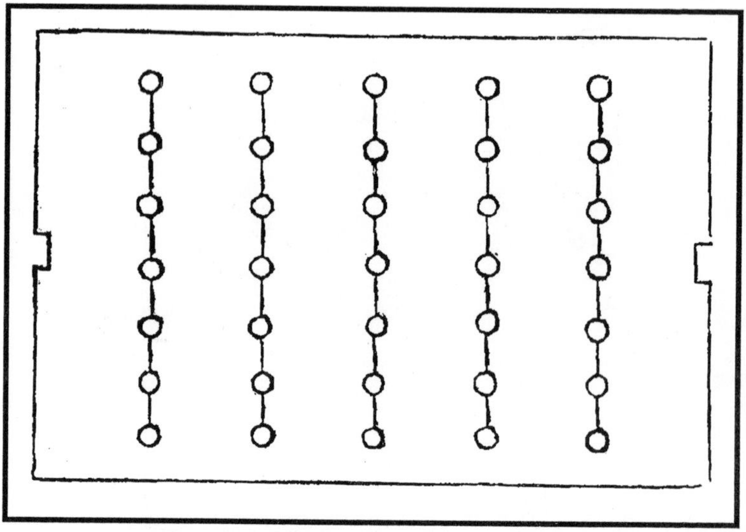

the lid, but must be pierced all over, and the holes connected by a continuous length of elastic braid. The braid is lifted with a peg, the flower inserted, the braid presses against the stalk and keeps it fast. It is of course a merely mechanical matter to enlarge this plan by having a deeper box and a series of trays, each being fitted with handles that just touch the bottom of the tray next above.

Chapter 21

ON BUYING NEW ROSES

If chess-playing develops skill in generalship, and whist educates the mind in casuistry, rose growing should surely favour the foundation of a cautious, decisive, and discriminating character. Very early in the experiences of the amateur rosarian will he become conscious of great desires and of an unaccountable faith in temporalities that are as yet unseen. Forgetting the good old roses that have weathered many a storm, and that have never suffered by comparison with flowers of later date, he will become possessed of a desire to buy the newest of the new, and will hunger for the annual lists, as he that watcheth for the morning. To advise complete renunciation of novelties would be folly, because it is one of the peculiar delights of floriculture to watch for the unfolding of new flowers at the earliest moment at which they can be obtained from the raiser's hands. The rosarian must cultivate, not roses only, but the art of saying NO, for his pursuit is encompassed with temptations, and it is always to be regretted when innocent aims and pardonable pride lead a man to illustrate the proverb which asserts that "fools and their money are soon parted". Buy the new roses, friend, if you like, but bear in mind that we have done our duty to warn you to expect in every such purchase a source of disappointment and vexation unless you have knowledge and judgment, and the courage to say "no", to guide you safely through the peril.

For many and many a years past, there have been introduced to the market some fifty or sixty new roses annually. The number of varieties offered by the French raisers has more than once of late years, reached seventy; but we may assume the average to be fifty with perfect safety. If we count up all the really good roses that have been introduced in the past ten years, and find them to amount to fifty, it will follow that in addition to these fifty good ones, there were four hundred and fifty bad ones brought into the market, and as new roses meet with a ready and extensive sale, there must have been much disappointment experienced by the purchasers. That at least one thousand roses were introduced to this country from the Continent during the past twenty years cannot be a matter of doubt; but a doubt may reasonably be entertained if amongst this immense number there are very many beyond one hundred varieties that could properly be described as of first-class quality, and hence worthy of a permanent place in the rose garden. It not unseldom happens that the new roses are in many respects inferior to varieties that they really ought to supersede in order to justify their candidature, and so if we neglect the old ones to look overmuch after the new ones, our collections will surely degenerate, and it will be found that when we thought we were going forward we were really going backward, like the gentleman on the slippery pavement who lost two steps for everyone he gained. He got home, the story says; but the rosarian who does this will get abroad and lose his way, and his chief pleasure will consist in parting with his money.

It is generally understood that we are indebted to the French raisers for new roses, but this is not so strictly correct as at first sight appears. It is true that our neighbours on the other side of the channel send us a batch of fifty or sixty annually, but the proportion of bad to good roses in these consignments is enormous. On the other hand, the English raisers annually offer a few, and these are usually good, so that as the English raisers pretty well compensate in *quality* for defect of *quantity* as compared with the French raisers, the disparity is not so great as it is generally considered. However, if a severe scrutiny were to be made, the French would win the day, notwithstanding that they continue every year to deluge the English market with rubbish described as "new roses".

It will be asked why, if there is some check on English raisers tending to the limitation of their selections of seedlings, a similar check cannot be imposed on the French raisers? The case is easily explained the Frenchmen cannot send their flowers in advance, and not many of them are seen by competent judges from this side in time to ensure sufficient guidance to the purchaser. It is therefore the custom of the nurserymen who trade in roses largely, to buy all that are offered and wait for the discovery of the relative value of their purchases. Very few amateurs venture on so hazardous a step. The experienced rosarian who buys to keep and not to sell, is principally guided in his selection by the names of the raisers and their descriptions of their novelties; for certain of the commercial rose growers on the other side are more fortunate, more particular, and more conscientious than the rest, the result being that having succeeded in raising first-class novelties, they select for sale only the most novel and distinct amongst them, and daringly sacrifice the rest, rather than tarnish a good reputation; others are in greater haste to make money, and annually send out a lot of second and third-rate seedlings, with one or two good ones amongst them to "spice up" the lot.

This being the case with the sale of imported roses here, it remains to be said that home-grown varieties, if not intrinsically better (comparing best with best), have a quite different kind of claim on the attention of the rosarian. The organizations of floriculture require our raisers to exhibit their novelties before they offer them as articles of sale to the public. Thus they pass through an ordeal of probation and criticism on their way to the market, and by the time that plants are ready and a price is named, we know something about them. As a matter of fact, the merits of new English roses are canvassed in the gardens and the exhibitions, long before the season for purchasing arrives, and although the wisest may make mistakes, the case is very different as between the purchase of "things not generally known", and things that everybody has seen and admired many times over.

It follows then that the prudent buyer of new roses will be a diligent student of trade catalogues. He will be fortified with the means of anticipating with some degree of accuracy, the ultimate value of all the new roses on offer. When we know the general character of a man's work, we can fairly guess what his next performance may be. It will be found that certain of the raisers of both our own country and France, have contributed largely to the rose garden of its choicest flowers, while others have sent but few that are good and many that are bad.

Some raisers send out novelties but rarely, and never many at one time. Generally speaking, these are to be trusted for something good. It does not follow, however, that those whose names appear more regularly, are dispensers of mere rubbish, because the larger men not only raise but purchase seedlings, and hence, if they are really conscientious in their work, their contributions may prove as important for quality as quantity.

At this point we might perhaps, to the advantage of the reader, institute some comparisons of roses in connection with the names of their raisers, to indicate as, nearly as might be, the relative positions of raisers as established by their work. In such a matter however, it is easy to do mischief, and utterly impossible to be just without "leaning a little". In a work intended to be of permanent value, the names of traders should be mentioned only when some peculiar necessity requires, and here the necessity does not arise, because the buyer of roses will derive greater advantage from comparisons of his own making than any we can provide for the purpose. Those who know nothing of catalogues or raisers and "all that sort of thing", have but to be content with established varieties, and for them the difficulty of selecting roses for the garden is completely disposed of. And when these "unlearned" amateurs wish to venture further, they may take the advice of the "Garden Oracle" or of writers in horticultural periodicals, who are known to make a study of roses and who *have no commercial interest in the sale of any of them.* A few amongst the many writers who offer counsel to rosarians, contrive to see most of the forthcoming roses while they are in flower in the seed beds, and these can speak by a better rule than guess-work; moreover, being familiar with the products of the several raisers and the reputation of each in the market, they are better enabled to judge of things they have not seen than those who have had no such training and are dependent solely on the descriptions in the trade catalogues.

Chapter 22

CURIOSITIES OF ROSE GROWING

The observant cultivator may expect considerable entertainment in the way of odds and ends, in addition to the pleasure to be anticipated as the result of the normal development of the art of rose growing. That the garden should produce an abundance of beautiful roses, answering in their characters to the panegyrics of the catalogues, is the primary object of the money and time and care bestowed upon it; but ugly roses may occur, and very curious roses, and perhaps valuable novelties, and these things will afford amusement, and in happy instances, something more. The amateur may even hope for blue roses, and black roses, and yellow moss roses, and roses flowering winter and summer without ceasing, and for the rose that Michael Angelo had in view in his immortal sonnet:

"In chaste hearts, uninfluenced by the power
Of outward change, there blooms a deathless flower
That breathes on earth the air of paradise."

There are on record many curious kinds of roses that to the superficial appear to belong properly to the land of dreams, but the wise man will not banish them thither in great haste, for history has given him abundant warning of the mischief that dodges the sceptical spirit. The Amazonian army of Diodorus Siculus passed for a fiction for centuries, but the fact was revealed at last as matter of commonplace in the hideous kingdom of Dahomey. The Unicorn has ceased to be regarded as a myth; the Leviathan is snugly housed in the Zoological Gardens; the Anthropophagi are much too plentiful; as they are also too fastidious, for the Fijian cannibals disdain cold missionary unless accompanied with tomato sauce. As for dragons, giants, and two-headed humanities, they have become so cheap that showmen have enough and to spare of them, and we may any day expect to meet a lot of them on change. The consideration of these facts should encourage the rosarian to hope for a few wonders or curiosities, and should they never come, it will be found that the exercise of patience has proved most excellent discipline.

The best blue rose that has come within our own cognizance was that seen by an amateur rosarian, and graphically, indeed pathetically, described by him in the *Gardeners' Magazine* for December 23rd, 1865. It was like some other fancy flowers, of very brief duration, and its proper home was where our friend met with it, the land of dreams. In the "Essay on Roses" of the Marquis D'Orbessan, it is stated that blue roses may be produced at will by watering the plants with a solution of indigo; the simplicity of the process is, we fear, its sole recommendation; but we must confess, with shame, that we have hot tested the efficacy of a plan that needs only a blue-bag storm from the laundry, for carrying it into effect. History affirms–so, indeed, we are told–that blue roses were grown in the gardens of the Alhambra, and the latest English catalogues of roses will be found to contain the names of several varieties that a fanciful florist might describe as blue–painting them for the express purpose with a new *couleur de rose*. The reader, curious in such matters, would of course, like to have the names of these hypothetically blue roses, and here they are: *Captain Ingram*, rich purple; *Celine Noiret*, purple shaded with rose; *Duhamel du Monceau*, rich red shaded with violet; *Elie Morel*, rosy lilac; *Exposition de Brie*, crimson shaded with purple; *Felix Genero*, rose shaded with violet; *Ferdinand de Lesseps*, purple shaded violet; *Gloire de Ducker*, dark purple; *James Veitch*, deep violet shaded with carmine; *La Fontaine*, purplish crimson; and lastly, *Unique*, a lovely blue-tinted lilac Tea rose, which occasionally, when aided by warm, cloudy, damp weather, makes a near approach to the pure blue of the delphinium. That none of these are blue in the proper sense of the term need not be insisted on; it is sufficient that they suggest the probability of the occurrence of a veritable blue rose "some day" in the future, and it may not be unreasonable to conclude that they are really as blue as those that have been described as such.

Generally speaking, the ancients found no difficulty in affecting unions, that are now regarded as impossible, as may be seen on reference to Pliny, and the second book of the Georgics. The products of the impossible unions were, of course, as curious as their parentage, and black roses were to be found amongst them in abundance. Since gardening books have been written in the English language, it has been believed and taught that the rose might be grafted on the black currant tree, and the result would be a plentiful production of black flowers. So recently as 1822, Mr. Loudon spoke of roses "quite black", as having been raised by L. Villaresii, of Monza. These have been less fortunate than the black tulips that M. Dumas celebrated in a tremendous fiction, for no, story-teller has raised them to the region of romance, and if they remain not amongst the serious facts, we shall find them amongst the prosy fancies. However, supposing we are as near black as to blue, the following list will serve to indicate the best of the blackest roses: *Baron Chauraud*, scarlet with blackish centre; *Black Prince*, well named, crimson shading to purplish black; *Cardinal Patrizzi*, crimson shading to black; *Louis Van Houtte*, red shading to blackish crimson and purple-this ought, perhaps, to be in the list of blues—*Monsieur Boncenne*, blackish purple; *Souvenir de William* Wood, the blackest of the black, a fine rose, with rich shadings of red and purple; *Xavier Olibo*, velvety black shaded with fiery red.

Making ample allowance for the vagaries of a hopeful imagination, we know of no proper reason for doubting that both blue and black roses are within the range of floral possibilities. We have a red delphinium (*D. nudicaule*), and a blue tropaelum (*T. azureum*); we have green roses, green dahlias, a green ixia; and of flowers that may be called black there is no scarcity, though we may, perhaps, soonest find examples amongst the pansies, tulips, and nemophilas. A "really black" flower does not exist, for when the petal of the blackest is held up in a strong light, it is found to be of a deep maroon or purple colour. But so long as it appears black when viewed as an opaque body, it is black, and may be described "as really black". It may be that the extremes of colour in the roses known to the modern rosarian, were also known from the earliest date at which the flower was cultivated, for we have no reason to suppose the flower more variable now than it was thousands of years ago. In such a case, our interest centres in the description rather than the fact, and we may hand over the subject to the grammarian, and consider that the horticulturist has fairly done with it. But, on the other hand, if we pin our faith to words and conclude, that amongst the many varieties of roses that have been necessarily and inevitably lost, were some that surpassed the most distinctive blues and blacks of the present day, then the problem falls into the hands of the experimental cultivator, whose hope it must be to recover from chaos, by systematic hybridizing and crossing, the treasures that time has devoured.

As compared with many other flowers that have been long in cultivation, the rose is certainly not particularly sportive. A few–very few–of the named varieties have originated as sports, but the majority, no one can doubt, are veritable seedlings. The commonest of sports is the occurrence of stripes and blotches on a flower that should be self coloured. As a rule, these sports are too indecisive to be regarded otherwise than as defects, and when they happen to be worth perpetuating, it is difficult to keep them, even by propagating from the buds nearest the sportive flower, or the wood that bears it. We frequently receive blotched and mottled flowers for opinion of their merits, and we invariably advise instant propagation from the shoots that produced the sports, but rarely is the same or a similar flower seen again, except as an original sport, which in its turn will probably pass away. Undesirable sports are more common than pretty ones, and may be produced with some degree of certainty, whereas the pretty ones come in their own way, and it appears to be impossible to command them.

The question will here arise, to what extent may cultivation be made to promote variation, without resorting to the practice of raising seedlings? There are several methods proposed, and we will first consider the most simple. This consists in overfeeding the plant by means of strong manures and abundance of water. If carried to a certain point, it will simply kill the roses, but if kept within the destructive line, it will certainly cause them to produce flowers out of character, and these will for the most part be ugly, though they will probably be curious. We will endeavour to prescribe a safe course of action. Prepare for a bed by taking out the soil to the depth of two feet. Fill the excavation by first laying down a fat manure from the pigstye. Upon this lay a mixture of turfy loam and fat stable manure, about half-rotten, up to the depth of fifteen inches, and then plant, keeping the roots as high up as possible, and covering them with fine dry soil, and finish by treading them in carefully. Now put on a thin coating of quit rotten manure, two or three inches deep. The plantation will now be above the level, but will soon sink below it, and allow room for successive heavy top dressings with fat manure, and of these there must be no stint. Any time before the end of March prune severely, leaving only two or three buds to every strong shoot. Towards the end of April give a heavy watering. Repeat the watering the first week in May. In the last week of May give another heavy watering, and this time add to the water genuine Peruvian guano, or good phospho-guano, at the rate of one ounce to one gallon. All through June and July give copious supplies of water; using plain soft water alternately with the solution of guano, for if that be administered constantly, it will cause death in the ranks. At the end of July cease watering for the season, to afford the trees some chance of ripening the gross shoots, of which they will have begun to make plenty. If, however, you are fired with ambition to obtain knowledge at any price, continue the treatment, or instead of using guano water, supply them with fine old port, at about ninety shillings a dozen. The result in this case, probably, will be that you will lose your roses *Moderata durant*.

One of the results of a moderate plethoric treatment will be a tremendous growth. You may enjoy surprise at that, but you will expect something more surprising. If you continue the treatment through two seasons, you will not be disappointed. In the first instance, you will have some flowers wonderful for size and beauty, especially if you thin judiciously. Such varieties as *Madame Domage*, *Madame Boll*, *John Hopper*, and *Colonel de Rougenmont*, will endeavour to fill a hat-box with a single flower, and nearly succeed, but *you* must provide the hat-box. But some other curious results may be looked for. Flowers will appear with huge coarse petals spreading out like cabbage leaves or young pantiles, and enclosing tufts of green stuff like tangled knots of Berlin wool. Fortune is now smiling on you through the medium of these green eyed monsters, some of which will throw out leaves, or better still, produce supplementary and supernumerary (but we will not say superfluous) shoots, bearing smaller roses—that is to say, amongst the deformed flowers, some will be proliferous, the flower itself giving birth to other flowers and on rare occasions these monstrous growths will have some amount of beauty. You must derive as much enjoyment as possible from such curiosities, because, unless you carry the business in a very secret manner, you will be accused of having paid a high price to make a burlesque of a pleasant pastime, and only inward satisfaction can compensate you for having become a target for the shafts of sarcasm. But having thus learned how to produce green-centred and proliferous roses, you will know how to prevent their occurrence, for, as a matter of fact, they rarely occur when manurial matters are applied judiciously.

We have now to speak of another method by which it is alleged that new varieties may be obtained. In the *Revue Horticole*, 1870, appeared an article from the pen of M. Du Breuil, in which the veteran horticulturist suggested a definite plan for ensuring the production of striped and spotted flowers of varieties that are normally self coloured. He says: "In the month of July ,1867 , I visited, at Bagnères-de-Bigorre, the garden of a great amateur of trees and flowers. He showed me several standard roses, and amongst them Géant des Batailles, of which, on some trees all the flowers (which were of a fine deep red), were marked with numerous spots of pale rose-colour. I observed the same peculiarity in other varieties of a light red, such as General Jacqueminot. All these rose trees in other respects were in a very fine condition of growth, and presented all the other characters of the varieties to which they belonged. The proprietor assured me that this variegation was constant, and that the trees which I saw had then been eight years budded. He also assured me that the peculiarity was perpetuated by budding. What could be the cause of this singularity ? M. X. informed me that, being obliged some years ago, for want of better, to take from the bottom of a shoot some shield-buds which apparently had no eyes, he nevertheless obtained from them a shoot which produced a rose-bush of which all the flowers presented the peculiarity I have just mentioned. He attributed this abnormal colouring to the imperfect condition of the bud employed. He repeated the same experiment, obtained the same result, and now produces this variegation whenever he pleases to do so, by the process which has just been described. The origin of this phenomenon may, I think, be explained thus: Although the leaves at the bottom of a shoot have no apparent eyes, they nevertheless exist in a rudimentary state under the epidermis. The disturbance to which they are subjected in the removal of the bud suspends their development, by depriving them for a time of the nutritive fluid which they received. This suspension of their natural course of development produces a certain derangement of their mechanism, which afterwards manifests itself in the abnormal colouring of the flowers. Something analogous takes place when cuttings of pear or apple trees bearing unexpanded flower- buds are used for grafts. The fruits which these produce are always more or less deformed, and this deformity is more marked. in proportion to the rudimentary condition of the flower-buds when the graft is made. I have no pretensions to infallibility; I think, however, that, with regard to the explanation of the indisputable facts which I have witnessed, I am not very far from the truth, and I further invite the attention of physiologists to this question".

The selection of incipient buds, recommended by M. Du Breuil, is probably the mode adopted by the Honourable Signor Zenone Zea, of Venice, who was reported to have obtained new varieties of roses by simple grafting. Much—perhaps, too much—was heard of the operations of this gentleman; but hitherto nothing has been properly seen. The results of the process have apparently been as carefully concealed as the *modus operandi*, and all the evidence we have of its efficiency consists in the somewhat vague affirmation of Professor di Visiani, and Doctor Zanardini, who were appointed by the Royal Institution of Venice, to report upon the subject. A translation of the full text of their report will be found in the *Gardeners' Magazine* for March 8th, 1873: the essence of it may be conveyed in a few words. It is stated that Signor Zea practises shield-budding, and obtains flowers very different in form, in tint, and in certain markings of a very intense colour. The reporters summarize the results as follows:

1. "That in the second, and still more so in the third year, when the grafts become stronger and more vigorous, the markings are much more pronounced and the colours generally brighter, as we saw in other older varieties obtained by him in the same way, the markings of which were very decided and the colours truly brilliant.
2. That the varieties so obtained remain constant when layered or grafted by cleft-grafting or shield-budding in the ordinary way.

3. That if they are lost they can be reproduced by repeating the operation under similar conditions.
4. That all varieties of roses do not give equally good results. Some give varieties of finer come and better marked than others.

Being unacquainted with those portion the process beyond that of ordinary shield-budding; bound to confine ourselves to a simple attestation of the fact, that the blooms seen by us were very different from those on the branches from which the buds were taken.

Signor Zea, in his letter, has shown himself disposed to communicate his method of operation to this institution. This would be very desirable, as it is only when the process is known that we can look to science for a possible explanation of the results so obtained".

An exhaustive chapter on the curiosities of rose growing, would probably exhaust the patience of the reader, and will not here be attempted. In order to keep the subject within reasonable limits, we shall conclude with a proposal for a curious and not ignoble feature of the rose garden. Procure first a lot of English briers, ranging over ten feet in height, and plant them in pairs, five feet apart, on either side of a walk, which should be at least, six or seven feet wide. Draw them together at the top to form a close arcade, and graft them by the common side graft. When they are well united, bud them with free growing Noisettes to form a flowery roof, and in due time you will have a bower of roses of the grandest possible character, such as, perhaps, you would not find by Bendemeer's stream. Another mode of procedure might be adopted to form a berceau bower. For this purpose, plant the tall briers three feet apart, and cross them herring-bone fashion, or in such a way as to form a line in which the letter **X** would be continuously repeated. They would have to be grafted together at the point of junction, and would require the support of stout stakes, or of an iron fence for two seasons, after which they would hold each other up, and defy the tempest. In this case, Noisettes would be quite suitable for "crowning the edifice", but we should prefer the most showy perpetuals. Such practice as this is only to be thought of in a district peculiarly favourable to rose growing, for gigantic briers are not plentiful, and when obtained, must have the advantage of a strong deep soil and a genial climate, or they will very soon undergo a process of shortening without the aid of the knife. In a particularly kind climate a bower walk or arcade could be soon produced and long kept by means of own-root Teas and Noisettes, and, of course, the most vigorous growers should be selected. The secret of success would consist in securing a few exceedingly strong shoots in the first instance, and crossing and grafting these to form a herring-bone wall, from which overhead the flowering growth should be produced abundantly.

Chapter 23

REMINDERS OF MONTHLY WORK

January

During frosty weather is a good time to have manure wheeled on for top-dressing the plantations. During open weather spread it over the surface and fork or rather "prick" it in, and in doing so be careful not to tear or cut the roots of the roses. If the roses are in regular rows, it is a good plan to open a trench eighteen inches deep midway between every two rows, and half fill the trench with manure and return the earth, then proceed to lightly fork the rest of the ground so as to slightly cover the general coating of manure. This is not usually a good time to plant roses, but a good season to get the ground ready for planting next month.

In the rose-house pruning and top dressing may be proceeded with, and a little heat must be allowed during very severe weather.

February

Get all planting done as early as possible, and when all are trodden up and finished, lay on a mulch of half rotten dung two or three inches deep to protect the roots from frost. If the dressing of the plantations was neglected last month, let it be done now; and when any plants appear sickly or deficient of vigour take them up, and remove to reserve ground; or, having pruned them root and branch, introduce some good turfy loam and rotten manure well broken over the stations, and replant without delay. Roses received from the nursery during frost, should be placed in a, dry dark cellar, without unpacking them, till the frost is gone. If received during bright open weather, unpack them directly, dip their roots in a puddle of clay, soot, and cow dung, beaten into a thick paint, and get them planted, staked, and mulched without delay. Towards the end of the month begin to prune the Provence, Moss, French, and Alba roses.

In the rose-house get all pruning and top dressing finished, and give air as often as possible, to prevent weakly growths.

March

Consider first what arrears are to be made good, and remember that if we have a long period of dry weather with east winds, every rose that has not been properly attended during the winter will suffer. Proceed with the pruning taking the Hybrid China and Hybrid Bourbon first, next the Hybrid Perpetuals, Bourbon, and the hardiest of the Noisettes. Tie out those that grow in a stiff upright manner to keep the heads open and handsome. This is a good time to plant dwarf roses out of pots, provided they have been kept very cool and, airy through the winter. If they have been kept growing and are full of bright green leaves, do not plant them for at least another month.

In the rose house examine every plant, and where you see a curled leaf hunt till you discover the cause of it, either maggot or fly. If much fly shut the house up close, give no water, and fumigate. Next morning syringe early and give no air till the leaves are partially dried, then give air as usual. Two days after fumigate again, whether you see fly or not. Syringe as before. By this treatment you will have no more fly for at least a month, perhaps no more all the season. Train out specimens in pots, be careful not to snap the wood in bringing the branches down.

April

Continue pruning, finishing up with Tea-scented, China, and Noisette. If the beds mulched during winter look unsightly through the predominance of straw in the material, sprinkle over it just enough fine earth to cover it. If any newly-planted roses have not yet been mulched, do it at once, it will possibly prevent some losses, and certainly dc good to all. If drought prevails for any length of time water heavily, and again in five or six days unless rain comes. Towards the end of the month is the best time in the whole year to plant out small plants from pots to form beds and groups of dwarf Hybrid Perpetuals, Chinas, Bourbons, etc. Be sure the plants are first well hardened, and if recently received from a nursery, keep them in an airy pit a week, then place them on a sheltered border for a week, then plant them.

In the rose-house many plants will now be coming into bloom, and air must be given with care to ensure a sturdy growth, and yet avoid any check, for the bright days are sometimes bleaker than the sunless ones. Give plenty of water, and try the borders to make sure that they are moist throughout.

May

Insects will abound among roses in the open air, and the only way to deal with them is to search them daily, and wherever there is a leaf curled discover the cause. No fear of fly yet out of doors. Where the heads are crowded thin the new shoots by pinching out, and, whether crowded or not, pinch out all shoots growing inwards and in positions and directions likely to spoil the symmetry of the heads. Suckers will begin to appear and must be removed. This is a good time to look over all the tallies and renew them where needful. If very dry weather give the rosery one very heavy soaking, and repeat in a week or so, unless there is a good fall of rain.

In the rose-house fumigate if the least occasion for it, for aphides propagate rapidly now unless swift destruction overtakes them in their youth. In the case of mildew give plenty of air, plenty of water at the roots, and dust with flour of sulphur when the leaves are damp. Trees op walls require to be smartly syringed night and morning.

June

Aphis will probably. abound out of doors, and the best remedy will be water. Ply them with the full force of one of Read's or Warner's engines every evening, and if this does not dislodge, and scatter, and, exterminate the vermin, resort to the use of tobacco powder or tobacco water. If practised in the use of the engine you will have no difficulty in wetting every leaf. As tobacco and all other infusions discolour the foliage, give plain water a fair trial first. There is nothing more certain to destroy aphis than immersion in water heated to 150° F., it is even more effectual than tobacco. To promote a fine bloom give water copiously two or three times a week, and thin out the buds where they cluster thickly, using for the purpose a small pair of scissors. The weight of the flowers will soon try the trees, so see that they are staked safely. Tie in the shoots from buds entered last summer, and if bloom buds show nip them out. By judicious stopping, fine heads may be formed this season, so as to fit the trees for good places in the rosery next year. Begin budding wherever the bark rises freely and suitable buds can be got, the saving of a few weeks in entering the bud is sometimes equivalent to the saving of a whole season in the growth after budding.

The rose-house must be freely ventilated night and day, and be abundantly supplied with water. Prune the roses that are out of bloom, and prepare them for flowering again in the autumn.

July

Before any of the early blooms are past go over the whole stock catalogue in hand and see if the tallies are right, and determine the characters of new varieties as better or worse than old ones in the same class of form and colour. Budding on briers out of doors is the great business of the month. During dull, rainy, close weather neglect everything else to get as many buds in as possible. The manner in which the several varieties bloom will afford better lessons on ever culture and especially on prunning then all the barks that were written. Gather all the fading flowers daily, place the petals in open baskets in a shady place to dry, and let the ladies have them for their perfume jars. If you desire seed of any variety allow a few of the first blooms to expand, remove all the rest, give the tree no water and leave the rest to nature and to fate. If you impregnate with selected pollen, tie the impregnated flower in a right muslin bag. To induce, any particular variety to seed, keep it on poor diet and give it very little water, the blooms will then come comparatively single, and will furnish or receive pollen, as may be desired. If the flower intended to receive the pollen is not open at the same time as the father flower, the pollen may be taken off with a dry camel's-hair pencil, and be preserved between silver paper till required.

In the rose-house give air night and day, deluge the place it with water, train in all this season's growth; do not shade, except for special reasons, as when yellow roses are just opening, then a little shade is good. Assist the Teas with some good fertilizer on the surface to help them in the autumn bloom. There is nothing so good as half rotten dung, but as it is unsightly, a mixture of guano and wood ashes is to be preferred, and it should be carefully pricked in.

August

Continue budding; all the brier stocks not fit hitherto will now take buds nicely. Loosen the ties of those first budded. Manettis will take buds at the end of the month. In the early part of the month put in cuttings of short nearly ripe shoots, and also of shoots that have flowered. In all cases keep cuttings and eyes alive and fresh by sprinkling their tops frequently rather than making the soil they are in very wet, they will in fact callus quicker if the soil is nearly dry.

In the rose-house give air night and day, and abundance of water. Where flower buds show plentifully thin them. Pot roses should be looked to, as the time has arrived for repotting or top dressing them to prepare for an early bloom.

September

Finish all budding as soon as possible. Loosen the ties of those budded early, taking notice if there is a pretty good junction between bud and stock, in which case tie again loosely, merely to protect from the atmosphere; if no apparent junction tie again. Some growers cut the tie at the back and leave it to fall away by the swelling of the bud, which it does in time, but not usually until it has done some mischief by resisting the swelling of the wood. Better to untie and tie again than to leave the bud to fight it out. This is the principal season for budding Manettis. At the end of the month put cuttings in the open borders or in pits, where they are to remain all winter.

In the rose-house there will now be a grand display of the lovely blooms of Teas, and perhaps of mildew, in which case give plenty of water and frequent dustings of sulphur. Give air now with caution, as the dull cold days may injure the bloom, but as a rule ventilate freely.

October

Continue to put in cuttings in the open ground. Prepare for making new plantations, and have the ground ready for planting next month. The best way to secure immediate effect is to purchase strong plants that have flowered in nursery quarters, and have them transplanted in November. Make up the list of varieties now, and let all earthwork and manuring be finished as quickly as possible. The reports in the journals of the last season's rose-shows, will be a great help in determining what additions to make to the rosarium, but better than any learned opinions of the merits of roses is your own opinion after having seen them yourself. A few well-firmed plants with ripe wood may be selected from the rosery and taken up for potting. Pot them at once, prune them hard, and put them in a cold frame with the pots plunged to the rim till wanted to force.

In the rose-house alterations and repairs may be made. It is a good time to renew and to plant borders. Pot roses must be under cover, and if not required to flower early, must be kept cool and airy.

November

Planting is the work of the season, but it must only be done when the soil is comparatively dry; if the weather is unfavourable, lay the plants in by the heels and wait for better times. Get in briers and Manettis, and plant in nursery rows for operating on next season. Earth up the dwarf teas, by drawing sufficient soil about them to bury the shoots of the previous season to a depth of about six inches.

In the rose-house planting and pruning may be carried on, and pot roses must be got into shape and otherwise prepared for next season's work.

December

It is best not to protect any of the tender roses until they have felt a little frost. But take care it is but little, and having given them a taste, protect with loose, light, dry materials which admit of being quickly removed. See that all the standards are safely staked, as if they rock about during gales they will be greatly injured. Newly planted roses should be mulched at once.

In the rose-house put the first batch in to force, always beginning, if possible, with Common Cabbage and a few of the Teas, as they bear early forcing best of any. Be very cautious in employing heat, for a sudden rise of the temperature will cause the buds to fall unopened. A dry heat will bring green fly and red spider, therefore promote a genial humidity as the heat is increased.

Chapter 24

THE ROSE SHOW

And what a wilderness of flowers !
It seem'd as though from all the bowers
And fairest fields of all the year,
The mingled spoils were scattered here.

—Moore

The Rose Show is a modern institution, and one of the most successful of its class. Its rapid and unchecked development affords the best argument for its necessity and usefulness, and suggests that were it possible to blot it out of existence suddenly, the loss would be deeply and painfully felt. Probably the subject is as well adapted to afford matter for profitable speculation to the moral philosopher, as to the florist, who feels that his pursuits and recreations play their part in modifying the complexion of society, although in promoting and preparing a flower show he may have no ambition whatever to initiate an agency for any except strictly floral purposes. Whatever may have been the effect on what we call civilization, of the special exhibitions of roses that are now so common, it is certain that they have operated in a most decisive and beneficial manner in the promotion of rose growing, the splendour of the rose as thus displayed, making impressions that books were all unequal to, and that were not to be expected even from the ordinary aspects of the rose garden in the height of the season. Institutions that may be classed as "fashionable", are not unseldom ephemeral, and at the best many avow their dislike of them, and interruptions of their prosperity may reasonably be anticipated. Now the rose show belongs to the category of "fashionable" entertainments, but it was never known in the course of the 36 years that have elapsed since their first establishment, that any sane person has had the courage to avow a dislike of them, or that a single failure has occurred. The beginning was humble enough, but the start once made in the metropolis, was quickly imitated in other towns, and the probability is all in favour of the increase, rather than the diminution of such gatherings, for amateurs of roses increase in numbers rapidly and the augmentation of the ranks is not accompanied with any perceptible decline of enthusiasm.

The founder of the rose show was the Right Rev. the Dean of Rochester (Rev. S. Reynolds Hole). There is no more ardent lover of the rose, and no better judge of its exhibition qualities, and no one more expert in its cultivation, than this huge veteran florist, who occasionally makes the playful boast, that he is the "greatest clergyman of the Church of England." Dean Hole has told his own story in his delightful "Book about Roses." Our business is to treat the rose show from our own point of view, and in the hope of rendering some service to the amateur.

The experiment with which Dean Hole led the way, consisted in forming an association called "The National Rose Show", the first exhibition of which took place in St. James's Hall, on the 1st of July , 1858. The surprise, the delight, and the promise of this novel entertainment, filled the public mind with the happy consciousness that *a new pleasure had been discovered*. The success was complete, but it was not the less owing to the wise heads and willing hands of those amongst whom the world was divided, than to the exquisite beauty of the display, and the absolute newness of its distinctive features. The second National Rose Show was held in Hanover Square Rooms, on the 23rd of June, 1859, when the contributions represented no less than twenty English counties. In 1860, the year when the sun lost his way, and Jupiter Pluvius held a four months' jubilee, the National Rose Show was held in the Crystal Palace, on the 12th of July, and thenceforward, rose shows were multiplied, and generally speaking, the plan prepared by Dean Hole in the first instance, was adopted as the basis of them all. The most important of these gatherings are those which occur annually in the Crystal Palace and two provincial centres under the auspices of the National

Rose Society; and those held at Gloucester, Helensburgh, Hereford, Manchester, Reigate, Richmond, and Worksop, by local societies. Let us suppose we have found our way to a rose show for the first time. If the affair has only average merit, we shall be agreeably startled. There will be a broad table of great length furnished on both sides with stands of cut roses of all colours, forming two distinct banks of the most glorious flowers. The crowd press to the ropes and contend–not unkindly-for front places, and those who obtain them scan the flowers eagerly as they pass slowly along: on every hand may be seen note-books in use, while everywhere may be heard exclamations of wonder and admiration and ecstacy. As for note-books, indeed, they are to be seen in use in all festive gatherings of a public nature, but never in such plenty or for such earnest use as at a rose show. Take warning from the fact, brother, to have your labels nicely written when you send your roses to the show; for the admirers of your flowers may be pressed and hustled, and required by the imperious policeman to "pass on", at the very moment when the names of a choice twenty-four are being entered in the note-book, with perhaps your name as the happy owner of them.

When the long lines of lovely flowers and excited and delighted faces of their admirers, have made their proper impression on you, and the rich spicy odour that pervades the place has not yet begun to satiate the sense, you will begin to consider the matter critically, and from that moment the world of roses will begin to expand and will soon become too vast for easy grasping. If you will condescend to recognise the writer of this as companion for awhile, with free license to talk at you as well as with you, some things may be noted that would escape your attention, and that some day you might sigh for a knowledge of, because of their appertaining to the public love of the Queen of Flowers.

Why are there no pot roses at this show? As a matter of fact, there may be a few and we shall have to find them, but the first glance shows that pot roses do not constitute a distinctive feature. This you will say is a mistake, and in a certain sense it is; but if we may speak in a way that sounds irreverent, but is really not so, we would observe that the mistake is not man's but Nature's. It is an interesting fact that classes have been many times provided for pot roses at summer rose shows, and a good exhibition of plants has never once rewarded the brave spirits who invited them. The delicate leafage and exquisitely folded flowers of first class specimen roses can only be obtained in the days of spring by means of slow forcing most judiciously conducted. By the time the open garden supplies flowers for exhibition, pot roses are past their best, and it is rather by accident than design when a collection is seen at a rose show in a condition of freshness and richness to justify their being there. Now, here is a task for the enthusiast who loves to begin with a difficulty, to establish pot roses as a normal feature of the summer exhibitions.

The rush that ensued when the barriers were removed and the judges retired, has now given place to an orderly inspection, and we shall find it pleasant work to admire and criticise the individual flowers. As you wish to make notes for your own particular use, it will be well to have a look at the twelves and forty-eights while you and they are fresh, for they will teach you more to begin with than the seventy-twos and ninety-sixes. To obtain first place in a good competition in the forty-eight class, requires really wonderful flowers. The trade lots will probably be the best, because the trade grower has thousands or trees to select from, and he and his men are adepts in the business. As a rule, nine times in ten, nay, ninety-nine times in a hundred, a first prize forty-eight will consist of sorts everyone of which the amateur rosarian should have, whether new or old, or of whatever colour. There may be half a dozen good stands of forty-eight and a dozen or more of twelve, and from these you may select with little fear of making a mistake, for of course when you come to boxes dotted with things like ragged button covers, or rosettes that have been crushed in an election squabble, you will pause in note making and push on to see something better. At every rose show, however good as a whole, you will be sure to see some collections that surprise by their smallness, raggedness, and impurity; but laugh not at them, for they represent a gentle hope and an honourable pride. You will find that they are the contributions of amateurs who have everything to learn. They have been overjoyed with their roses at home; they have been fired with ambition to win prizes with them. They have, with trembling hands and throbbing hearts, entered the lists, and only now, when it is too late to avert disappointment, do they truly know how high the standard is, and how conspicuous are their own shortcomings. The big classes and the special classes will furnish us with the names of many fine varieties that we did not meet with in the smaller groups, and if we give up note making when we arrive at these, we shall perhaps enjoy them all the more, for a first-class seventy-two, ranging nicely in boxes of the same make, and put up as a seventy-two man, that is to say, as a first-class trader grower can put them up, is a sight for the Gods. And we shall find boxes filled with *A.K. Williams*, or *Marechal Niel*, or *Madame Cusin*, or *Perle de Lyon*, or *La France*, or *Marchioness of Londonderry*, and we shall be bound to linger over them and remember that we came here to enjoy ourselves.

In the course of your comparisons you will meet with certain varieties again and again, and the repetition will not tie you. Bad roses do not appear frequently in first and second prize groups, but good ones do, and those few that appear everywhere may be booked with safety as the best of roses. Now we have made note of many such, and have thus far dealt with things seen; but what of things unseen? What of roses known to fame, of which we fail to find examples? Here arises one of the delights of the rosarian critic. He has been looking for *Isabella Sprunt*, or *Madame Margottin*, or the almost blue Unique, or the winter-flowering moss that was whispered about, or the yellow perpetual that was actually described in the papers. Why are none of these here? Really, brother, a prompt answer to the question is not ready; but how likely it is that on this particular date in this particular season, none of them are fit for show, and that is the reason nobody has presented them. Matter for reflection and inquiry here. We shall meet some of the veterans presently, and the talk will be all of roses, so we will hope to hear about these absent ones, whether they have been "cast as rubbish to the void", or are simply out of time, and hence unpresentable.

Not less interesting than roses of renown that do not appear, are those that are known to nobody, and that on particular occasions startle everybody by their splendid qualities, and especially by their aid in finishing a grand twenty-four or forty-eight. At the Royal Horticultural Society's Rose Show at Bath, in 1873, there appeared in the great trade class arose labelled "Marquise de Gibot". The judges quickly singled it out, the reporters made note of it, and soon afterwards the amateurs crowded round the stand containing it, and it was booked by hundreds as a rare and glorious find. Who raised it? When was it sent out? were the questions that over-ruled all others throughout the continuance of the show, and at luncheon and dinner tables afterwards, and again at night, when the florists met over grog and cigars, and found the labours and enjoyments of the day sufficient food for merriment. When we turned to our catalogues next day we found that *Marquise de Gibot* had been out some years, and had fallen into obscurity through lack of first-class merit; its splendid appearance on this occasion being somewhat of a fluke, or, at all events, an illustration of the axiom that every rose has its season.

Observe, now, in the very stand before us, a smallish neatly-folded, nicely-finished rose, of an exquisite plum colour, enriched by shades that tend here to rich vinous purple, there to deepest indigo blue. It is a marvellous bit of colouring, and, of course, we shall book the name, Louis XIV. Nowhere else in all the show does this lovely purple rose appear, and the fact, if our axiom is sound, affords a hint that it is not to be depended on, for whoever could cut such a flower would not fail to take advantage of it for a twenty-four or forty-eight. The advent of Louis XIV is quite fresh in our recollection; we "bought it in", as the gardeners say, with others of its season, and in due time secured a nice lot of plants. Alas! it proved to be one of the shyest varieties ever seen; its flowers were like angels' visits, and notwithstanding its exquisite beauty, we were glad to exchange away our plants, reserving only one, just to keep it in the list as a lovely curiosity. If you enquire into the case of varieties rarely seen you will certainly gain useful information, and you will soon learn that a rose is not of necessity to be condemned because it is rarely shown, for some of the most useful roses are simply not good enough for show, and others flower at a time when the shows have not commenced or are all over.

It is time we had a look at the new roses. Were we companioning an adept instead of chaperoning a beginner, we should probably have sought out the new roses first of all, to make sure of seeing them at their best, and before the first sense of fatigue began to tell on our powers of comparison. The first thing to be done is to count up the classes and look for the contributions, so as to understand in the first instance how far the new varieties are numerically represented. You see we have eight lots of twelve of the newest; three collections, comprising the new roses of the past three years; and a considerable number of competitions in particular varieties. To get at something useful quickly, we may adopt the same rule as before, that is, take note of the sorts that are most frequently repeated. It will be observed that in everyone of the eight twelves, four varieties are repeated, and in three out of the eight no less than seven varieties are repeated, and this favoured seven includes the still more-favoured four.

We may conclude that the seven are good, or they would not be so frequently presented. The concurrence of exhibitors in their favour is a most important point, for it is evident that in seven different gardens, widely separated, these were capable of supplying, on the day of the show, flowers of fine quality. Having compared the new varieties amongst each other, we must also compare them with old varieties of the highest renown in their several sections and classes. For example, here is a grand new yellow rose, of which two samples are shown in two separate stands; in one case it is described as a Noisette, and in the other as a Tea. We will have a good look at it and get it well into our heads, and then go over yonder and have a look at the best blodms of *Maréchal Niel, Perle de Lyon*, and *Celine Forestier*. Here is a delicious Perpetual in the way of *Marie Baumann*; let us carry it in our mind's eye to that established beauty, and compare and judge. We must moreover judge them as they stand without the aid of comparisons with particular varieties. Can you find a yellow eye in the centre of that huge camellia-like crimson flower? Has that pretty white a pale or dark leafage? Is it, think you, a Perpetual as the label describes it, or something else? Look at these commonplace flowers that have not one quality to distinguish them as valuable novelties; we will book them all as bad, and if any of them turn out good, as perhaps they may, we shall fear no reproaches from within or without, for we judged them as they appeared, by the best samples the best cultivators could put upon the table. Keep in mind what a new rose should be, considering what roses we already possess; be not led away by mere prettiness, and in any and every case take note of the growth, for if that is weak and wiry, the variety, however attractive, is only too likely to turn out comparatively worthless.

In due time we shall see in the horticultural papers the reports of the experts, and then we will compare them with our own notes and remembrances. We shall find, perhaps, that we have made some mistakes, and we may discover not a few mistakes on the other side, for even the papers are fallible, reporting is usually done in a hurry, and in proportion as a pursuit is followed as a matter of business, the genuine enthusiasm that begot it fades away; hence the observations of a genuine amateur are often far more accurate and discriminating than those of the most experienced and eclectic of literary florists.

LABELS FOR ROSE TREES

It is of the utmost importance to keep rose trees neatly and effectually labelled. The common wood tallies used for the purpose answer for a time, but if they are not periodically looked over and renewed before the wood decays or the writing is obliterated, it is only too probable that the names of the roses will be lost, and no small part of the delight they should afford will cease with the disappearance of the names. A large collection can be kept in order effectually by means of a catalogue with numbers attached to the names, the trees having labels bearing corresponding numbers. Names are ephemeral, numbers are permanent. We may for example have cast out Great Western long ago, and if so, the label bearing the name has ceased to be of any use. But if that variety was entered as No. 9, we shall find a use still for No.9 label, and if the numbering and cataloguing plan be adopted, it will be worth while to have substantial metal labels bearing the numbers in strong relief. There are many kinds of metal plant labels in the market, but none to surpass in hardness, neatness, legibility, and cheapness, the Shakespearian Labels, made by Mr. Smith, of Stratford-on-Avon. These can be provided with names as well as numbers, and of every shape and size that fancy or convenience may suggest.

The best material for attaching all kinds of labels is copper wire of about the thickness of this line ▬. If very thin it is apt to cut; if too stout, it is difficult to twist it with the fingers; and it is waste of money to provide wire so stout that pliers or pincers are required in using it. The soft stuff called "horticultural wire" is worse than useless, for it perishes quickly and lets the label fall to rot or be trodden into the ground.

The cheapest label, and one that may be considered indestructible, is made of zinc, and written upon by means of a quill pen and a prepared ink. A new sheet of zinc should be obtained for the purpose, and it should be cut up into convenient lengths, the corners nicely rounded off and a hole pierced at one end for the wire. In respect of making the inscription, there are at least half-a-dozen modes of accomplishing it, but the simplest of all, and not the least effective, is to proceed as follows: Prepare a solution of, blue vitriol, so weak that when you write with it on hard white paper it makes only a pale blue mark. Scrub the labels with fine sand or pounded brick with a little moisture. When dry write upon them, and the moment they are written plunge them in clear water, and wave them about in it, and put them aside to dry. Those who prefer a more complicated process may proceed as follows: Take half an ounce of verdigris, half an ounce of salammoniac, and a quarter of an ounce of lamp-black. Pound them in a mortar, and stir up with five ounces of water. This ink is to be applied with a quill pen. We employ labels of this kind for trees and shrubs, taking care every year to examine them all, and loosen the wires of such as require it.

The small wooden labels that are tied up in bundles in red tape and sold in the city shops are very neat and very bad. The clear white face upon them is produced by smearing them with strongly-sized whiting, on which the inscription is to be placed. The rain washes off the whiting and the writing together, and the label is made a blank for evermore. Those who buy ready-made labels should ensure having them whitened with lead, or without any such finishing at all. Old wooden tallies may be put into use again by slivering off the surface with a sharp knife, and putting on a thin smear of white lead.

Chapter 25

SELECTIONS OF ROSES

The experienced amateur will not be bound up by any ready-made selection; but the following lists, may prove useful as aids when purchasing and planting occupy the attention of the rosarian, and they should in all cases be closely followed by those who are not well acquainted with the relative merits of varieties:

100 Hybrid Perpetuals for Exhibition

(Arranged according to their colours)

White and White-tinted

Madame Lacharme, Margaret Dickson, Merveille de Lyon, and Violette Bouyer.

Light Pink and Flesh Colour

Baroness Rothschild, Captain Christy, Clio, Duchesse de Valombrosa, La France, Madame Gabriel Luizet, Marguerite de St. Amand, and Madame Hippolyte Jamain.

Deep Pink and Pale Rose

Abel Grand, Catherine Soupert, Centifolia rosea, Comtesse de Paris, Comtesse de Serenye, Her Majesty, Duchesse de Morny, Egeria, Edouard Morren, Elie Morel, Jeannie Dickson, Mrs. John Laing, Mdlle. Eugénie Verdier, Marie Cointet, Marie Finger, Mons. Noman, Pride of Waltham, Queen of Queens, Spenser, Suzanne Marie Rodocanachi.

Deep Rose, Carmine, and Cerise

Annie Laxton, Alphonse Soupert, Antoine Ducher, Caroline Testout, Countess of Rosebery, Dupuy Jamain, Hippolyte Jamain, John Hopper, Lady Sheffield, Madame Prosper Langier, Marchioness of Exeter, Marie Verdier, Marquise de Castellane, Mary Bennett, Star of Waltbam, and Victor Verdier.

Crimson-scarlet, Blackish-crimson, and Purple shaded

Abel Carriere, Baron de Bonstetten, Bruce Findlay, Charles Lefebvre, Crimson Queen, Devienne Lamy, Duke of Edinburgh, Duke of Teck, Duke of Wellington, Earl of Pembroke, Ferdinand de Lesseps, Horace Vernet, Jean Liabaud, Louis van Houtte, Pierre Notting, Prince Arthur, Jean Soupert, Prince Camille de Roban, Victor Hugo, Reynolds Hole, and Xavier Olibo.

Red-scarlet, Red, Rose-crimson, and Deep carmine

Alfred Colomb, Alfred K. Williams, Annie Wood, Auguste Rigotard, Beauty of Waltham, Comte Raimbaud, Camille Bernardin, Charles Gater, Countess of Oxford, Dr. Andry, Duchess of Bedford, Eclair, E. Y. Teas, Fisher Holmes, General Jaqueminot, Gustave Piganeau, Henri Ledechaux, Lady Helen Stewart, Le Havre, Lord Macaulay, Madame Henri Pereire, Madame Victor Verdier, Maréchal Vaillant, Marie Baumann, Marie Rady, Maurice Bernardin. Mrs. Charles Wood, Pride of Reigate, Salamander, Senateur Vaisse, Star of Waltham, and Ulrich Brunner.

72 Hybrid Perpetuals for Exhibition

(Arranged in order of merit)

A. K. Williams, Earl of Dufferin, Gustave Piganeau, Countess of Oxford, Duke of Edinburgh, Etienne Levet, Madame Gabriel Luizet, Her Majesty, Marie Baumann, Susanne Marie Rodocanachi, Alfred Colomb, Charles Lefebvre, Dr. Andre, Dupuy Jamain, Horace Vernet, Louis van Houtte, Mrs. John Lang, Merveille de Lyon, Ulrich Brunner, Baroness Rothschild, Duke of Wellington, Heinrich Schultheis, La France, Marie Rady, Xavier Olibo, Duchess of Bedford, Francois Michelon, Madame Victor Verdier, Camille Bernardin, Countess of Rosebery, Duke of Teck, Fisher, Holmes, Marie Verditr, Marquise de Castellane, Prince Arthur, Senateur Vaissé, Victor Hugo, Captain Christy, General Jacqueminot, La Duchesse de Morny, Beauty of

Waltham, Comte de Raimbaud, Jeannie Dickson, Pride of Waltham, Charles Darwin, E. Y. Teas, Lady Mary Fitzwilliam, Margaret Dickson, La Havre, Prince Camille de Rohan, Reynolds Hole, Sir Rowland Hill, Star of Waltham, Violette Bouyer, Abel Carriere, Duchesse de Valambrosa, M. Noman, Viscountess Folkestone, Marie Finger, Madame Eugene Verdier, Annie Wood, Victor Verdier, Alphonse Soupert, Lady Henry Stewart, Maurice Bernardin, Auguste Rigotard, John Stuart Mill, Marguerite de St. Amand, Pierre Notting, Lady Sheffield, Thomas Mills, and Marchioness of Dufferin.

36 Hybrid Perpetuals for Exhibition

(Arranged in order of merit)

A. K. Williams, Charles Lefebvre, Marie Baumann, Mrs. John Laing, Alfred Colomb, Her Majesty, Ulrich Brunner, Madame Gabriel Luizet, Louis van Houtte, Merveille de Lyon, Etienne Levet, Horace Vernet, La France, Duke of Edinburgh, Francois Michelon, Dupuy Jamain, Gustave Piganeau, Earl of Dufferin, Susanne Marie Rodocanachi, Baroness Rothschild, Duchess of Bedford, Countess of Oxford, Dr. Andre Marquise de Castellane, Prince Arthur, Heinrich Schultheis, Comte de Raimbaud, Duke of Wellington, Lady Mary Fitzwilliam, Victor Hugo, Marie Verdier, Marie Finger, Captain Christy, Marie Rady, Xavier Olibo, and Margaret Dickson.

50 Teas and Noisettes for Exhibition

(Arranged according to their colours)

White and White tinted

Grace Darling, Innocente Pirola Madame Willermoz, Niphetos, Rubens, Souvenir de Paul Neyron, Souvenir de S. A. Prince, The Bride, and White Perle.

Yellow and Yellow shaded

Amazone, Belle Lyonnaise, Caroline Kuster, Edouard Gautier, Etoile de Lyon, Francisca Kruger, Jean Ducher, Isabella Sprunt, Madame Berard, Madame Hoste, Madame Hippolyte Jamain, La Boule d'Or, Madame Lambard, Maréchal Niel, Marie van Houtte, Perle des Jardins, Princess Beatrice, Princess of Wales, Sappho, and Souvenir de Madame Levet.

Blush, Flesh Colour, Rose, and Crimson

Alba Rosea, Anna Olivier, Catherine Mermet, Cleopatra, Comtesse de Nadaillac, Corinna, Comtesse Panesse, Devoniensis, Ernest Metz, Hon. Edith Gifford, Jean Guillaumez, Jules Finger, Madame Bravy, Madame Cusin, Madame de Watteville, May Rivers, Rubens, Souvenir d'un Ami, Souvenir d'Elise Vardon, Souvenir de Madame Pernet, Souvenir de Gabriel Drevet, Souvenir de Madame Metral, and Souvenir de Therese Levet.

24 Teas and Noisettes for Exhibition

(Arranged in order of merit)

The Bride, Comtesse de Nadaillac, Maréchal Niel, Marie Van Houtte, Souvenir d'Elise Vardon, Catherine Mermet, Souvenir de S. A. Prince, Souvenir d'un Ami, Anna Olivier, Hon. Edith Gifford, Ernest Metz, Madame de Watteville, Innocente Pirola, Madame Cusin, Rubens, Madame Hoste, Francisca Kruger, Princess of Wales, Niphetos, Jean Ducher, Madame Lambard, Caroline Kuster, Ethel Brownlow, and Cleopatra.

18 Teas and Noisettes for Exhibition

(Arranged in order of merit)

Catherine Mermet, Souvenir d'Elise Vardon, The Bride Comtesse de Nadaillac, Innocente Pirola, Maréchal Niel Marie Van Houtte, Anna Olivier, Souvenir de S. A. Prince, Hon. Edith Gifford, Madame Cusin, Madame de Watteville, Niphetos, Ernest Metz, Souvenir d'un Ami, Ethel Brownlow, Jean Ducher, and Cleopatra.

44 Roses for Pot Culture

Hybrid Perpetuals

Alphonse Soupert, Annie Laxton, Baroness Rothschild, Beauty of Waltham, Crimson Queen, Camille Bernardin, Dr. Andry, Duke of Edinburgh, Duke of Teck, Edouard Morren, Francois Michelon, La France, Merveille de Lyon, Madame Victor Verdier, Marquise de Castellane, Ulrich Brunner, Violette Bouyer, and Victor Verdier.

Tea-scented and Hybrid Teas

Catherine Mermet, Cheshunt Hybrid, Corinna, Ernest Metz, Etoile de Lyon, Grace Darling, Hon. Edith Gifford, Innocente Pirola,

Lady Mary Fitzwilliam, Madame Margottin, Madame Hoste, Madame de Watteville, Madame Willermoz, Marie van Houtte, Madame Lambard, Medea, Niphetos, Sappho, Souvenir d'un Ami, Souvenir d'Elise Vardon, and The Bride.

Noisettes

Céline Forestier, Madame Caroline Kuster, Triumphe de Rennes.

Roses for Garden Decoration

Hybrid Perpetual

Abel Grand, Alphonse Soupert, Annie Laxton, Annie Wood, Baroness Rothschild, Boule de Neige, Bruce Findlay, Camille Bernardin, Centifolia Rosea, Charles Lamb, Charles Lefebvre, Cheshunt Scarlet, Comtesse Cecile de Chabrillant, Comtesse d'Oxford, Crown Prince, Dr. Andry, Duke of Connaught, Duke of Edinburgh, Dupuy Jamain, Earl of Pembroke, Fisher Holmes, Général Jacqueminot, Gloire de Margottin, Gloire de Rosoméne, Glory of Cheshunt, Henri Ledechaux, Heinrich Schultheis, Jeannie Dickson, John Hopper, Jules Margottin, Madame Bellenden Kerr, Madame Clemence Joigneaux, Madame Gabriel Luizet, Madame Victor Verdier, Magna Charta, Maréchal Vaillant, Marie Finger, Marie Rady, Miss Hassard, Merveille de Lyon, Mrs. Harry Turner, Mrs. John Laing, Paul Neyron, Pride of Waltham, Senateur Vaisse, Ulrich Brunner. Lette Bouyer, White Baroness, William Warden.

Teas and Noisettes

Aimée Vibert (N), Anna Olivier, Belle Lyonnaise, Caroline Kuster, Celine Forestier (N), Climbing Devoniensis, Climbing Niphetos, Climbing Perle des Jardins, Comtesse Riza du Parc, Dr. Grill, Emilie Dupuy, Francisca Kruger, Gloire de Dijon, Goubault, Homere, Isabella Sprunt, Lamarque (N), L'Ideal (N), Luciole, Ma Capucine, Madame Berard, Madame Charles, Madame Chedane Guinoisseau, Madame Falcot, Madame Hoste, Madame Lambard, Madame Van Houtte, Madame Willermoz, Ophirie (N), Rève d'Or, Rubens, Safranv, W. A. Richardson (N).

Hybrid Teas

Bardou Job, Camoens, Cannes la Coquette, Captain Christy Cheshunt Hybrid, Gloire Lyonnaise, Gustave Regis, Lady Henry Grosvenor, La France, Marquess of Salisbury, Reine Marie Henriette, Viscountess Folkestone.

Bourbon

Armosa, Madame Isaac Pereire, Mrs. Paul, Setina, Souvenir de la Malmaison.

China

Cramoisie Superieure, Ducher, Fabvier, James Sprunt, Laurette Messimy, Mrs. Bosanquet, Old Blush or Common Monthly, Old Crimson, Red Pet, White Pet.

Moss

Baron de Wassenaer, Blanche Moreau, Célina, Common or Old, Comtesse de Murinais, De Meaux, Gloire des Mousseuses, Lanei, Little Gem, White Bath.

Hybrid Chinas, Bourbons and Noisettes

Blairi, No.2, Charles Lawson, Chénedole, Coupe d'Hebé, Fulgens, Madame Plantier.

Polyantha

Cecile Brunner, Clothilde Soupert, Gloire des Polyantha, Madame Anna Maria de Montravel, Ma Paquerette, Lignonette, Perle d'Or.

Japanese

Alba, Blanc Double de Courbert, Madame Georges Bruant, Rubra.

Single

Hebe's Lip, Paul's Single White, Rosa alpina, Bracteata, Brunoni, Moschata, Indica, Lucida, Macrantha, Moschata Nivea, Multiflora, Pomifera, Rubrifolia.

French and Damask

Commandant Beaurepaire, Ceillet Parfait, Red Damask, Rosamundi, Village Maid, York and Lancaster.

Alba

Celestia, Felicité, Maiden's Blush.

Austrian Briers

Austrian Copper, Austrian Yellow, Harrisonii, Persian Yellow.

Sweet Briers

Common, Double Scarlet, Janet's Pride.

60 Varieties Succeeding in the Neighbourhood of Towns

Hybrid Perpetuals

Alfred Colomb, Anna Alexieff, Baroness Rothschild, Baronne Prevost, Beauty of Waltham, Charles Lefebvre, Comte de Nanteuil, Comtesse de Jaucourt, Docteur Andry, Duke of Edinburgh, Duchesse de Morny, Elizabeth Vigneron, Elie Morel, Eugene Appert, Francois Treyve, Francois Lacharme, Général Jacqueminot, Gloire de Ducher, La France, Jean Goujon, John Hopper, Jales Margottin, Lord Raglan, Louise Darzins, Madame Charles Wood, Madame Domage, Madame Knorr, Madame V. Verdier, Paul Neron, Pierre Notting, Victor Verdier.

Bourbon Perpetuals

Catherine Guillot, Comtesse Barbantanne, L'Avenir, Louis Odier, Madame Charles Baltet.

Bourbons

Mrs. Paul, Prince Albert, Souvenir de la Malmaison.

China

Common China, Mrs. Bosanquet.

Moss

Baronne de Wassenaer, Common, Luxembourg.

Hybrids of China and Bourbons

Charles Lawson, Coupe d'Hébé, Paul Ricaut, Paul Perras, Vivid, William Jesse.

Pillar, Trellis and Wall Roses

(*C. Climber. P. Pillar.*)

Hybrid Perpetuals

Anna Alexieff, *P.*; Annie Wood, *C.*; Climbing Charles Lefebvre, *P.*; Climbing Edouard Morren, *P.*; Climbing Jules Margottin, *P.*; Climbing Queen of Queens, *C.*; Climbing Victor Verdier, *P.*; Gloryof Waltham, *P.C.*; Red Rover, *C.*; Sophie Stern, *P.*; Red Dragon, *C.*

Bourbons and China

Blairi No. 2. *C.*; Charles Lawson, *P.*; Chenedole, *P.*; Coupe d'Hebé, *P.*; Fulgens, *C.*; Paul Verdier, *P.*; Paul Perras, *P.*; Vivid, *C.*

Teas, Noisettes and Hybrid Teas

Bouquet d'Or, *C.*; Cheshunt Hybrid, *P.*; Fortune's Yellow, *C.*; Gloire de Dijon, *C.*; Madame Berard, *P.*; Emilie Dupuy, *P.*; Madame Eugéne Verdier, *P.*; Pink Rover, *C.*; Reine Marie Henriette, *C.*; Reine Olga de Wurtemburg, *C.*; Maréchal Niel, *C.* (under glass); Waltham Climber, No.2, *C.*

Ayrshire

Bennett's Seedling or Thoresbyana, *C.*; Dundee Rambler, *C.*; Queen of the Belgians, *C.*; Ruga, *C.*

Evergreen

Félicite Perpetué, *C.*; Flora, *C.*; Leopoldine d'Orleans, *C.*; Princess Marie, *C.*; Rampant, *C.*

Banksian

Alba or White, *P.*; Lutea or Yellow, *P.*

Boursalt

Amadis, *C.*; Gracilis, *C.*

Polyantha

Crimson Rambler (Turner's), *C.*; Grandiflora, *C.*; Single Polyantha, *C.*

SYNOPTICAL CATALOGUE OF ROSES

Abbreviations

A.B.–Austrian Brier; *Ben*–Bengal; *B.*–Bourbon; *H.B.*–Hybrid Bourbon; *C.*–China; *H.C.*–Hybrid China; *Da.*–Damask; *Gal.*–Gallica; *H.*–Hybrid of unknown origin; *H.P.*–Hybrid Perpetual; *Mic.*–Microphylla; *M.*–Moss; *Mu.*–Multiflora; *P.M.*–Perpetual Moss; *N.*–Noisette; *H.N.*–Hybrid Noisette; *Pra.*–Prairie; *T.*–Tea.scented; *H.T.*–Hybrid Teas.

Abbé Berlèze, H.P., *Guillot fils* (1864), cerise red, medium, vigorous.

Abbé Bramerel, H.P., *Guillot fils* (1871), deep crimson, large, vigorous.

Abbé Girardin, B., *Bernaix* (1882), rose, large, vigorous.

Abbé Giraudier, H.P., *Levet* (1869), bright rose, medium, vigorous.

Abbé Lauray, H.P., *Trouillard* (1864), bright rose, medium, moderate.

Abbé Reynaud, H.C., *Guillot fils* (1863), carmine, large, vigorous.

Abbé Thomasson, T., *Schwartz* (1888), salmon, small, vigorous.

Abbé Veniere, H.P., *Guillot pere* (1867), clear rose, medium, vigorous.

Abd-el-Kader, H.P., *Verdier* (1860), bright crimson, medium, moderate.

Abel Carrière, H.P., *E. Verdier* (1875), marone crimson, large, vigorous.

Abel Chatenay, H.P., *E. Verdier* (1889), coral red, large, vigorous.

Abel Grand, H.P., *Damaizin* (1865), light rose, large, vigorous.

Abraham Zimmerman, H.P., *Levêque* (1879), purple red, large, vigorous.

Abricoté, T., *Dupuis*, apricot yellow, medium, moderate.

A Bouquets, T., *Cherpin* (1872), yellow white, medium, moderate.

Achille Gonod, H.P., *Gonod* (1864), carmine red, large, vigorous.

Acidalie, B., *Rousseau* (1838), blush white, large, vigorous.

Adam, T., *Adam* (1833), rose salmon, large, moderate.

Adanson, H.P., *Schwartz* (1874), red amaranth, medium, vigorous.

Adélaide Fontaine, H.P., *Fontaine* (1856), light rose, medium, moderate.

Adelaide de Meynot, H.P., *Gonod* (1883), rose cerise, medium, moderate flash-left. Adélaide de Savoie, H.P., *Moreau* (1864), satiny rose, medium, vigorous.

Adéle Bécar, H.C., *Laffay* (1847), bright rose, large, moderate.

Adéle Bourdeau, B., *Vigneron* (1873), light rose, large, vigorous.

Adéle de Bellabre, T., *J. Ducker fils* (1888), peach, large, vigorous.

Adéle Dufresnoy, H.P., *Robert* (1876), rosy flesh, medium, vigorous.

Adéle Jougand, T., *Ledeckaux*, yellow, small, moderate.

Adelina Patti, H.P., *Fontaine*, carmine rose, medium, moderate.

Adelina Viviand-Morel, T. (1890), apricot yellow, medium, vigorous.

Adeline Outrey, T, *Nabonnand et fils* (1889), yellow, medium, vigorous.

Admiral Coubert, H.P., *Dubreuil* (1885), carmine red, medium. moderate.

Admiral Gravina, H.P., *Mor. et Rob.*, purple, medium, moderate.

Admiral Nelson, H.P., *Ducher* (1859), bright red, large, vigorous.

Admiral Seymour, H.P., *Liabaud* (1883), purple red, large, vigorous.

Adolphe Brongniart, H.P., *Margottin* (1868), carmine red, medium, vigorous.

Adolphe Noblet, H.P., *Ledechaux* (1861), bright red, medium, vigorous.

Adolphe Poulain, H.P., *E. Verdier*, red, medium, vigorous.

Adrian Marx, H.P., *Bernardin* (1866), cerise, large, vigorous.

Adrienne de Cardoville, B., *Guillot fils* (1864), delicate rose, medium, vigorous.

Adrienne Christophle, T., *Guillot fils* (1868), apricot, large, vigorous.

Adrienne de Montebello, H.P., *Margottin* (1868), satiny rose, large, moderate.

A. Geoffroy St. Hilaire, H.P. *E. Verdier* (1878), red crimson, medium, moderate.

Aimée Vibert, N., Vibert (1828), white, medium, vigorous.

Aimęe Vibert scandens, N., *curtis* (1841), white, medium, robust.

Aimée Vibert variegata, N., *Schwartz* (1878), white, medium, vigorous.

Alba, B.K. (1807), white, small, vigorous.

Alba carnea, H.P., *Touvais* (1868), blush white, medium, vigorous.

Alba floribunda, H.P., *Touvais* (1868), flesh, medium, vigorous.

Alba mutabilis, H.P., *E. Verdter* (1865), rose tinted, large moderate.

Alba rosea, T., *Guillot pére* (1848), flesh-white, large, vigorous.

Albane d'Arneville, H.N, *Schwartz* (1885), white, medium, vigorous.

Albert la Blotais, H.P., *Mor. et Rob.* (1882), purple-red, medium, moderate.

Albert Durean, M., *E. Verdier* (1869), bright red, medium, moderate.

Albert Payne, H.P., *Touvais* (1873), flesh-pink, large, vigorous.

Albert de Stella, H.P., *Guillot* (1858), cherry-red, medium, moderate.

Albion, H.P., *Liabaud* (1869), cerise-red, large, vigorous.

Alcindor, H.P., *Lartey*, rose, medium, vigorous.

Alexander Chomer, H.P., *Liabaud* (1874), deep red, large, vigorous.

Alexander Dickson, H.P., *Dickson* (1873), rose, large, moderate.

Alexander Dumas, H.P., *Margottin* (1860), dark crimson, medium, vigorous.

Alexander Dupont, H.P., *Liabaud* (1883), red crimson, large, vigorous.

Alexander Dutitre, H.P., *Levéque* (1842), rose, medium, moderate.

Alexandre de Humboldt, H.P. *C. Verdier* (1869), bright rose, large, moderate.

Alexandrine Bechmeteff, H.P. (1853), bright carmine, large, vigorous.

Alexandrine Belfroy, H.P., *Fontaine* (1859), rose pink, medium, moderate.

Alexina Ben., *Beluze* (1841), rose, medium, moderate.

Alexis Lepère, H.P. *Vigneron* (1875), clear red, large, vigorous.

Alfred Colomb, H.P., *Lacharme* (1865), rich red, large, vigorous.

Alfred de Dalmas, P.M., *Portemer* (1855), flesh pink; medium, robust.

Alfred de Rougemont, H.P., *Lacharme* (1862), fiery crimson, large, vigorous.

Alfred K. Williams, H.P., *Schwartz* (1877), carmine red, large, vigorous.

Alice Dureau, H.P., *Vigneron* (1867), bright rose, large, vigorous.

Alice Leroy, M., Trouillard (1842), pink, small, moderate.

Aline Pierron, B., *Guillot* (1858), red, medium moderate.

Aline Rozey, H.N., *Schwartz* (1885), flesh, small, moderate.

Aline Sisley, T., *Guillot fils* (1874), rose red, large, vigorous.

Alpaide de Rotalier, H.P., *Campy* (1863), velvety red, large, robust.

Alphonse Berlin, H.P., *Gautreau* (1863), red cerise, medium, moderate.

Alphonse Damaizin, H.P., *Damaizin* (1861), bright crimson, medium, moderate.

Alphonse Fontaine, H.P., *Fontainc père* (1868), red carmine, large, vigorous.

Alphonse Karr, T., *Nabonnand* (1878), deep red, large, vigorous.

Alphonse Karr, H.P., *Portemer* (1845), flesh, medium, moderate.

Alphonse Karr, H.P., *Feuillet* (1855), rose, small, moderate.

Alphonse Lamartine, H.P., *Ducher* (1853), rose, medium, moderate.

Alphonse Mortelmans, T., *Md. Ducher* (1875), rose lilac, medium, vigorous.

Alphonse Soupert, H.P., *Lacharme* (1884), rose, large, vigorous.

Alsace-Lorraine, H.P., *Duval* (1879), deep crimson, large, vigorous.

Amadis, B., *Laffay* (1829), crimson, medium, vigorous.

A. Maille, B., *Moreau-Robert* (1889), rich carmine, large, vigorous.

A.M. Ampére, H.P., *Liabaud* (1882), purple, medium, moderate.

Amazone, T., Ducher (1872), deep yellow, medium, moderate.

Ambrogio Maggi, H.P., *Pernet* (1879), bright rose, large, vigorous.

Amédée Langlois, B., *E. Verdier* (1871), red purple, large, vigorous.

Amédée Philibert, H.P., *Levéque* (1879), purple and red, large, vigorous.

Amélie Hoste, H.P., *Gonod* (1874), light pink, large, vigorous.

America. N., *Page* (1859), pale yellow, medium, vigorous.

American Banner, N., *Cartwright* (1879), carmine, small, moderate.

American Beauty, H.P., *Bancroft* (1885), rose-pink, large, vigorous.

Amcena, H.P., *Soup. et Nott.* (1877), rose carmine, large, moderate.

Anacreon, H.P., *Schwartz* (1874), red, large. vigorous.

André Dunand, H.P., *Schwartz* (1871), tender rose, large, vigorous.

André Fresnoy, H.P., *Pernet* (1868), deep red, large, moderate.

André Gill, H.P., *R. Barrault* (1883), red carmine, large, vigorous.

André Leroy, H.P., *Pradel*, light rose, medium, moderate.

André Leroy d'Angers, H.P. *Trouillard* (1862), marone crimson, large, vigorous.

André Nabonnand, T., *Nabonnand* (1878), carmine red, large, moderate.

André Schwartz, T., *Schwartz* (1884), crimson, medium, vigorous.

Angèle Fontaine, H.B., *Fontaine* (1877), red carmine, medium, moderate.

Angélina Granger, H.P., *Granger* (1852), rose pink, medium, moderate.

Anicet Bourgeois, H.P., *Mor. et Rob.* (1880), cherry-red, medium, vigorous.

Anna Alexieff, H.P., *Margottin* (1858), clear rose, large, vigorous.

Anne Beluze, B., *Beluze* (1842).

Anna Blanchon, H.P., *Liabaud* (1874), bright rose, large, robust.

Anna de Diesbach, H.P., *Lacharme* (1858), bright rose, large, vigorous.

Anna Maria, Pra., *Feast* (1843), pink, small, moderate.

Anna Olivier, T. , *Ducher* (1872), flesh rose, large, vigorous.

Anne Marie de Montravel, Mu., *Rambaux* (1879), white, small, vigorous.

Annette Séant, T., *Levet* (1869), sulphur, medium, moderate.

Annie Laxton. H.P., *Laxton* (1871), rose crimson, large, moderate.

Annie Wood, H.P., *E. Verdier* (1866), bright red, large, vigorous.

Anisette, T., *Guillot* (1852).

Antoine Alleon, H.P., *Margottin fils* (1872), cerise red, large, vigorous.

Antoine Castel, H.P., *E. Verdier* (1873), rose red, large, moderate.

Antoine Chantin, H.P., *E. Verdier* (1883), rose, large, vigorous.

Antonia Decarli, T., *Levet* (1873), yellow, medium, moderate.

Antoine Devert, T., *Gonod* (1880), sulphur white, large, vigorous.

Antoine Ducher, H.P., *Ducher* (1866), purple red, large, robust.

Antoine Gauret, T., *Rebout* (1892), salmon rose, large, vigorous.

Antoine Mermet, H.T., *Guillot fils* (1884), carmine, medium, moderate.

Antoine Mouton, H.P., *Levet* (1874), rich rose, large, vigorous.

Antoine Quihou, H.P., *E. Verdier* (1879), purple marone, large, vigorous.

Antoine Riviore, H.P., *Liabaud* (1889), rich red, large, vigorous.

Antoine Schurz, H.P.. *Ketton frères* (1889). white, large, moderate.

Antoine Wintzer, H.P., *E. Verdier* (1884), red carmine, large, vigorous.

Antoinette Bouvagne, T., *Beluze* (1842).

Antonine Verdier. H.P., *Jamain* (1871), rose carmine, large, robust.

Apolline, B., *V. Verdier* (1848), rosy pink, large, vigorous.

Arch. Elizabeth d'Autriche, H.P., *Mor. et Rob.* (1882), rose, large, vigorous.

Archduc Charles, C., *Laffay*, crimson, medium, moderate.

Archduc Joseph, T., *Nabonnand* (1892), bright rose, large, vigorous.

Archevêque de Cambrai. B., *Guillot* (1851).

Archevêque de Paris, H.P., *Touvais* (1861), purple and violet, medium, vigorous.

Archimide, T., *Robert* (1856), fawn, medium, moderate.

Ardoisé de Lyon, H.P., *Plantier* (1865), violet rose, medium, vigorous.

Aristide Dupuis, H.P., *Trouillard* (1867), ruby red, large, robust.

Arles Dufour, H.P., *Liabaud* (1862), crimson purple, large, vigorous.

Armosa, B., *Marccheseau* (1840), pink, medium, moderate.

Artémise, H.P., *Mor. et Rob.* (1876), rose carmine, large, vigorous.

Arthur de Sansal, H.P. (1855), crimson purple, medium moderate.

Arthur Oger, H.P., *Oger* (1874), red purple, large, vigorous.

Aspasie, H.P., *Touvais* (1866), clear red, medium, moderate.

Attraction, H.T., *Dubreuil* (1886), carmine, large, vigorous.

Audubon, H.P. (1856), bright rose, medidm, moderate.

Augusta, N., *American* (1853), deep sulphur, medium, moderate.

Auguste Buchner, H.P., *Levêque* (1880), red scarlet, large, vigorous.

Auguste Mie, H.P., *Laffay* (1850), glossy pink, large, vigorous.

Auguste Neumann, H.P., *E. Verdier* (1869), bright red, large, moderate.

Auguste Oger, T., *Oger* (1856), coppery, medium, moderate.

Auguste Rigotard, H.P., *Schwartz* (1871), bright red, large, vigorous.

Auguste Rivière, H.P., *E. Verdier* (1864), red carmine, large, moderate.

Auguste Vacher, T., *Lacharme* (1853), deep yellow, large, moderate.

Augustine Guinoisseau, H.T., *Guinoisseau* (1889), rose, large, vigorous.

Aureus, T., *Ducher* (1873), coppery yellow, medium, moderate.

Aurore, H.P., *Touvais* (1861), rose, copper, large, moderate.

Aurore Boreale, H.P., *Oger* (1865), brilliant red, large, robust.

Aurore du Guide, B. (1850), violet crimson, medium, moderate.

Aurore du Matin, H.P., *Robert* (1867), bright rose, large, vigorous.

Avocat Duvivier, H.P., *Levêque fils* (1875), purple red, large, vigorous.

Avocat Lambert, H.P., *Besson* (1884), satiny rose, large, vigorous.

Bacchus, H.P., *Paul & Son*, (1855), crimson, medium, moderate.

Baltimore Belle, Pra., *Feast* (1843), blush, small, vigorous.

Baptiste Desportes, H.P., *Trouillard* (1864), red, medium, moderate.

Barillet Deschamps, H.P., *Vigneron* (1867), brilliant rose, large, vigorous.

Baron de Bonstetten, H.P., *Liabaud* (1871), velvety crimson, large, vigorous.

Baron Chaurand, H.P., *Liabaud* (1869), purple red, medium, moderate.

Baron L. de St. Genies, H.P., *Granger* (1867), rosy red, large, robust.

Baron G[illegible]nella, B.P., *Guillot père* (1859), rosy pillk, large, vigorous.

B[illegible]nn, H.P., *Levêque fils* (1867), poppy red, large,

Baron de [illegible]ouiley, H.P.. *Vigneron* (1876), purple red, large, vigorous.

Baron Larray, H.P. (1854), pink, medium, moderate.

Baron A. de Rothschild, H.P., *Lacharme* (1862), bright red, large, vigorous.

Baron de Rothschild, H.P., *Guillot fils* (1862), red, large, vigorous.

Baron Taylor, H.P., *Dugat* (1879), pale rose, medium, moderate.

Baron A. de Vrints, T., *Gonod* (1880), red pink, medium, vigorous.

Baron de Wassenaër, P.M. (1853), rose, large, vigorous.

Baron Wolseley, H.P., *E. Verdier* (1883), crimson, large, vigorous.

Baroness Rothschild, H.P., *Pernet* (1869), pale flesh, large, vigorous.

Baronne Blochausen, H.P., *Ketten freres* (1885), flesh, medium, moderate.

Baronne de Beauverger, H.P., *Gautreau*, rose, medium, vigorous.

Baronne Barge, T., *Pernet père*, rose and yellow, medium, moderate.

Baronne d'Estrange, T. *Lemarque* (1892), salmon rose, large, vigorous.

Baronne Maurice des Graviers, H.P., *E. Verdier* (1866), red cerise, large, vigorous.

Baronne Haussmann, H.P., .*E. Verdier* (1866), carmine red, large, vigorous.

Baronne Hallez, H.P. (1850), dark red, medium, moderate.

Baronne Pelletin de Kinkelin, H.P., Granger (1853), deep red, medium, moderate.

Baronne Henriette de Laew, T. *Nabonnand et fils* (1888), pale rose, small, vigorous.

Baronne M. de Lustende, H P., *Pergravand* (1892), rose, large, vigorous.

Baronne de Maynard, B., *Lacharme* (1865), white, medium, moderate.

Baronne de Medem, H.P., *E. Verdier*, cerise, large, vigorous.

Baronne J.B. de Morand, T. *Schwartz* (1892), flesh anq yellow, medium, moderate.

Baronne de Noirmont, B. *Granger*, rose, small, moderate.

Baronne de Prailly, H.P., *Liabaud* (1871), bright red, large, vigorous.

Baronne J. Panvilliers, H.P., *Duval* (1879), bright rose, large, vigorous.

Baronne A. de Rothschild, H.P., *Pernet*, tender rose, medium, vigorous.

Baronne Nath. de Rothschild, H.P., *Pernet* (1885), rose, medium, moderate.

Baronne Prevost, H.P., *Desprez* (1843), bright rose, large, vigorous.

Baronne de Sinety, T., *Gonod* (1884), yellow, medium, vigorous.

Baronne Travot, H.P., *C. Verdier* (1885), rose, medium, moderate.

Baronne Louise Uxkull, H.P., *Guillot fils* (1871), rose carmine, large, moderate.

Baronne Vittat, H.P., *Liabaud* (1873), flesh rose, large, moderate.

Baronne M. Werner, T. *Nabonnand* (1885), white salmon, medium, vigorous.

Barthélemy Joubert, H.P., *Mor. et Rob.* (1877), cherry red, large, vigorous.

Barthélemy Levet, H.P., *Levet* (1878), bright rosc, medium, moderate.

Béatrix, H.P., *Cherpin* (1865), rose carmine, medium, moderate.

Beauté de l'Europe, T. *Gonod* (1882}, yellow, medium, vigorous.

Beauté Francais, H.P., *Lartey*, red, medium, moderate.

Beauté Inconstante, T., *Pernet, Ducher* (1892), orange red, medium, vigorous.

Beauté Lyonnaise, H.P., *Guillot* (1851), rose, medimn, moderate.

Beauté Séduisante, B., *Touvais* (1861), red marone, large, vigorous.

Beauty of Beeston, H.P., *Frettingham* (1872), crimson, medium, moderate.

Beauty of Greenmount, N., *Pentland* (1854), rosy red, small, vigorous.

Beauty of Stapleford, H.T.. *Bennett* (1878), rose pink, medium, moderate.

Beauty of Thame, H.P., *Walker* (1873), marone crimson, large, vigorous.

Beauty of Waltham, H.P., *W. Paul* (1862), rose carmine, large, vigorous.

Beauty of Westerham, H.P., *Cattell* (1864), red crimson, medium, vigorous.

Bedford Belle, H.T., *Laxton* (1884), blush white, medium, vigorous.

Belle Allemande, T., *Beluze* (1840), pink, medium, moderate.

Belle Américaine, H.P., *Boll* (1837), pink, small, moderate.

Belle Anglaise, H.P., *Ducher* (1856), rose flesh, small, moderate.

Belle Brune, H.P., *Lartey* (1861), violet, medium, moderate.

Belle Chartronnaise, T., *Lartey* (1861), crimson and cerise, large, moderate.

Belle Cuirrée T., *Pernet* (1866), yellow, medium, moderate.

Belle de Bourg-la-Rerne, H.P., *Margottin* (1859), rose, large, vigorous.

Belle de Segur, A., rose flesh, small, moderate.

Belle des Jardins, G. *Guillot fils* (1872), red str. white, medium, moderate.

Belle du Printemps, H.P., *Damaizin* (1862), pale rose, large, moderate.

Belle Fleur d'Anjou, T., *Touvaiș* (1872), rosy white, large, vigorous.

Belle Fille du Prrntemps, H.P. *Touvais* (1862), pale rose, large, moderate.

Belle Jardinière, H.P., *Crozy* (1853), rose, medium, vigorous.

Belle Lyonnaise, T., *Levet* (1869), salmon yellow, large, moderate.

Belle Lyonnaise, H.P., *Ducher* (1854), blush pink, medium, vigorous.

Belle Macônnaise, T., *Ducher* (1870), salmon rose, large, moderate.

Belle Normande, H.P., *Oger* (1864), silvery rose, medium, vigorous.

Bellina Guillot, N., *Schwartz* (1889), white, medium, vigorous.

Belzunce, H.P., *Mor. et Rob.* (1885), vermilion, large, vigorous.

Benjamin Drouet, H.P., *E. Verdier* (1878), purple red, large, vigorous.

Bennett's Seedling, Ayr., *Bennett* (1840), white, medium, robust.

Benoît Broyer, H.P., *Gonod* (1874), rich red, medium, vigorous.

Benoit Comte, H.P., *Schwartz* (1884), red, medium, moderate.

Benoit Cornet, H.P., *Cornet* (1863), rose, large, moderate.

Béranger, H,P., (1851), rose crimson, large, moderate.

Berberifolia Hardii, Mic., yellow, small, moderte.

Barceau Impérial, H.P., (1856), delicate rose, medium, vigorous.

Bernard Palissy, H.P., *Margottin* (1864), carmine red, large, vigorous.

Bernard Verlot, H.P., *Margottin* (1874), red scarlet, large, moderate.

Berthe Baron, H.P., *Veillard* (1869), silvery rose, large, vigorous.

Berthe Levêque, H.P., *Cochet* (1866), rose, medium, moderate.

Bessie Johnson, H.P., *Curtis* (1872), blush, large, vigorous.

Bicolor Incomparable, H.P., *Touvais* (1861), dark rose, medium, vigorous.

Bignonia, T., *Levet* (1872), red, medium, moderate.

Bijou de Lyon, P., *Schwartz* (1883), white, small, moderate.

Bijou des Prairies, Pra., *Schwartz* (1878), bright rose, medium, vigorous.

Black Prince, H.P., *W. Paul* (1866), dark crimson, large, vigorous.

Blairi No.2, H.C., *Blair* (1845), rose blush, large, vigorous.

Blanche de Beaulieu, H.P., *Margottin* (1851), pink, large, vigorous.

Blanche de Méru, H.P., C. *Verdier* (1869), bright rose, medium, vigorous.

Blanche Lafitte, B., *Pradel* (1851), blush, medium, moderate.

Blanche Moreau, P.M., *Mor. et Rob.* (1880), pure white, small, vigorous.

Blanche Portemer, H.P., *Portemer* (1851), pure white, medium, moderate.

Blanche Rebatel, P., *Bernaix* (1888), carmine red, small, vigorous.

Blanchfleur, Fr., *Vibert* (1846), blush, mediumm moderate.

Boccace, H.P., *Mor. et Rob.*, crimson, medium, vigorous.

Boieldieu, H.P., *Margottin* (1877), cherry red, large, vigorous.

Boileau, H.P., *Mor. et Rob.* (1884), rose, large, vigorous.

Bona Weillshot, H.T., *Soupert et Notting* (1889), rosy vermilion, large, vigorous.

Bon Silène, T., *Hardy* (1839), rose salmon, medium, vigorous.

Bougère, T., *Bougère* (1832), deep salmon, large, vigorous.

Boule de Nanteuil, G., crimson, small, moderate.

Boule de Neige, H.P., *Lacharme* (1867), pure white, medium, moderate.

Boule d'Or, T., *Margottin* (1860), yellow, medium, vigorous.

Bouquet de Marie, H.P., *Damaizin* (1858), flesh, small, moderate.

Bouquet d'Or, N., *Ducher* (1872), coppery yellow, large vigorous.

Bouquet Rose, H.P., *Touvais*, cerise, medium, moderate.

Bouquet de la Vierge, B., *Soup. et Not.* (1873), rose, white, small, moderate.

Bourbon Queen. B., *Manger* (1834), rose, medium, vigorous.

Bouton d'Or, T., *Guillot fils* (1866), deep yellow, medium, vigorous.

Brennus, H.C., *Laffay* (1830), light carmine, large, vigorous.

Brightness of Cheshunt, H.P., *Paul & Son* (1881), vivid red, medium, vigorous.

Brilliant, H.P., *W. Paul & Son* (1886), crimson, medium, vigorous.

Buffalo Bill, H.P., *E. Verdier* (1889), pale rose, large, vigorous.

Buffon, H.P., *Guillot père* (1859), crimson, medium, moderate.

Bunnert Fridolin, T., *Bernaix* (1882), yellow, medium, robust.

Burgmester, Karl Müller, H.P., *Soup. et Not.*, red, medium, moderate.

Calliope, H.P., *Mor. et Rob.* (1879), satiny rose, large, vigorous.

Camille Bernardin, H.P., *Gautreau* (1865), bright red, large, vigorous.

Camöens, H.T., *Schwartz* (1882), rose yellow, medium, moderate.

Canary, T., *Guillot père* (1852), yellow, medium, moderate.

Candide, H.P., *Touvais*, blush, small, moderate.

Cannes la Coquette, H.T., *Nabonnand* (1877), salmon, medium, moderate.

Captain Cherpin, H.P., *Guillot* (1851).

Captain Christy, H.P., *Lacharme* (1873), flesh colour, large, moderate.

Captain Louis Frère, H.P., *Vigneron* (1884), rose, medium, moderate.

Captain Ingram, M., *Laffay* (1856), velvety purple, medium, vigorous.

Captain Lamure, H.P., *Levet* (1870), deep red, medium, moderate.

Captain Paul, H.P., *Boyau* (1866), bright red, medium, moderate.

Captain Rognat, H.P., *Guillot père* (1864), brilliant red, large, moderate.

Capucine Liabaud, H.P., *Liabaud* (1882), red, medium, moderate.

Cardinal Patrizzi, H.P., *Trouillard* (1857), purplish crimson, medium, moderate.

Carl Coers, H.P., *Granger* (1865), crimson purple, large, vigorous.

Carlina (1888), white, medium, vigorous.

Carmen T., F. *Dubreuil* (1888), yellow rose, medium, vigorous.

Caroline, T., pink, large, vigorous.

Caroline Cook, T., *A. Cook* (1871), yellow, small, vigorous.

Caroline Marniesse, N., *Roeser* (1848), creamy white, small, moderate.

Caroline Milson, H.P., *Guillot* (1853), flesh, medium, moderate.

Caroline Riquet, B. (1858), white, medium, vigorous.

Caroline de Sansal, H.P., *Deprez* (1850), flesh pink, large, vigorous.

Caroline Schmitt, N., *Schmitt* (1881), yellow, medium, moderate.

Cassimir Perrier, H.P., *Schwartz* (1874), ruby red, large, vigorous.

Catherine Bell, H.P., *Bell & Son* (1877), rose, medium, moderate.

Catherine Bonnard, H.B , *E. Verdier* (1871), carmine rose, large, vigorous.

Catherine Fontaine, T., *Liabaud* (1892), creamy yellow, large, vigorous.

Catherine Guillot, B., *Guillet père* (1860), rosy purple, large, vigarous.

Catherine Mermet, T., *Guillot fils* (1869), flesh rose, large, vigorous.

Catherine Soupert, H.P., *Lacharme* (1879), peach, medium, moderate.

Catinat, H.P., *Oger* (1873), bright rose, medium, vigorous.

Cecile Brunner, P., *Ducher* (1880), bright rose, medium, moderate.

Celestial, A., flesh, small, modrate.

Céline, M., *Robert* (1855), crimson, small, moderate.

Céline Dubois, D.P. (1850), French white, medium, moderate.

Céline Forestier, N., *A. Leroy* (1858), pale yellow, medium, vigorous.

Céline Gonod, B., *Gonod* (1863), rose, medium, moderate.

Célestine Pourreaux, H.P., *Fontaine* (1873), bright cerise, large, vigorous.

Cels's multiflora, C., *Cels* (1838), flesh, small, moderate.

Cendres Napoleon, B, *Beluze* (1841).

Centifolia rosea, H.P., *Touvais* (1863), bright pink, large, vigorous.

Chamois, T., *Ducher* (1869), chamois, medium, moderate.

Charlemagne, H.P., *Oger* (1863), red cerise, large, moderate.

Charlemagne, B., *Dorisy* (1846), blush pink, large, moderate.

Charles Baltet, H P., *E. Verdier* (1877), carmine red, large, vigorous.

Charles Bosierre, H.P. (1849), carmine, medium, moderate.

Charles Darwin, H.P., *Laxton* (1879), dark crimson, large, vigorous.

Charles de Franciosi, T. (1890), chrome yellow, large, moderate.

Charles de Thezillat, T., *Nabonnand et fils* (1888), creamy yellow, large, vigorous.

Charles Dickens, H.P., *W. Paul & Son* (1886), rose, large, vigorous.

Charles Duval, H.P., *E. Verdier* (1877), bright red, medium, moderate.

Charles Fauquet, H.P., *Levêque* (1884), red, large, moderate.

Charles Fontaine, H.P., *Fontaine* (1868), crimson, medium, moderate.

Charles Gater, H.P., *Paul & Son* (1891), glowing crimson, medium, vigorous.

Charles Getz, B., *Cook* (1871), rose pink, medium, vigorous.

Charles Lamb, H.P., *W. Paul & Son* (1884), red, medium, vigorous.

Charles Lawson, H.B., *Lawson* (1853), rose carmine, large, vigorous.

Charles Lee, H.P., *Gautreau* (1868), red, medium, moderate.

Charles Lefebvre, H.P., *Lacharme* (1861), velvety crimson, large, vigorous.

Charles Legrady, T., *Pernet* (1885), rose, medium, vigorous.

Charles Levêque, T., *Nabonnand* (1885), red, medium, moderate.

Charles Margottin, H.P., *Margottin* (1864), carmine red, large, vigorous.

Charles Martel, B. , *Guillot* (1842)

Charles Ravolli, T., *Pernet* (1875), rose, small, moderate.

Charles Rouillard, H.P., *E. Verdier* (1865), bright rose, large, robust.

Charles Turner, H.P., *E. Verdier* (1865), bright red, large, vigorous.

Charles Turner H P., *Margottin* (1869), brilliant rose, large, vigorous.

Charles Verdier, H.P., *Guillot père* (1866), silvery rose, large, robust.

Charles Wood, H.P., *Portemer* (1864), dark red, large, vigorous.

Charlotte Corday, H.P., *Joubert* (1864), purple red, large, moderate.

Chateau des Bergeries, T., *Ledechaux* (1887), pale yellow, large, vigorous.

Chtâteaubriand, H.P., *Portemer* (1852), light pink, medium, moderate.

Cheshunt Hybrid, H.T., *Paul & Son* (1873), red carmine, large, vigorous.

Chevalier de Colquhoun, T., *Nabonnand* (1878), bright red, medium, moderate.

Chevalier Nigra, H.P., *C. Verdier* (1865), dark crimson, large, vigorous.

Christine Nilsson, H.P., *Levêque fils* (1867) , deep rose, large, vigorous.

Christine de Noue, T., (1890), red purple, large, vigorous.

Christian Puttner, H.C., *Oger* (1861), rose, medium, moderate.

Ciceron, H.P., *Ducher* (1854).

Cimabue H.B. (1858), rich crimson, large, vigorous.

Citoyen des Deux Mondes, Ben., *Lacharme* (1850).

Clair Carnot, N. *Guillot fils* (1873), rich yellow, medium, moderate.

Claire Jacquier, P., *Bernaix* (1888), yellow, small, vigorous.

Claire Renard, H.P., *Oger* (1866), bright rose, large, vigorous.

Claire Thierry, H.P., *Oger* (1874), rosy cerise, medium, moderate.

Clara Cochet, H.P., *Lacharme* (1886), rose, large, vigorous.

Claude Bernard, H.P., *Liabaud* (1878), deep rose, large, vigorous.

Claude Jacquet, H.P., *Liabaud* (1892), purple scarlet, large, moderate.

Claude Levet, H.P., *Levet* (1872). deep red, large, robust.

Claude Millon, H.P., *E. Verdier* (1863), velvety red, medium, vigorous.

Claudia Augustin, N., *Damaizin* (1868), white and yellow, medium, robust.

Clemence Delarue, H.P., *Fontaine*, rose, small, moderate.

Clemence Raoux, H.P., *Granger* (1869), satiny rose, medium, vigorous.

Clemence Thierry, H.P., *Oger* (1879), rose lilac, medium, vigorous.

Clement Nabonnand. T., *Nabonnand* (1877), salmon yellow, medium, moderate.

Climbing Bessie Johnson, H.P., *Paul & Son* (1878), pink, medium, vigorous.

Climbing Captain Christy, H.P., *Ducher* (1881), pink, niedium, vigorous.

Climbing Charles Lefebvere, H.P., *Cranston* (1876), crimson, large, moderate.

Climbing Comtesse d'Oxford, H.P., *Smith* (1875), red carmine, large, robust.

Climbing Devoniensis, T., *Pavitt* (1858), creamy white, large, vigorous.

Climbing Edouard Morren, H.P., *Paul & Son* (1879), rose, large, vigorous.

Climbing Jules Margottin, H.P., *Cranston* (1875), carmine rose, large, robust.

Climbing Mdlle, Eugénie Verdier, H.P., *Paul & Son* (1877), rose pink, medium, vigorous.

Climbing Niphetos, T., *Keynes Williams* (1888), white, medium, vigorous.

Climbing Queen of Queens, H.P., *W. Paul & Son* (1892), rose, medium, vigorous.

Climbing Victor Verdier, H.P., *Paul & Son* (1871), rose carmine, large, robust.

Clothilde, T., *Rolland* (1867), creamy white, medium, moderate.

Clothilde Soupert, N., *Soup. et Not.* (1889), pearly white, medium, vigorous.

Clotilde Rolland, H.P., *Rolland* (1867), cerise rose, large, moderate.

Cloth of Gold, N., *Coquereau* (1843), deep yellow, large, robust.

Clovis, H.P., *Ledechaux* (1868), rose purple, large, vigorous.

Coeur de Lion, H.P., *W. Paul* (1867), bright rose, large, vigorous.

Colonel Felix Breton, H.P., *Schwartz* (1884), red, large, vigorous.

Colonel de Cambriel, H.P., *Nor. et Rob.*, red, medium, moderate.

Colonel Robert Lefort, M., *E. Verdier* (1884), purple, medium, moderate.

Colonel de Rougemont, H.P., *Lacharme* (1854), clear carmine, large, vigorous.

Colonel de Sansal, H.P., *Jamain* (1874), carmine red, medium, moderate.

Commandant Beaurepaire, C., *Moreau Robert* (1875), bright rose, medium, robust.

Commandant Fournier, H.P., *Laffay* (1846), crimson, medium, moderate.

Commandant Fournier, H.P., *Mor. et Rob.* (1885), fiery red, large, vigorous.

Commandant de Lamalignie, H.P. (1890), scarlet, large, vigorous.

Commandant Mausuy, H.P., *Vigneron* (1868), bright red, large, moderate.

Comice de Taru et Garonne, B., *Pradel* (1852), carmine red, medium, moderate.

Comice de Seine et Marne, B., *Pradel* (1842), deep red, medium, moderate.

Comte de Beaufort, H.P. (1858), deep crimson, medium, moderate.

Comte de Bourmont, H.P. (1851), pale rose, large, vigorous.

Comte Florimonde de Bergeyck, H.P., *Soup. et Not.* (1879), rosy red, large, vigorous.

Comte Bobinsky, H.P. (1850), carmine, medium, moderate.

Comte Cavour, H.P., *Liabaud* (1856), bright rose, medium, moderate.

Comte Henri Rignon, H.T., *Pernet-Ducher* (1888), coppery yellow, large, vigorous.

Comte Horace de Choiseul, H.P., *Lévêque* (1879), vermilion, large, vigorous.

Comte d'Epremesnil, Rug., *Nabonnand* (1882), lilac, medium, moderate.

Comte d'Eu, B., *Lacharme* (1884), crimson, medium, moderate.

Comte de Flandres, H.P., *Lévêque* (1882), purple red, medium, moderate.

Comte de Falloux, H.P., *Trouillard* (1860), rich crimson, medium, moderate.

Comte Adrien de Germiny, H.P., *Lévêque* (1882), rose, medium, moderate.

Comte de Grivel, T., *Levet* (1871), pale yellow, large, vigorous.

Comte Litta, H.P., *E. Verdier* (1866), velvety red, large, vigorous.

Comte de Montijo, B. (1855), dark crimson, medium, moderate.

Comte de Mortemart, H.P., *Margottin* (1881), rose, medium, moderate.

Comte de Nanteuil, H.P., *Quietier* (1852), lilac rose, large, vigorous.

Comte Odart, H.P. (1851), deep red, medium, moderate.

Comte de Paris, T., *Mad. Pean* (1844), flesh, medium, moderate.

Comte de Paris, H.P., *Laffay* (1839), lilac, large, moderate.

Comte de Paris, H.P., *E. Verdier* (1864), rose red, medium, vigorous.

Comte de Paris, T., *Hardy* (1839), flesh colour, large, vigorous.

Comte de Paris, H.P., *Lévêque* (1887), poppy red, medium, vigorous.

Comte Raimbaud, H.P., *Rolland* (1867), cerise red, large, robust.

Comte de Ribaucourt, H.P., *Jemean*, red, medium, moderate.

Comte de Sembui, T., *Mad. Ducher* (1874), salmon pink, large, vigorous.

Comte Alphonse Serenye, H.P., *Touvais* (1865), purple red, large, robust.

Comte de Tavena, T., *Ducher* (1871), yellow, large, vigorous.

Comte de Thun-Hohenstein, H.P., *Lévêque* (1881), crimson, medium, moderate.

Comtesse Bertrand de Blacas, H.P., *E. Verdier*, delicate rose, large, vigorous.

Comtesse Cahen d'Anvers, H.P., *Ledechaux* (1885), rose, large, vigorous.

Comtesse d'Arnim, H.P., *Soup. et Not.*, carmine, medium, vigorous.

Comtesse d'Eu, H.P., *E. Verdier*, cerise rose, large, vigorous.

Comtesse de Barbantanne, B., *Guillot père* (1858), flesh white, medium, vigorous.

Comtesse de Bearn, H.P., *Lévêque* (1885), red, large, moderate.

Comtesse de Bessequier, B., *Beluze* (1842).

Comtesse de Bouchard, N. (1890), saffron, large, vigorous.

Comtesse de Bresson, H.P., *Guinoiseau*, (1873), lilac rose, large, vigorous.

Comtesse de Breteuil, T., *Pernet-Ducher* (1892), rosy salmon, large, vigorous.

Comtesse de Brossard, T., *Oger*, yellow, small, moderate.

Comtesse de Camondo, H.P., *Lévêque* (1880), deep rose, large, vigorous.

Comtesse de Casserta, T., *Nabonnand* (1877), copper red, medium, moderate.

Comtesse de Casteja, H.P., *Margottin* (1883), crimson, large, vigorous.

Comtesse de Chabrillant, H.P., *Marest* (1858), deep pink, medium, moderate.

Comtesse H. de Choiseul, H.P., *Moreau* (1878), cherry red, large, vigorous.

Comtesse Henriette Combbs, H.P., *Schwartz* (1881), satin rose, medium, moderate.

Comtesse Doria, H.P (1853), crimson, medium, moderate.

Comtesse Duchatel, H.P., *Laffay* (1844), rose purple, medium, vigorous.

Comtesse Eva Stahemberg, T. (1890), creamy yellow, large, moderate.

Comtesse de Falloux, H.P., *Trouillard* (1867), purple rose, large, robust.

Comtesse de Flandres, H.P., .*E. Verdier* (1877), satin rose, medium, moderate.

Comtesse de Frigneuse, T., *Guillot* (1885), yellow, medium, vigorous.

Comtesse O'Gorman, T., *Nabonnand* (1892), rose and yellow, medium, moderate.

Comtesse Festelics Hamilton, T., *Nabonnand* (1892), carmine red, large, vigorous.

Comtesse F. de Thurn Hohenstein, H.P., *Levêque* (1880), carmine crimson, large, vigorous.

Comtesse d'Indre, H.P., *E. Verdier* (1879), carmine red, large, vigorous.

Comtesse Jaubert, H.B., *Laffay* (1847), rose, medium, moderate.

Comtesse de Jaucort, H.P., *Cochet* (1866), rose flesh, large, vigorous.

Comtesse Julie Hunyady. T., *Soupert et Not.* (1888), deep yellow, large, vigorous.

Comtesse Julie de Schulenburg, H.P., *Soupert et Notting* (1888), deep purple, large, vigorous.

Comtesse Louise de Kergolay, H.P., *Touvais*, purple, medium, moderate.

Comtesse Nathalie de Kleist, H.P., *Soupert et Notting* (1880), coppery red, large, vigorous.

Comtesse de Labarthe, T., *Bernède* (1857), pink, medium, moderate.

Comtesse de Lacepede, H.C., blushm medium, vigorous.

Comtesse de Leuse, T., *Nabonnand* (1878), salmon rose, medium, moderate.

Comtesse de Ludre, T., *E. Verdier* (1879), red, medium, moderate.

Comtesse de Mailly Nesle, H.P., *Lévêque* (1883), rose, large, vigorous.

Comtesse de Maussac, H.P., *Vigneron* (1873), clear rose, large, vigorous.

Comtesse Hélène Mier, H.P., *Soupert et Notting* (1876), clear rose, large, robust.

Comtesse F. Morgues, H.P., *Pernet* (1866), bright red, large, moderate.

Comtesse de Mosbourg, B., *Pradel* (1861), satiny rose, large, moderate.

Comtesse de Murinais, M., *Vibert* (1843), flesh white, large, robust.

Comtesse de Naidaillac, T., *Guillot fils* (1871), rose, large, vigorous.

Comtesse Ouvaroff, T., *Margottin* (1860), creamy rose, large, moderate.

Comtesse de Palikao, H.P., *E. Verdier* (1865), rose, medium, moderate.

Comtesse Riza du Parc, T., *Schwartz* (1876), rose, medium, moderate.

Comtesse de Paris, H.P., *E. Verdier* (1864), lively rose, large, moderate.

Comtesse de Paris, H.P., *Lévêque* (1883), rose, medium, moderate.

Comtesse de Polignac, H.P., *Granger*, red, medium, moderate.

Comtesse de Rocquigny, H.P., *Vaurin*, salmon red, medium, moderate.

Comtesse de Saint Andeol, H.P., *Renaud Guepet* (1889), deep rose, large, moderate.

Comtesse de Seguier, H.P., *Lévêque fils* (1861), dark red, large, moderate.

Comtesse de Serenye, H.P., *Lacharme* (1874), silvery pink, medium, vigorous.

Comtesse Vally de Serenye, H.P., *Fontaine* (1875), amaranth, large, vigorous.

Comtesse de Serincourt, T., *Pradel*, salmon, medium, moderate.

Comtesse Anna Thurn, T., *Soupert et Notting* (1887), yellow, medium, vigorous.

Comtesse de Turenne, H.P., *E. Verdier* (1866), flesh, large, vigorous.

Comtesse de Vallier, H.P., *Damaizin* (1866), purple violet, medium, vigorous.

Comtesse de Witzthun, T. (1890), bright yellow, large, vigorous.

Comtesse Alban de Villeneuve, T., *Nabonnand* (1882), yellow rose, medium, moderate.

Comstant Lusseau, H.P., *Trouillard* (1864), clear red, medium, moderate.

Constantin Fretiakoff, H.P., *Jamain* (1877), rose crimson, large, vigorous.

Copper Austrian, A.B., reddish copper, small, moderate.

Coquette des Alpes, H.P., *Lacharme* (1867), blush white, medium, moderate.

Coquette des Blanches, H.P., *Lacharme* (1871), pure white, medium, vigorous.

Coquette de Lyon, T., *Ducher* (1870), canary yellow, medium, vigorous.

Corinna, T., *Paul & Son* (1892), salmon, large, vigorous.

Cornelia Koch, T., *Koch*, (1855), creamy white, large, moderate.

Countess of Oxford, H.P., *Guillot père* (1869), carmine red, large, vigorous.

Countess of Pembroke, H.T., *Bennett* (1882), satin rose, medium, vigorous.

Countess of Rosebery, H.P., *Postans* (1879), bright carmine rose, large, vigorous.

Coupe de Cynthée, B., *Guillot* (1846).

Coupe d' Hébé. H.B., *Laffay* (1840), deep pink, large, robust.

Couquette de Normande, H.P., *Oger*, white, medium, moderate.

Couronne de Parterre, H.P., *Touvais* (1861), velvety crimson, large, vigorous.

Cramoisi Superieur, C., *Plantier* (1834), crimson, medium, vigorous.

Crested, or Cristata, Prov. *Vibert* (1827), rose pink, medium, moderate.

Crimson Bedder, H.P., *Cranston* (1874), crimson, large, moderate.

Crimson Globe, H.M., *W. Paul & Son* (1890), crimson, large, vigorous.

Crimson Queen, H.P., *W. Paul & Son* (1890), velvety crimson, full, vigorous.

Crown Prince, H.P., *W. Paul & Son* (1880), deep crimson, large, vigorous.

Curé de Charentay, H.P., *Ducher* (1867), rose purple, medium, vigorous.

Curt Schnlthei., T., *Nabonnand* (1882), rose yellow, medium, moderate.

D'Aguesseau, G., crimson, medium, moderate.

Dames Patronesses d'Orleans, H.P., *Vigneron* (1877), crimson, large, vigorous.

Danaë, H.P., *Touvais* (1865), cerise rose, large, vigorous.

Danmark, H.P., *W. Paul & Son* (1890), rose, large, vigorous.

Darzens, H.P., *Ducher* (1860), yellowish rose, large, vigorous.

David Pradel, T., *Pradel* (1851), lilac rose, large, moderate.

Dean of Windsor, H.P., *Turner* (1878), vermilion, large, vigorous.

De la Grifferaie, H.P., deep rose, small, vigorous.

Delille, P.M., *Robert* (1852), red, medium, moderate.

Delphine Gaudot, T., *Beluze* (1840).

De Meaux, M., *Or. Taunton* (1825), pink, small, moderate.

Dennis Hélye, H.P., *Gautreau* (1864), rosy carmine, large, vigorous.

De Reymont, P., *Aleqatiere* (1888), red crimson, small, vigorous.

Desgasches, H.B., *Plantier*, (1850), carmine, medium, moderate.

Desprez, N., *Desprez* (1838), red buff, large, vigorous.

Deuil du Dunois, H.P., *Vigneron*, crimson, medium, moderate.

Deuil de Paul Fontaine, M., *Fontaine* (1873), red, medium, moderate.

Deuil de l'Empereur du Mexique, H.P., *Cordier* (1867), red, large, moderate.

Deuil du Prince Albert, H.P., *Gonod* (1862), dark crimson, large, vigorous.

Deuil du Col. Dentert, H.P., *Margottin* (1878), marone purple, large, vigorous.

Deuil du Prince Jerome, H.P., *Lartay*, velvet crimson, medium, moderate.

Deuil du Mad. Willermoz, H.P., *Lacharme* (1853), dark crimson, medium, moderate.

Devienne-Lamy, H.P., *Lévêque fils* (1868), carmine red, large, moderate.

Devoniensis, T., Foster (1838), creamy white, large, moderate.

Diana, H.P., *W. Paul* (1874), deep pink, large, vigorous.

Dingee Conard, H.P., *E. Verdier* (1875), crimson, medium, moderate.

Directeur Alphand, H.P., *Lévêque* (1884), scarlet, large, moderate.

Directeur Réné Gerard, T., *Pelletiér* (1892), flesh yellow, large, modeate.

Directeur N. Jensen, H.P., *E. Verdier* (1884), red carmme, medium, moderate.

Distinction, H.T., *Bennet* (1882), peach, medium, vigorous.

Docteur Douet, H.P., *Tesnier* (1889), fiery red, large, vigorous.

Domingo Aldrufeu, H.P., *Pernet*, rose, medium, moderate.

Douglas, B., *V. Verdier* (1848), crimson, medium, moderate.

Dowager Duchess of Marlborough, H.P., *Paul & Son* (1890), rose, large, moderate.

Dr. Andry, H.P., *E. Verdier* (1864), dark red, large, vigorous.

Dr. Antoine Carlès, T., *Nabonnand* (1885), yellow, medium, moderate.

Dr. Arnal, H.P., *Roeser* (1848), crimson, small, moderate.

Dr. Auguste Krell, H.P., *E. Verdier* (1877), cherry red, large, moderate.

Dr. Baillon, H.P., *Margottin* (1878) crimson purple, large, robust.

Dr. Bastien, H.P. (1890), magenta rose, large, moderate.

Dr. Berthet, B., *Damaizin* (1858), cherry red, large, moderate.

Dr. Berthet, T., *Pernet* (1878), pale rose, large, vigorous.

Dr. Brechemier, H.P., *Vigneron* (1873), crimson, medium, vigorous.

Dr. Bretonneau, H.P., *Trouillard* (1858), deep red, large, moderate.

Dr. Chopart, B. (1890), bright rose, medium, vigorous.

Dr. de Chalus, H.P., Touvais (1871), brilliant red, large, vigorous.

Dr. Dor, H.P., *Liabaud* (1885), red, medium, moderate.

Dr. Garnier, H.P., *Mor. et Rob.* (1883), cerise red, large, vigorous.

Dr. Guepin, H.P., *Mor. et Rob.* (1872), velvety red, medium, moderate.

Dr. Henon, H.P., *Léon Lille* (1853), white, medium, moderate.

Dr. Hogg, H.P., *Laxton* (1880), violet purple, large, vigorous.

Dr. Hooker, H.P., *Paul & Son* (1876), bright crimson, medium, moderate.

Dr. Hurta, H.P., *Soupert et Notting* (1867), rosy purple, large, robust.

Dr. Jenner, H.P., *Margottin* (1878), carmine red, large, vigorous.

Dr. Julliard, H.P. (1850), rose, medium, moderate.

Dr. Kane, N., *Pentland* (1856), sulph, yellow, large, moderate.

Dr. Larray, H.P., *Mor. et Rob.* (1866), vinous red, large, vigorous.

Dr. Lemée, H.P., *Touvais* (1871), velvety purple, large, vigorous.

Dr. Lipdley, H.P., *W. Paul* (1866), dark crimson, large, moderate.

Dr. Marjolin, H.P., *Laffay* (1842), rose crimson, small, dwarf.

Dr. Marx, H.P., *Laffay* (1842), crimson, large, moderate.

Dr. Marx, H.P., *Laffay* (1858), carmine, large, vigorous.

Dr. Pasteur, H.T., *Mor. et Rob.* (1888), carmine, medium, vigorous.

Dr. Rushpler, H.P. (1856), clear rose, large, robust.

Dr. Sewell, H.P., *Turner* (1879), crimson scarlet, large, vigorous.

Dr. Vingtrinier, H.P., *Fontaine* (1863), red carmine, medium, moderate.

Dr Wilhelm Neubert, H.P., *Soupert et Notting* (1873), cherry red, large, vigorous.

Du Guesclin, H.P., *Mor. et Rob.* (1875), rich rose, medium, vigorous.

Duarte de Oliviera. N., *Brassac* (1879), rose salmon, medium, vigorous.

Duc d'Aumale, H.P., *E. Verdier* (1875), dark cerise, large, vigorous.

Duc de Cazès, H.P., *Touvais* (1860), dark purple, large, moderate.

Duc de Chartres, H.P., *E. Verdier* (1876), red purple, large, vigorous.

Duc d'Harcourt, H.P., *Mor. et Rob* carmine, medium, moderate.

Duc de Magenta, T., *Margottin* (1859), coppery rose, large moderate.

Duc de Malakoff, H.P., *Plantier*. (1856), red, large, moderate.

Duc de Montpensier, H.P., *Lévêque fils* (1875), red crimson, large, vigorous.

Duc de Nassau, H.P., *Pradel* (1873), red purple, medium, moderate.

Duc d'Orleans, H.P., *E. Verdier* (1888), vermilion red, large, vigorous.

Duc de Rohan, H.P., *Lévêque fils* (1861), bright red, large, moderate.

Duc de Wellington, H.P., *Granger* (1864), crimson, large, moderate.

Duoher, C., *Ducher* (1869), pure white, medium, moderate.

Durhess of Albany, H.P., *W. Paul & Son* (1888), rose pink, medium, robust.

Ducness of Bedford, H.P., *W. Paul & Son* (1879), scarlet crimson, large, vigorous.

Duchess of Connaught, H.P., *Bennett* (1878), silvery rose, large, moderate.

Duchess of Connaught, H.P., *Noble* (1883), crimson, large, vigorous.

Duchess of Edinburgh, T, *Nabonnand* (1874), bright red, large, moderate.

Duchess of Edinburgh, H.P., *Beunett* (1874), pink, large, vigorous.

Duchess of Fife, H.P., *Cocker* (1892), silvery red, large, vigorous.

Duchess of Norfolk, H.P., *Margottin* (1853), deep crimson, large, robust.

Duchess of Rutland, H.P., *Bennett* (1888), flesh pink, large, moderate.

Duchess of Sutherland, H.P., *Laffay* (1839), flesh pink, medium, moderate.

Duchess of Westminster, H.T., *Bennett* (1878), bright cerise, medium, moderate.

Duchess d'Alencon, H.P., *Mor. et Rob.* (1861), rose, medium, moderate.

Duchesse d'Aoste, H.P., *Margottin* (1867), glossy rose, large, vigorous.

Duchesse de Bragance, T., *Dubreuil* (1887), yellow, large, vigorous.

Duchesse de Cambacérès, H.P., *Fontaine* (1854), rich rose, large, vigorous.

Duchesse de Caylus, H.P., *E. Verdier* (1864), bright carmine, large, moderate.

Duchesse de Chartres, H.P., *E. Verdier* (1875), rose, medium, moderate.

Duchesse de Dine, H.P., *Paul & Son* (1891), crimson, medium, moderate.

Duchesse de Dino, H.P., *Levêque et. fils* (1889), carmine, large, vigorous.

Duchesse d'Harcourt, H.P., *Oger* (1873), rose lilac, medium, moderate.

Duchesse d'Istrie, M., *Portemer* (1857), rose, medium, moderate.

Duchesse de Magenta, H.P., *Guillot père* (1859), white, medium, moderate.

Duchesse de Medina Caeli, H.P., *Marest* (1864), red purple, medium, vigorous.

Duchesse Marie Salviati, T., *Soupert et Notting* (1889), yellow, large, vigorous.

Dnchesse d'Orleans, H.P., *Quetier* (1852), blush, large, moderate.

Duchesse d'Ossuna, H.P., *Jamain* (1876), rosy red, large, vigorous.

Duchesse de Thuringe, B., *Guillot père* (1847), blush-white, medium, moderate.

Duchesse Antonine d'Ursel, H.P., *Soup. et Not.* (1884), red, large, vigorous.

Duchesse de Valombrosa, H.P., *Nabonnand* (1879), red yellow, large, vigorous.

Duchesse de Valombrosa, H.P., *Schwartz* (1875), pink, rarge, vigorous.

Duhamel du Monceau, H.P., *Hugues* (1872), brilliant red, large, vigorous.

Duke of Albany, H.P., *W. Paul & Son* (1883), crimson, large, vigorous.

Duke of Cambridge, H.P., *Margottin* (1857), bright rose, large, moderate.

Duke of Connaught, H.T., *Bennett* (1878), deep crimson, large, moderate.

Duke of Connaught, H.P., *Paul & Son* (1876), bright crimson, medium, vigorous.

Duke of Edinburgh, H.P., *Paul & Son* (1868), crimson, large, vigorous.

Duke of Fife, H.P., Cocker (1892), crimson-scarlet, large, vigorous.

Duke of Marlborough, H.P., *Lèvêque* (1885), crimson, large, vigorous.

Duke of Teck, H.P., *Paul & Son* (1880), scarlet, large, vigorous.

Dumnacus, H.P., *Mor. et Rob* (1880), carmine red, large, vigorous.

Dundee Rambler, Ayr., *Martin*, pink, medium, robust.

Dupetit Thouars, B., *Portemer* (1844), red, medium, vigorous.

Dupuy Jamain, H.P., *Jamain* (1868), cerise red, large, vigorous.

Dybowski, H.P., *Lèvêque* (1892), vermilion red, large, moderate.

Earl of Beaconsfield, H.P., *Christy* (1880), carmine, medium, moderate.

Earl of Beaconsfield, H.P., *Schwartz* (1878), rosy crimson, large, vigorous.

Earl of Dufferin, H.P., *Dickson & Son* (1887), crimson, large, vigorous.

Earl of Pembroke, H.P., *Bennett* (1882), crimson, large, vigorous.

Ecae, Afgh., *In. fr. Afghn.* (1884), yellow, small, moderate.

Eclaire, H.P., *Lacharme* (1884), fiery red, medium, vigorous.

Eclair de Jupiter, N., crimson, medium, vigorous.

Edgar Jolibos, H.P., *E. Verdier* (1884), scarlet, medium, moderate.

Edith de Murat, B., *Ducher* (1858), flesh, medium, moderate.

Edmund Wood, H.P., *E. Verdier* (1875), dark cerise, large, vigorous.

Edouard André, H.P., *E. Verdier* (1879), rich red, large, vigorous.

Edouard Desfosses, B., *Renard* (1840), carmine rose, medium, moderate.

Edouard Dufour, H.P., *Lévêque fils* (1877), rich crimson, large, vigorous.

Edouard Fontaine, H.P., *Fontaine* (1878), silvery rose, large, moderate.

Edouard Gautier, T., *Ducher* (1884), white, small, moderate.

Edouard Hervé, H.P., *E. Verdier* (1885), crimson, medium, moderate.

Edouard Michel, H.P., *E. Verdier* (1888), rose carmine, large, vigorous.

Edouard Morren, H.P., *Granger* (1868), bright rose, large, vigorous.

Edouard Pynaert, H.P., *Schwartz* (1877), rich red, large, vigorous.

Egeria, H.P., *Schwartz* (1878), rose-pink, medium, vigorous.

Ella Gordon, H.P., *W. Paul & Son* (1884), cherry-red, large, vigorous.

Elie Morel, H.P., *Boucharlet* (1867), rosy lilac, large, vigorous.

Elise Fugier, T. (1890), white, medium, vigorous.

Elise Boelle, H.P., *Guilot père* (1869), pale rose, medium, vigorous.

Elise Flory, Ben., *Guilot père* (1851), rose, medium, moderate.

Elise Sauvage, *Miellez* (1818), yellow, medium, moderate.

Elise Schüle, H.T., *Giesler* (1892), cerise red, large, vigorous.

Elizabeth de la Rocheterie, H.P., *Vigneron* (1882), rose, medium, moderate.

Elizabeth Vigneron, H.P., *Vigneron* (1865), rose pink, large, vigorous.

Emile Bardiaux, H.P., *Lévêque et fils* (1889), carmine, large, vigorous.

Emilie Dulac, H.P., *Guillot* (1861), rose, large, moderate.

Emilie Dupuy, T., *Levet*, salmon, medium, vigorous.

Emilie de Girardin, P.M. (1854), rose, medium, moderate.

Emilie Hausburg, H.P., *Lévêque fils* (1869), satiny rose, large, vigorous.

Emilie Plantier, H.N., *Schwartz* (1878), bright yellow, large, vigorous.

Emily Laxton, H.P., *Laxton* (1877), red rose, large, vigorous.

Emma Coombey, H.P., *Gonod* (1872).

Emotion, B., *Guillot père* (1862), fiesh-white, medium, moderate.

Empéréur Alexandre III., H.P., *Soup. et Not.* (1885), carmine, large, vigorous.

Empéréur de Brésil, H.P., *Soup. et Not.* (1880), red, medium, vigorous.

Empéréur de Maroc, H.P., *Guinoisseau* (1858), crimson, medium, vigorous.

Emperor, H.P., *W. Paul & Son* (1884), crimson, small, vigorous.

Emperor Napoleon, H.P. (1854), crimson, medium, moderate.

Empress, H.P., *W. Paul & Son* (1884), pink, small, vigorous.

Empress of India, H.P., *Laxton* (1876). dark crimson, large, vigorous.

Enfant d'Amaugny, H.P., *Ducher* (1867), rose, large, vigorous.

Enfant du Mont Carmel, H.P., *Cherpin* (1851), rose, large, vigorous.

Enfants de Lyon, N., *Crozy* (1858).

Ennemond Boule, H.P., *Liabaud* (1879), bright red, medium, vigorous.

Erhprinzessin Marie von Ratibor, T., *Taske* (1892), capucin red, medium, moderate.

Ernest Boncenne, H.P., *Cherpin* (1867), brilliant rose, medium, vigorous.

Ernest Herger, H.P., *E. Verdier* (1873), bright purple, large, vigorous.

Ernest Metz, T., *J.B. Guillot* (1888), rose, large, robust.

Ernest Prince, H.P., *Ducher* (1882), rose, medium, vigorous.

Erzherzog Franz Ferdinand, T., *Soupert et Notting* (1892), red and gold, medium, moderate.

Etendard de Jeanne d'Arc, T., *Margottin*, (1884), white, medium, vigorous.

Etendard de Lyon, H.P., *Gonod* (1885), red, medium, moderate.

Etendard de Sebastopol, H.P., *Ducher* (1856), crimson, medium, moderate.

Etienne Dubois, H.P., *Damaizin* (1873), silvery rose, large, vigorous.

Etienne Dupuy, H.P., *Levet* (1873), silvery rose, large, vigorous.

Etienne Furst, H:P., *Soup. et Not.*, crimson, medium, vigorous.

Etienne Lecrosnier, H.P., *Oger* (1861), amaranth, medium, moderate.

Etna, M., *Laffay* (1845), crimson, medium, moderate.

Eioile d'Angers, T. (1890), coppery yellow, large, vigorous.

Etoile de Lyon, T., *Guillot* (1882), yellow, large, vigorous.

Etoile d'Or, N., *Dubreuil* (1889), yellow, medium, vigorous.

Eugène Appert, H.P., *V. Trouillard* (1869), crimson, large, vigorous.

Eugène Beauharnais, Ben., *Moreau* (1865), crimson, medium, moderate.

Eugène Boucier, H.P., *E. Verdier* (1861), purplish red, large, vigorous.

Eugène Petit, H.P., *Touvais*, carmine, medium, moderate.

Eugène Transon, H.P., *Vigneron* (1882), rose, medium, moderate.

Eugène Verdier, H.P.. *Guillot* (1863), red, medium, vigorous.

Eugène de Savoie, P.M., *Mor. et Rob.* (1861), bright red, medium, vigorous.

Eugène Savary, T., *Gonod* (1872), rosy yellow, medium, moderate.

Eugène Scribe, H.P., *Gautreau* (1866), fiery red, large, vigorous.

Eugène Sue, H.P., *Ducher* (1852), satiny rose, large, moderate.

Eugénie Bréon, B., *Berlet* (1847), flesh, small, moderate.

Eugénie Desgaches, T., *Plantier* (1835), clear rose, large, vigorous.

Eugénie Dubus, H.P., *Fontaine* (1861), red, medium, vigorous.

Eugénie Guinoisseau, M., *Guinoisseau* (1865), red, medium, moderate.

Euphrasie Rousseau, H.P., *Rousseau*, rose, medium, moderate.

Euryanthe, H.P., *Peters* (1866), dark red, medium, moderate.

Evelyn Turner, H.P., *E. Verdier*, rose, medium, moderate.

Evêque de Luxembourg, H.P., *Soup. et Not.* (1877), velvety crimson, medium, vigorous.

Evêque de Nîmes, H.P., *Plantier* (1857), scarlet crimson, large, moderate.

Exadelphé, T., *Nabonnand* (1886), yellow, large, vigorous.

Exposition de Brie, H.P., *Granger* (1865), bright red, large, vigorous.

Exposition du Havre, H.P., *Gautreau* (1869), rose-carmine, medium moderate.

Fabvier, C., *Laffay*, crimson, medium, moderate.

Fair Rosamond, C.H., *W. Paul & Son* (1890), rosy pink, large, vigorous.

Fata Morgana, T., *Drogemeller* (1892), satiny rose, medium, moderate.

Fanny Petzold, H.P., *Fontaine* (1865), satiny rose, large, vigorous.

Felicien David, H.P., *E. Verdier* (1872), carmine red, medium, moderate.

Félicité Parmentier, Ayr., blush, large, moderate.

Félicité Perpétué, E., *Jacques* (1828), flesh colour, medium, robust.

Félicité Rigaud, H.P., *Fontaine* (1824), satin rose, medium, moderate.

Felix Genero, H.P., *Damaizin* (1866), purple rose large, vigorous.

Felix Mousset, H.P., *E. Verdier* (1885), rose purple, medium, moderate.

Felix Ribeyre, H.P., *E. Verdier* (1888), bright rose, large, vigorous.

Fellenberg, N., crimson, medium, vigorous.

Ferdinand Chaffolte, H.P., *Pernet* (1879), bright red, large, vigorous.

Ferdinand de Lesseps, H.P., *E. Verdier* (1869), crimson, large, vigorous.

Fiancailles de la Princesse Stephanie, T. *Levet* (1880), orange yellow, medium, moderate.

Fimbriata, H.C., *Jacques* (1831), red, medium, moderate.

Firebrand, H.P., *Labruyère* (1873), brilliant crimson, large, robust.

Fisher Holmes, H.P., *E. Verdier* (1865), red scarlet, large, robust.

Flavescens, T., *In. fr. China* (1824), yellow, medium, moderate.

Flora, S., deep rose, small, vigorous.

Flora, P., *Schwartz* (1888), creamy white, small, vigorous.

Florence de Calquhoun', T., *Nabonnand* (1879), red lilac, medium, vigorous.

Flora Nabonnand, T., *Nabonnand* (1877), yellow medium, moderate.

Florent Pauwels, H.P., *Soup. et Not.* (1879), rose lilac, large, vigorous.

Fontenelle, M., Vibert (1849), rose, small, moderate.

Fontenelle, H.P., *Mor. et Rob.* (1877), carmine red, large, vigorous.

Fortunei, Bk, *In. fr. China* (1850), white, medium, vigorous.

Fortnne's Yellow, Bk., *In. fr. China* (1845), yellow, medium, vigorous.

Frances Bloxam, H.C., *Paul & Son* (1892), salmon medium, vigorous.

Francesco Ingegnoli, P., *Bernaix* (1888), red, medium, vigorous.

Francis the First, H.P., *Trouillard* (1859), crimson, medium, moderate.

Francisque Barillet, H.P., *Damaizin* (1866), cherry red, large, vigorous.

Francisque Kruger, T., *Nabonnand* (1880), flesh, large, vigorous.

Francisque Rive, H.P., *Schwartz* (1884), cerise, large, vigorous.

François Arago, H.P., *Trouillard* (1858), crimson, medium, moderate.

François Courtin, H.P., *E. Verdier* (1873), rich cerise, large, vigorous.

François Dubois, H.P., *Damaizim* (1866), crimson red, large, vigorous.

François Dugommier, B., *Mor. et Rob.* (1873) purple red, large, vigorous.

François Fontaine, H.P., *Fontaine* (1867), crimson, medium, vigorous.

François Gaulain, H.P., *Schwartz* (1878), deep purple, large, vigorous.

François Goeschke, H.P., *Soup. et Not.* (1865) rose lilac, large, vigorous.

François Herincq, H.P., *E. Verdier* (1878), poppy red, medium, moderate.

François I., H.P., *Trouillard* (1858), amaranth, medium, moderate.

François Lacharme, H.P., *V. Verdier* (1861), carmine, medium, moderate.

François Levet, H.P., *Levet* (1880), rose pink, medium, vigorous.

François Louvat, H.P., *Touvais* (1861), lilac red, large, vigorous.

François Menard, T., *Tesnier* (1892), crimson red, large, vigorous.

François Olin, H.P., *Ducher* (1882), red cerise, medium, vigorous.

François J. Pfister, H.P., *E. Verdier* (1876), red cerise, medium, vigorous.

François Premier, H.P., *Trouillard* (1858), red medium, moderate.

François Treyve, H.P., *Liabaud* (1866), red scarlet, large, vigorous.

F.M. Dos Santos Vianna, T., *Nabonnand* (1882), rose, medium, moderate.

Fredelick Wood, H.P., *E. Verdier*, cherry red, medium, vigorous.

Fringed, Musk, white, medium, vigorous.

Froissart, H.P., Miellez, carmine, small, moderate.

Fulgens, H.C., *Malton*, crimson, medium, vigorous.

Furstin Johanna Auersperg, H.P., *Soup. et Not.* (1884), rose, medium, moderate.

Gabriel Martel, H.P., T., *Levet* (1873), coppery yellow, large, vigorous.

Garden Favourite, H.P., *W. Paul* (1884), pink, large, vigorous.

Garibaldi, H.P., *Damaizin* (1859), rosy lilac, medium, moderate.

Gaspard Monge, H.P., *Mor. et Rob.* (1874), bright red, large, vigorous.

Gaston Chandon, T., *Schwartz* (1885), rose yellow, medium, moderate.

Gaston Lévêque, H.P., *Lévêque* (1878), bright crimson, large, vigorous.

Géant des Batailles, H.P., *Nerard* (1846), rich red, medium, moderate.

Gem of the Praries, Pra., *Burgess* (1865), red white, small, vigorous.

General Appert, H.P., *Schwartz* (1885), red purple, medium, vigorous.

Général Barral, H.P., *Damaizin* (1867), violet rose, medium, moderate.

Général Bedeau, H.P., *Margottin* (1851), carmine, medium, moderate.

Général Championnet, H.P., *Mor. et Rob.* (1866), rose red, large, moderate.

Général Castellane, H.P., *Guillot père* (1851), crimson, large, vigorous.

Général Cavaignac, H.P. (1851), light carmine, large, moderate.

Général Chargarnier, H.C., *Laffay* (1847), purple red, large, moderate.

Général de Cissey, H.P., *E. Verdier* (1875), scarlet, large, vigorous.

Général Dessaix, H.P., *Mor. et Rob.* (1867), fiery red, large, vigorous.

General Dumouriez, H.P., *Moreau*, cerise, medium, moderate.

General Grant, H.P., *E. Verdier* (1869), crimson scarlet, large, vigorous.

Général d'Hautpoul, H.P., *E. Verdier* (1864), red scarlet, large, moderate.

Général Jacqueminot, H.P., *Roussel* (1853), brilliant red, large, vigorous.

Général Jacqueminot, H.C., *Laffay* (1846), shaded lake, large, moderate.

Général Lamartinière, H.P., *Jamain* (1869), rose crimson, large, vigorous.

Général MacMahon, H.P. (1858), rose carmine, large moderate.

Général Mertschansky, T. (1890), pink, large, vigorous.

Général Milordowitch, H.P., *Lèvêque fils* (1869), red carmine, large, vigorous.

Général Mirandol, H.P., *Oger* (1864), deep red, medium, moderate.

Général von Moltke, H.P., *Bell* (1873), redt mediumt moderate.

Général Negzier, H.P., (1851), peach rose, mediumt, moderate.

Général Pelissier, H.P., *Ducher* (1855), light rose, large, vigorous.

Général Schlablikine, T., *Nabonnand* (1878), rose, medium, moderate.

Général Simpson, H.P., *Lacharme* (1854), carmine, large, vigorous.

Général Terwange, H.P., *Gautreau* (1874), brilliant rose, large, vigorous.

General Washington, H.P., *Granger* (1860), red crimson, large, moderate.

General Sir E. Wood, H.P., *Cant* (1882), rose, large, moderate.

George Baker, H.P., *Paul & Son* (1881), cerise laket medium, moderate.

George Moreau, H.P., *Mor. Rob.* (1881), red, large, vigorous.

George Patinot, H.P., *Gautreau* (1879), cerise, medium, vigoroue.

George Paul, H.P., *E. Verdier* (1863), bright rose, medium, moderate.

George Peabodyt B., *Pentland* (1857), crimson, small, moderate.

George Pernet, P., *Pernet fils* (1887), rose, small, vigorous.

George Prince, H.P., *E. Verdier* (1863), rose-red, medium, vigorous.

George Simont H.P., *Oger* (1863), bright red, medium, vigorous.

George Vibert, Prov., *Roberts* (1853), purple, medium, moderate.

Georges Furber, T., *Bernaix* (1889), purple, large, tnoderate.

Georges Schwartz, Mult., *Schwartz* (1889), rosy carmine, medium, robust.

Gigantèsque, T., *Odier* (1845), rose, medium, moderate.

Gipsy, H.T., *Laxton* (1884), dark red, medium, vigorous.

Gloire d'Angiers, H.P., *Boyau* (1846), bright rose, large, moderate.

Gloire de Bordeaux, T., *Lartey* (1861), lilac rose, large, vigorous.

Gloire de Chatillon, H.P., *Fontaine* (l861), red, medium, moderate.

Gloire de Cuivres, T., *Tesnier* (1889), coppery yellow, large, moderate.

Gloire de Dijon, T., *Jacofot* (1853), salmon bufft large, vigorous.

Gloire de Ducher, H.P., *Ducher* (1865), crimson purple, large, vigorous.

Gloire de l'Exposition de Bruxelles, H.P., *Soupert et Notting* (1889), purple amaranth, large, vigorous.

Gloire de France, H.P., *Margottin* (1854), crimson shaded, large, vigorous.

Gloire de Lyon, H.P., *Ducher* (1857), purplish red, medium, vigorous.

Gloire Lyonnais, H.T., *Guillot* (1885), white, medium, vigorous.

Gloire de Margottin, H.P., *Margottin* (1888), cerise, large, vigorous.

Gloire de Margottin, H.P., *Margottin* (1889), rich crimson, medium, moderate.

Gloire de Montplaisir, H.P., *Gonod* (1866), bright rose, large, vigorous.

Gloire des Mousseuses, M., *Laffay* (1852), blush, large, vigorous.

Gloire d'Orléans, H.P., *Vigneron* (1879), carmine red, large, vigorous.

Gloire de Polyantha, P., *Guillot et fils* (1888), bright rose, smallt vigorous.

Gloire de Bourg-la-Reine, H.P., *Margottin* (1879), red, large, vigorous.

Gloire de Rosomene, H.P., *Vibert*, crimson, large, robust.

Gloire de Santenay, H.P., *Ducher* (1859), purple red, medium, moderate.

Gloire de Thelwitz, H.P., *Peters* (1866), rose lake, medium, moderate.

Gloire de Vitry, H.P., *Masson* (1854), rose carmine, large, vigorous.

Gloriosa, H.P., *Touvais*, tender rose, small, moderate.

Glory of Cheshunt, H.P., *Paul & Son* (1880), crimson, large, vigorous.

Glory of Waltham, H.P., *Vigneron* (1864), rich crimson, large, robust.

G. Nabonnand, T., *Nabonnand et fils* (1888), rosy yellow, large, vigorous.

Gonsoli Gaelano, H.P., *Pernet* (1874), satiny rose, medium, moderate.

Goubalt, T., *Goubalt* (1843), bright pink, medium, moderate.

Goliath, H.P., *Trouillard* (1861), rose, edge white, large, vigorous.

Grace Darling, T., *Bennett* (1884), tinted white, medium, vigorous.

Gracilis, Bour., *Shailler* (1796), pink, medium, robust.

Grandeur of Cheshunt, H.P., *Paul & Son* (1883), crimson, large, vigorous.

Grand Duc Alexis, H.P., *Lévêque* (1892), blood red, large, vigorous.

Grand Duke Nicholas, H.P., *Lévêque fils* (1877), brilliant red, large, moderate.

Grand Mogul, H.P., *W. Paul & Son* (1887), crimson, large, vigorous.

Great Western, H.P., *Laffay* (1840), crimson scarlet, large, vigorous.

Gribaldo Nicola, T. (1890), nankin yellow, medium, vigorous.

Guillaume Guillemot, H.P., *Schwartz* (1880), rose, large, vigorous.

Gustave Courax, H.P., *Duval*, purple, medium, moderate.

Gustave Nadand, T., *Soup. et Not.* (1889), vermilion, large, vigorous.

Gustave Persin, H.P., *Fontaine* (1865), fiery red, large, vigorous.

Gustave Piganeau, H.P., *Pernet fils-Ducher* (1889), red, large, vigorous.

Gustave Revilliod, H.P., *Schwartz* (1875), bright rose, large, vigorous.

Gustave Rosseau, H.P., *Fargeton* (1862), violet red, medium, vigorous.

Gustave Thierry, H.P., *Oger* (1881), cherry red, medium, moderate.

Gustave Regis, H.T. (1890), canary yellow, medium, moderate.

Hans Makart, H.P., *E. Verdier* (1885), scarlet, medium, vigorous.

Harrison Weir, H.P., *Turner* (1879), velvety crimson, large, vigorous.

Harrison's Yellow, A.B., *Harrison* (1830), golden yellow, small, moderate.

Hebe, H.P., *Mor. et Rob.* (1884), rose, medium, moderate.

Heinrich Schultheis, H.P., *Bennett* (1882), rose, large, vigorous.

Helen, H.P., *Paul* (1854), rosy blush, medium, moderate.

Helen Paul, H.P., *Lacharme* (1882), blush pink, large, vigorous.

Héliogable, H.P., *Guinoisseau*, red, large, vigorous.

Helvetia, T., *Ducher* (1873), rose salmon, large, vigorous.

Henri Lecoq, T., *Ducher* (1871), shaded rose, medium, vigorous.

Henri Meynadier, T., *Nabonnand* (1885), rose, medium, moderate.

Henriette Pettite, H.r., *Margottin* (1879), amaranth rose, large, vigorous.

H.W. Beecher, H.P., *E. Verdier* (1874), purple red, large, vigorous.

Henry Bennett, H.P., *Lacharme* (1875), rosy carmine, large, vigorous.

Henry Bennett, T., *Levet* (1872), rosy sulphur, medium, moderate.

Henry Brichard, H.T. (1890), white, large, moderate.

Henry IV., H.P., *C. Verdier*, purple, medium, moderate.

Henry Ledechaux, H.P., *Ledechaux* (1868), carmine, large, moderate.

Henri Martin, M. , *Portemer* (1862), red, small, moderate

Henri Pagés, H.P., *Levet* (1870), bright rose, large, robust.

Henri Vilmorin, H.P., *Lévêque fils* (1878), rich red, large, vigorous.

Her Majesty, H.P., *Bennett* (1882), pink, large, robust.

Hermosa, B., *Marcheseau* (1840), bright rose, medium, vigorous.

Herodiade, N., *Brassac* (1888), rose, medium, vigorous.

Hippolyte Flandrin, H.P., *Damaizin* (1865), soft rose, large, moderate.

Hippolyte Jamain, H.P., *Faudin* (1869), rose, large, moderate.

Hippolyte Jamain, H.P., *Lacharme* (1874), carmine rose, large, vigorous.

Hippolyte Marchand, H.P., *Vigneron* (1882), rose, large, vigorous.

Homer, T., *Robert* (1859), salmon rose, medium, vigorous.

Hon. George Bancroft, H.T., *Bennett* (1878), rose, large, vigorous.

Hon. Edith Gifford, T., *Guillot* (1883), flesh, medium, vigorous.

Horace Vernet, H.P., *Guillot fils* (1866), purple red, medium, moderate.

Hortense Mignard, H.P., *Baltet* (1873), cherry red, medium, moderate.

Hortense Vernet, P.M., *Rob. et Mor.* (1861), pink, small, moderate.

Hortensia, T., *Ducher* (1870), rose salmon, large, vigorous.

Ida, T., *Mdme. Ducher* (1875), pale yellow, medium, moderate.

Imbricata, M., *Ducher* (1869), light rose, medium, moderate.

Impératrice Charlotte, H.P., *E. Verdier* (1867), rose, large, robust.

Impératrice Eugénie, B., *Beluze* (1855), rose, medium, moderate.

Impératrice Eugénie, P.M., *Guillot* (1855).

Impératrice des Francais, H.P., *Oger* (1855), flesh, large, vigorous.

Impératrice Maria Alexandra, H.P., *Damaizin* (1862).

Impératrice Marie Féodorowia, H.P., *Lévêque* (1892), rose, large, vigorous.

Inermis, H.P., *Lacharme* (1850), pink, small, moderate.

Ingegnoli Prediletta, T., *Bernaix* (1892), rose-mauve, largo, moderate.

Inigo Jones. H.P., *W. Paul & Son* (1886), dark rose, medium, vigorous.

Innocente Pirola, T., *Mdme. Ducher* (1878), white, large, vigorous.

Intendant Perrier, H.P., *Vigneron* (1882), cerise red, large, moderate.
Isabella, T., *Cels* (1838), white, small, moderate.
Isabella Gray, N., *Gray* (1855), yellow, medium, robust.
Isabella Sprunt, T., *Sprunt* (1866), pale yellow, large, vigorous.
Jacob Pereire, H.P., *Moreau*, purple red, medium, moderate.
Jacques Cartier, H.P., *Mor. et Rob.* (1868), clear rose, large, vigorous.
Jacques Lafitte, H.P., *Vibert* (1846), bright rose, large, moderate.
Jacques Plantier, H.P., *Damaizin* (1871), flesh rose, medium, moderate.
James Dickson, H.P., *E. Verdier* (1861), crimson, large, moderate.
James Mitchell, P.M., *E. Verdier* (1861), lilac rose, medium, moderate.
James Sprunt, B., *Sprunt* (1856), velvety crimson, medium, vigorous.
James Veitch, P.M., *E. Verdier* (1864), rosy purple, medium, vigorous.
James Watt, H.P., *Mor. et Rob.* (1873), lake, large, vigorous.
Jane Mossop, T., *Nabonnand* (1879), flesh white, medium, moderate.
Jaune Desprez, N., *Desprez* (1838), fawn and pink, medium, vigorous.
Jaune d'Or, T., *Oger* (1863), deep yellow, medium, moderate.
Jaune Nabonnand, T., *Nab.* (1890), chrome yellow, farge, vigorous.
J.B. Varrone, T., *Guillot et fils* (1889), rosy pink, large, moderate.
J.D. Pawle, H.P., *Paul & Son* (1890), crimson, large, vigorous.
Jean Bart, H.P., *Margottin* (1860), reddish violet, medium, vigorous.
Jean Bodin, M., *Vibert* (1847), rose, medium, moderate.
Jean Brosse, H.P., *Ducher* (1867), clear rose, medium, vigorous.
Jean Cherpin, H.P., *Liabaud* (1865), velvety red, large, moderate.
Jean Dalmais, H.P., *Ducher* (1873), cerise red, large, vigorous.
Jean Ducher, T., *Mad. Ducher* (1874), salmon yellow, large, vigorous.
Jean France, H.P., *Levet* (1866), dark purple, medium, moderate.
Jean Goujon, H.P., *Margottin* (1862), deep rose, large, vigorous.
Jean B. Guillot, H.P., *E. Verdier* (1861), purple red, medium, moderate.
Jean Hardy, N., *Hardy* (1859), yellow, medium, moderate.
Jean Lambert, H.P., *E. Verdier* (1865), dark red, large, vigorous.
Jean Lelièvre, H.P., *Oger* (1879), red crimson, large, vigorous.
Jean Liabaud, H.P., *Liabaud* (1875), velvety crimson, large, vigorous.
Jean Lorthois, T., *Ducher*, (1879), rose, medium, vigorous.

Jean Monford, M., *Robert* (1852), rose, small, moderate.

Jean Pernet, T., *Pernet* (1867), clear yellow, large, vigorous.

Jean Rosenkrantz, H.P., *Portemer fils* (1864), rich red, large, vigorous.

Jean Sisley, H.T., *Bennett* (1878), rose lilac, medium, moderate.

Jean Soupert, H.P., *Lacharme* (1875), velvety purple, large, moderate.

Jean Touvais, H.P., Touvais (1863), purple red, medium, vigorous.

Jeanne Abel, T., *Guillot* (1883), rose, medium, vigorous.

Jeanne d'Arc, N., *V. Verdier* (1848), white, medium, vigorous.

Jeanne d'Arc, N., *Ducher* (1869), light yellow, medium, moderate.

Jeanne Chevalier, H.P., *Rambaux* (1879), bright red, medium, vigorous.

Jeanne Drivon, P., *Schwartz* (1884), tinted white, small, moderate.

Jeanne Guillaumez, T., *Bonnaire* (1889), red, large, vigorous.

leanne Guillot, H.P., *Liabaud* (1869), satiny rose, large, vigorous.

Jeanne Hachette, H.P., *Oger*, carmine, medium, moderate.

Jeanne Hely d'Oissel, H.P., *Ledéchaux* (1889), red, medium, vigorous.

Jeanne Renou, H.P.. *Oger*, rose, medium, vigorous.

Jeanne Sury, H.P., *Fandon* (1868), claret crimson, large, moderate.

Jenny Lind, H.M., (1845), crimson, medium, moderate.

Joacnim du Bellay, H.P., *Mor. et Rob.* (1883), vermilion, medium, vigorous.

John Bright, H.P., *Paul & Son* (1878), scarlet, large, vigorous.

John Cranston, P.M., *E. Verdier* (1861), violet red, medium, vigorous.

John Fraser, H.P., *E. Verdier* (1876), red crimson, large, vigorous.

John Fraser, P.M., Lévêque (1861), red and carmine, medium, vigorous.

John Grier, H.P., *E. Verdier* (1865), bright red, large, vigorous.

John Harrison, H.P., *E. Verdier* (1873), purple crimson, large, vigorous.

John Hopper, H.P., Ward (1862), rosy crimson, large, vigorous,

John Keynes, H.P., *E. Verdier* (1864), bright red, large, vigorous.

John Laing, H.P., *E. Verdier* (1872), bright crimson, small, moderate.

John Stuart Mill, H.P., *Turner* (1874), clear red, large, vigorous.

John Saul, H.P., *Mad. Ducher* (1878), carmine red, medium, vigorous.

John Gould Veitch, H.P., *Lévêque fils* (1864), purple, large, moderate.

Joseph Bernachi, N., *Ducher* (1878), pale yellow, medium, vigorous.

Joseph Chappaz, H.P., *Schmidt* (1883), lilac, medium, moderate.

Joseph Decaisne, H.P. (1852), bright rose, medium, moderate.

Joseph Degueld, H.P. (1890), bright carmine, large, moderate.

Joseph Metral, T., *Bernaix* (1888), magenta, large, vigorous.

Joseph Metral, H.P. *Liabaud* (1884), garnet red, medium, moderate.

Joseph Tasson, H.P., *Soup. et. Not.* (1883), purple, medium, vigorous.

Joseph Teysier, T., *Dubreuil* (1892), rose yellow, medium, moderate.

Josephine Beauharnais, H.P., *Guillot fils* (1865), rose, large, vigorous.

Josephine Clement, B:, *Guillot* (1858), pink, medium, moderate.

J. Prowe, H.P., *Lévêque* (1892), red, large, moderate.

Jules Bourgeois, H.P., *Ledechaux* (1867), velvety red, medium, moderate.

Jules Bourquin, T., *Chauvry* (1892), yellow and lilac, large, vigorous.

Jules Calot, H.P., *E. Verdier* (1866), red carmine, large, vigorous.

Jules César, B., *E. Verdier* (1865), rose cerise, large, vigorous.

Jules Chrétien, H.P., *Damaizin* (1869), satiny rose, large, vigorous.

Jules Chrétien, H.P., *Schwartz* (1877), puple crimson, large, vigorous.

Jules Desponds, H.P., *Liabaud* (1888), cinnabar red, large, vigorous.

Jules Finger, T., *Mad. Ducher* (1879), blush white, large, vigorous.

Jules Jurgensen, B., *Schwartz* (1879), purple crimson, large, vigorous.

Jules Lavay, H.P., *Damaizin* (1864), rosy flesh, large, vigorous.

Jules Marquinant, H.P., *Vigneron* (1883), red, large, moderate.

Jules Margotin, H P., *Margottin* (1853), rosy red, large, vigorous.

Jules Mongès, H.P., *Guillot* (1882), carmine, large, vigorous.

Jules Seurre, H.P., *Liabaud* (1869), carmine red, medium, vigorous.

Julie de Mersant, M., rose, medium, vigorous.

Julie Fontaine, H.P., *Fontaine* (1878), salmon rose, large, vigorous.

Julie Touvais, H.P., *Touvais* (1868), rose flesh, large, vigorous.

Julie Treyve, H.P., *Liabaud* (1868), pale rose, large, vigorous.

Juliette Berthand, B., (1890), white, medium, vigorous.

Julius Finger, H.P., *Lacharme*, (1879), rosy red, large, vigorous.

Juno, H.C., *Laffay* (1847), light rose, large, vigorous.

Jury, B., *Guillot* (1885), cherry red, medium, moderate.

Kaiserin Augusta Victoria, T., *Lambert* (1890), yellowish white, medium, moderate.

Kaiserin Friedrich, T., *Drogemuller* (1890), yellow, large, vigorous.

Karl Müller, H.P., *Soup. et Not.*, amaranth, medium, vigorous.

Karl Marie von Weber, P., *Turque* (1892), carmine and yellow, medium, moderate.

Kate Hausburg, H.P., *Granger* (1863), rose pink, large, vigorous.

Katkoff, H.P., *Mor. et Rob.* (1888), carmine, large, vigorous.

Kean, G., purple, medium, vigorous.

King of the Prairies, Pra. , *Feast* (1843), rose, small, vigorous.

King's Acre, H.P., *Cranston* (1864), vermilion, large, moderate.

Kleber, H.P., *Boyau* (1872), crimson red, medium, moderate.

Krimhilde, T., *Drogemeller* (1892), yellow, medium, moderate.

Kronprinzessin Victoria, B., *Spath* (1888), white, large, vigorous.

L'Abondance, H.P., *E. Verdier* (1864), bright red, medium, vigorous.

L'Abondance, N., *Mor. et Rob.* (1888), pure white, small, vigorous.

L'Idea1, N., *Nabonnand* (1888), yellow, medium, vigorous.

La Lisette de Béranger, H.P., *Moreau* (1867), flesh, medium, moderate.

La Tour d'Auvergne, G., rose, medium, vigorous.

La Valliante Bergère, H.P., *Cherpin* (1847).

La Boule D'Or, T., *Margottin* (1860), yellow, large, moderate.

La Bouquetière, B, *Laffay*, (1843), rose, medium, moderate.

La Brillante, H.P., *E. Verdier*, (1861), bright carmine, medium, moderate.

La Caleta, T., *Priez & Ketten* (1892), white yellow, large, moderate.

La Chanson, T., (1890), rosy carmine, large, vigorous.

La Favorite, H.P., *Guillot* (1871), tender rose, medium, moderate.

La Fontaine, H.C. *Guinoisseau* (1855), red, medium, moderate.

La France H.P., *Guillot fils* (1867), bright pink, large, vigorous.

La France de 89, H.T., *Moreau-Robert* (1889), red, large, vigorous.

Laforcade, H.P., *Lévêque et fils* (1889), carmine, large, vigorous.

La Grandeur, T., *Nabonnand* (1877), rose, large, vigorous.

La Jonquille. T., *Ducher* (1871), deep yellow, medium, moderate.

La Lune, T., *Nabonnand* (1878), creamy yellow, large, vigorous.

La Madeleine, H.P., *Nabonnand* (1882), ruby red, medium, moderate.

La Duchesse de Morny. H.P., *E. Verdier* (1863), rose, large, vigorous.

La Motte Sanguine, H.P., *Vigneron*, (1869), crimson, large, robust.

La Nuance, T., *Guillot fils*, (1875), rosy white. large, vigorous.

La Princesse Vera, T., *Nabonnand* (1878), creamy white. medium, moderate.

La Quintinie, H.P., (1853), deep crimson, large, moderate.

La Reine, H.P., *Laffay* (1843), rosy pink, large, moderate.

La Rosiere, H.P., *Damaizin* (1874), dark crimson, medium, moderate.

La. Saumonée H.P., *Margottin* (1877), salmon rose, large, moderate.

La Séduisante H.P., *Lacharme*, (1850), carmine, medium, moderate.

La Sirène, H.P., *Soup. et Not.* (1867), amaranth purple, small, vigorous.

La Souveraine, H.P., *E. Verdier* (1874) magenta rose, large, robust.

La Sylphide, T., *Laffay*, cream, large, moderate.

La Toulousaine, H.N., *Brassac* (1877), rose white, small, moderate.

La Tulipe, T., *Ducher* (1868), white rose, medium, moderate.

La Ville de Bruxelless, D., *Vibert* (1836), rose, medium, moderate.

La Ville de St. Denis, H.P., *Thomas*, rosy carmine, large, moderate.

Lady Alice, H.T., *Paul & Son*, (1888), flesh pink, medium, moderate.

Lady Mary Fitzwilliam. H.T., *Bennet*, (1882), flesh, large, vigorous.

Lady Fordwick, H.C., *Laffay*, (1838), rose, medium, moderate.

Lady Henr, Grosvenor, H.T., *Bennett*, (1892), pale flesh, large, vigorous.

Lady of the Lake, H.P., *Paul & Son*, (1884) peach, large, vigorous.

Lady Emily Peel, H.N., *Lacharme*, (1862), carmine, medium, vigorous.

Lady Sheffield. H.P., *Postans* (1881), rosy cerise, large, vigorous.

Lady Shelley, H.P., *Mitchell* (1853), shaded crimson, large, vigorous.

Lady Helen Stewart, H.P., *Dickson & Son*, (1886), scarlet, large, vigorous.

Lady Stnart, H.C., *Portemer* (1852), pink, medium, moderate.

Lady Suffield, H.P., *W. Paul* (1866), purple crimson, large, vigorous.

Lacépède, H.P., *C. Verdier* (1865), clear red, medium, moderate.

Laelia, H.P., *Crozy* (1857), rose pink, large, vigorous.

Laelia, H.P., *Laffay* (1844), rose lilac, laige, moderate.

Laïs, T., *Damaizin*, (1863), yellow, medium, moderate.

Lamarque N., *Maréchal*, (1830), sulphur white, medium, vigorous.

Lamarque à Fleurs Jaunes, N., *Ducher* (1869), yellow, medium, moderate.

Lamartine, H.B., *Guillot* (1842).

Lanei, M., *Laffay* (1845), rose crimson, large, vigorous.

Laura Davoust, Mult., pink, small, vigorous.

Laure Redmond, H.P., *Lacharme* (1850), blush, medium, moderate.

Laure Fontaine, T., *Fontaine* (1867), creamy white, medium, moderate.

Laurent Carle, H.P., *E. Verdier* (1889), rosy carmine, medium, vigorous.

Laurent de Rillé, H.P., *Lévêque* (1885), cerise, medium, moderate.

Laurente Descours, H.P., *Liabaud*, (1862), velvet purple, medium, moderate.

Lays, N., *Guillot*. (1848).

Le Blanqui, T., *Ducher* (1871), white, large, vigorous.

Le Bignonia, T., *Levet* (1873), orange yellow, medium, moderate.

L'Eblouissante, H.P., *Touvais* (1861), crimson, large, moderate.

Le camée, B., *Beluze* (1845).

L'Elegante, T., *Guillot*, (1883), yellow pink, medium, vigorous.

L'Enfant du Mont-Carmel, H.P., *Cherpin* (1851), rose, large, vigorous.

L'Etincelante, H.P., *E. Verdier* (1875), bright red, large, vigorons.

Le Royal Epoux, H.P., *Damazin*, pink, medium, moderate.

L'Esperance, H.P., *Fontaine* (1871), cherry red, large, moderate.

L'Esperance, H.P., *Lartay*, rose, medium, vigorous.

La Florifère T., *Ducher* (1870), salmon white, medium moderate.

Le Havre, H.P., *Eude* (1870), vermilion, large, vigorous.

L'Ideale, N., *Paul & Son* (1890), rich apricot, medium, vigorous.

Le Khedive, H.P., *Barrault* (1883), crimson, medium, moderate.

Le Loiret, H.P., *Ribault* (1883), carmine, large, vigorous.

Le Mont Blanc, T., *Ducher* (1869), white yellow, large, vigorous.

Le Nankin, T., *Ducher* (1871), white rose, large, vigorous.

Le Pactole, T., *Pean*, cream, large, moderate.

Le Rhône, H.P., *Guillot fils* (1862), scarlet crimson, large, moderate.

Le Roitelet, B., *Soup. et Not.* (1868), satiny rose, small, moderate.

Lecocq-Dumesnil. H.P., *E. Verdier* (1883), red, large, vigorous.

Lena Turner, H.P., *E. Verdier* (1869), cerise red, large, vigorous.

Léonce Giessen, H.P., *Lacharme* (1875).

Léonie Osterrieth, T., *Soup et Not.* (1892), white yellow, medium, moderate.

Léon Duval, H.P., Lévêque (1879), red carmine, medium, vigorous.

Léon Renault, H.P., *Ledechaux* (1878), cherry red, medium, vigorous.

Leon Say, H.P., *Lévêque* (1883), red lilac, large, vigorous.

Leon XIII., T., *Soup. et Not.* (1892), white yellow, medium, moderate.

Léopold I., H.P., *Vanasche* (1863), deep red, large, vigorous.

Léopold II., H.P., *Margottin* (1868), rosy red, large, robust.

Léopold de Bauffremont, H.C., pink, medium, vigorous.

Léopold Hausburg, H.P., *Granger* (1864), bright carmine, large, vigorous.

Leopold Vauvel, H.P., *E. Verdier* (1889), rosy red, large, vigorous.

Letty Coles, T., *Keynes* (1875), rose carmine, large, vigorous.

Leveson Gower, H.T., *Beluze* (1846), rose salmon, medium, moderate.

Leon des Combats, H.P., *Lartay* (1853), carmine, large, vigorous.

Lichas, B., *Guillot* (1845).

Lisette de Beranger, H.P., *Guillot fils* (1867), rosy flesh, large, vigorous.

Little Gem, M., *W. Paul* (1880), crimson, small, vigorous.

Longfellow, H.P., *Paul & Son* (1885), crimson, large vigorous.

Longworth Rambler, E., *Liabaud* (1880), crimson, medium, robust.

Lord Bacon, H.P., *W. Paul & Son* (1883), crimson, large, vigorous.

Lord Beacosfield, H.P., *Bennett* (1878), dark crimson, large, vigorous.

Lord F. Cavendish, H.P., *Frettingham* (1883), scarlet, medium, vigorous.

Lord Clyde, H.P., *Paul & Son* (1863), red crimson, large, vigorous.

Lord Eldon, T., *Coppin* (1872), saffron yellow, large, moderate.

Lord Elgin, H.P., *Guillot père* (1858), dark purple, medium, moderate.

Lord Herbert, H.P., *W. Paul* (1862), deep carmine, medium, moderate.

Lord Macaulay, H.P., *W. Paul* (1863), deep crimson, large, robust.

Lord Palmerston, H.P., *Margottin* (1857), carmine, medium, moderate.

Lord Raglan, H.P., *Guillot père* (1854), crimson, medium, moderate.

Louis d'Arzens, H.N., *Lacharme*, (1861), blush, medium, moderate.

Louis d'Autriche, H.P., (1858), violet red, large, vigorous.

Louis Barlet, T., *Mdme. Ducher* (1875), almon white, medium, moderate.

Louis Brassic, H.P., *Brassac*, satiny rose, large, moderate.

Loujs Builliat, H.P., *Gonod* (1867), red crimson, large, vigorous.

Louis Chaix, B., *Lacharme* (1857), deep crimson, medium, moderate.

Louis Donadine, H.P., J.M., *Gonod* (1887), dark marroon, large, vigorous.

Louis Dore, H.P., *Fontaine* (1878), red, medium, moderate.

Louis XIV., H.P., *Guillot fils* (1859), velvety red, large, weak.

Louis Gigot, T., *Ducher* (1871), white rose, medium, moderate.

Louis Gimurd, M., *Pernet* (1877), bright red, medium, moderate.

Louis Guilland, T., *Nabonnand et fils* (1888), rose, large, vigorous.

Louis van Houtte, H.P., *Granger* (1863), rich carmine, large, vigorous.

Louis van Houtte, H.P., *Lacharme* (1869), red crimson, large, moderate.

Louis Lille, H.P., *Dubreuil* (1887), bright red, large, vigorous.

Louis Margottin, H.P., *Margottin* (1862), pale rose, medium, moderate.

Louis Noisette, H.P., *Ducher* (1865).

Louis Odier, B., *Margottin* (1861), rich rose, large, vigorous.

Louise Phillippe Albert d'Orleans, H.P., *E. Verdier* (1885), cerise, medium, vigorous.

Louis Richard, T., *Mdme. Ducher* (1877), rosy yellow, medium, vigorous.

Louis Spath, H.P., *Soup. et Not.* (1876), rose pink, large, moderate.

Louisa Gretton, H.P., *Cranston* (1882), crimson, medium, moderate.

Louisa Wood, H.B., *E. Verdier* (1869), bright rose, large, vigorous.

Louise Nabonnand, T., *Nabonnand* (1892), rose yellow, large, vigorous.

Louise Damaizin, H.P., *Damaizin* (1863), rosy red, large, vigorous.

Louise Darzens, H.N., *Lacharme* (1861), pure white, medium, vigorous.

Louise Odier, H.P., *Margottin* (1850), bright rose, medium, moderate.
Louise Peyronny, H.P., Lacharme (1844), rose pink, large, vigorous.
Louise de Savoie, T., *Ducher* (1853), pale yellow, large, vigorous.
Luciole, T., *Guillot* (1887), rosy red, large, vigorous.
Lucrèce, T., *Oger* (1866), salmon rose, medium, moderate.
Lusidas, T., *De Costo* (1885), yellow, medium, vigorous.
Lutea, B.K. (1827), yellow, small, vigorous.
Luxembourg, M., crimson, medium, vigorous.
Lyonnais, H.P., *Lacharme* (1871), bright pink, large, vigorous.
Ma Capucin, T., *Levet* (1871), bright yellow, medium, moderate.
Ma Frisée, H.P., *Vigneron*, red, medium, moderate.
Ma Pivoine, H.P., *Levet* (1866), purple-violet, large, vigorous.
Ma Ponctuée, P.M., *Guillot père* (1858), spotted rose, medium, vigorous.
Ma Surprise, M.I.C., *Guillot fils* (1872), salmon pink, medium, moderate.
Ma Surprise, H.P., *Levet* (1884), red, medium, moderate.
Mabel Morrison, H.P., *Broughton* (1878), white, large, vigorous.
MacMahon, H.P., *E. Verdier* (1872), rose, large, moderate.
Mdme. Albani, H.P., *E. Verdier* (1877), brilliant red, medium, moderate.
Mdme. Alboni, M., *V. Verdier* (1850), pink, medium, moderate.
Mdme. Caradori Allen, P., *Feast* (1843), pink, medium, moderate.
Mdme. Alice Allatina, H.P., *Nabonnand* (1889), red, large, vigorous.
Mdme. Alegatière, P., *Alegatiere* (1888), bright rose, medium, vigorous.
Mdme. Amadieu, T., *Pernet* (1881), rose, medium, moderate.
Mdme. Eugene Appert, H.P., *Trouillard* (1865), rosy salmon, medium, vigorous.
Mdme. d'Arblay, MUSK., white, small, vigorous.
Mdme. Arntzenius, H.P., *Soup et Not.* (1874), carmine, large, vigorous.
Mdme. Alphonse Aubert, H.P., *Fontaine* (1875), carmine, large, vigorous.
Mdme. Amélie Baltet, H.P., *E. Verdier* (1878), rose, large, vigorous.
Mdme. Charles Baltet, B.P., *E. Verdier* (1865), rose, small, moderate.
Mdme. Jean Bausillon, T., *Godard* (1892), straw white large, vigorous.

Mdme. Lauriol de Barny, H., *Trouillard* (1868), rose, large, vigorous.

Mdme. Barriot, H.P., *Damaizin* (1867), carmine rose, medium, vigorous.

Mdme. Bellon, H.P., *Pernet* (1871), tender rose, medium, moderate.

Mdme. Bérard, T., *Levet* (1870), salmon rose, large, vigorous.

Mdme. Alexandre Bernaix, H.T., *Guillot fils* (1877), rose, large, vigorous.

Mdme. Bernard, T., *Levet* (1876), creamy rose, medium, moderate.

Mdme. Lefebvre Bernard, H.P., *Levet* (1871), rose, large, vigorous.

Mdme. Bernutz, H.P., *Jamain* (1874), satin rose, large, moderate.

Mdme. Bertrand, H.P.. *Pernet père* (1889), rose, large, vigorous.

Mdme. Anna de Besobrassoff, H.P., *Gonod* (1877), carmine rose, medium, moderate.

Mdme. Martin de Bessé, H.P., *Granger* (1866), tinted rose, medium, moderate.

Mdme. F. Besson, H.P., *Besson* (1882), flesh pink, large, vigorous.

Mdme. Marie Bianchi, H.P., *Guillot* (1882), lilac, large, vigorous.

Mdme. Alfred Bleu, H.P., *E. Verdier* (1885), crimson, medium, moderate.

Mdme. Boll, H.P., Boll (1859), carmine rose, large, vigorous.

Mdme. Gustave Bonnet, H.P., *Lacharme* (1860), pink, medium, moderate.

Mdme. Gustave Bonnet, N., *Lacharme* (1864), rose white, small, vigorous.

Mdme. Maxime Bonnet, B., *Pradel* (1861), cerise red, large, vigorous.

Mdme. Jeanne Bouger, H.P., *Gonod* (1877).

Mdme. Arséne Bouneau, H.P., *Bouneau*, rose, moderate, vigorous.

Mdme. Martha du Bourg, T., *Bernaix* (1889), yellow, large, vigorous.

Mdme. Boutin, H.P., *Jamain* (1861), crimson red, large, vigorous.

Mdme. Jean Bouyer, H.P., *Gonod* (1877), rose pink, large, moderate.

Mdme. Emilie Boyau, H.P., *Boyau* (1864), rose flesh, large, vigorous.

Mdme. Bravy, T., *Guillot père* (1848), creamy white, large, moderate.

Mdme, Bremond, T., *Guillot et fils* (1866), deep red, medium, moderate.

Mdme. G. Bruant, H.R., *Bruant* (1888), white, large, vigorous.

Mdme. Bruel, H.P., *Levet* (1882), rose carmine, large, moderate.

Mdme. Bruny, H.P., Plantier (1858), rose, small, moderate.

Mdme. F. Buchner, H.P., *Lévêque* (1885), rose, medium, moderate.

Mdme. Anna Bugnet, B., *Gonod* (1866), flesh white, medium, moderate.

Mdme. William Bull, H.P., *E. Verdier* (1876), rose, medium, vigorous.

Mdme. Jules Caboche, H.P., *Vigneron*, rose, medium, vigorous.

Mdme. Martin Cahusac, T., *Lévêque* (1892), rose yellow, large, vigorous.

Mdme. Caillat, H.P., *E. Verdier* (1861), bright cerise, large, vigorous.

Mdme. Ernest Calvat, B., *Schwartz* (1888), rose pink, large, vigorous.

Mdme. Camille, T., *Guillot fils* (1871), salmon rose, large, vigorous.

Mdme. Canrobert, H.P., *Gonichon* (1868), carmine, medium, vigorous.

Mdme. Canrobert, H.P., *Liabaud* (1862), pale lilac, medium, moderate.

Mdme. Carl, H.T., *Bernaix* (1887), red, medium, vigorous.

Mdme. Louis Carique, H.P., *Fontaine* (1859), crimson, large, vigorous.

Mdme. Carnot, N., *Moreau-Robert* (1889), golden yellow, medium, vigorous.

Mdme. Sadi Carnot, T., *Renand Guepet* (1889), salmon, large, robust.

Mdme. Caro, T., *Levet* (1880), salmon, large, vigorous.

Mdme. Alfred Carrière, N., *Schwartz* (1879), flesh colour, large, vigorous.

Mdme. Miolan Carvalho, N., *Lévêque* (1875), sulphur, large, vigorous.

Mdme. Chabal, H.P., *Schwartz* (1889), rose, medium, vigorous.

Mdme. Eugène Chambeyran, H.P., *Gonod* (1878), rose, large, vigorous.

Mdme. Raoul Chandon, H.P., *C. Verdier* (1885), rose, small, moderate.

Mdme. Charles, T., *Damaizin* (1864), apricot yellow, medium, vigorous.

Mdme. Rose Charmeux, H.P., *Gautreau* (1874), purple red, medium, moderate.

Mdme. Chaté, H.P., *Fontaine* (1871), cherry red, medium, moderate.

Mdme. L. Chaure, H.P., *Vigneron* (1885), red cerise, large, vigorous.

Mdme. Chaveret, T., *Levet* (1872). apricot yellow, large, vigorous.

Mdme. Elize de Chenier, B. (1858), bright pink, medium, moderate.

Mdme. Chierot, H.P., *Pernet* (1877), bright rose, large, vigorous.

Mdme. Chignard, H.T., *Vigneron* (1877), clear red, large, vigorous.

Mdme. Chirard, H.P , *Pernet* (1867), fresh rose, large, vigorous.

Mdme. Marie Cirodde, H.P., *C. Verdier* (1867), pink, large, vigorous.

Mdme. Clavel, H.P., *Lacharme* (1856).

Mdme. Clurt, H.P., *Gonod* (1868), rosy salmon, large, vigorous. .

Mdme. Scipion Cochet, H.P., *Desmazures* (1871), cherry, large, vigorous.

Mdme. Scipion Cochet, T. (1887), yellow, large, vigorous.

Mdme. Collet, B., *Liabaud* (1864), rosy white, medium, vigorous.

Mdme. de la Collonge, H.P., *Level père* (1889), bright rose, large, vigorous.

Mdme. Emma Combey, H.P., *Gonod* (1872), carmine, large, vigorous.

Mdme. Contesse, B. (1858), peach, medium, vigorous.

Mdme. Adeline Cote, H.P., *Schmidt* (1882), red crimson, large, vigorous.

Mdme. Marcus Cote, H.P., *Guillot fils* (1872), rosy red, large, vigorous.

Mdme. Coulombler, H.P., *Lévêque* (1884), rose red, medIum, moderate.

Mdme. Charles Crapelet, H.P., *Fontaine* (1859), rose red, large, vigorous.

Mdme. Creyton, H.P., *Gonod* (1868), bright carmine, large, robust.

Mdme. Crozy, H.P., *Levet* (1882), pink, medium, moderate.

Mdme. Cuzin, T., *Guillot* (1882), rose yellow, medium, vigorous.

Mdme. Damaizin, T., *Damaizin* (1858), salmon, large. vigorous.

Mdme. Julie Daran, H.P., *Touvais* (1861), rosy crimson, large, vigorous.

Mdme. Debray, H.P., T. *Ribault* (1885), rose, medium, vigorous.

Mdme. Decour, H.P., *Pernet* (1868), rich rose, large, robust.

Mdme. Th. Delacour, H.P., *E. Verdier* (1885), carmine, metlium, moderate.

Mdme. Lelievre Delaplace, H.P., *E. Verdier* (1883), red, large, vigorous.

Mdme. Delaville, T., *Oger* (1873), sulphur yellow, medium, moderate.

Mdme. Dellevaux H.P., *Besson* (1884), satin rose, large, vigorous.

Mdme. Denis, T., *Gonod* (1872), sulphur white, medium, moderate.

Mdme. Desbordeaux, H.P., *Oger* (1873), satiny rose, medium, moderate.

Mdme. Joseph Desbois, H.T., *Guillot* (1886), flesh, large, vigorous.

Mdme. Barillet Deschamps, T., *Bernède* (1855), yellow, medium, moderate.

Mdme. Therese Deschamps, T., *Nabonnand et fils* (1888), bright red, large, vigorous.

Mdme. Honoré Defresne, T., *Levet* (1886), deep yellow, large, vigorous.

Mdme. Desir, H.P., *Pernet* (1886), bright rose, large, vigorous.

Mdme. Baptiste Desportes, H.P., *Trouillard* (1865), rose, medium, moderate.

Mdme. Just Detry, B., *Detry* (1869), red carmine, large, moderate.

Mdme. Devaucoux, T., *Mdme. Ducher* (1874), canary, medium, moderate.

Mdme. Devert, H.P., *Pernet* (1876), rose pink, medium, moderate.

Mdme. Angèle Dispott. H.P., *Dauvesse* (1869), fiery red, medium, moderate.

Mdme. Domage, H.P., *Margottin* (1854), rosy crimson, large, vigorous.

Mdme. Louis Donadine, H.P., *Gonod* (1877), pink, large, moderate.

Mdme. Doré, B., *Foniaine* (1863), rose purple, medium, moderate.

Mdme. Dorgerc, T. (1890), large, moderate.

Mdme. Dorlia, H.P., *Fontaine* (1877), bright cerise, medium, vigorous.

Mdme. Derreux Douville, H.P., *Lévêque* (1863), tender rose, large, vigorous.

Mdme. E. Dreol, H.P., *Dreol* (1861), rose lilac, medium, moderate.

Mdme. Dubuisson, H.P., *Baudry* (1861), carmine, medium, moderate.

Mdme. Dubois, H.P., *Fontaine* (1866), vermilion red, medium, moderate.

Mdme. Ducamp, H.P., *Fontaine* (1863), purple red, medium, moderate.

Mdme. Ducher, T., *Ducher* (1869), clear yellow, medium, moderate.

Mdme. Ducher, H.P., *Levet* (1879), cerise red, large, moderate.

Mdme. Emilie Dunau, N., *Nabonnand* (1879), tender rose, large, moderate.

Mdme. Michel Dupré, H.P., *Gonod* (1876), brilliant red, large, vigorous.

Mdme. Emilie Dupuy, T., *Levet* (1870), yellow, medium, vigorous.

Mdme. Durand, T. (1890), bright yellow, large, vigorous.

Mdme. Alice Dureau, H.P., *Vigneron* (1869), rose, medium, moderate.

Mdme. André Duron, H.T., *Bonnaire* (1887), clear red, large, vigorous.

Mdme. Dustour, H.P., *Pernet* (1869), carmine red, large, vigorous.

Mdme. Emain, H.P., *Pernet* (1872), purple red, large, vigorous.

Mdme. Bonnet Eymard, T., *Pernet* (1874), yellow, medium, moderate.

Mdme. Falcot, T., *Guillot fils* (1858), apricot yellow, medium, vigorous.

Mdme. Farfouillon, H.P., *Liabaud* (1868), satiny rose, large, vigorous.

Mdme. Fauvennier, H.P., *Fontaine* (1878), rose, medium, moderate.

Mdme. Ocker Ferenez, T., *Bernaix* (1892), canary and carmine, large, vigorous.

Mdme. Fillion, H.P., *Gonod* (1865), flesh rose, medium, vigorous.

Mdme. Marie Finger, H.P., *Rambaux* (1873), flesh rose, large, vigorous.

Mdme. A. Fitler, H.P., *Faudon* (1873), salmon rose, large, vigorous.

Mdme. Fanny. de Forest, H.N., *Schwartz* (1883), salmon, medium, moderate.

Mdme. E. Forgeot, H.P. (1890), cerise red, large, vigorous.

Mdme. Appoline Foulon, H.P., *Vigneron* (1883), rose salmon, medium, vigorous.

Mdme. Freeman, H.N., *Guillot père* (1862), white, medium, moderate.

Mdme. Frémion, H.P., *Margottin* (1860), rose carmine, medium, moderate.

Mdme. Eugène Frèmy, H.P., *E. Verdier* (1885), rose, large, vigorous.

Mdme. Frenlon, T., *Moreau Roberts* (1892), white and rose, large, moderate.

Mdme. Fresnoy, H.P., *Pernet* (1864), lively rose, medium, vigorous.

Mdme. Sophia Fropot, H.P., *Levet* (1876), rosy pink, large vigorous.

Mdme. Furtado, H.P., *V. Verdier* (1860), bright rose, large, moderate.

Mdme. Gadel, H.P., *Perdet* (1872), lilac rose, large, moderate.

Mdme. Gaillard, T., *Ducher* (1870), salmon yellow, medium, moderate.

Mdme. Louis Gaillard, T., *Liabaud* (1892), white yellow, large, vigorous.

Mdme. Marie Garnier, H.P., *Gonod* (1882), flesh piuk, large, vigorous.

Mdme. Alice Van Geert, H.P., *Lévêque* (1884), red rose, medium, moderate.

Mdme. de St. Genêt, H.P., *Lartay*, violet red, large, moderate.

Mdme. Anna Gerold, H.P., *Soup. et Not.* (1882), rose, medium, moderate.

Mdme. D. Giraud, H.P., *Haussy* (1854), striped, medium, moderate.

Mdme. Fanny Giron, H.P., *Schmidt* (1883), satin rose, medium, moderate.

Mdme. Joseph Godier, T., *Pernet* (1887), rose, large, vigorous.

Mdme. Gonod, H.P., *Mor. et Rob.* (1867), satiny rose, large, moderate.

Mdme. J.M. Gonod, H.P., *Gonod* (1875), red crimson, large, vigorous.

Mdme. Grawitz, H.P., *Soup. et Not.* (1878), rose, medium, moderate.

Mdme. Henri Greville, T., *Tesnier* (1892), yellow salmon, large, vigorous.

Mdme. Jules Grèvy, H.P., *Schwartz* (1882), pink, medium, moderate.

Mdme. Grondier, H P., *Gonod* (1867), salmon rose, large, vigorous.

Mdme. James Grog, H.P., *Baumann* (1864), carmine, medium, moderate.

Mdme. Guillaumez, T., *Bonnaire* (1892), silver yellow, large, vigorous.

Mdme Guillot, H.P., *Guillot* (1851), rose pink, large, vigorous.

Mdme. Pierre Guillot. T., *Guillot et fils* (1888), copper yellow, large, vigorous.

Mdme. Chedane Guinoisseau, T., *Lévêque* (1880), sulphur, large, vigorous.

Mdme. Emma Hall, H.P., *Liabaud* (1876), rose carmine, large, vigorous.

Mdme. Marthé d'Halloy, H.P., *Lévêque* (1882), carmine, medium, moderate.

Mdme. Joseph Halphen, T., *Margottin* (1858), blush, medium, moderate.

Mdme. Hardy, D., *Hardy* (1832), white, large, vigorous.

Mdme. Helody, H.P. (1836), silvery rose, medium, moderate.

Mdme. James Hennessy, H.P., *Duval* (1879), satiny rose, large, vigorous.

Mdme. Louis Henry, N., *Ducker* (1879), pale yellow, small, vigorous.

Mdme. la Marquise d'Hervey, H.P., *Vigneron* (1877), red, large, vigorous.

Mdme. Herivaux, H.P., *Jamain* (1875), rich red, large, vigorous.

Mdme. Hilaire, H.P. (1850), blush, medium, moderate.

Mdme. Hoche, M., *Mor. et Rob.* (1859), white, small, moderate.

Mdme. Hoste, H.P., *Gonod* (1865), rosy flesh, large, moderate.

Mdme. Hoste, T., *Guillot fils* (1887), white, large, vigorous.

Mdme. Van Houtte, H.P., *Morgottin* (1857), rosy pink, medium, moderate.

Mdme. Hovart, H.P., *Vigneron* (1883), vermilion, large, moderate.

Mdme. Hunnebelle, H.P., *Fontaine* (1873), carmine rose, large, vigorous.

Mdme. Adèle Huzard, H.P., *C. Verdier* (1867), rose, large, moderate.

Mdme. Azélie Imbert, T., *Levet* (1870), salmon yellow, large, vigorous.

Mdme. Jacquier. H.P., *Guillot fils* (1868), deep purple, large, vigorous.

Mdme. Angèle Jacquier, T., *Guillot fils* (1879), yellow, large, vigorous.

Mdme. E. Jaenisch, H.P., *Soup. et Not.* (1869), white red, medium, moderate.

Mdme. F. Jamain, H.P., *Ledechaux* (1875), rose carmine, large, vigorous.

Mdme. H. Jamain, T., *Guillot fils* (1869), white yellow, large, vigorous.

Mdme. H. Jamain, H.P., *Garron* (1871), light pink, medium, moderate.

Mdme. Francois Jamain, T., *Levet* (1872), orange, medium, moderate.

Mdme. Jard, B., *Guillot père* (1858), cherry, large, vigorous.

Mdme. Léon de St. Jean, T., *Levet* (1875), rosy salmon, large, vigorous.

Mdme. Morane Jeune, H.P., *Jamain* (1878), silvery rose, large, vigorous.

Mdme. Clémence Joigneaux, H.P., *Liabaud* (1861), red lilac, large, vigorous.

Mdme. Jolibos, H.P., *E. Verdier* (1879), rose carmine, medium, vigorous.

Mdme. de St. Joseph, T., salmon pink, large, vigorous.

Mdme. Jean Joubert, B., *Margottin* (1877), carmine, medium, moderate.

Mdme. Alex. Jullien, H.P., *Vigneron* (1883), rose, large, vigorous.

Mdme. Lacourt Jury, H.P., *Guillot* (1854), yellow, medium, vigorous.

Mdme. Dr. Jutte, T., *Levet* (1872), white, medium, moderate.

Mdme. Bellenden Ker, H.P., *Guillot père* (1866).

Mdme. Oswald de Kerchove, H.P., *Schwartz* (1879), salmon rose, large, vigorous.

Mdme. Knorr, G., *V. Verdier* (1855), blush rose, medium, moderate.

Mdme. Philippe Kuntz, T., *Bernaix* (1889), rosy carmine, large, vigorous.

Mdme. Maurice Kuppenheim, T., *Mdme. Ducher* (1877), salmon yellow, medium, moderate.

Mdme. Caroline Kuster, N., *Pernet* (1872), yellow, large, vigorous.

Mdme. de Laboulaye, H.P., *Liabaud* (1877), rose, medium, moderate.

Mdme. Pauline Labonte, T., *Pradel* (1852), salmon, large, moderate.

Mdme. Eugène Labruyere, H.P., *Gonod* (1883), salmon, medium, vigorous.

Mdme. Lacharme, H.P., *Lacharme* (1873), blush, large, moderate.

Mdme. Lacroix, H.P., *Guillot* (1853), pale rose, medium, moderate.

Mdme. Laffay, H.P., *Laffay* (1839), purple rose, medium, vigorous.

Mdme. Marie Lagrange, H.P., *Lagrange* (1883), carmine, large, moderate.

Mdme. Lambard, T., *Lacharme* (1877), rosy red, large, moderate.

Mdme Eliè Lambert, T. (1890), pale rose, medium, moderate.

Mdme. Lamon, H.P., *Lartey* (1861), cerise red, large, vigorous.

Mdme. Lamoricère, H.P., *Mor. et Rob.* (1852), bright pink, medium, moderate.

Mdme. Landeau, M., *Mor. et Rob.* (1873), light red, medium moderate.

Mdme. Julie Lasseu, N., *Nabonnand* (1882), rose, medium, moderate.

Mdme. Prosper Laugier, H.P., *E. Verdier* (1875), bright rose, large, vigorous.

Mdme. Laurent, H.P., *Granger* (1869), rose cerise, medium, moderate.

Mdme. Alphonse Lavallée, H.P., *E. Verdier* (1878), cherry red, large, vigorous.

Mdme. Marie Lavallée, H.T., *Nabonnand* (1882), rose, large, vigorous.

Mdme. Charles Lavot, H.P., *Vigneron* (1882), rose, medium, moderate.

Mdme. Clorinde Leblond, H.P., *Dauvesse* (1869), red, medium, moderate.

Mdme. Lefrancois, H.P., *Oger* (1869), flesh rose, medium, moderate.

Mdme. Legrand, P.M., *Fontaine* (1863), rose carmine, medium, moderate.

Mdme. Legras, A., cream, medium, moderate.

Mdme. Lemesle, H.P. (1890), red purple, large, vigorous.

Mdme. André Leroy, H.P., *Trouillard* (1864), rose, medium, moderate.

Mdme. Louis Lévêque, H.P., *Lévêque* (1873), rose, large, moderate.

Mdme. Louis Lévêque, T., *Lévêque* (1892), rose yellow, large, moderate.

Mdme. Levet, T., *Levet* (1869), salmon yellow, large, moderate.

Mdme. Barthélemy Levet, T., *Levet* (1879), yellow, medium, moderate.

Mdme. Etienne Levet, H.T., *Levet* (1878), cerise yellow, large, vigorous.

Mdme. Liabaud, H.P., *Gonod* (1869), flesh white, large, vigorous.

Mdme. Saison Lierval, H.P., *E. Verdier* (1873), carmine, medium, vigorous.

Mdme. Lilienthal, H.P., *Liabaud* (1878), bright rose, large, vigorous.

Mdme. Leonard Lille, H.T., *Nabonnand* (1879), fiery red, medium, moderate.

Mdme. H. de Luesmans, H.P., *Soup. et Not.* (1884), carmine, large, vigorous.

Mdme. Luizet, B., *Liabaud* (1867), bright rose, medium, moderate.

Mdme. Gabriel Luizet, H.P., Liabaltd (1877), pink, large, vigorous.

Mdme. B. Mackart, H.P., *E. Verdier* (1884), rose, large, vigorous.

Mdme. Maeker, H.P., *Damaizin* (1863), deep blush, medium, moderate.

Mdme. Chabaud de St. Mandrier, N., *Nabonnand* (1882), salmon, medium, moderate.

Mdme. Mangonette, T., *Soup. et Not.* (1888), yellow, medium, vigorous.

Mdme. Maninier, H.P., *Liabaud* (1875).

Mdme. Pierre Margery, H.P., *Liabaud* (1882), rose, medium, moderate.

Mdme. Margottin, T., *Guillot fils* (1866), citron yellow, large, vigorous.

Mdme. Jules Margottin, T., *Levet* (1871), rose yellow, large, vigorous.

Mdme. Galli-Marie, H., *E. Verdier* (1876), rich rose, large, vigorous.

Mdme. Theodore Martel, H.P., *Ducher* (1854), flesh, small, moderate.

Mdme. Masset, B., *Lacharme* (1853), rose, medium, moderate.

Mdme. Masset, N., *Lacharme* (1857), rose, tinted white, small, vigorous.

Mdme. Massicault, H.P., *Schwartz* (1885), rose, medium, moderate.

Mdme. Clement Massier, N., *Nabonnand* (1885), rose, medium, vigorous.

Mdme. Masson, H.P., *Masson* (1854), reddish crimson, large, vigorous.

Mdme. Claire Mathieu, H.P., *Vigneron* (1874), soft rose, large, vigorous.

Mdme. Maurin, T., *Guillot Père* (1853), white salmon, small, moderate.

Mdme. Gabrielle Meritte, H.P., *Vigneron* (1882), lilac, medium, moderate.

Mdme. Charles Meurice, H.P., *Lévêque fils* (1878), velvety purple, large, vigorous.

Mdme. Emile Metz, H.T., *Soup. et Not.* (1892), rose, large, moderate.

Mdme. B. du M. de Montchauveau, H.P., *Jamain* (1876), rose pink, large, vigorous.

Mdme. Hortense Montefiore, H.T., *Soup. et Not.* (1889), white, large, vigorous.

Mdme. Montet, H.P., *Liabaud* (1880), soft rose, large, vigorous.

Mdme. Guillot de Montfavet, H.P., *Gonod* (1871), rose, medium, moderate.

Mdme. de Monseignat, B., *Pradel* (1861), cerise, large, moderate.

Mdme. Grandin Monville, H.P., *E. Verdier* (1875), bright cerise, medium, vigorous.

Mdme. Moreau, H.P., *Gonod* (1864), deep crimson, large, robust.

Mdme. Moreau, P.M., *Mor. et Rob.* (1872), vermilion, large, vigorous.

Mdme. Moreau, T., *Moreau-Robert* (1889), capper yellow, large, vigorous.

Mdme. Anna Moreau, H.P., *Mor. et Rob.* (1884), rose, large, vigorous.

Mdme. Leopold Moreau, H.P., *Vigneron* (1883), rose, large, vigorous.

Mdme. Francisque Morel, T. *Liabaud*, (1888), white, medium, vigorous.

Mdme. Viviand-Morel, H.P., *Schwartz* (1883), carmine, small, moderate.

Mdme. Motier, H.T., *Vigeron* (1889), silver white, large, vigorous.

Mdme. Nachury, H.P., *Damaizin* (1873), delicate rose, large, vigorous.

Mdme. Norman Neruda, H.P., *Paul & Son* (1885), carmine, medium, vigorous.

Mdme. Céline Noirey, T., *Guillot fils* (1868), tender rose, large, vigorous.

Mdme. Noman, H.P., *Guillot père* (1867), white, medium, moderate.

Mdme. Pierre Oger, B., *Oger* (1878), blush, medium, vigorous.

Mdme. Olga, T , *Lévêque et fils* (1889), white, large, vigorous.

Mdme. Hersilie Ortgies, B., *Mor. et Rob.* (1868), salmon white, medium, vigorous.

Mdme. Edouard Ory, P.M., *Robert* (1854), crimson, medium, moderate.

Mdme. Louis Paillet, H.P., *E. Verdier*, rose, large, vigorous.

Mdme. Thérèse de Parrieu, H.P., Gautreau, rose, large, vigorous.

Mdme. Albert Patel, T., *Godard* (1892), white flesh, large, vigorous.

Mrs. Paul, B., *Paul & Son* (1890), rose pink, large, vigorous.

Mdme. George Paul, H.P., *E. Verdier* (1866), flesh rose, large, vigorous.

Mdme. Marmy Paul, T., *Marmy* (1885), yellow, medium, moderate.

Mdme. W. Paul, H.P., *V. Verdier* (1863), crimson, medium, moderate.

Mdme. W. Paul, P.M., *Mor. et Rob.* (1869), bright rose, large, vigorous.

Mdme. Pauvert, B., *Rambaux* (1876), pale pink, large, moderate.

Mdme. Pauwells, T., *Soup. et Not.* (1885), yellow, small, moderate.

Mdme. Marie Pavie, T., *Nabonnand et fils* (1888), rose, large, vigorous.

Mdme. Isaac pereire, H.B., *Margottin* (1880), carmine, large, vigorous.

Mdme. P. Pernet, T., *Nabonnand* (1879), canary, medium, moderate.

Mdme. Auguste Perrin, H.N., *Schwartz* (1878), rose, medium, moderate.

Mdme. Henri Perrin, H.P., *Schwartz* (1892), lilac and carmine, large, vigorous.

Mdme. Ernest Piard, H.T., *Bonnaire* (1887), bright rel, large, vigorous.

Mdme. Francois Pettit, H.N., *Lacharme* (1877), white, small, vigorous.

Mdme. Gustave Pierret, H.P., *Vigneron* (1885), lilac, medium, moderate.

Mdme. Pitaval, H,B., *Liabaud* (1885), red, large, moderate.

Mdme. Place, H.P., *Margottin* (1854), rose pink, medium, moderate.

Mdme. Platz, P.M., *Moreau* (1864), rose lilac, medium, moderate.

Mdme. Plantier, H.B., *Plantier* (1835), white, large, vigorous.

Mdme. Vve. A. Pommery, H.P., *Lévêque* (1883), rose, medium, moderate.

Mdme. Fey Pranard, H.P., *Cherpin* (1869), pale rose, large, moderate.

Mdme. Prud'homme, H.B., *Mor. et Rob.* (1872), cerise large, vigorous.

Mdme. de St Pulgent, H.P., *Gautreau* (1871), vermilion, large, moderate.

Mdme. Pulliat, H.P., *Ducher* (1866), deep rose, medium, vigorous.

Mdme. Puissant, H.P., *Mor. et Rob.* (1868), rose red, large, robust.

Mdme. Rambaux, H.P., *Ramhaux* (1883), carmine, large, vigorous.

Mdme. Récamier, H.P., *Lacharme* (1853), flesh white, medium, moderate.

Mdme. Remond, T., *Lambert* (1883), yellow, medium, moderate.

Mdme. Renshy, H.P., *Guillot et fils* (1889), rosy carmine, large, vigorous.

Mdme. Renard, H.P., *Mor. et. Rob* (1864), deep rose, medium, moderate.

Mdme. Retornaz, T., *Guillot père* (1865), coppery yellow, medium, moderate.

Mdme. Richer, H.P., *Faudon* (1869).

Mdme. de Ridder, H.P., *Margottin* (1871), amaranth, medium, moderate.

Mdme. Adélaïde Ristori, B., *Pradel* (1861), cerise, medium, moderate.

Mdme. Rival, H.P., *Gonod* (1866), tender rose, medium, vigorous.

Mdme. Rivière, H.C., *E. Verdier* (1874), light rose, large, vigorous.

Mdme. Maurice Rivoire, H.P., *Gonod* (1876).

Mdme. Maurice Rivoire, H.P., Gonad (1878), rose flesh, large, moderate.

Mdme. Rochet, H.P., *Liabaud* (1883), rose, medium, moderate.

Mdme. Mxme. de la Rocheterie, H.P., *Granger* (1881), rose, large, moderate.

Mdme. Marie Roederer, H.P., *Lévêque* (1882), cerise, medium, moderate.

Mdme. Roger, H.P., *Mor. et Rob.* (1877), pale rose, medium, vigorous.

Mdme. Rolland, H.P., *Mor. et Rob.* (1867), rosy flesh, large, vigorous.

Mdme. Rollet, H.P., *Gonod* (1875), rosy salmon, large, moderate.

Mdme. Rose Romarin, T., *Nabonnand et fils* (1888), red, large, vigorous.

Mdme. de Forcade la Roquette, H.P., *Gautreau* (1869), red, medium, moderate.

Mdme. Charles de Rostang, H.P. (1890), rose pink, medium, vigorous.

Mdme. la Bnne. de Rothschild, H.P., *Pernet* (1867), rose, large, vigorous.

Mdme. A. de Rougemont, H.N., *Lacharme* (1862), pink, medium, vigorous.

Mdme. Rougier, H.P., *Jamain* (1874), clear red, medium, vigorous.

Mdme. Rousset, H.P., *Guillot fils* (1864), tender rose, large, vigorous.

Mdme. Marie Roussin, T., *Nabonnand et fils*, yellow, large, vigorous.

Mdme. Charles Salleron, P.M., *Fontaine* (1867), crimson, large, moderate.

Mdme. Schmitt, H.P., *Schmitt* (1855), rose lilac, medium, moderate.

Mdme. Schultz, N., *Beluze* (1856), pale yellow, small, vigorous.

Mdme. George Schwartz, H.P., *Schwartz* (1871), rose. large, vigorous.

Mdme. Joseph Schwartz, T., *Schwartz* (1880), flesh rose, medium, vigorous.

Mdme. Scipion, H.P., *Cochet* (1871), cerise rose, large, vigorous.

Mdme. de Loeben Sels, H.P., *Soup. et Not.* (1879), pink, large, moderate.

Mdme. Charles Séguret, B., *Pradel* (1861), crimson, medium, moderate.

Mdme. Théobald Sernin, H.P., *Brassac* (1877), carmine, medium, moderate.

Mdme. Sertot, T., *Pernet* (1848), white, medium, moderate.

Mdme. de Sévigné, B, *Mor. et Rob.* (1874), soft rose, large, vigorous.

Mdme. Louis Seydoux, H.P., *Fontaine* (1867), clear rose, large, moderate.

Mdme. Simon, T. (1890), white and rose, large, vigorous.

Mdme. Nathalie Simon. H.P., *Vigneran* (1883), red, medium, moderate.

Mdme. Max Singer, T., *Soup et Not.* (1887), yellow, medium, vigorous.

Mdme. J. Sisley, Ben., *Dubreuil* (1885), white, small, moderate.

Mdme. Raphael de Smet, T., *Nabonnand* (1885), rose, small, moderate.

Mdme. Margarite de Soras, T.. *Nabonnand et fils* (1889), chrome yellow, large, vigorous.

Mdme. Soubeyron H.P., *Gonod* (1872), bright rose, small, moderate.

Mdme. Soupert, P.M., *Soup. et Not.* (1871), cerise, medium, vigorous.

Mdme. de Staël, P.M. (1858), rosy flesh, medium, moderate.

Mdme. Standish, H.P., *Trouillard* (1860), satiny rose, large, vigorous.

Mdme. E. Stchegoleff, T., *Nabonnand* (1882), rose, medium, moderate.

Mdme. de Stella, B., *Guillot père* (1863), bright rose, medium, vigorous.

Mdme. Hermann Stenger, H.P., *Gonod* (1864), rose, large, moderate.

Mdme. Stingue, H.P., *Liabaud* (1885), red, medium, moderate.

Mdme. Stoltz, D., pale lemon, medium, vigorous.

Mdme. Adolphe de Tarle, T., *Tesnier* (1889), satiny white, large, vigorous.

Mdme. de Tartas, T., *Bernède*, rose, small, moderate.

Mdme. Elise Tasson, H.P., *Lévêque* (1879), cerise, large, vigorous.

Mdme John Taylor, T., *Nabonnand*, sulphur, medium, moderate.

Mdme. Olympe Terestchenko, H.P., *Lévêque* (1883), tinted white, large, vigorous.

Mdme. Caroline Testout, H.T., *Pernet fils* (1890), pink, large, vigorous.

Mdme. Thevenot, H.P., *Jamain* (1869), red, medium, moderate.

Mdme. Thibaut, H.P., *Lévêque et fils* (1889), soft rose, large, vigorous.

Mdme. Thiers, B., *Pradel*, rose, medium, moderate.

Mdme. Trifle, T., *Levet* (1869), salmon yellow, large, vigorous.

Mdme. Charles Truffaut, H.P., *E. Verdier* (1878), satiny rose, large, vigorous.

Mdme. Ambroise Truillet, H.P., *Moreau* (1869), salmon, medium, moderate.

Mdme. John Twombly, H.P., *Schwartz* (1882), bright red, large, vigorous.

Mdme. Trotter, H.C., *Granger* (1855), red, small, vigorous.

Mdme. Trudeau, H.P., *Boll* (1850), rose lilac, medium, moderate.

Mdme. Marie Ussher, T., *Nabonnand et fils* (1889), rosy carmine, large, vigorous.

Mdme. Vachez, B., *Ducher* (1864), rosy white, small, moderate.

Mdme. Valembourg, H.P., *Oger*, purple, medium, moderate.

Mdme. Valton, B., *Nabonnand*, pink, medium, vigorous.

Mdme. Henriette Vapereau. H.P., *Pradel*, cerise, large, moderate.

Mdme. de Vatry, T., *Guerin* (1855), pink, large, vigorous.

Mdme. Dos Santos Vianna, H.P., *Soulp. et Not.* (1883), rose carmine, large, moderate.

Mdme. Guvot de Villeneuve, H.P., *Gautreau*, tender rose, large, vigorous.

Mdme. Baron Veillard, B., *Vigneron* (1889), lilac, large, vigorous.

Mdme. Charles Verdier, H.P., *Lacharme* (1864), bright rose, large, vigorous.

Mdme. Eugène Verdier, H.P., *V. Verdier* (1859), flesh, medium, moderate.

Mdme. Eugène Verdier, H.P., *E. Verdier* (1878), silvery rose, large, rob.

Mdme. Eugène Verdier, T., *Levet* (1883), chamois, large, vigorous.

Mdme. Victor Verdier, H.P., *E. Verdier* (1863), bright red, large, vigorous.

Mdme. Verlot, H.P., *E. Verdier* (1876), bright cerise, large, vigorous.

Mdme. Rival Verne, H.P., *Liabaud* (1873), salmon rose, medium, vigorous.

Mdme. Ambroise Verschaffelt H.P., *E. Verdier* (1804), pale rose, medium, moderate.

Mdme. Angelique Veysset, H.T. (1890), bright rose, large, vigorous.

Mdme. George Vibert. H.P., *Mor. et Rob.* (1879), carmine, large, vigorous.

Mdme. Vidot, H.P., *Couturier* (1854), flesh white, medium, moderate.

Mdme. Vignat, H.P., *Liabaud* (1892), light red, large, vigorous.

Mdme. Vigneron, H.P., *Vigneron* (1858), peach, large, vigorous.

Mdme. Louis Vigneron, H.P., *Vigneron* (1883), rose, medium, moderate.

Mdme. Melanie Vigneron, H.P., *Vigneron* (1883), lilac, medium, moderate.

Mdme. de Villars, P.M., *Beluze* (1885).

Mdme. Elise Vilmorin, H.P. Lévêque (1864), rose carmine, medium, vigorous.

Mdme. Henri Vilmorin, T., *Nabonnand* (1882), yellow, medium, moderate.

Mdme. Emilie Viaeberghs, T., *Soup. et Not.* (1888), pale yellow, medium, vigorous.

Mdme. Watteville, T., *Guillot* (1884), tinted white, medium, moderate.

Mdme. Julie Weidman, H.P., *Soup. et Not.* (1881), salmon rose, medium, vigorous.

Mdme. Welche, T., *Mdme. Ducher* (1878), pale yellow, medium, moderate.

Mdme. de Wettstein, H.P., *Levet* (1885), cerise, large, moderate.

Mdme. William, T., *Larty* (1857), fawn and white, medium, moderate.

Mdme. Mlanie Willermoz, T., *Lacharme* (1845), white salmon, large vigorous.

Mdme. Wilson, H.P., *Vigneron* (1884), rose, medium, moderate.

Mdme. Rosalie de Wincop, H.P., *Vigneron* (1882), lilac, medium, vigorous.

Mdme. Charles Wood, H.P., *E. Verdier* (1861), rich crimson, large, vigorous.

Mdme. William Wood, H.P., *E. Verdier* (1876), rose red, large, vigorous.

Mdme. Charles Frederic Worth, H.P., *Schwartz* (1889), deep carmine, large, vigorous.

Mdme. Yorke, H.P., *Mor. et Rob.* (1882), vermilion, medium, vigorous.

Mdlle. Ilona d'Adorjan, H.P., *E. Verdier* (1874), salmon rose, medium, moderate.

Mdlle. Amélie Alphen, H.P., *Margottin* (1864), rose carmine, large, moderate.

Mdlle. Juliette Alphen, H.P., *Margottin* (1869), clear rose, large, vigorous.

Mdlle. Amand, T., *Lartey* (1861), cerise red, medium, moderate.

Mdlle. Marie Andre, H.P., *Soup. et Not.* (1882), rose carmine, medium, moderate.

Mdlle. Thérèse Appert, H.P., *Trouillard* (1866), light rose, iarge, vigorous.

Mdlle. Marie Arnaud, T., *Levet* (1872), canary yellow, large, moderate.

Mdlle. Louise Aunier, H.P., *Liabaud* (1884), rose, medium, vigorous.

Mdlle. Berthe Baztheral, H.P., *Fontaine* (1869), cerise, medium, moderate.

Mdlle. H. de Beauvau, T., *Lacharme* (1886), yellow, large, vigorous.

Mdlle. Bergier, B., *Pernet* (1885), rose, small, moderate.

Mdlle. Cécile Berthod, T., *Guillot fils* (1871), sulphur yellow, large, vigorous.

Mdlle. Marie Berton, T., *Levet* (1873), straw white, medium, moderate.

Mdlle. Camille Bigotteau, H.P., *Vigneron* (1883), red cerise, medium, moderate.

Mdlle. Blanche, T., *Guillot fils* (1877), rosy pink, medium, moderate.

Mdlle. Bonnaire, H.P., *Pernet* (1859), rose white, medium, moderate.

Mdlle. Marguerite Boudet, H.P., *Guillot et fils* (1888), rose lilac, medium, moderate.

Mdlle. Suzanne Bouyer, H.P., *Gonod* (1879), red carmine, large, vigorous.

Mdlle. Alexandrine Bruel, T., *Levet* (1885), white, small, moderate.

Mdlle. Cécile Brunner, MU. *Mad. Ducher* (1880), rose, medium, moderate.

Mdlle. Germaine Caillot, H.T., *Pernet* (1886), flesh, large, vigorous.

Mdlle. Charlotte Card, H.P., *Vigneron* (1876), red cerise, large, moderate.

Mdlle. Marie Castel, H.P., *E. Verdier* (1877), cherry red, medium, moderate.

Mdlle. Elise Chabrier, H.P., *Gautreau*, tender rose, medium, moderate.

Mdlle. Berthe Chanu, H.P., Fontaine (1886), rose carmine, large, vigorous.

Mdlle. Margte. Chatelaine, B., *Vigneron* (1879), pale rose, large, vigorous.

Mdlle. Marie Chauvet, H.P., *Besson* (1882), rose, large, vigorous.

Mdlle. Louise Chrétien, H.P., *Liabaud* (1884), rose salmon, medium, moderate.

Mdlle. Marie Closon, H.P., *E. Verdier* (1883), rose, medium, moderate.

Mdlle. Mare Cointet, H.P., *Guillot fils* (1872), bright rose, large, moderate.

Mdlle. Annie Cote, H.N., *Guillot fils* (1875), lilac white, largo, vigorous.

Mdlle. Thérèse Coumer, H.P., *Liabaud* (1866), bright rose, large, vigorous.

Mdlle. Hélène Croissandeau, H.P., *Vigneron* (1883), rose, large, vigorous.

Mdlle. Anne Marie Danloux, H.P., *Vigneron* (1877), rosy white, medium, vigorous.

Mdlle. Marie Deschamps, H.P., *Pradel*, pink, medium, moderate.

Mdlle. Louise Dessayre, B., *Pradel* (1861), tinted white, medium, moderate.

Mdlle. Marie Digat, H.P., *Levet* (1883), crimson, medium, vigorous.

Mdlle. Margte. Dombrain, H.P., *E. Verdier* (1865), satiny rose, large, vigorous.

Mdlle. Henriette Dubus, H.P., *Fontaine* (1858), purplish crimson, large, moderate.

Mdlle. Dumaine. H.P., *Pernet* (1873), tender rose, medium, moderate.

Mdlle. Blanche Durrschmidt, T., *Guillot fils* (1877), pink, medium, moderate.

Mdlle. Julie Dymonier, H.P., *Gonod* (1879), pale rose, medium, moderate.

Mdlle. Emain, B., *Pernet* (1861), rosy white, large, vigorous.

Mdlle. Marguerite Fabisch, T., *Godard* (1889), rose, medium, vigorous.

Mdlle. Marie Finger, H.P., *Rambaux* (1873), flesh rose, large, vigorous.

Mdlle. Loide de Falloux, H.P., *Trouillard* (1864), pale rose, medium, moderate.

Mdlle. Favart, B., *E. Verdier* (1869), rose striped white, medium, moderate.

Mdlle. Emilie Fontaine, H.P., *Fontaine* (1882), purple crimson, large, vigorous.

Mdlle. F. de la Forest, H., *Margottin fils* (1872), rose pink, large, vigorous.

Mdlle. Marie Gagnière, T., *Nabonnand* (1878), yellow, medium, moderate.

Mdlle. Annette Gamon, H.T., *Godard* (1889), pale rose, medium, vigorous.

Mdlle. Marie Gapnière, T., *Nabonnand* (l878), yellow, medium, moderate.

Mdlle. Julie Gautain, H.P. , *Liabaud* (1884), rose, large, moderate.

Mdlle. Thérèse Genevay, T., *Levet* (1874), peach pink, large, vigorous.

Mdlle. Léonie Giessen, H.P., *Lacharme* (1875), rosy white, large, vigorous.

Mdlle. Julia Grévy, H.P., *Gauireau* (1879), deep red, medium, vigorous.

Mdlle. Godard, H.P. (1858), Jilac rose, large, vigorous.

Mdlle. Genevieve Godard, T., *Godard* (1889), bright rose, large, vigorous.

Mdlle. Marie Gonod, H.P., *Gonod* (1871), white, medium, moderate.

Mdlle. Josephine Gyot, B., *Touvais* (1863), bright red, medium, vigorous.

Mdlle. Victoire Hèlyve, H.P., *E. Verdier* (1878), tender rose, large, vigorous.

Mdlle. Nathalie Imbert, T., *Nabonnand* (1885), salmon, medium, moderate.

Mdlle. Francisca Kruger, T., *Nabonnand* (1879), yellow rose, medium, moderate.

Mdlle. de Labathe, H.P., Bernède (1856), bright rose, medium, moderate.

Mdlle. Mathilde Lenaerts, T., *Levet* (1879), rosy white, medium, vigorous.

Mdlle. Alice Leroy, H.P., *Trouillard* (1855), rose, medium, moderate.

Mdlle. Léa Lévêque, H.P., *E. Verdier* (1884), rose, medium, moderate.

Mdlle. Berthe Levet, H.P., *Cochet* (1865), rose, medium, moderate.

Mdlle. Thérèse Levet, H.P., *Levet* (1866), brilliant rose, large, vigorous.

Mdlle. Gabrielle Loanville, H.P., *Pradel* (1861), coppery rose, medium, moderate.

Mdlle. Lobry, H.P., *Guillot père* (1863) rosy white, medium, moderate.

Mdlle. Marie Magat, H.P., *Liabaud* (1889), clear red, large, vigorous.

Mdlle. Marguerite Manoin, H.P., *Fontaine* (1879), cerise-purple, large vigorous.

Mdlle. Louise Margerand, H.P., *Liabaud* (1876), tender rose, large, vigorous.

Mdlle. Jeanne Marix, H.P., *Liabaud* (1866), deep rose, large, vigorous.

Mdlle. Lydia Marty, H.P., *Liabaud* (1878), rose lilac, medium, moderate.

Mdlle. Henriette Matthieu, H.P., *Vigneron* (1885), satiny rose, medium, moderate.

Mdlle. Claire Merle, T., *Nabonnand* (1885), rose, small, moderate.

Mdlle. Marie Metral, HoP., *Liabaud* (1888), salmon rose, medium, vigorous.

Mdlle. Hélène Michel, H.P., *Vigneron* (1854), rose, medium, vigorous.

Mdlle. Marguerite Michou, H.P., *Vigneron* (1883), red, medium, moderate.

Mdlle. Marie Moreau, BEN., *Nabonnand* (1879), rose, medium, moderate.

Mdlle. Annette Murat, T., *Levet* (1885), yellow, small, moderate.

Mdlle. Jeanne Naudin, T., *Nabonnand* (1878), rose, medium, moderate.

Mdlle. Claudine d'Offroy, H.P., *Touvais* (1861), clear red, large, vigorous.

Mdlle. Julie Pereard, H.P., *Pernet* (1872), rose, large, moderate.

Mdlle. Leonie Persain, H.P., *Fontaine* (1864), silvery rose, medium, moderate.

Mdlle. Gabrielle de Peyronny, H.P., *Lacharme* (1863), bright rose, medium, moderate.

Mdlle. Lazarine Poizeau, T., *Levet* (1876), orallge-yellow, medium, vigorous.

Mdlle. Portier, H.P., *Guillot père* (1864), pale rose, medium, moderate.

Mdlle. Rachel, T., *Damaizin* (1860), yellow, medium, moderate.

Mdlle. Rachel, T., *Beluze* (1841), white, small, moderate.

Mdlle. Marie Rady, H.P., *Fontaine* (1865), bright red, large, vigorous.

Mdlle. Caroline Riquet, B., *Lacharme*, white, medium, moderate.

Mdlle. Suzanne Rodocanachi, H.P., *E. Verdier* (1880), rose-carmine, large, vigorous.

Mdlle. Marie Rodocanachi, H.P., *Lévêque* (1884), rose, medium, moderate.

Mdlle. Marie Roë, H.P., *Liabaud* (1875), rose-purple, large, vigorous.

Mdlle. Camille de Rochetaille, N., *Bernaix* (1889), white and carmine, medium, vigorous.

Mdlle. Berthe Sacavin, H.P., *E. Verdier*, satin rose, medium, vigorous.

Mdlle. Eugénie Savary, H.P., *Gonod* (1872), flesh-white, medium, moderate.

Mdlle. Catherine Soupert, H.P., *Lacharme* (1879), delicate rose, large, vigorous.

Mdlle. Clothilde Soupert, T., *Levet* (1884), rose-carmine, large, vigorous.

Mdlle. Félicité Truillot, B., *E. Verdier* (1861), rose, medium, vigorous.

Mdlle. Emilie Verdier, H.P., *E. Verdier*, carmine, medium, vigorous.

Mdlle. Eugénie Verdier, H.P., *Guillot fils* (1869), flesh-rose, large, vigorous.

Mdlle. Eugénie Verdier, P.M., *Schwartz* (1872), crimson-red, large, vigorous.

Mdlle. Marie Verdier, H.P., *E. Verdier* (1875), bright rose, large, vigorous.

Mdlle. Marie Verlot, H.P., *E. Verdier* (1884), rose, medium, moderate.

Mdlle. Marie Villeboisnet, H.P., *Trouillard* (1866), tender lose, large, vigorous.

Mdlle. Sophie Villeboisnet, H.P., *Touvais* (1867), rose, medium, moderate.

Mdlle. Brigitte Violet, H.T., *Levet* (1878), rose-salmon, large, vigorous.

Mdlle. Eugénie Wilhelm, H.P., *Soup. et Not.* (1873), amaranth, medium, moderate.

Mdlle. Annie Wood, H.P., *E. Verdier* (1866), bright red, large, vigorous.

Madeleine d'Aoust, T., *Bernaix* (1889), pale rose, large, vigorous.

Madeline Nonin. H.P., *Ducher* (1866), salmon-rose, medium, moderate.

Madeline de Vauzelles, B., *Vigneran* (1882), tender rose, large, moderate.

Mafilatre, H.P., *Oger*, red, medium, vigorous.

Magna Charta, H.P., *W. Paul* (1876), carmine-pink, large, vigorous.

Mai fleuri, T., *Tesnier* (1892), satiny white, large, vigorous.

Malmaison Rouge, B., *Gonod* (1880), red, large, vigorous.

Maman Cochet, T., *Scipion Cochet* (1889), rosy flesh, large, vigoious.

Marcel Grammont, H.P., *Vigneron* (1868), deep red, large, vigorous.

Marcelin Rhoda, T., *Ducher* (1872), white-yellow, large, vigorous.

Marcella, H.P., *Liabaud* (1865), salmon rose, medium, moderate.

Marchioness of Exeter, H.P., *Laxton* (1877), cherry rose, large, vigorous.

Marchioness of Lorne, H.P., *W. Paul & Sons* (1888), rich rose, large, vigorous.

Maréchal Bazaine, H.P., *Defaure* (1864), rose carmine, medium, vigorous.

Maréchal Bugeaud, T., bright rose, large, vigorous.

Maréchal Canrobert, H.P., *Pernet* (1863).

Maréchal Forey, H.P., *Margottin* (1864), red crimson, large, vigorous.

Maréchal Niel, N., *Pradel* (1864), deep yellow, large, vigorous.

Maréchal Niel, H.P., *Pradel jun.* (1861), clear rose, large, moderate.

Maréchal Robert, T., *Mad. Ducher* (1875), pale lemon, large, vigorous.

Maréchal Souchet, H.P., *Damaizin* (1863), rose carmine, large, vigorous.

Maréchal Souchet, H.P., *Guillot fils* (1863), crimson, large, vigorous.

Maréchal Vaillant, H.P., *Jamain* (1861), purple crimson, large, vigorous.

Margaret More, *Ware* (1888), blush, large, moderate.

Margarita, N., *Guillot fils* (1868), yellow, medium, vigorous.

Marguerite, T., *Guillot fils* (1868), bright yellow, medium, moderate.

Marguerite de St. Amand, H.P., *Sansal* (1864), light pink, large, vigorous.

Marguerite d'Anjou, H.P., *Boyau* (1847), satin rose, medium, moderate.

Marguerite d'Anjou, H.P., *Trouillard* (1862), red edged white, large, moderate.

Marguerite de Thezillat, T., *Nabannand et fils* (1889), red and yellow, large, vigorous.

Marguerite Bonnet, B., *Liabaud* (1864), flesh white, large, vigorous.

Marguerite Brassac, H.P., *Brassac* (1875), velvety carmine, large, vigorous.

Marguerite Breslier, T., *Jean Ducher* (1892), rose, large, vigorous.

Marguerite Jamain, H.P., *H. Jamain* (1873), flesh rose, large, vigorous.

Marguerite Lecureux, H.P., *Cherpin* (1853), carmine, small, moderate.

Marguerite Marchais, T., *Nabonnand* (1878), coppery yellow, large, vigorous.

Marguerite de Roman, H.P., *Schwartz* (1883), flesh, large, vigorous.

Marie Accary, N., *Guillot fils* (1872), rose yellow, medium, vigorous.

Marie Aviat, H.P., (1856), lilac rose, medium, moderate.

Marie Baumiann, H.P., *Baumann* (1863), carmine crimson, large, vigorous.

Marie de Blois, M, *Mor. et Rob.* (1852), rose, small, moderate.

Marie Boisse, H.P., *Oger* (1864), pale rose, medium, moderate.

Marie de Bourgoyne, P.M., *Mor. et Rob.* (1854), deep rose, small, dwarf.

Marie Bremond, T., *Guillot fils* (1866), purple red, medium, vigorous.

Marie Charge, N., shaded yellow, small, robust.

Marie Cordier, H.P., *Fontaine*, red carmine, large, vigorous.

Marie Ducher, T., *Ducher* (1868), clear rose, large, moderate.

Marie Duncan, H.P., *Lacharme* (1872), tender rose, large, moderate.

Marie Guillot, T., *Guillot fils* (1873), white yellow, medium, vigorous.

Marie Van Houtte, T., *Ducher* (1871), white yellow, large, vigorous.

Marie Jailla.t, T., *Mad. Ducher* (1877), rose, medium, moderate.

Marie Lafone, H.P., *Pradel* (1861), cerise and purple, large, moderate.

Marie Larpin, B , *Guillot fils* (1867), delicate rose, medium, moderate.

Marie Opoix, T., *Schwartz* (1874), white yellow, medium, moderate.

Marie Pavie, P., Alegatiere (1888), pale rose, large, vigorous.

Marie Louise Pernet, H.P., Pernet (1876), bright rose, large, vigorous.

Marie Perrachon, H.P., *Ducher* (1864), violet purple, medium, moderate.

Marie Portemer, H.P., *Portemer* (1858), purplish red, large, vigorous.

Marie Rambaux, T, *Rambaux* (1879), canary yellow, medium, vigorous.

Marie Sage, H.P., *Dubreuil* (1889), soft rose, medium, vigorous.

Marie de Caroline de Sartoux, T., *Nabonnand* (1882), white, medium, vigorous.

Marie Sisley, T., *Guillot fils* (1868), yellow white, large, vigorous.

Marie Theresa, H.P., *Ducher* (1872), pale rose, medium, vigorous.

Marie Thierry, H.P. (1858), lilac rose, large, moderate.

Marie Louise de Vitry, H.P., Masson (1856), carmine, medium, moderate.

Marietta de Besobrasoff, T., *Nabonnand* (1876), carmine, medium, moderate.

Mariette Biottey, H.P., *Gonod* (1875), satiny rose, medium, moderate.

Marquis Balbiano, B., *Lacharme* (1855), silvery rose, medium, vigorous.

Marquise de Castellane, H.P., *Pernet* (1869), bright rose, large, robust.

Marquise de Forton, T., *Charreton* (1889), saffron, medium, vigorous.

Marquise de Ohambon, H.P., *Gautreau*, salmon rose, medium, moderate.

Marquise de Gibot, H.P., *De Sansal* (1868), clear rose, large, vigorous.

Marquise d'Hervey, H.P., *Vigneron* (1877), velvety red, large, vigorous.

Marquise de Lingeris, H.P., *Guenoux* (1869), carmine rose, large, vigorous.

Marquise de McMahon, H.P., *Pernet* (1865), bright rose, medium, moderate.

Marquise de Mortemart, H.P., *Liabaud* (1868), flesh white, large, weak.

Marquise de Murat, H.P., *Ducher* (1855), carmine, medium, vigorous.

Marquise Adéle de Murinais, H.P., *Schwartz* (1876), pink, large, moderate.

Marquis of Salisbury, H.P., *Paul & Son* (1879), rosy crimson, large, vigorous.

Marquis de Sanima, T., *Ducher* (1875), coppery rose, larqe, vigorous.

Marshall P. Wilder, H.P., *Ellwanger & Barry* (1885), carmine, large, moderate.

Martin Cahuzac, H.P., *Lévêque et fils* (1889), rosy carmine, large, vigorous.

Mary Bennett, H.P., *Bennett* (1884), cerise, large, moderate.

Mary Pochin, H.P., *Pochin* (1881), deep crimson, large, vigorous.

Masterpiece, H.P., *W. Paul* (1880), rosy crimson, large, vigorous.

Mathilde, T., *Granger* (1877), white, medium, moderate.

Mathurin Regnier, H.P. (1855), pink, large, vigorous.

Maupertuis, P.M., *Mor. et Rob.* (1868), velvety red, large, vigorous.

Maurice Bernardin, H.P., *Granger* (1861), vermilion, large, vigorous.

Maurice Lepelletier, H.P., *Mor. et Rob.* (1868), vermilion, medium, vigorous.

Maurice Lévêque de Vilmorin, H.P., *Lévêque et fils* (1889), clear red, large, vigorous.

Maurice Perault, H.P., *Vigneron* (1869), cherry red, large, vigorous.

Maurice Rouvier, T. (1890), rose, large, vigorous.

Maxime de la Rocheterie, H.P., *Vigneron* (1871), purple red, large, vigorous.

Maximilan II., H.P., *V. Verdier* (1858), purplish crimson, medium, moderate.

May Quennell, H.P., *Postans* (1871), magenta carmine, large, moderate.

May Rivers, T., *Rivers & Son* (1888), creamy wnite, large, moderate.

May Turner, H.P., *E. Verdier* (1874), rose pink, large, robust.

Medea, T., *W. Paul & Son* (1890), lemon, large, vigorous.

Melanie Oger, T., *Oger* (1851), white, medium, moderate.

Melanie Soupert, T., *Nabonnand* (1882), white, large.

Mere de St. Louis, H.P., *Lacharme* (1852), blush, medium, moderate.

Mèrveille d'Anjou, H.P., *Touvais* (1867), rosy red, large, vigorous.

Mèrveille de Lyon, H.P., *Pernet* (1883), white, large, vigorous.

Mesdames Soeurs Chevandier, H.P., *Pernet* (1864), deep red, large, vigorous.

Meyerbeer, H.P., *E. Verdier* (1867), fiery red, large, vigorous.

Micaela, P.M., *Moreau* (l864), cerise, medium, moderate.

Michael Buchner, H.P., *Scupert et Notting* (1892), rose red, large, moderate.

Michael Saunders, H.T., *Bennett* (1878), bright pink, large, vigorous.

Michael Strogoff, H.P., *Barrault* (1883), crimson, large, moderate.

Michel Angé, H.P., *Oger* (1863), red purple, medium, moderate.

Michel Bonnet, B., *Guillot père* (1864), lively rose, medium, vigorous.

Mignard. H.P, (1858), crimson rose, medium, moderate.

Mignonette, P., *Guillot* (1882), rose, small, moderate.

Mignonne, T., *Nabonnand* (1878), rose flesh, small, moderate.

Minerve, H.P., *Gonod* (1868), fiery red, medium, vigorous.

Minutifolia alba, *Bennett* (1888), white, small, vigorous.

Miniature, P., *Alegatière* (1885), pale rose, small, vigorous.

Miranda, H.P., *Sansal*, tender rose, small, moderate.

Miller Hays, H.P., *E. Verdier* (1874), crimson, medium, moderate.

Miss Ethel Brownlow, T., *Dickson & Son* (1886), salmon pink, large, vigorous.

Miss Hassard, H.P., *Turner* (1875), delicate pink, large, vigorous.

Miss Hillier, H.P., *E. Verdier* (1873), crimson red, large, vigorous.

Miss Ingram, H.C. *Ingram* (1868), blush white, large, vigorous.

Miss Marston, T., *Ketton fréres* (1889), yellow and white, large, vigorous.

Miss May Paul, T., *Levet* (1882), tinted white, large, vigorous.

Miss Poole, H P., *Turner*, silvery rose, medium, vigorous.

Miss Wenn, T. (1890), rose pink, medium, vigorous.

Modèle de Perfection, B., *Guillot fils* (1861), bright pink, medium, moderate.

Moire, T. *Moire* (1844), fawn, medium, moderate.

Mousseline, *Mor. et Rob.* (1882), rose, small, moderate.

Mr. Gladstone, H.P., *Paul & Son* (1870), rose, medium, weak.

Mrs. Baker, H.P., *Laxton* (1876), carmine red, large, vigorous.

Mrs. J. Berners, H.P., *Ward* (1866), magenta rose, large, vigorous.

Mrs. George Dickson, H.P., *Bennett* (1884), pink, large, vigorous.

Mrs. Dombrain, H.P., *Trouillard* (1862), red and black, large, moderate.

Mrs. Elliott, H.P., *Laffay* (1840), rose, medium, moderate.

Mrs. Jowitt, H.P., *Cranston* (1880), lake crimson, large, vigorous.

Mrs. John Laing, H.P., *Bennett* (1886), pink, large, vigorous.

Mrs. Laing, H.P., *E. Verdier* (1872), rosy carmine, large, vigorous.

Mrs. Laxton, H.P., *Laxton* (1878), rosy crimson, large, moderate.

Mrs. Opie, T., *Bell & Son* (1877), salmon rose, medium, moderate.

Mrs. Paul, B., *Paul & Son* (1892), blush white, large, vigorous.

Mrs. Pierce P., *Pierce* (1850), blush, small, moderate.

Mrs. Rivers, H.P., *Guillot* (1850), flesh, medium, vigorous.

Mrs. Standish, H.P., *Trouillard* (1860), pure crimson, medium, moderate.

Mrs. Caroline Swailes, H.P., *Swailes* (1885), flesh, large, moderate.

Mrs. Harry Turner, H.P., *Turner* (1880), crimson-scarlet, large, vigorous.

Mrs. Veitch, H.P., *E. Verdier* (1872), bright rose, large, moderate.

Mrs. Ward, H.P., *Ward* (1866), rose-pink, large, vigorous.

Mrs. Charles Wood, H.P., *E. Verdier* (1861), bright red, large, vigorous.

Mrs. Veitch, H.P., *E. Verdier* (1872), bright rose, large, moderate.

Monplaisir, T., *Guillot fils* (1868), salmon-yellow, large, vigorous.

Monseigneur Fournier, H.P., *Lévêque* (1875), bright red, large, vigorous.

Mons. Chaix d'Est Aage, H.P., *Lévêque* (1866), bright red, large, moderate.

Mons. Loriol de Barny, H.P., *Trouillard* (1866), vinous red, medium, vigorous.

Mons. Berthiere. H.P., *Vigneron* (1885), crimson, large, moderate.

Mons. Paul Bestion, B., *Nabonnand* (1879), red-crimson, large, vigorous.

Mons. Boncenne, H.P., *Liabaud* (1864), red-crimson, medium, vigorous.

Mons. Benoit Comte, H.P., *Schwartz* (1884), scarlet, large, vigorous.

Mons. Jean Cordier, H.P., Gonod (1871), clear rose, large, vigorous.

Mons. Eugene Delaire, H.P., *Vigneron* (1879), fiery red, large, vigorous.

Mons. Desir, T., *Pernet père* (1888), red crimson, large, vigorous.

Mons. Druet, H.P., *Rambaux* (1876), rose-carmine, large, vigorous.

Mons. Alfred Dumesnil. H.P., *Margottin fils*, deep rose, large, vigorous.

Mons. Albert Dureau, H.P., *Vigneron* (1869), red, medium, moderate.

Mons. Fillion, H.P., *Gonod* (1876), rosy magenta, large, vigorous.

Monseigneur Fournier, H.P., *Lévêque* (1875), bright red, large, vigorous.

Mons. Eurtado, T., *Laffay* (1866), sulphur-yellow, medium, moderate.

Mons. Gerberon, H.P., *Vigneron* (1879), brilliant red, medium, vigorous.

Mons. Hoste, H.P., *Liabaud* (1885), crimson, medium, moderate.

Mons. Jard, B., *Guillot* (1857), red, medium, moderate.

Mons. Joigneaux, H.P., *Liabaud* (1861), purple-red, medium, moderate.

Mons. Journeaux, H.P., *Marest* (1868), red-scarlet, large, vigorous.

Mons. Lapierre, H.P., *Gonod* (1878), crimson-red, medium, vigorous.

Mons. Alfred Leveau, H.P., *Vigneron* (1881), carmine, medium, moderate.

Mons. Etienne Levet, H.P., *Levet* (1871), carmine, large, vigorous.

Mons. Fransoise Michelon, H.P., *Levet* (1871), carmine, large, vigorous.

Mons. Jules Monges, H.P., *Guillot* (1881), rose, large, moderate.

Mons. Montigny, H.P. (1857), deep rose, large, vigorous.

Mons. Moreau, H.P., *Guillot père* (1864), red-purple, medium, vigorous.

Mons. Normon, H.P., *Guillot père* (1867), tender rose, large, vigorous.

Mons. Alexandre Palletiere, B., *Duval* (1879), rose, medium, vigorous.

Mons. Augnste Perrin, H.P., *Schwartz* (1887), cherry-red, large, vigorous.

Mons. Plaisangon, H.P., *Ducher* (1866), bright carmine, large, vigorous.

Mons. de Pontbriant, H.P., *Damaizin* (1864), carmine red, large, vigorous.

Mons. Ravel, H.P., *Guillot* (1856), crimson-scarlet, medium, moderate.

Mons. Francisque Rive, H.P., *Schwartz* (1884), cerise, large, moderate.

Mons. E.Y. Teas, H.P., *E. Verdier* (1874), cerise, large, vigorous.

Mons. Theirs, H.P., *Trouillard* (1866), brilliant red, large, vigorous.

Mons. Thouvenel, H.P., *Vigneron* (1880), velvety red, large, vigorous.

Mons. Gabriel Tournies, H.P., *Levet* (1876), deep rose, large, vigorous.

Mons. Trievoz, H.P., *Schwartz* (1888), carmine rose, medium, vigorous.

Mons. Eugène Vavin, H.P., Duval cerise, medium, vigorous.

Mons. Woolfield, H.P., *Guillot père* (1866), bright rose, large, vigorous.

Monte Christo, H.P., *Fontaine* (1861), crimson, medium, moderate.

Monte Rosa, T., *Ducher* (1872), rosy salmon, medium, vigorous.

Morphée, H.P., *Schwartz* (1887), crimson, medium, vigorous.

Murillo, H.P., *Fontaine* (1862), velvety-purple, medium, moderate.

Nancy Lee, H.T., *Bennett* (1879), satin-rose, small, moderate.

Napoléon III., H.P., *E. Verdier* (1866), red-scarlet, large, vigorous.

Narcisse, N. (1845), pale yellowt medium, vigorous.

Narcisse de Salvandy, Prov. *Van Houtte* (1845), crimson and white, medium, moderate.

Nardy Freres, H.P., *Ducher* (1865), purple rose, large, vigorous.

Nard, T., *Nabonnand et fils* (1888), yellow, large, robust.

Nataschv Metschersky, T., *Nabonnand* (1878), rosy salmon, medium, moderate.

Newton, H.P., *Gonod* (1869), red, small, weak.

Nicholas d'Assas, H.P. (1854), clear rose, large, vigorous.

Niphetos, T., *Bougere* (1844), white, large, vigorous.

Noémi, H.P. (1852), light rosem medium, moderate.

Notaire Bonnefon, H.P., *Liabaud* (1868), red purple, large, vigorous.

Notre Dame de Fourvierds, H.P., *Ducher* (1861), rose, large, moderate.

Nuits de Young, P.M., *Laffay* (1845), deep crimson, medium, moderate.

Octavie , N., *Vibert* (1845), bright red, medium, vigorous.

Oderic Vital, H.P., *Oger* (1858), rose, medium, vigorous.

Ceillet Fantasie, B., *Guillot fils* (1871), velvet red, striped white, medium, vigorous.

Ceillet Flamand, B., *Oger* (1866), rose, striped crimson, medium, moderate.

Ceillet Parfait, G., *Foulard* (1841), white, striped crimson, small, moderate.

Old Crimson, G., *Evans* (1810), crimson, medium, moderate.

Olga Marix, H.P., *Schwartz* (1873), flesh white, medium, moderate.

Olivier de Clisson, H.P., *Mor. et Rob.* (1866), vermilion, large, vigorous.

Olivier Delhomme, H.P., *V. Verdier* (1861), bright red, large, vigorous.

Olivier Metra, H.P., *E. Verdier* (1885), cerise, large, moderate.

Ophelia, T., *Ducher* (1873), clear yellow, medium, vigorous.

Ophirie, N., *Goubault* (1841), coppery yellow, medium, vigorous.

Oriflamme de St. Louis, H.P. (1858), carmine, large, vigorous.

Ornement des Jardins, H.P., *Mor. et Rob.* (1855), crimson, medium, moderate.

Oscar Lamarche, H.P., *Schwartz* (1875), amaranth, large, vigorous.

Oscar Leclerc, P.M., *Robert* (1853), red, medium, moderate.

Oscar II. Roi de Suede, H.P., *Soupert et Notting* (1889), carmine, large, vigorous.

Oxonion, H.P., *Turner* (1876), deep rose, large, vigorous.

Paeonia, Pra., *Lacharme* (1855), red, large, vigorous.

Pallida, H.P., *Feast* (1843), blush small, moderate.

Panachèe Langrois, H.P., *Rambaucourt* (1873), cherry red, large, vigorous.

Panachée de Luxembourg, H.P., *Soup. et Not.* (1866), purple, striped salmon, medium, vigorous.

Panaché d'Orleans, H.P., *Dauvesse* (1854), rose striped, medium, vigorous.

Papillon, H.P, *Nabonnand* (1878), salmon rose, medium, vigorous.

Paquerette, P., *Guillot* (1875), white, small, moderate.

Parmentier, H.P. *Guillot fils* (1860), pale rose, medium, moderate.

Paul Dupuy, H.P. (1853), amaranth, large, vigorous.

Paul de Fabry, H.P., *Liabaud* (1879), bright red, large, vigorous.

Paul Feval, H.P., *Guillot* (1861), pink, medium, moderate.

Paul Floret, T., *Nabonnand* (1882), rose, medium, moderate.

Paul Jamain, H.P., *Jamain* (1878), bright red, large, vigorous.

Paul Joseph, B., *Portemer* (1842), violet red, medium, moderate.

Paul Marot, H.T., *Bonnaire* (1892), pale rose, medium, moderate.

Paul de la Meilleraye, H.P., *Guillot fils* (1863), cerise rose, large, vigorous.

Paul Nabonnand, T., *Nabonnand* (1876), satiny rose, medium, moderate.

Paul Neyron, H.P., *Levet* (1869), dark rose, large, vigorous.

Paul Perras, H.P., pale rose, medium, vigorous.

Paul Ricaut, H.B., *Portemer* (1845), bright crimson, large, vigorous.

Paul Verdier, H.P., *C. Verdier* (1866), bright rose, large, vigorous.

Paul's Early Blush, H.P., *Paul & Son* (1892), silvery blush, large, vigorous.

Paul's Single Crimson, H.P., *Paul & Son* (1882), crimson, medium, vigorous.

Paul's Single White, H.P., *Paul & Son* (1882), white, medium, vigorous.

Pauline Buonaparte, H.P. (1850), white, small, moderate.

Pauline Lansezeur, H.P., *Lansezeur* (1854), crimson, medium, moderate.

Pauline Plantier, T., *Plantier* (1835), white lemon, medium, moderate.

Pauline Talabot, H.P., *E. Verdier* (1874), carmine red, medium, moderate.

Pavillion de Pregny, H.N., *Guillot père* (1863), rosy red, medium, vigorous.

Peach Blossom, H.P., *W. Paul* (1873), delicate pink, large, vigorous.

Pearl, H.T., *Bennett* (1878), flesh white, medium, moderate.

Perle Blanche, H.P., *Touvais* (1869), pale rose, medium, moderate.

Penelope Mayo, H.P., *Davis* (1878), carmine red, large, vigorous.

Perfection de Blanches, H.P., *Schwartz* (1873), white, medium, moderate.

Perfection de Lyon, H.P., *Ducher* (1888), rose lilac, large, vigorous.

Perfection de Montplaisir, T., *Levet* (1871), yellow, medium, moderate.

Perle d'Angers, H.P., *Mor. et Rob.* (1879), pale rose, medium, vigorous.

Perle Blanche, H.P., *Touvais* (1862), pale rose, medium, moderate.

Perle des Blanches, H.N., *Lacharme* (1872), white, medium, moderate.

Perle des Jardins, T., *Levet* (1874), canary yellow, large, vigurous.

Perle de Lyon, T., *Ducher* (1872), apricot yellow, moderate.

Perle d'Or, P., *Dubreuil* (1884), yellow, small, moderate.

Perle de Panachées, G., striped rose, medium, moderate.

Persian Yellow (from Persia), A.B., *Willock* (1837), yellow, large, moderate.

Petite Amante, B., *Soup. et Not.* (1866), rose red, medium, vigorous.

Philibert Pellet, H.P., *Gonod* (1873), rose, medium, moderate.

Philomene, H.P., *Crozy* (1857), pink, medium, moderate.

Pierre Carnot, H.P., *Levet* (1878), deep red, medium, vigorous.

Pierre Dunand, H.P., *Pernet* (1882), rose, medium, vigorous.

Pierre Guillot, H.T., *Guillot* (1879), red, medium, moderate.

Pierre Isambart, H.P., *Gautreau* (1871), red crimson, medium, moderate.

Pierre Marcardier, T., *Jean Ducher* (1892), creamy yellow, large, moderate.

Pierre Notting, H.P., *Portemer* (1863), blackish red, large, vigorous.

Pierre Seletzky, H.P., *Levet* (1872), bright red, large, vigorous.

Pilar Domedel, T., *Pries & Ketton* (1892), rose white, medium, moderate.

Pink Rover, H.T., *W. Paul & Son* (1890), pale pink, medium, moderate.

Pitord, H.P., *Lacharme* (1867), claret red, large, moderate.

Pius IX, H.P., *Vibert* (1849), violet rose, medium, vigorous.

Pline, H.P., *Guillot fils* (1865), vermilion red, large, vigorous.

Polyantha grandiflora, P., *Paul & Son* (1888), white, medium, robust.

Pomponette, B., *Soup. et Not.* (1878), salmon rose, medium, vigorous.

Pompon Blanc Parfait, A.B., *E. Verdier* (1875), flesh white, small, vigorous.

Portland Blanche, D., *Vibert* (1836), tinted white, medium, vigorous.

P. Riffaut, T., *Nabonnand et fils* (1888), bright rose, large, robust.

Pourpre d'Orleans, H.P., *Dauvesse* (1861), purple, medium, moderate.

Préfet Limbourg, H.P., *Margottin fils* (1878), velvety red, large, vigorous.

Premier Essai, Mic., *Geschwind* (1866), flesh white, small, vigorous.

President, T., *Paul & Son* (1860), rose salmon, large, vigorous.

President Joachim Crespo, H.P., *Lévêque* (1885), rose, medium, moderate.

Président Dutailly, prov., *Dubreil* (1888), fiery red, medium, vigorous.

Président Grévy, H.P., *E. Verdier* (1872), purple red, medium, vigorous.

President Hardy, H.P., *E. Verdier* (1873), carmine, medium, moderate.

Président Léon de St. Jean, H.P., *Lacharme* (1875), dark crimson, large, vigorous.

Président Lenaertes, H.P., *Soup. et Not.* (1883), deep red, medium, moderate.

Président de Lestrade, T., *Puyradard* (1891), bright rose, large, vigorous.

President Lincoln, H.P., *Granger* (1862), cerise red, large, vigorous.

Président Mas, H.P., *Guillot fils* (1865), velvety red, large, vigorous.

Président Porcher, H.P., *Vigneron* (1866), rose carmine, large, vigorous.

Président Schlachter, H.P.; *E. Verdier* (1877), crimson, medium, moderate.

Président Senelar, H.P., *Schwartz* (1882), cherry red, medium, vigorous.

President Thiers, H.P., *Lacharme* (1871), fiery red, large, vigorous.

President Willermoz, H.P., *Ducher* (1867), bright rose, large, vigorous.

Pride of Reigate, H.P., *Brown* (1885), carmine striped white, large, vigorous.

Pride of Waltham, H.P., *W. Paul* (1881), rose pink, large, vigorous.

Prince Albert, H.B., *Laffay* (1852), crimson, medium, moderate.

Prince Prosper d'Aremberg, T., *Soup. et Not* (1881), salmon red, medium, moderate.

Prince Arthur, H.P., *Canl* (1875), deep crimson, medium, vigorous.

Prince Eugéne de Beauharnais, H.P., *Mor. et Rob.* (1864), red scarlet, large, vigorous.

Prince de Beira, H.P., *E. Verdier* (1888), vermilion red, large, vigorous.

Prince Cretwertinsky, N., *Nabonnand et fils* (1888), yellow, large, vigorous.

Prince Paul Demidoff , H.P., *Guillot fils* (1873), carmine rose, large, vigorous.

Prince Humbert, H.P., *Margottin* (1867), purple red, large, moderate.

Prince Imperial, H.P. (1856), rose carmine, medium, moderate.

Prince de Joinville, H.P., *W. Paul* (1864), rich rose, large, vigorous.

Prince Léon, H.P., *Marest* (1853), cerise, large, moderate.

Prince Leopold, H.P., *W. Paul* (1869), deep red, large, robust.

Prince de la Moskowa, H.P. (1853), deep red, medium, moderate.

Prince Napoleon, B., *Pernet* (1864), bright rose, large, vigorous.

Prince Noir, H.P. (1854), velvety crimson, medium, moderate.

Prince Henri de Pays-Bas, H.P., *Soup. et Not.* (1862), deep crimson, medium, moderate.

Prince de Portia, H.P., *E. Verdier* (1865), vermilion red, large, vigorous.

Prince Cam. de Rohan, H.P., *E. Verdier* (1861) , crimson, large, vigorous.

Prince Stirbey, H.P., *E. Verdier* (1871), rose flesh, medium, moderate.

Prince of Wales, H.P., *Laxton* (1871), pink, large, moderate.

Princess Adelaide, M., *Laffay* (1845), pale rose, medium, vigorous.

Princess A1ice, M., *Paul* (1853), shaded pink, medium, moderate.

Princesse Charles d'Aremberg, H.P., *Soup. et Not.* (1876), rose carmine, large, moderate.

Princesse Julie d'Aremberg, H.P., *Soup. et Not.* (1885), canary, medium, moderate.

Princesse Prosper d'Aremberg, T., *Soup. et Not.* (1881), salmon, medium, vigorous.

Princess Beatrice, H.P., *W. Paul* (1872), deep pink, large, vigorous.

Princess Beatrice, T., *Bennett* (1887), yellow, large, vigorous.

Princesse Imperiale du Bresil, H.T., *Soup. et Not.* (1882), carmine, large, vigorous.

Princess Mary of Cambridge, H.P., *Paul & Son* (1866), pale rose, large, vigorous.

Princess Christian, H.P., *W. Paul* (1870), rosy peach, large, vigorous.

Princesse Clémentine, H.P., *E, Verdier* (1876), tender rose, large, vigorous.

Princesse Mary Dolgorouky, H.P., *Gonod* (1878), satiny rose, large, vigorous.

Princesse Hélène, H.P., *Laffay* (1837), rose purple, medium, moderate.

Princess Lichtenstein, H.P., *W. Paul* (1864), white, large, moderate.

Princess Louise, H.P., *Laxton* (1871), flesh colour, medium, moderate.

Princess Louise, E., *Jacques* (1828), creamy white, medium, moderate.

Princess Mathilde, H.P., *Liabaud* (1860), crimson, medium, moderate.

Princess Marguerite d'Orleans, H.P., *E. Verdier* (1888), rose, large, vigorous.

Princess Marguerite d'Orleans, T. (1890), rosy carmine, large, vigorous.

Princess May, T., *W. Paul & Son* (1892), delicate blush, medium, vigorous.

Princesse de Metternich, H.P., *Sansal* (1858), rose, large, vigorous.

Princess de Monaco, T., *Dubreill* (1892), creamy yellow rose, large, vigorous.

Princesse de Nassau, Musk, cream, medium, vigorous.

Princesse Olympe, H.P, *Beluze* (1885), white, medium, moderate.

Princesse Amélie d'Orleans, H.P., *Lévêque* (1872), rose, medium, moderate.

Princesse Amélie des Pays Bas, H.P., *Liabaud* (1884), purple, large, vigorous.

Princesse W. des Pays-Bas, P., *Soup. et Not.* (1886), white, small, moderate.

Princesse Radziwell, H.P., *Lévêque* (1846), red, medium, vigorous.

Princess Royal, M., *Portemer* (1874), flesh rose, medium, moderate.

Princesse de Sagan, T., *Dubreuil* (1887), crimson, medium, vigorous.

Princess Sarsina, T. (1890), rose and yellow, medium, vigorous.

Princesse Ant. Strozzio, H.P., *E. Verdier* (1877), rose, medium, moderate.

Princesse C. de la Tremouille, H.P., *Lévêque* (1872), rose, medium, moderate.

Princess Louise Victoria, H.P., *Knight* (1872), flesh pink, small, robust.

Princess of Wales, T., *Bennett* (1884), yellow. medium, vigorous.

Princess of Wales, H.P., *W. Paul* (1864), vivid crimson, large, vigorous.

Principe Bacciochi, M., *Mor. et Rob.* (1885), rose, medium, vigorous.

Professor Chevereul, H.P., *C. Verdier* (1865), vermilion, large, vigorous.

Professor Duchartre, H.P., *E. Verdier* (1861), red, medium, vigorous.

Professor Jolibois, H.P., *E. Verdier* (1888), carmine, medium, vigorous.

Professor Koch, H.P., *E. Verdier* (1884), dark crimson, large, vigorous.

Professor E. Regel, H.P., *E. Verdier*, carmine, large, moderate.

Progress, H.T., *Paul & Son* (1890), bright carmine, medium, vigorous.

Prospérité, H.P., *Lartay*, red, medium, moderate.

Prosper Laugier, H.P., *E. Verdier* (1884), scarlet, medium, vigorous.

Prudence Besson, H.P., *Lacharme* (1865), carmine red, large, vigorous.

Purpurine, H.P., *Liabaud* (1865), red purple, medium, moderate.

Queen, Ayr. *Rivers* (1836), purple, medium, robust.

Queen of Bedders, B., *Noble* (1876), crimson, large, vigorous.

Queen of Bourbons, B., *Manger* (1834), rose, medium, moderate.

Queen of Denmark, H.P., *Granger* (1856), flesh, large, vigorous.

Queen Eleanor, H.P., *W. Paul* (1876), rich pink, large, vigorous.

Queen of Mosses, H. M., *Laffay* (1845), crimson, medium, moderate.

Queen of the Prairies, Pra., *Feast* (1843), rosy red, small, vigorous.

Queen of Queens, H.P., *W. Paul & Son* (1883), rose, large, vigorous.

Queen's Scarlet, Ben., *Hallock & Thorpe* (1880), crimson, medium, moderate.

Queen Victoria, H.P., *Fontaine* (1850), pale pink, large, vigorous.

Queen of Waltham, H.P., *W. Paul* (1875), cherry rose, large, vigorous.

R. C. Sutton. H.P., *Frettingham* (1882), rose, medium, moderate.

Red Dragon, H.P., *W. Paul* (1878), brilliant crimson, large, robust.

Red Gauntler, H.P., *W. Paul & Son* (1882), crimson, large, vigorous.

Red Rover, H.P., *W. Paul* (1863), fiery red, large, robust.

Reine des Amateurs, H.P., *Oger* (1879), salmon rose, large, vigorous.

Reine Blanche, P.M., *Robert* (1858), white, medium, moderate.

Reine Blanche, H.P., *Damaizin* (1868), blush white, large, moderate.

Reine Blanche, *Ladham* (1891), white, large, vigorous.

Reine de Castile, D., *Pernet* (1863), rose white, large, vigorous.

Reine de la Guillotière, H.P., *Plantier* (1835), rose, medium, moderate.

Reine Marie Henriette, H.T., *Levet* (1878), cerise red, large, vigorous.

Reine des Massifs, N., *Levet* (1874), coppery yellow, medium, vigorous.

Reine du Midi, H.P., *Rolland* (1867), bright rose, large, robust.

Reine Emma des Pays-Bas, T., *Nabonnand* (1879), salmon yellow, medium, moderate.

Reine Marie Pia, T., *Schwartz* (1880), deep rose, large, vigorous.

Reine du Portugal, T., *Guillot fils* (1867), golden yellow, large, vigorous.

Reine Victoria, B., *Labruyère* (1872), bright rose, large, vigorous.

Reine des Vierges, B., *Beluze* (1884), rose, medium, moderate.

Reine des Violettes, H.P., *Mille-Malet* (1860), violet, medium, vigorous.

Reine Olga de Wurtemburg, H.T., *Nabonnand* (1882), red, medium, vigorous.

Rembrandt, H.P., *Mor. et. Rob.* (1884), vermilion, medium, vigorous.

Rène Daniel, H.P., *Damaizin* (1868), cerise red, large, vigorous.

Rêve d'Or, N., *Ducher* (1869), deep yellow, large, vigorous.

Rev. J.B.M. Camm, H.P., *Turner* (1875), rosy pink, large, vigorous.

Rev. H. Dombrain, H.B., *Margottin*, (1863), brilliant red, large, vigorous.

Rev. Trautmann, H.P., *Soup. et Not.* (1877), lake red, medium, moderate.

Reveil, B., *Guillot père* (1854), purple shaded black, large, moderate.

Reveil des Printemps, H.P., *Oger* (1884), flesh, large, moderate.

Reynolds Hole, H.P., *Paul & Son* (1872), marone crimson, medium, moderate.

R. Dudley Baxter, H.P., *W. Paul* (1879), marone crimson, large, vigorous.

Richard Laxton, H.P., *Laxton* (1878), red crimson, large, vigorous.

Richard Smith, H.P., *Verdier* (1861), purple red, medium, moderate.

Richard Wagner, H.T., *Tucke* (1892), salmon yellow, large, vigorous.

Richard Wallace, H.P. *Lévêque* (1871), bright rose, large, moderate.

Richesse de Couleur, H.P., *Touvais* (1861), purple, large, vigorous.

Rivers, H.P., *Laffay* (1839), rose, large, vigorous.

Robert Burns, H.P., *Paul* (1850), bright crimson, medium, vigorous.

Robert de Brie, H.P., *Granger*, salmon rose, medium, moderate.

Robert Fortune, H.P., *Ducher* (1861) , bright rose, medium, moderate.

Robert Marnock, H.P., *Paul & Son* (1878), crimson, medium, moderate.

Robusta, B., *Soup. et Not.* (1877), fiery red, medium, robust.

Roger Lambelin, H.P. (1890), deep carmine, medium, moderate.

Roi de Bavière, H.P. (1857), maroon crimson, medium, moderate.

Roi d'Espagne, H.P., *Fontaine* (1864), bright red, medium, vigorous.

Rosa Bonheur, H.P., *Fontaine* (1871), rose carmine, large, vigorous.

Rosa Mundi, H.P., *Ducher* (1864), rosy blush, medium, moderate.

Rosalie, T., *Hallock and Thorpe* (1885), pink, small, moderate.

Rose â Bois Jape, H.P., *Brassac* (1877), bright cerise, large, vigorous.
Rose Button, LUCIDA, *Veitck & Sons* (1885), rose, small, moderate.
Rose Perfection, H.P., *Touvais* (1866), bright rose, large, vigorous.
Rose du Roi, D., *Lelieur* (1812), crimson, medium, moderate.
Rosieriste Harms, H.P., *E. Verdier* (1879), velvety red, large, vigorous.
Rosieriste Jacobs, H.P., *Mad. Ducher* (1880), blackish red, large, vigorous.
Rosine Margottin, H.P., *Margottin* (1856), pink, medium, moderate.
Rosy Morn, H.P., *W. Paul* (1878), rose peach, large, vigorous.
Royal Epoux, H.P., *Damaizin* (1859), bright rose, large, moderate.
Royal Standard, H.P., *Turner* (1874), satiny rose, large, vigorous.
Rubens. T. *Robert* (1859), rose white, large, vigorous.
Rubens, H.P., *C. Verdier* (1864), velvety red, medium, moderate.
Rushton Radclyffe, H.P., *E. Verdier* (1864), red cerise, large, vigorous.
Safrano, T., *Beauregard* (1839), bright apricot, small, vigorous.
Safranot à Fleur Rouges, T., *Oger* (1869), red yellow, small, moderate.
Salet, P.M., *Lacharme* (1854), pale rose, medium, vigorous.
St. George, H.P., *W. Paul* (1874), dark crimson, large, vigorous.
Salamander, H.P., *W. Paul & Son* (1890), scarlet crimson, large, vigorous.
Sapphe, T., *W. Paul & Sons* (1888), nankin yellow, large, vigorous.
Secretaire Nicolais, H.P., *Schwartz* (1884), purple red, large, vigorous.
Secretaire Noe, T., *Nabonnand et fils* (1888), bright red, large, vigorous.
Semiramis, H.P., *Touvais* (1864), flesh-rose, large, moderate.
Sénateur Chevreau, H.P., *Pernet* (1869), bright red, large, vigorous.
Sénateur Reveil, H.P., *Damaizin* (1863), bright rose, large, vigorous.
Sénateur Vaisse, H.P., *Guillot père* (1859), brilliant red, large, vigorous.
Setina, B., *Henderson* (1859), rose, medium, moderate.
Shirley Hibberd, T., *Levet* (1873), yellow buff, small, moderate.
Siegfried, T. *Drogemeller* (1892), salmon, large, moderate.
Silver Queen, H.P., *W. Paul & Son* (1887), crimson, large, vigorous.
Silver Queen, H.P., *W. Paul & Sons* (1889), silvery pink, medium, moderate.

Simon St. Jean, H.P., *Liabaud* (1861), purple, small, moderate.

Sir Joseph Paxton, B., *Laffay* (1852), deep red, medium, moderate.

Sir de Ludovic Talausé, T. , *Pelletier* (1892), blush, large, vigorous.

Sir Garnet Wolseley, H.P., *Cranston* (1875), vermilion red, large, vigorous.

Skobeleff, H.P., *Eug. Verdier* (1889), rosy lilac, large, vigorous.

Socrates, T., *Mor. et Rob.* (1858), fawn, medium, moderate.

Soeur des Anges H.P., *Oger* (1862), flesh white, large, vigorous.

Soeur Athanase, H.P., *Fontaine*, carmine, large, vigorous.

Soeur Severin, T., *Reboul* (1892), white, large, vigorous.

Soeur Thècle, H.P., *Fontaine* (1866), rose carmine, large, vigorous.

Soleil d'Austerlitz, H.P., *Lacharme* (1850), crimson, medium, vigorous.

Solfaterre, N., *Boyau* (1843), sulphur yellow, large, vigorous.

Sombreuil, T., *Bobert* (1850), rose white, large, vigorous.

Soupert et Notting, P.M., *Pernet* (1874), rosy red, medium, vigorous.

Souv. d'un Ami, T., *Defougere* (1846), salmon rose, large, vigorous.

Souv. de la Reine d'Angleterre, H.P., *Cochet* (1854), rose, large, moderate.

Souv. de l' Arquebuse, B. (1854), crimson, medium, moderate.

Souv. d'A. Bahivet, H.P., *Cochet* (1867), velvety crimson, large, vigorous.

Souv. de la Reine des Belges, H.P., *Cochet* (1850), brigbt carmine, medium, moderate.

S. du Pr. Royal de Belgique, H.P., *Gautreau* (1869), red, medium, moderate.

Souv. de Bellanger, H.P., *Eude* (1871), red purple, medium, moderat.

Souv. de Mad. Berthier, H.P., *Berthier* (1882), red, large, vigorous.

Souv. de Mous. Boll, H.P., *Boyau* (1866), cerise red, large, vigorous.

Souv. de Geneviève Godard, H.T., *Godard* (1892), dark rose, large, moderate.

Souv. de Gregoire Bordillon, H.P., *Moreau Robert* (1889), bright red, large, vigorous.

Souv. de Lord Brougham, BEN, *Nabonnand* (1879), rich red, large, vigorous.

Souv. de Bruel, B., *Levet père* (1889), brilliant red, large, vigorous.

Souv. de Caillat, H.P., *E. Verdier* (1867), violet purple, medium, moderate.

Souv. de Petit Caporal, H.P., *Guillot père* (1854), lilac, medium, moderate.

Souv. de Comte Cavour, H.P., *Margottin* (1861), crimson, large, vigorous.

Souv. de Comte Cavour, H.P., *Mor. et Rob.* (1861), red, medium, moderate.

Souv. de Mad. Auguste Charles, B, *Mor. et Rob.* (1866), flesh colour, medium, moderate.

Souv. de Clairvaux, T. (1890), rose pink, medium, vigorous.

Souv. de Henry Clay, S., *Boll* (1854), pale rose, medium, moderate.

Souv. de Madame Corval, H.P., *Gonod* (1867), salmon rose, medium, vigorous.

Souv. de l'Amiral Courbet, T., *Pernet père* (1885), red, medium, vigorous.

Souv. de l'Expos. de Darmstadt, H.P., *Soup. et Not.* (1871), dark crimson, large, vigorous.

Souv. de Romain Desprez, H.P., *Jamain* (1872), flesh rose, medium, moderate.

Souv. de Mdlle. Marie Detry. T., *Mad. Ducher* (1877), salmon rose, large, moderate.

Souv. de Général Douai, H.P., *Pernet* (1871), satiny rose, medium, moderate.

Souv. de Mons. Droche, H.P., *Mad. Ducher* (1881), rose, medium, moderate.

Souv. de G. Drevet, T., *Guillot* (1885), salmon, large, vigorous.

Souv. de Ducher, H.P., *E. Verdier* (1874), bright red, medium, vigorous.

Souv. de Claude Dupont, T., *Godard* (1892), dark rose, large, vigorous.

Souv. de Pierre Dupuy, H., *Levet* (1876), rich red, medium, vigorous.

Souv. de Lady Eardley, H.P., *Guillat père* (1861), amaranth, large, vigorous.

Souv. de Victor Emmanuel, H.P., *Mor. et Rob.* (1878), vermilion red, large, vigorous.

Souv. de Victor Emmanuel, H.P., *Pernet* (1878), pale rose, medium, moderate.

Souv. de Mons. Faivre, H.P., *Levet* (1879), rosy red, large, vigorous.

Souv. d'Aline Fontaine, H.P., *Fontaine* (1879), carmine, medium, vigorous.

Souv. de Mère Fontaine, H.P., *Fontaine* (1874), rose carmine, large, vigorous.

Souv. de Leon Gambetta, H.P., *Gonod* (1884), carmine, medium, moderate.

Souv. de Louis Gaudin, B., *Trouillard* (1864), red purple, large, moderate.

Souv. de Francois Goulain, T., *Guillot et fils* (1889) magenta, large, vigorous.

Souv. de Victor Gautreau, H.P., *Gautreau* (1888), carmine red, medium, moderate.

Souv. du Gomot, H.P., *Schwartz* (1889), fiery red, large, vigorous.

Souv. de Gonod, H.P., *Paul & Son* (1891), cherry rose, large, moderate.

Souv. de Leon Gonod, H.P., *Gonod* (1871), rich rose, large, vigorous.

Souv. du Rosieriste Gonod, H.P., *Ducher* (1889), cerise, large, vigorous.

Souv. de Mdlle. Marie Gourdrn, T., *Nabonnand* (1879), rose yellow, medium, moderate.

Souv. de Leveson Gower, H.P., *Guillot père* (1852), ruby red, large, moderate.

Souv. de Mdme. H. Heunevue, T., *Bernaix* (1892), rose, medium, vigorous.

Souv. de Louis van Houtte, H.P., *E. Verdier* (1876), bright crimson, large, vigorous.

Souv. de Dr. Jamain, H.P., *Lacharme* (1865), crimson, large, moderate.

Souv. de l'Ami Labruyere, H.P., *Gonod* (1885), pink, medium, vigorous.

Souv. de Mons. Laffay, H.P., *E. Verdier* (1878), crimson red, medium, vigorous.

Souv. de Victoire Landeau, H.P., *Mor. et Rob.* (1885), rose, medium, moderate.

Souv. de Victor Landeau, B. (1890), red, large, vigorous.

Souv. deAdèle Launav., P.M., *Mor. et Rob.* (1872), rose, large, vigorous.

Souv. Alphonse Lavallee, H.P., *C. Verdier* (1885), red, large, vigorous.

Souv. d'Auguste Legros, T., *Bonnaire* (1889), fiery red, large, vigorous.

Souv. de Rène Lèvêque, H.P., *Lèvêque* (1881), red purple, medium, vigorous.

Souv. de T. Levet, T., *Levet* (1883), red, large, vigorous.

Souv. d'A. Lincoln, H.P., *E. Verdier* (1865), purple, medium, vigorous.

Souv. de I'Ex de Londres, B., *Guillot père* (1851), amaranth, large, moderate.

Souv. de la Malmaison, B., *Beluze* (1843), flesh colour, large, vigorous.

Souv. du Capt. Marc, H.P., *Oger* (1874), crimson red, medium, moderate.

Souv. de Champ de Mars. H.P., *Fontaine* (1867), red purple, large, vigorous.

Souv. de Maximilian, T., *Mor. et Rob.* (1867), red white, medium, vigorous.

Souv. d'une Mère, H.P., *Touvais* (1864), tender rose, medium, moderate.

Souv. de Mad. A. Michaut, H.P., *Vigneron* (1873), deep red, large, vigorous.

Souv. de Charles Montault, H.P., *Mor. et Rob* (1863), red, medium, vigorous.

Souv. De Paul Neyron, T., *Levet* (1871), salmon yellow, large, vigorous.

Souv. de l'Ami Pancher, H.P., *E. Verdier* (1879), crimson, medium, vigorous.

Souv. du Docteur Passot, T., Godard (1889), crimson, large, vigorous.

Souv. du Dr. Payen, A.P., *Vigneron* (1892), bright red, large, vigorous.

Souv. de Joseph Pernet, H.P., *Pernet père* (1888), crimson, large, vigorous.

Souv. de Mdlle. Jenny Pernet, T. , *Pernet* (1863), rose red, large, vigorous.

Souv. de Mad. Pernet, T., *Pernet* (1875), salmon pink, large, vigorous.

Souv. de B. St. Pierre, H.P., *Guillot fils* (1864), red, medium, moderate.

Souv. de Mons. Poiteau, H,P., *Margottin* (1868), pink, large, vigorous.

Souv. de Francois Ponsand, H.P., *Touvais* (1867), bright rose, large, vigorous.

Souv. de Mons. Ponsard, H.P., *Liabaud* (1867), clear rose, large, vigorous.

Souv. de Poncet, H.P., *Pernet* (1892), rose, medium, moderate.

Souv. de President Porcher, H.P., *Granger* (1881), rose, medium, moderate.

Souv. de S.A. Prince, T., *Prince* (1889), white, medium, vigorous.

Souv. de Redoute, H.P., *Fontaine* (1867), red purple, medium, vigorous.

Souv. du General Richard, H.P., *Liabaud* (1889), red, large, vigorous.

Souv. d'Auguste Riviere, H.P., *E. Verdier* (1877), crimson, large, vigorous.

Souv. de Mad. Robert, H.P., *Mor. et Rob.* (1877), pink, medium, moderate.

Souv. du Baron de Rochetaüle, H.P., *Liabaud*, purple red medium, vigorous.

Souv. de Baron de Rothschild, B., *Crozy* (1868), red, medium, vigorous.

Souv. de Mons. Rousseau, H.P., *Lévêque* (1861), carmine, large, vigorous.

Souv. de Georges Sand, T., *Mad. Ducher* (1876), rosy salmon, large, vigorous.

Souv. d'Arthur Sansal, H.P., *Guenoux* (1876), bright rose, large, vigorous.

Souv. de Baron Semur, H.P., *Lacharme* (1874), purple red, large, vigorous.

Souv. de Spà, H.P., *Gautreau* (1873), crimson red, large, vigorous.

Souv. de Charles Sumner, H.P., *E. Verdier* (1874), carnline, large, moderate.

Souv. d'Adolphe Thiers, H.P., *Mor. et Rob.* (1877), crimson, large, moderate.

Souv. d'Elise Vardon, T., *Marest* (1854), creamy white, large, vigorous.

Souv. de J.G. Veitch, H.P., *E. Verdier* (1872), crimson, large, vigorous.

Souv. de Pierre Verdier, P.M., *Mor. et Rob.* (1867), carmine, large, vigorous.

Souv. Mad. Victor Verdier, H.P., *E. Verdier* (1884), rose, large, moderate.

Souv. de Victor Verdier, H.P., *E. Verdier* (1878), crimson large, vigorous.

Souv. de Pierre Vibert, P.M., *Moreau Rob.* (1867), dark red, large, vigorous.

Souv. de Mad. W. Wood, H.P., *E. Verdier* (1877), rose, medium, vigorous.

Souv. de William Wood, H.P., *E. Verdier* (1864), violet purple, large, vigorous.

Spenser, H.P., *W. Paul* (1892), bright rose, large, vigorous.

Standard of Marengo, H.P., *Guillot père* (1851), scarlet red, large, vigorous.

Stanwell Perpetual, P.S., rosy blush, medium, moderate.

Star of Waltham, H.P., *W. Paul* (1875), deep crimson, large, moderate.

Sulphureux, T., *Ducher* (1869), sulphur, medium, moderate.

Sultan of Zanzibar, H.P., *Paul & Son* (1876), maroon, medium, moderate.

Sunset, T., *Henderson* (1884), red striped, medium, moderate.

Superba, P., *Feast* (1843), pink, small, vigorous.

Surpasse Comice de Seine-et-Marne, B., *Guillot* (1852), crimson, medium, vigorous.

Susanna Wood, H.P., *E. Verdier* (1869), bright rose, large, vigorous.

Sydonie, H.P., *Dorisy* (1846), rose, medium, vigorous.

Tatiana Onequine, H.P., *Lévêque* (1882), carmine red, large, moderate.

Théocrite, H.P. (1851), rosy pink, large, vigorous.

Théodore Buchelet, H.P., *E. Verdier* (1873), purple, large, moderate.

Théodore Bullier, H.P., *E. Verdier* (1879), carmine, large, vigorous.

The Meteor, H.T., *W. Paul & Son* (1887), dark crimson, large, vigorous.

The Puritan, H.P., *Evans* (1887), white, large, vigorous.

The Shah, H.P., *Paul & Son* (1876), dark crimson, medium, moderate.

Thérèse Genevay, T., *Levet* (1875), rose, medium, moderate.

Thérèse Loth, T., *Liabaud* (1874), blush pink, medium, moderate.

Thiron Montauban, T., Puyradard (1892), bright red, large, moderate.

Thomas Methven, H.P., *E. Verdier* (1869), carmine, large, vigorous.

Thomas Mills, H.P., *E. Verdier* (1873), rosy carmine, large, vigorous.

Thomas Rivers, B. (1858), lilac, large, moderate.

Thorin, H.P., *Lacharme* (1866), bright rose, large, vigorous.

Thunberg, H.P., *E. Verdier* (1867), purple violet, large, vigorous.

Thyra Hammerich, H.P., *V. Verdier* (1868), rosy flesh, large vigorous.

Toujour Fleuri, H.P., *Cherpin* (1855), purple crimson, medium, moderate.

Tour Bertrand, T., *Ducher* (1869), clear yellow, large, moderate.

Tournefort, H.P., *Liabaud* (1867), bright rose, large, vigorous.

Tourville, H.P., *Mor. et Rob.* (1879), rose carmine, large, vigorous.

Triomphe d'Alencon, H.P., *Chauvet*, red, large, moderate.

Triomphe d'Amiens, H.P., *Mille-Malet* (1861), crimson, medium, vigorous.

Triomphe d'Angers, H.P., *Mor. et Rob.* (1863), crimson, medium, moderate.

Triomphe d'Avranches, H.P. (1855), bright red, large, moderate.

Triomphe des Beaux Arts, H.P., *Fontaine* (1857), crimson, medium, moderate.

Triomphe de Beauté, H.P., *Oger* (1853), crimson, medium, vigorous.

Triomphe de Caen, H.P., *Oger* (1861), crimson, medium, moderate.

Triomphe de l'Exposition, H.P., *Margottin* (1855), reddish crimson, medium, moderate.

Triomphe des Francais, H.P., *Pernet* (1864), crimson, medium, vigorous.

Triomphe de France, H.P., *Margottin* (1875), carmine, large, vigorous.

Triomphe de Guillot fils, T., *Guillot fils* (1861), white and rose, large, vigorous.

Triomphe de la Guillotiere, Mic., *Guillot père* (1864), rose, medium, moderate.

Triomphe de Lyon, H.P., *Cordier* (1859), velvety crimson, medium, moderate.

Triomphe de Luxembourg, T., *Hardy* (1836), buff, large, moderate.

Triomphe de Milan, T., *Mdme. Ducher* (1876), yellow, large, vigorous.

Triomphe de Montrouge, H.P. (1858), crimson, large, vigorous.

Triomphe de Nancy , H. P. , *Crousse*, crimson, large, vigorous.

Triomphe de Paris, H.P. (1852), dark crimson, large, vigorous.

Triomphe de Pernet père, H.T. (1890), bright rose, large, moderate.

Triomphe de Rennes, N., *Lansezeur* (1857), canary yellow, large, vigorous.

Triomphe de Rouen, H.P., *Gargon*, rose, medium, moderate.

Triomphe de la Terre des Roses, H.P., *Guillot père* (1864), violet rose, medium, moderate.

Triomphe de Rosomanes, H.P., *Gonod* (1873), crimson, large, vigorous.

Triomphe de Soissons, H.P., *Fontaine* (1866), salmon rose, large, vigorous.

Triomphe de Toulouse. H.P., *Brassac* (1873), carmine, large, vigorous.

Triumphant, Pra., *Piercc* (1850), deep rose, small, vigorous.

Turenne, H.P., *V. Verdier* (1861), bright crimson, large, vigorous.

Ulrich Brunner fils, H.P., *Levet* (1882), cerise, large, vigorous.

Unique, T., *Guillot fils* (1869), white, purple, medium, moderate.

Unique, P., *Grimwood* (1777), white, medium, moderate.

Unique Jaune, N., *Mor. et Rob.* (1872), red yellow, medium, vigorous.

Vainqueur de Goliath, H.P., *Pernet* (1872), cherry red, medium, vigorous.

Validé, P.M., *Laffay* (1858), rosy carmine, medium, moderate.

Vallée de Chamounix, T., *Ducher* (1872), coppery, medium, moderate.

Vandermersch Mertens, T., *Nabonnand* (1882), yellow, medium, moderate.

Vase d'Election, H.P., *Ducher* (1864), clear rose, medium, vigorous.

Vaucanson, H.P., *Schwartz* (1871), vinous red, medium, moderate.

Velours Pourpre, H.P., *E. Verdier* (1866), purple, large, moderate.

Vicomte Maison, H.P., *Fontaine* (1868), cerise carmine, large, vigorous.

Vicomte Vigier, H.P., *V. Verdier* (1861), violet red, large, vigorous.

Vicomtesse de Cazès, T., *Pradel* (1844), deep yellow, large, vigorous.

Vicomtesse Folkestone, H.T., *Bennett* (1886), pink, large, vigorous.

Vicomtesse de Montesquieu, H.P., *Quetier* (1861), flesh, large, moderate.

Vicomtesse du Terrail, B., *Vigneran* (1884), flesh, medium, moderate.

Vicomtesse de Vezins, H.P., *Gautreau* (1868), rose, large, vigorous.

Victor le Bihan, H.P., *Guillot père* (1859), carmine, medium, moderate.

Victor Emmanuel, B., *Guillot père* (1867), purple crimson, large, moderate.

Victor Hugo, H.P., *Schwartz* (1885), crimson, medium, moderate.

Victor Puillat, T., *Ducher* (1870), yellow white, large, vigorous.

Victer Trouillard, H.P., *Trouillard* (1855), deep crimson, large, dwarf.

Victor Trouillard père, H.P., *Trouillard* (1868), red, large. vigorous.

Victor Verdier, H.P., *Lacharme* (1859), rose carmine, large, vigorous.

Victor Verne, H.P., *Damaizin* (1871), deep red, large, vigorous.

Villaret de Joyeuse, H.P., *Damaizin* (1874), carmine, large, vigorous.

Ville de Clamart, H.P., *Fontaine* (1879), bright rose, medium, vigorous.

Ville de Lyon, H.P., *Ducher* (1866), silvery rose, large, moderate.

Vincent Duval, H.P., *Duval* (1879), rosy carmine, large, vigorous.

Violette Bouyer, H.P., *Lacharme* (1882), flesh, large, vigorous.

Violet Queen, H.P., *Paul & Son* (1892), crimson violet, large, moderate.

Virgile, H.P., *Guillot père* (1871), salmon-rose, larloe, moderate.

Virginal, H.P., *Lacharme* (1858), white, medium, moderate.

Viscomte de Lauviere, H.P., *Liabaud* (1889), purplish red, large, vigorous.

Viscountess Falmouth. H.T., *Bennett* (1878), rose-pink, large, vigorous.

Vivid, H.B., *W. Paul* (1853), bright red, large, vigorous.

Vorace. B., *Lacharme* (1852), velvety crimson, large, vigorous.

Vulcain, H.P., *V. Verdier* (1850), purple, red, large, moderate.

Waban, T., *Wood* (1892), rose, large, moderate.

Waltham Climbers, Nos. 1, 2, 3, H.T., *W. Paul & Son* (1885), crimson, large, vigorous.

White Baroness, H.P., *Paul & Son* (1882), white, large, vigorous.

White Bath, M., *Slater* (1810), white, large, vigorous.

White Lady, H.T., *W. Paul & Son* (1888), white, large, vigorous.

Wilhelm Liffa, H.T., *Ketton frères* (1889), carmine, large, moderate.

William Francis Bennett, T., *Bennett* (1885), purple, medium, vigorous.

William Bull, H.P., *E. Verdier* (1861), rosy cerise, large, vigorous.

William Griffith, H.P., *Portemer* (1854), satiny rose, large, robust.

William Jesse, H.C., *Laffay* (1850), rosy crimson, large, vigorous.

William Koelle, H.P., *Pernet* (1878), bright red, large, vigorous.

William Lobb, M., *Laffay* (1855), red, medium, moderate.

William Paul, H.P., *Guillot père* (1862), red, crimson, medium, moderate.

William Pfitzer, H.P., *E. Verdier* (1861), brilliant red, medium, vigorous.

W.A. Richardson, N., *Mad. Ducher* (1878), orange-yellow, large, vigorous.

William Rollisson, H.P., *E. Verdier* (1865), cherry-rose, medium, moderate.

William Warden, H.P., *Mitchell* (1879), rose-pink, large, vigorous.

Wilson Saunders, H.P., *Paul & Son* (1874), crimson, medium, moderate.

Woodland Marguerite, N., *Pentland* (1859), blush, medium, vigorous.

Xavier Olibo, H.P., *Lacharme* (1864), blackish crimson, large, moderate.

Ye Primrose Dame, T., *Bennett* (1886), yellow, medium, vigorous.

Yolande d'Aragon, H.P., *Vibert* (1843), lilac-rose, medium, moderate.

INDEX

I

J

K

L

M

N

O